THE
ANCIENT
WORLD

THE ANCIENT WORLD

GENERAL EDITOR : ESMOND WRIGHT

HAMLYN
London · New York
Sydney · Toronto

List of contributors
Sir Mortimer Wheeler
Nicholas Postgate
L. K. Young
David Hawkins
Thomas Trautmann
John Coles
Richard Cowell
Paul Wietzel
Anthony Bryer
Barry Kemp

Published by
The Hamlyn Publishing Group Limited
London · New York · Sydney · Toronto
Astronaut House, Hounslow Road, Feltham,
Middlesex, England.

Original text
© The Hamlyn Publishing Group Limited 1969
Revised and updated 1979
This edition
© The Hamlyn Publishing Group Limited 1979
Second impression 1982

ISBN 0 600 30323 3

Filmset in the United Kingdom by Tradespools Ltd.,
Frome, Somerset
Printed and bound in Yugoslavia

Part I
THE AWAKENING OF MAN
Page 8

Introduction

Part I

THE AWAKENING OF MAN

Introduction

Many of man's achievements, though usually considered to be the products of civilization were in fact the result of his activities as a nomadic hunter in prehistoric times. Other important advances in human society were made almost as soon as the first peasant communities were founded. The achievements of man the hunter and man the farmer provide a background to the extraordinary advances made by urban societies in the ancient Near East.

Though man's presence on the earth has been attested, as long ago as 2,000,000 years compared with the age of the earth itself, this is an insignificant period of time. What is it that has set man apart from his animal ancestors? The position in which man finds himself today, more powerful than all other living things, must be the result of his culture, of many millennia of traditions and experience, and not of his physical characteristics, which are in many respects inferior to those of other animals.

From archaeological evidence it can be shown that the reason for man's behaviour in early times was the constant improvement in his way of life, an improvement brought about not only by the harsh realities of his environment but also by his own ingenuity and imagination. Archaeologists speak of revolutions in man's activities, periods when advances vital to his future were made, and although it is evident that the earliest revolutions—the neolithic and the urban—were the result of centuries of experience, nevertheless they stand our among the achievements of early man. Just as the establishment of farming led to the eventual development of urban communities, so the urbanization of man provided the foundation for the later achievements of the Greeks and Romans.

Man's biological background played an important part in the development of human society. Man is a primate, and it is likely that his physiological development involved not only continuously potent males and highly receptive females but also the necessity for a lengthy nurturing period for the young. In addition, and unlike other primates of the present day, man relied at least in part upon animal food, more difficult to obtain than vegetable food and involving endurance and the exertion of male strength.

The result of these activities must have been a division of labour on the basis of sex, and it is probable that sexual partnerships comprising a single man and woman developed because of the difficulty of obtaining sufficient food. The problem of finding food would in itself tend to bring together men who could hunt more successfully as a group than as individuals. Such a group would develop characteristic and traditional modes of existence, in which social evolution as distinct from biological evolution would begin to play an important part.

One of the first necessities for the evolution of human society was speech, by which traditional methods of food gathering might be explained to the young, ideas transmitted and exchanges made. Such transmission of thoughts may well have led to the development of tool making. Although other creatures, both animals and birds, use material objects for immediate purposes, only man was able to produce tools to a standard pattern and to arrange that such tools became traditional in both style and function. Equally important for the evolution of early man was his ability to adapt himself to varied environments. The result of this may be contrasted with the relatively static position of other primates, such as the great apes, which are confined to parts of Africa and number less than a million. These basic features of mankind—speech, tools and adaptability—had already become a part of man's cultural heritage 250,000 years ago.

The archaeologist tries not only to understand the major economic and political events of past times, events which in literate societies were usually recorded and which may be deduced through the excavation of prehistoric monuments, but also to appreciate the life of the anonymous people who made up the basis of these societies. The archaeologist tends, out of necessity, to overlook the private individual or the small family who may not have contributed anything original to human development. Those glimpses of hunters, peasants and shopkeepers which have been afforded through excavation of caves, farmsteads and urban houses, or through the recovery of such items as toys and rattles in children's graves, underline man's petty interests, his loyalties, and his sense of frustration at the irrevocable nature of death. The deliberate burial of the dead, provided with food and equipment for an existence beyond the grave, must have stemmed from a desire to avoid what seemed to be the futility of life.

The life of the hunter must have been hazardous, but at least it guaranteed the freedom of the individual, and both danger and freedom of expression must have played their part in the appearance of religious concepts, art and music during man's existence as a hunter. Freedom in a permanently settled society, however, was not that of the nomad, and there is little doubt that the establishment of farming communities marked the end of leisure for the majority of people, who were destined to toil in the fields or pastures for the communal good. Such farming villages were probably at first self-supporting and independent of other centres of population, but provided a basis for the eventual growth of towns. With the emergence of urban civilization, the personal freedom of the individual began to be eroded and, broadly speaking, this process continued until the establishment of more democratic institutions by the Greeks.

The development of urban civilization represents a period when settled communities began to expand and to multiply in many areas. In Mesopotamia, cities such as Uruk (the Erech of the Old Testament), which eventually formed the Sumerian nation, had appeared before 3500 BC complete with elaborate temples, public buildings and an organized political system. The word 'city' should not be taken to indicate size so much as organization. It would take only seven minutes to walk around the walls of Homeric Troy, and although the walls around Uruk were greater, the city itself was small by present standards. The Sumerian civilization, like the civilizations of Egypt, involved much more than mere urban development and town planning.

With increased densities of population, such activities as pottery-making and metalworking could become the specialized pursuit of a few craftsmen. Trade in commodities and ideas, which had existed for many centuries on a small scale, could be expanded, and in towns it must have soon reached the stage of extensive and complex commercial transactions requiring written records and the services of scribes. Archaeology shows that a system of writing was first invented in Mesopotamia, in the early Sumerian cities.

At the same time, the growth of towns brought other rewards. For a few people, gifted in some way, urbanization provided opportunities for elevation to positions of power or prestige, which had hardly been attained in earlier societies. For a very small number of people the new circumstances permitted the accumulation of wealth which the greatest hunter could never have achieved, a durable wealth which could be transferred to succeeding generations. The treasure in the tomb of Tutankhamun in Egypt is a spectacular example of the accumulation of wealth for one individual, but its social implications are matched by Sumerian and Assyrian tombs where riches and, in some cases, servants were obliged to accompany their master into the afterlife.

Urbanization also brought less attractive concepts into the lives of people. The contrast between those who led and those who laboured must have continued to grow, and the urban centres of Sumer, Assyria and Egypt contained slums as well as palaces. As disappointing to the student of human behaviour is the overall impression of apparently inevitable and unending conflict

On page 8, figure of a mother goddess from Hattusas, Anatolia, c. 5700–5600 BC.

Left, a procession of men and women, perhaps part of a religious ritual: detail of a painting from Tassili-des-Ajjer.

between different urban centres and between different nations. The history of Assyrian and Hittite conquests tells little of the human suffering involved in the seemingly endless efforts to extend and maintain territory. Yet it should not be forgotten that pressures of war generally bring out some of the best qualities in man, and it may be that knowledge of the use of iron was achieved through Hittite need in times of conflict.

War between groups of people probably had existed from the earliest times, but increased urbanization brought concentrations of wealth and power which fostered endemic conflict. Territory, treasure, women, slaves—all were there for the taking. Devastation, disease and famine were part of the lot of the ordinary man. Such circumstances as these undoubtedly contributed to the increasing influence of religion as a supernatural means of escape from the problems at hand.

Man must always have been curious about past events. Knowledge was dependent at first upon oral traditions, later supplanted by written records of past events, and stimulated by the visible monuments of half-remembered episodes.

Active interest in the past as a record of human behaviour is, however, of recent origin. The Greeks and the Romans acknowledged the existence of a remote past, but did not attempt to uncover the material remains of their ancestors. In the Middle Ages, any interest in the ancient world was effectively suppressed by teachings of the Christian Church which presented an ordered list of events since the Biblical beginning of the world in 4004 BC. In the seventeenth century, however, the antiquities of the Classical world began to excite the imagination of scholars, and their interest was soon extended to western Asia and its riches. Knowledge of the antiquities of Egypt was obtained by Napoleon's expedition there, and at the same time, interest in the early history of Mesopotamia was aroused.

From 1860, excavations were carried out in Mesopotamia and Egypt. This date marks the beginning of gradual acceptance of the biological evidence for the great antiquity of man. Since then over a century of excavation and research has enormously increased knowledge of human evolution. It can be seen that the legacy of the past does not extend only to Greece and Rome. The essential features of human society had been present for centuries before the rise of these Mediterranean civilizations. The Greeks and the Romans were fortunate in that they inherited the achievements of the ancient Near East, but they were also capable of developing their own concepts of human evolution. The awakening of man was an essential preliminary to the conscious development of those ideas of freedom and personal initiative that contributed so much to the development of mankind.

Chapter 1

Man before History

The creature we call man, because he made tools, first appeared in Africa during the early part of the geological epoch called the Pleistocene or Great Ice Age. For many thousands of years he existed side by side with animals which, although similar in appearance, lacked this vitally important skill. With tools man could begin to control his environment and his fellow creatures. The most primitive stone axe, roughly chipped from a pebble, enabled him to gather food more easily by killing or collecting.

From his African homeland man the tool-maker moved slowly into Europe and southern Asia. In successive migrations, which were virtually completed 250,000 years ago, he penetrated much of the Old World that was not covered by the periodic advances of great ice-sheets from the highlands to the north.

In time the separation of primitive man into isolated groups led to the development of different physical types possessing varying cultures. New inventions brought a greater range of specialized tools, and a new form of man, *Homo sapiens*, appeared on the scene. He was able to cope with the environment of northern regions and prospered both economically and culturally under the stimulus of colder conditions. He hunted such animals as the mammoth and reindeer and pushed as far north as the Arctic Circle and into the North American continent. However, in tropical Africa and the Far East, in areas where climatic changes, even seasonal ones, were not so marked, cultural developments lagged behind those of the north.

Perhaps the most significant event of this era was the emergence about 50,000 years ago of a belief in life after death, as shown by the careful burial of the dead with provisions of food and weapons. This tradition of burial opened the way to a fuller appreciation of the mysteries of life and death and stimulated the development in western Europe of the remarkable paintings and engravings of animals and other objects in cave sanctuaries. This art and its associated hunting and fertility rituals lasted for about 20,000 years until the end of the Pleistocene period—about 10,000 years ago.

It was at this time that the final melting of the ice-sheets which had at times covered much of northern Europe and North America took place. The consequent changes in climate and vegetation led to the dispersal to the northeast of those animals which had flourished under colder conditions. Early man found it difficult to adapt himself to the new environment thus created and the economic and cultural groups into which he had been formed tended to break up. Although men went on to occupy areas from which the ice had retreated, in Europe at least human progress lost its momentum.

Agriculture and the domestication of animals

The next major advance took place in the Near East with the establishment of agriculture and the domestication of animals. This achievement was the result of centuries of specialized hunting and food gathering which had led man to concentrate upon those animals and plants that by their nature could most readily become useful to him. Varieties of wheat and barley were available in a broad belt stretching from Anatolia to Iran, and goats and sheep were even more widely dispersed throughout the Near East. The careful and persistent gathering of these resources led imperceptibly to cultivation and domestication. Once the implications of these novel ideas for food collection had been realized, a rapid transformation in human society took place.

The development of agriculture meant that a large population could survive on the produce of a relatively small area of suitable land, from which unwanted plants and

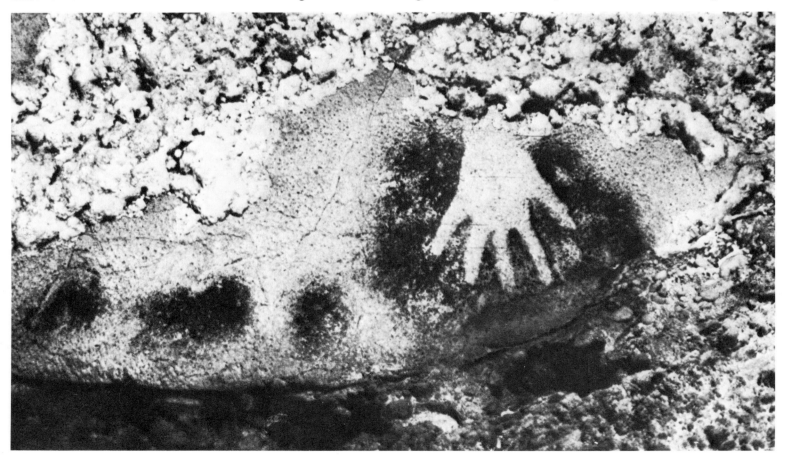

Reindeer from the wall-paintings in the Lascaux caves, France.

Left, rock painting from the neolithic settlement at Tassili-des-Ajjer on the North African coast: the woman, who is masked and carries what looks like a bowl, is thought to be participating in a religious ceremony.

Opposite, a human hand, thought to have been stencilled for magical purposes, from the Pech-Merle cave, France.

animals could be excluded. This concentration of effort upon a small area contrasted sharply with the traditional way of life of the hunter and a more sedentary form of economy emerged. The alteration in the structure of human society was relatively abrupt. In the Near East permanent settlements with stone-built houses and walls and towers were established by 7000 BC, although only 1,000 years before this the indigenous economy had still followed the basic pattern of hunting and food gathering of the previous 100,000 years.

The development of farming and the establishment of permanent settlements transformed man's precarious existence as a hunter and led eventually to an increase in population. At the same time, the growth of a pastoralist economy made it possible for normally sedentary animals, such as sheep and cattle, to survive, under human care, in new and alien environments.

Radiocarbon dating methods show that agricultural communities were well established in the Near East by 6000 BC, and that the spread of agriculture to the north and west, bringing waves of new people into Europe, and possibly into North Africa, took place before 4000 BC. The first movement of peasant communities into western Europe and into the Sahara was complete before 3000 BC.

Well before this time, however, other important developments had been made in western Asia. Of the many advances which seem to have resulted from settled community life in this area, the making of pottery and the casting of copper and bronze were perhaps the most important. Handmade pottery was being produced in many regions by 6000 BC, and metal working was well established by the fifth millennium.

Linked with these developments was the emergence of religious beliefs, which at first took the form of the widespread production of female figurines of clay, for use in fertility cults in the home at a time when agriculture was only newly established. Later, cult shrines were built for more complex rituals. At Jericho, a number of human skulls had facial features modelled in clay, with shells for eyes, and several had painted representation of hair. These heads may have been used for ancestor worship. At Catal Huyuk in Anatolia, a complex cult appeared involving female statues, leopards and vultures, as well as bulls and rams.

The development of urban civilization

The growth of peasant communities along the Tigris and Euphrates rivers, as in Egypt and in the Indian subcontinent, led to the establishment of urban societies. One of the greatest of these was the Ubaid, which appears to have developed in 4000 BC at the head of the Persian Gulf. It was a simple agricultural community which flourished through the careful use of resources, the development of methods of water-conservation and irrigation of the adjacent semi-desert and the organization of extensive trading connections. Eventually, settlements were made in the northern regions of Mesopotamia and the basis for historical Sumer was laid.

From this central area, it is likely that cultural achievements in architecture, writing, and modes of transport, were spread to North Africa, southern Europe and southern Asia. Fostered by the arts and crafts of these various regions, they gave rise to the civilizations which history has recorded.

Left, ditch, wall and tower in the early Neolithic fortifications at Jericho.

Opposite top, relief from Ubaid, the centre of the first prehistoric culture of southern Mesopotamia, c. 2600–2400 BC, depicting Imdugud, the benevolent lion-headed eagle of Sumerian mythology, protecting two stags; it was probably placed above the entrance to a temple. British Museum, London.

Opposite bottom, human skull modelled in plaster with cowrie shell eyes: found at Jericho, it dates from between 7000 and 6000 BC. Amman Museum, Jordan.

Chapter 2

The Achievement of Sumer

Where the two great rivers of Mesopotamia flow into the Persian Gulf, there now stretches a wide area of marshland, inhabited by the marsh Arabs. Above these marshes there extends northwards a flat plain through which the Tigris and the Euphrates flow. On the east it is bounded by mountains, on the west by desert, and on the north by the high mountains of eastern Turkey.

In the summer this plain is desperately hot, and no plant can grow unless it is watered, as no rain falls. Life on the plain is impossible without the water brought by the Tigris and Euphrates—names which they bore as far back as they can be traced. However, although, like the Nile, they flood when the winter snows melt in the mountains at their sources, unlike those of the Nile, the floods come at a most inconvenient time for the farmer. All the time his corn, sown in November, is growing, there is a shortage of water, but by March, when it is nearly ripe, the rivers are in full flood, and it is only with the greatest difficulty that the careful farmer can prevent their waters from sweeping over his fields and carrying away all his hard-earned crops.

It is, therefore, certain that the first people to live in this land—the land of Sumer—understood not only how to grow corn and other crops, but also how to control the rivers, by leading off water through ditches and canals when it was scarce, and by building dams and escape channels to keep the floods away from the fields. The challenge of the new surroundings and the need for mutual cooperation to make good use of the water supply must have acted as stimulants which helped to create the civilization which was born there.

At the time of the Ubaids, however, Sumer was no more advanced than the countries around it. They all shared a knowledge of agriculture, pottery, and even, to a limited extent, of how to work metals. In Sumer people built houses of mud bricks—the material of most buildings in the Near East to this day—and although their prosperity can have grown only very slowly, we can watch their temples being built again and again, each time a little larger and more splendid than the last. The wealth of the village shrine is a sure indication of the wealth of the worshippers who use it.

Uruk, the first city

Where all the land is flat and no single height or pass can command a strategic advantage over the rest of the country, only chance may determine where great cities will be found. Thus, throughout the history of Sumer, power and wealth shifted from one city to another. Just before 3000 BC Uruk enjoyed a time of great prosperity, when a whole complex of elaborate shrines and temples within the city were built, some of a size comparable to a Gothic cathedral. Many of them, uncovered by archaeological excavations, showed much of their original decoration, with cones of various colours embedded like nails in their outer walls, making zigzag bands of colour which resemble the trunks of palm trees when applied to the half-columns which form part of the façades.

Buried among these ruins were some of the treasures of the temple. These included beautifully worked silver and copper animal

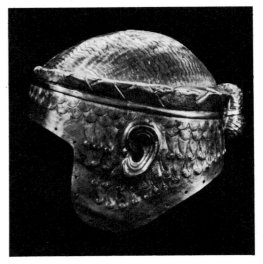

figurines, inlaid stone bowls, and many other carved stone objects which were probably the products of craftsmen employed by the temple itself. The finest object of all was a stone vase, about three feet high, on the outer side of which are three bands of sculptured decoration showing a procession bearing offerings. Sheep, goats and cattle, which with corn were the basis of the temple's wealth, form part of the procession, while the head of the procession is the goddess Inanna, always the chief deity of Uruk. From Uruk, too, comes the first known piece of life-size sculpture, a wonderfully naturalistic head of a woman—perhaps a priestess.

However admirable the vigorous, classical art of this period, it is not its most

significant cultural feature. It is from Uruk at this time that the first written records have been preserved. A primitive form of picture writing, scratched, recorded lists of domestic items and the dealings of the temples. Signs for sheep, pigs and oxen, ploughs and boats, and for many other items indispensable to the agricultural economy of the temples can immediately be recognized.

It is not possible to tell what language these first writers spoke because a picture of a boat indicates that they had a word for boat, but not what that word was. Very soon methods developed by the scribes to show the pronunciation of these signs made it possible to say that the language they wrote was Sumerian. It is therefore highly likely that the inventors of this script—and probably the first people ever to use writing —were the Sumerians.

The first examples of picture writing were drawn, often in considerable detail, in the clay, but, from at least 2000 BC onwards, a quicker method was in use which, while reducing the pictorial element of the sign, eased the process of writing. Instead of each line being laboriously drawn, the triangular point of a sharpened reed was jabbed into the clay, while one edge of the reed made a tail to the triangle, which stood for a line in the original sign. Once this method had been adopted, curved lines were no longer possible, and this was the first step which converted quite recognizable pictures into clusters of wedge-shaped lines called cuneiform.

Below, statue of Ebih-il, governor of Mari, third millennium BC. Musée du Louvre, Paris.

Below left, the ruins of Uruk, the first city of ancient Sumer.

Left, head of a god from Lagash, c. 2800 BC. Musée du Louvre, Paris.

Opposite top, golden helmet belonging to King Meskalamdug, ruler of Ur in about 2600 BC. Iraq Museum, Baghdad.

Opposite bottom right, Eannatum, ruler of Lagash in about 2400 BC, leading his victorious troops against the city of Umma: one side of the Stela of the Vultures, sculpted to commemorate Enannatum's triumphs. Musée du Louvre, Paris.

Opposite bottom left, statue of a male figure from temple at Tell Asmar, after c. 2400 BC. Oriental Institute, University of Chicago.

17

The cities of Sumer

Records of the period before 2300 BC come from various cities of Sumer: from Uruk, from Ur and from the ancient sites of Lagash and Shuruppak. Together they tell us much about the life of these first literate men. Although all the cities recognized their common unity as Sumerian, and although the city of Nippur, with its god Enlil, was the religious focal point for all Sumer, there was no one seat of political power. Each of the cities or towns of Sumer was the head of a small city state, with striking resemblances to the cities of Classical Greece, and as in Greece there was continual bickering between neighbours.

One city state might obtain control over other, temporarily weaker, cities, and then its ruler might merit the title of 'king'. An example of the changeable nature of politics at this time is furnished by the fortunes of the city of Lagash. At one time the 'king of Kish', Mesalim, interceded in a land dispute between Lagash and its bitter rival Umma; a generation later, although still preoccupied with its dispute with Umma, Lagash, under the leadership of Eannatum, defeated a ruler of Mari, a city lying north of Kish on the middle Euphrates.

The Sumerian head of a city state was called an *ensi*, and it is clear that his power was considered to be delegated to him by the god of the city. He was the chief religious member of the community, and represented the people in his dealings with the city god. The victory of one state over another was seen as a reflection on earth of similar events

Left, reconstruction of a bull-headed lyre found at Ur, c. 2600 BC. British Museum, London.

Opposite top, sacrificial scene from Mari, Musée du Louvre, Paris.

Left, the Ziggurat (a complex of religious buildings) at Ur, c. 2150–2050 BC; a temple to the moon god Nanna probably surmounted it, but no trace now remains.

Opposite centre right, female head from Uruk, c. 3200–3000 BC; known as the 'Lady of Warka', it is made from white marble. Iraq Museum, Baghdad.

Opposite bottom right, limestone votive plaque from Lagash, c. 2600–2350 BC: Urnansche, ruler of Lagash, is carrying a basket of mud on his head to make the first bricks of a new temple; at the   .. bottom of the plaque he is shown celebrating the completion of the work. Musée du Louvre, Paris.

Opposite left, alabaster vase from Uruk, c. 3200–3000 BC, showing crops and cattle—the fruits of the earth—being offered to the goddess of fertility. Iraq Museum, Baghdad.

involving their respective gods. Moreover, the 'kingship' of Sumer, awarded by the god Enlil from his seat at Nippur, was also thought to be a matter decided in heavenly council.

Interesting light has been thrown on the position of the *ensi* by excavations at the city of Ur. There a vast cemetery was discovered, which contained tombs so conspicuous for their ostentatious wealth that they can only have belonged to the members of a royal house. To accompany them in their afterlife the dead had been supplied with massive quantities of gold, silver, other metals and precious stone, worked exquisitely into jewellery, vessels, armour and even musical instruments. In addition to these, they contained grim evidence that slaves too were a man's possessions in ancient Sumer, and if the ruler was to live in the next world as he had in this, then slaves must accompany him. In one tomb more than seventy bodies were found, lying neatly ordered outside the central chamber, which housed the king's body.

The temples also retained much of their wealth, and often had a considerable labour force to work their lands. Besides the staple corn, the temple priests cultivated dates, grew onions and other garden plants, kept herds, and ran fresh and seawater fisheries. Between them, the *ensi* and the temple exercised complete economic control over the city, and we even hear of priests participating in the local wars.

The empire of Agade

The minor squabbles of the Sumerian cities were dramatically cut short when Sargon I, the founder of the dynasty of Akkad, conquered them between about 2400 and 2350 BC. Sargon had an Akkadian name, Akkadian being a Semitic language, akin to Hebrew and Arabic, which had long been spoken in northern Sumer and was soon to replace Sumerian altogether. Sargon was most likely of Semitic race himself. He founded his own capital, called Agade, near Kish, and then, with astonishing speed, achieved supremacy over the whole of Sumer.

Sargon and his successors, of whom Naram-Sin was the most notable, controlled by military force an area which reached from Tell Brak, on the headwaters of the Habur river, down to Elam, where they held the local princes subject. Like the later kings of Assyria, they ventured as far as the Mediterranean, and drew on the cedar supplies of the Amanus mountains in northern Syria.

Throughout the century or so of its domination, the empire of Agade suffered from internal dissensions. Instead of adopting the old Sumerian custom of exercising kingship in Sumer, while leaving the Lord

of each city more or less independent, Sargon and his descendants seem to have abolished the local dynasties, thus rousing the whole of Sumer against them. Another reason for Sumer's hostility towards Sargon, was that he diverted the Persian Gulf trade in copper, precious stones, and other luxuries to Agade.

Earlier, Ur and Lagash had almost monopolized this valuable commerce, which brought them into contact with the countries of Magan and Meluhha, and ultimately with the cities of the Indus Valley. The loss of this trade meant impoverishment for them. It is also possible that Sargon incurred hostility because he belonged to a different race.

The Gutian invasion

The Akkadian Empire fell as swiftly as it had risen. The period of its fall is poorly documented, but it is known that a people from the hills, called Gutians, were responsible for the final collapse (*c*. 2270 BC). A later literary composition describes how the gods had cursed Agade for impiety, how the 'fresh water of Agade turned to salt water' and how trade was interrupted so that 'long grass grew where the boats had anchored, the plants of lamentation grew where chariots had passed'. However, if the downfall of the dynasty was remembered, so were its achievements. Legends which have survived concerning the exploits of Sargon and Naram-Sin show that the example of conquest they set lasted longer in the memories of later generations than the fate which overcame them.

Northern Sumer suffered the effects of the Gutian invasion more directly than the south. Soon after the invasion the ruler of Uruk in the south, Utu-hegal, relates how he defeated and captured the Gutian king. To judge from his fairly accurate account of the campaign, Ur and the old rivals Lagash and Umma were also independent of the Gutian yoke, so that, at least in southern Sumer, life was resumed much as before, after the power of Agade had been broken.

During this period, while the north was being ruled by the Gutians, Lagash flourished, particularly during the reign of Gudea, who is well known today through the many statues of him. In addition to more than twenty statues, some of which bear his inscriptions, there remain two large clay cylinders, which are inscribed with hymns relating to the dedication of a temple to Bau, the goddess of the city of Girsu in his dominion. He tells how he was instructed in a dream to build the temple, and then how he collected the raw materials to equip it. Wood from Elam, Magan and Meluhha, copper and blocks of stone, pitch or bitumen, were all brought in at the command of the goddess for the building of the

Left, Akkadian cylinder seal, c. 2350–2150 BC, depicting a scene from mythology. British Museum, London.

Opposite top, Gilgamesh strangling a lion: by the eighth century BC, the date of this relief, Gilgamesh had become a mythological hero, but he was a real person and reigned over Uruk in the third millennium BC. Musée du Louvre, Paris.

Left, black basalt votive figure of Gudea, governor of Lagash, possibly from one of his temples; Gudea's hands are clasped in the ritual attitude of prayer. British Museum, London.

Far left, bronze head—possibly of Sargon I—from Nineveh, c. 2350–2150 BC. Iraq Museum, Baghdad.

Left, silver vase, dating from c. 2600–2350 BC, found at Lagash; the lion-headed eagle god Imdugud is shown with a pair of lions. Musée du Louvre, Paris.

Far left, alabaster statue of Gudea. Musée du Louvre, Paris.

Opposite bottom, stela of Naram-Sin, king of Akkad, c. 2300 BC: Naram-Sin is standing triumphant over his Elamite enemies, wearing the horned helmet of divinity and protected by the emblems of his gods above him. Musée du Louvre, Paris.

temple. Gudea never mentions his relations with other cities, and he presents a picture of a self-sufficient community, desiring not to extend its boundaries, but to grow in wealth and piety towards the gods—always the necessary precondition of prosperity.

Birth of a new empire

Soon after Utu-hegal had broken Gutian power in Sumer, he himself was made subject to the Lord of Ur, Ur-Nammu. Although little more is known about this king's victories in Sumer, the situation when his son, Shulgi, succeeded him makes it clear that he had extended his control over most of the land.

According to Ur-Nammu's own account this control was not inhuman. In his introduction to the earliest known collection of 'laws' or regulations, he records, in phrases which recur throughout Mesopotamian history, his offerings to the gods, his establishment of law and order in the land, and his defence of the fatherless and the widow. One of the regulations by which he hoped to achieve law and order reads: 'If a man has accused someone of adultery with a free man's wife, and the accused has been cleared of this accusation by river ordeal, the accuser shall pay twenty shekels of silver.'

By wise government Ur-Nammu laid a solid foundation for his empire, and when Shulgi assumed power his chief preoccupation was the maintenance of the frontiers which his father had created. In particular, much attention was needed on the eastern borders, where the tribes of the Zagros Mountains gave constant trouble. Year after year they were visited by punitive expeditions from the kings of Ur, but the nature of the terrain made a complete subjugation of the area impracticable. It is possible that

the empire of the third dynasty of Ur extended as far as had the Akkadian Empire.

While Ur-Nammu seems to have left the local government of the Sumerian cities in the hands of their traditional rulers. Shulgi and his successors gradually transferred the posts of governor to their own nominees, and thus began to break down the traditional pattern of Sumerian city-states. Similarly, further afield, Assur on the Tigris and Susa in Elam were given governors appointed by the central authority at Ur.

While the country's borders were being maintained attention was also given to internal administration, and here Shulgi was an undoubted innovator. Under his rule every department of government kept accounts, down to the smallest detail, of its receipts and issues of materials for which it was responsible. There are records of yearly statements involving enormous quantities of foods, wool, metals and vast numbers of livestock, handled by the king's deputies. Smaller accounts deal with the issue of supplies to the many messengers who collected their rations at government stores along their route, and also with the organization and payment of work on government buildings, canals and agricultural projects.

Very soon after the accession of Ibbi-Sin there are signs that all was not well. Tribute to the third dynasty of Ur from the outlying cities were no longer recorded in the lists, prices began to climb, and by the tenth year of his reign starvation was threatening the city of Ur itself. The correspondence of Ibbi-Sin with Ishbi-erra, one of his officials in the north, illustrates at once his desperate need for corn to feed the city, and the weakness of his control. Ishbi-erra describes the difficulties he encountered in gathering and transporting the corn, difficulties which were much increased by the hostile nomads apparently in command of the open country.

However, it was not these nomads from the western desert who dealt the kingdom of Ur its death blow. At the end of the third millenium a marauding band from Elam, with assistance from the mountain tribes, overthrew and plundered the cities of Sumer. They occupied Ur and left a garrison there. Ibbi-Sin, as later tradition records, was carried off to Elam where he spent his remaining days. For the Sumerians this reversal of fortunes could have come about only as the result of a curse by the gods, and they felt that the moon goddess, Ningal, had deserted her city of Ur.

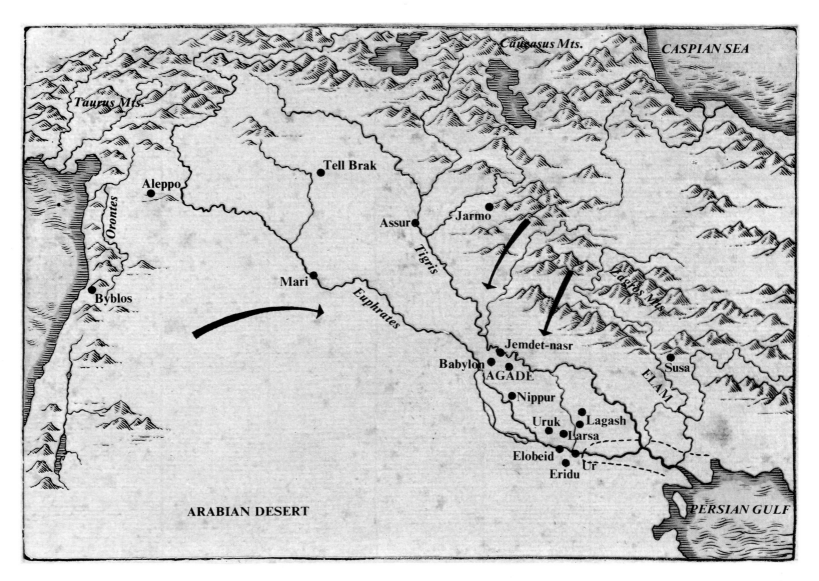

The mother Ningal stands like an enemy outside the city, she weeps loud over her ruined shrine of Ur. 'An [the chief of the gods] has ruined my city, Enlil has destroyed my temple, has struck it with his axe . . . . Earth has gathered in my city's canals, foxes have made their holes there.'

The first 'dead language'

The downfall of the third dynasty of Ur entailed more than the collapse of a political structure. Although Sumerian had remained the official language of the empire during the reigns of the third dynasty kings, the last two, Shu-Sin and Ibbi-Sin, bore Akkadian names. Very soon after the transference of power to the Amorite rulers Sumerian ceased to be a spoken language. It did not die out, however.

Most of the Sumerian texts which have come down to us were written during this Old Babylonian period by students and scholars who preserved the language and scribal traditions of their predecessors.

Kings wrote their inscriptions in Sumerian, although often with an Akkadian version as well. The influence of Sumerian religion with its concept of a supreme god (Enlil) and its myths, which encompassed the idea of a search for eternal life, permeated all branches of cuneiform writing to the end.

A considerable amount is known about the schools of Sumer. At Ur archaeological excavations actually revealed a schoolroom with mud-brick benches in rows for the students and in the same room their exercises—round tablets with a sentence written by the teacher on the front and copied on the back, with varying success, by the student. The schools also used long lists of words which the pupils had to learn by heart. They included legal terms, names of animals, plants and foods, and objects made of wood or metal. These lists are particularly useful for the modern scholar, especially since the scribes added to them the Akkadian translation of each Sumerian word. A favourite with the scribes was the proverb, and stories of school life, with the usual tales of bad behaviour and beatings, were also understandably popular.

Among other texts which these early schools have preserved, the most interesting

Above, map of Mesopotamia (the word is Greek for 'between two rivers'), the fertile trade route sandwiched between desert and mountains.

Opposite top, the stela of Ur-Nammu, king of Ur. University Museum, Philadelphia.

Opposite bottom, the standard of Ur, a panel dating from c. 2600–2400 BC, found in one of the earliest tombs in the royal cemetery at Ur. It depicts scenes of war: from top to bottom, the king receiving prisoners, helmeted lancers and defeated enemies, and, along the bottom, chariots driving across the bodies of the fallen. British Museum, London.

are undoubtedly the stories about gods and heroes. The series of legends which centre on the figure of Gilgamesh are strongly reminiscent, in their mixture of reality and fairy tale, of the poems of Homer. They are mostly short stories, each relating one episode, and concern such exploits as an expedition against the giant, Huwawa, in the Cedar Mountains, Gilgamesh's victory over the Bull of Heaven, sent against him by the love-goddess Inanna because he had rejected her advances, and a clash with his one-time overlord, the King of Kish, which is an illuminating account of intercity politics in the pre-Akkadian period.

The stories about the gods are no less varied, and show a liveliness of invention hardly equalled by later Semitic writers. One, for example, tells of the rescuing of Dumuzi, a god of fertility, from the underworld, by his sister, who obtains his release by agreeing to stay there as his substitute for half the year, while he completes the other half. Sumerian also has the earliest known account of the great flood, and of one man's escape from it in an ark.

The Sumerian language soon ceased to be anything more than a scholastic achievement. Nevertheless, the advances made by the Sumerians in technical knowledge, such as metalworking, and their mastery of the sciences of irrigation and agriculture, laid the economic basis for the prosperity of Mesopotamia for thousands of years to come. Even the advent of iron hardly changed the way of life pioneered by the Sumerians in the third millennium BC.

The Amorites

The chief threat to the civilization established in the plain of Sumer came from the mountain tribes in the east and the nomadic tribes of the western deserts, who were torn between scornful distrust of the soft city dweller of Babylon and grudging envy of his wealth. Incursions by bands of these tribes, who spoke a Semitic language called Amorite, added to the anarchy surrounding the downfall of the third dynasty of Ur. Before Ibbi-Sin's final defeat Ishbi-erra established himself as an independent ruler of the ancient city of Isin, and thus founded the first Amorite dynasty in Sumer.

The Amorites gained control of most of the old cities of Sumer and of many states which had once formed part of the Ur empire of the third dynasty, and so shared the same cultural heritage. After a period of

confusion strong Amorite dynasties had become established in the south at Larsa (which had already defeated and annexed the kingdom of Isin), at Babylon in northern Sumer or Akkad, at Eshnunna, east of the Tigris, and at Mari on the middle Euphrates. Amorite dynasties had also appeared around the Tigris on territory which later became Assyrian, and there were, moreover, a host of smaller principalities scattered over northern Mesopotamia.

A letter from the palace at Mari shows the political conditions of the times. Each of the major kings has a following of ten, fifteen or (in the case of Aleppo in Syria) twenty client kings, an indication of how delicately the balance of power was preserved. Other letters from Mari record details of the town's dealings with the south, where the two chief powers were Larsa, under the rule of Rim-Sin, and its northern neighbour, Babylon, whose king, Hammurapi, had considerably enlarged his territory during his early years. Although he must have maintained cordial relations with Rim-Sin to his south, we suddenly hear of Rim-Sin's defeat and find that in the thirtieth year of his reign, Hammurapi is master of all Sumer. Later he extended his power still further, conquering Mari, and receiving the submission of Shamshi-Adad's successor in Assyria.

It was after these achievements that Hammurapi had a monument prepared which has preserved his fame more effectively than any temporal conquest. On a tall stela he inscribed a long and detailed description of the regulations by which he wished his country's laws to be administered. Some of the provisions are harsh, but it is more significant that recognition is shown of the distinction between intentional and accidental homicide or injury. Moreover, the position accorded by the code to women is a more honourable one than in many countries today. The code includes many detailed clauses about various classes and professions and this has made it a priceless source of knowledge about contemporary society. Although it is no longer the oldest code of laws known, it is by far the most detailed from ancient Mesopotamia.

Hammurapi's conquests were the last great political event of his age. His successors gradually lost most of the territory he had so quickly won, although no power emerged strong enough to challenge the fading strength of Babylon. The lasting result of Hammurapi's campaigns is only to be seen later, when the pre-eminence which he had thus gained for Babylon, an upstart among the cities of Sumer, was reaffirmed by the succeeding Kassite kings, who chose it as their capital, and fostered at Babylon the learned traditions of ancient Sumer. The conclusive proof of Babylon's political insignificance came only in the year 1595 BC when the Hittite king, Mursilis, swept down the Euphrates in a sudden raid, and sacked the national shrine.

Opposite right, statue from Mari, an outlying region that provided the most lively and inventive sculpture in Sumeria during the mid-third millennium BC.

Opposite left, detail from the Stela of Hammurapi, showing Hammurapi with the sun god Shamash, who holds a ring and staff in his hands; beneath the figures starts the 'Code of Hammurapi,' the king's description of his laws. Musée du Louvre, Paris.

SUMER FROM ITS ORIGINS TO HAMMURAPI

Date	Ruling cities of Sumer	Domestic history	Foreign history	Culture	Date	Ruling cities of Sumer	Domestic history	Foreign history	Culture
3000 2900	Kish dynasties			Cuneiform writing First temples	2200	Naram-Sin		Invasion of the Gutians	
		Struggles between the cities: Ur, Uruk and Lagash			2100 2000	Gudea of Lagash	Sumerian revival Empire of Ur		Artistic revival Great ziggurat of Ur
2600	1st Dynasty of Ur			Triumphs of Sumerian art—royal tombs of Ur	1900 1800	Rise of Mari	Amorite domination	Emergence of Assyria	Royal palace of Mari
2500	Lagash 2nd Dynasty of Ur		Infiltration of Semites		1700	Hammurapi Samsuilunas		Aryans lay waste Iran Kassite invasion in	Hammurapi's Code
2400	and Uruk				1600			Babylonia	
2300	Lugalzaggisi Sargon of Agade	Unification of Babylonia under Akkadian rule							

Chapter 3

The Hittite Contribution

The written history of Anatolia (modern Turkey) goes back almost to the year 2000 BC. Even before that date a high standard of civilization had been reached, but it was illiterate and has left no written records. Nothing is therefore known of the names of the peoples and cities, what language they spoke, or what happened to them. Shortly after 2000 BC however, we have the first group of written documents in the shape of the archives of the Assyrian merchant colony of Kanesh. These are written in Old Assyrian cuneiform script on clay tablets which have been excavated by archaeologists from the area of the great mound which marks the site of the ruined city of Kanesh.

Thus it was that writing was first imported into Anatolia from the land of its invention, Mesopotamia. The Assyrian merchants who brought it travelled across the wide plains and rivers of upper Mesopotamia, through the narrow passes of the formidable Taurus mountains and up to the Anatolian highlands, in search of the metals which their country needed—copper, silver and gold. To exchange for these they took the fine woven cloth of Assyria and another metal, tin, which they themselves imported from the East. In Anatolia they set up merchant colonies from which to conduct their trade. Kenesh was the greatest of these, and is today the best known. In these colonies, which were usually situated outside the walls of the native cities, the Assyrians lived and wrote down the details of their business transactions on clay, in the form of bills, receipts and letters.

These documents provide much information about Assyrian trade and the state of the country itself at that time. From them it can be seen that Anatolia like Sumeria was divided up into a large number of small city-states, each of which was governed by its own native prince. The cities mentioned are much the same as those also known from a later date. One of these merchant colonies was settled at the city of Hattusas, which was later to become the capital of the Hittite Empire.

The texts give no direct information about the races and languages of the native peoples. However, a study of their personal names, as written down by the Assyrians,

seems to show that there were already a large number of Hittites and their kinsmen, the Luwians, present in Anatolia, but that, as later, the population was very mixed. The population also included Hurrians, a people from the east, across the river Euphrates, and Hattians, who were perhaps the original inhabitants of the land before the Hittites arrived on the scene.

The local princes of the city-states seem to have been on the whole completely independent of each other, but the presence of the well-organized Assyrian traders forming a network throughout the country might have subjected them to certain pressures. However, there was a tendency for one or other of these princes to conquer the cities of his neighbours and then to assume the title of 'great prince', showing that he had succeeded in unifying at least part of the land. Some time after 1840 BC the city and merchant colony at Kanesh were attacked and burnt. It is not known for certain who was responsible for this but it seems likely that it was the work of one of the Anatolian princes who was attempting to assert his authority.

After a period in which the city stood deserted and in ruins, the Assyrian merchants returned and continued their trade. There then appeared on the scene a prince whose exploits exceeded all those of his

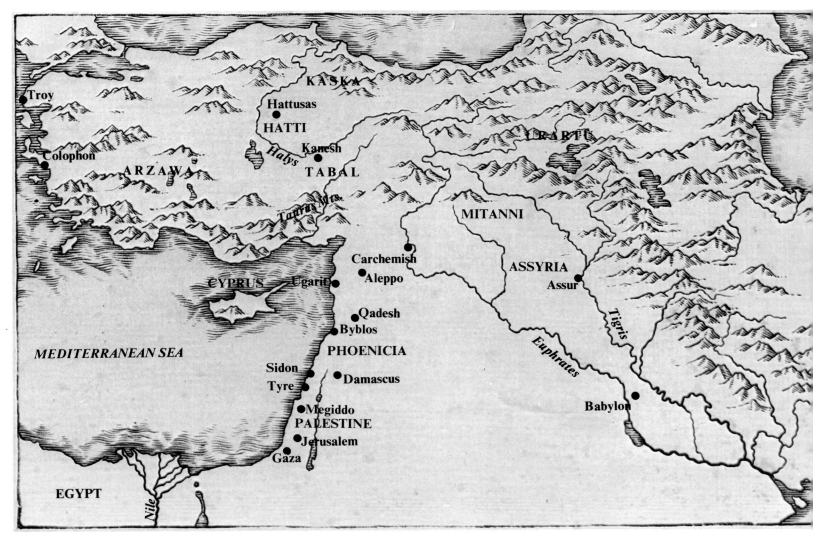

Above, map of the world as it was known to the Hittites.

Left, one of the sphinxes that guard the gateway, built in the mid-fourteenth century BC, to Alaja Huyuk, one of the main Hittite cities known to archaeologists.

Opposite top, the sanctuary of Yazilikaya, Anatolia, c. 1360–1250 BC.

Opposite, funerary stela from Marash, eighth century BC: the scribe Tarhunpiyas is standing on the knees of a woman—maybe his mother or perhaps a goddess; he holds a stylus in one hand, a falcon in the other. Musée du Louvre, Paris.

predecessors and which were remembered even in the days of the Hittite Empire. His name was Anittas, of the city of Kussara, and his own narrative of his deeds is preserved on a tablet from the Hittite royal library. He seized the city of Kanesh, known in Hittite as Nesa, and made it his capital. He subjugated all the other cities, taking for himself the title of 'great king'. He destroyed the city of Hattusas and put a curse on it, sowing the ruins with mustard seed.

The Hittite Old Kingdom

It is not known what became of the dynasty of Anittas after it had been transferred from Kussara to Kanesh. The second settlement at Kanesh was once again burnt and abandoned for a long period. It was during this time that the mass of the Hittites must have arrived in Anatolia, and when historical records begin again, some time after 1700 BC, a Hittite kingdom proper has been established. For more than sixty years archaeologists have been excavating the ancient city of Hattusas, the Hittite capital, near the modern Turkish village of Boghazkoy. There they have discovered a huge mountain stronghold, surrounded by massive walls more than two miles in length, pierced by at least seven gates.

Inside these walls lies the ancient citadel, perched on a rocky crag with the remains of the Hittite palace and guard-houses, and below this in the lower town an enormous temple dedicated to the storm god, the head of the Hittite pantheon. At some distance outside the walls, at a place now known as Yazilikaya ('inscribed cliff'), another temple was found standing in front of a rocky grotto, the sides of which were decorated with processions of Hittite gods leading up to the central scene where the storm god faces his consort.

In the ruins of the palace and the temple of the storm god excavations have revealed thousands of clay tablets and fragments. These formed part of the great royal library and archives of the Hittite empire. They were written in the cuneiform script borrowed from Mesopotamia, for the most part in the language which is now known as Hittite. The Hittite people, however, called their language 'Nesite' (i.e., the language of the city of Nesa), and their kingdom 'Hatti', borrowing the name from the previous inhabitants of the land. Thus it was that their neighbours, the Babylonians and Egyptians, called them 'the people of Hatti', while to the Hebrews of the Old Testament they were the 'sons of Heth', from which the modern term 'Hittite' is taken.

This language, Hittite, was deciphered in 1916 by a Czech scholar, and proved to be an Indo-European language—that is, related to Latin and Greek. Other languages used in Hatti were Luwian and Palaic, which were closely connected with Hittite. The language of the previous inhabitants of the land, known as Hattian, was partly remembered and used for ritual purposes. The Hittites also employed the language of their eastern neighbours, the Hurrians, and, more especially, the language of Mesopotamia, Akkadian, which was in general use among the powers of the Near East for writing letters and drafting treaties.

Although the Hittites remembered Anittas as the 'great king', they regarded Labarnas as the founder of their kingdom. He was a legendary figure whose name was used as a title by all subsequent Hittite rulers. His successor, Labarnas II, was the first historical Hittite king. This Labarnas moved his capital from Kussara to Hattusas from which he took the name Hattusilis by which he is usually known. By a series of hard-fought campaigns he united central Anatolia into the kingdom of Hatti and carried his forces eastwards through the Taurus mountains as far as the Euphrates.

His heir and grandson Mursilis in a short but glorious reign won victories for Hatti never again equalled. After defeating the Hurrians in Syria and destroying the city of Aleppo, he marched down the Euphrates against Babylon, where in about 1515 BC he

brought to an end the declining dynasty of Hammurapi. He did not attempt to hold conquered Babylonia. Leaving the enjoyment of his victories to others, he returned to Hattusas where he was murdered in a palace conspiracy.

This led to some 200 years of weakness and confusion in Hatti. At home conspiracy and murder flourished within the royal family and abroad revolts in Hittite-held territories and incursions of hostile peoples from the mountains threatened the state. Even the sequence of kings would have been lost but for the work of one significant king of the period, Telipinus, who must have reigned about 100 years after Mursilis (c. 1500 BC). He not only succeeded in temporarily securing the country's safety against attack but also attempted far-reaching internal reforms. It is to the 'Decree of Telipinus', which sets out his reforms, that we owe most of our knowledge of the earlier Hittite history. The purpose of his reforms was to re-establish the position of the king against the threat of murder and usurpation and to enlist the assembled nobility in his support.

The Hittite Empire

The century following the death of Telipinus is very poorly documented, even the exact number and order of kings being uncertain. The evidence available seems to show that it was a period of growing weakness when Hatti was faced with a severe crisis with all its enemies attacking at once. These included the Luwians to the west, the barbarous mountain-dwelling Kaskas in the northern province and further east across the Euphrates the Hurrian kingdom of Mitanni, which was at its height of power, having won control of the Syrian cities which had previously been dominated by Egypt. Such was the desperate situation which faced Suppiluliumas, the king who checked the period of decline and inaugurated two centuries of an expanded Hittite empire.

Suppiluliumas came to the throne about 1380 BC after his elder brother, Tudhaliyas the Younger, had been assassinated by the army. His first task was to secure Hatti against the attacks of its neighbours and this required many years' fighting. Looking beyond this, however, he realized that his country's strength must depend on Hatti's domination of Syria, so to this end he directed the major effort of his reign.

In a series of wars he broke the power of Mitanni. He installed his sons as kings of Aleppo and Carchemish, and bound other Syrian princes to himself as vassals by means of treaties. Egypt under the declining Eighteenth Dynasty was too weak to interfere. In fact, an Egyptian queen, the widow

Above, rock relief showing a king—possibly Warpalawa—paying homage to a god of vegetation, c. 1750 BC.

Above left, one of the guardian lions on the Lion Gate at Malatya, ninth century BC. Archaeological Museum, Ankara, Turkey.

Opposite, the lion gate at Hattusas, c. 1600 BC.

of Tutankhamun begged Suppiluliumas for one of his sons in marriage to become King of Egypt. In about 1336 BC Suppiluliumas died of plague which the army had brought back from the Syrian campaigns.

His heir, Arnuwandas II, also succumbed to the plague shortly after his accession and was succeeded by his brother Mursilis II. Mursilis proved to be as able as his father in handling an almost equally difficult situation. Preoccupied with Syria, Suppiluliumas had allowed the security of Anatolia to deteriorate once more, and at his death, Arzawa, never properly subdued, revolted again. Mursilis spent the first ten years of his reign campaigning in western Anatolia and also in the north against the ever restless Kaska people. Later in his reign he had to face a crisis in Syria on the death of his brother, the King of Carchemish, but the structure of the empire bequeathed to him held together and he was able to maintain it.

Some interesting personal details have been preserved about Mursilis, who seems to have been particularly superstitious. He attributed the plague which was ravaging Hatti to the wrath of the gods for the impious assassination of Tudhaliyas the Younger, and attempted to appease them with long and abject prayers. At one critical moment with trouble impending on the northern frontier and in Syria, he attributed his predicament to the neglect of certain rites of Suppiluliumas, and hurried off to perform them, leaving the fighting to his generals.

He was on the worst possible terms with his mother, accusing her of bringing about the death of his wife by black magic, and also of afflicting him with a curious speech impediment (perhaps the effects of a slight stroke). For this impediment he also blamed the wrath of the storm god, and therefore went through elaborate purification rituals 'written down on an ancient tablet'. He died in about 1310 BC after a reign of some twenty-five years.

His son and successor, Muwatallis, seems to have maintained the power of Hatti in Anatolia without any drastic measures. In this he was much assisted by his younger

brother, Hattusilis, who had command of the northern frontier. During the reign of Muwatallis, however, the Egyptian interest in Syria revived under the vigorous kings of the Nineteenth Dynasty. This led to the great battle of Qadesh in 1300 BC between Muwatallis and Rameses II. The boastful terms in which the Egyptian king described this engagement concealed his defeat, which he barely saved from becoming a disaster. The Hittite grip on Syria remained firm and its frontier post at Qadesh was quite undisturbed.

Muwatallis died in about 1294 BC and was succeeded first by his illegitimate young son, Urhi-Teshub, and then by his uncle, Hattusilis, who seized power and exiled Urhi-Teshub to Cyprus. Hattusilis made peace with Rameses of Egypt in a famous treaty of 1284 BC, preserved in Egyptian and Hittite, which acknowledged the Hittite possessions in Syria and Palestine. Hattusilis also made an alliance with Babylon. These pacific gestures were designed to secure his kingdom against a new and dangerous enemy from the east, the Assyrians.

Tudhaliyas IV succeeded his father, Hattusilis, in about 1265 BC. Late in his reign the Assyrian, Tukulti-Ninurta I (1244–1208 BC), crossed the Euphrates in a great raid in which he carried off nearly 30,000 Hittites. The Hittites responded by compelling their Syrian vassals to place a trade embargo on Assyria.

A more serious threat to Hatti than the Assyrians (and ultimately to prove fatal) now appeared in the west. On the edge of the Hittite world there had always existed a country which was known to the Hittites as 'the land of Ahhiyawa', and where the king was a 'great king', the equal of the Hittite king himself. It has been suggested that the people of Ahhiyawa were the Achaean Greeks who were known to Homer as the 'Achaiwoi'. The most that can be said for

certain is that the two names are very likely the same, but it does not seem that Ahhiyawa could have been situated as far away as Mycenae. It seems more likely that Ahhiyawa was a settlement of Mycenaean Greeks on the coast or islands of Asia Minor.

In the reign of Tudhaliyas IV the King of Ahhiyawa engaged in plotting with Madduwattas, a western vassal of the Hittites. He also appeared to be fomenting trouble in Arzawa, which rose in revolt. Tudhaliyas fought against Arzawa and invaded Cyprus, the first serious attempt at an invasion by sea made by the non-seafaring Hittites. This was the first extension of the empire since the days of Mursilis II.

When Tudhaliyas IV was succeeded by his son, Arnuwandas III, the position of Hatti had deteriorated. The effects of the Arzawan campaign were slight, and there soon appeared an alliance between Madduwattas and the kings of Ahhiyawa and Arzawa. Arnuwandas, dying childless after a short reign, was succeeded by his brother, Suppiluliumas II, who, in spite of his illustrious name, was unable to face the gathering storm. Little is known about his reign or the disaster in which it ended. The Hattusas archives, as it typical of all ancient records, break off before the final collapse. All that is known is that the cities of the Hittite Empire were ruthlessly sacked and burnt about 1200 BC and the political domination of the Hittites in Anatolia was destroyed for ever.

Judging from Assyrian records it seems that it was the Phrygians who were responsible for the downfall of the Hittites, and, after a lapse of some four centuries, succeeded in rebuilding an Anatolian empire of

Above, Phrygian statue of the goddess Cybele flanked by a pair of flute-players.

Left, drinking horn in the form of a bull, c. 1400–1200 BC. Schimmel Collection, New York.

Opposite right, pendant in the form of a seated goddess, probably the sun goddess of Arinna, c. 1400–1200 BC. Schimmel Collection, New York.

Opposite centre, goose-like vase found in a tomb at Gordion, the Phyrgian capital. Archaeological Museum, Ankara, Turkey.

Opposite left, rock relief from the sanctuary at Yazilikaya, showing Sharruma, a Hurrite god, protecting King Tudhaliyas IV, c. 1400–1200 BC.

their own under King Midas. The Egyptians, however, attributed the disaster to the 'peoples of the sea', who later attacked their own country.

The achievements of the Hittites

In religion and general culture the Hittites were very much a part of the world in which they lived. Their chief god was the storm god, the wielder of thunder, who was worshipped under different names in different countries. His wife, too, was acknowledged as a powerful goddess. Besides these, a vast number of lesser gods, described collectively as the 'thousand gods of Hatti' also received attention. The king acted not only as the commander of the armies and chief judge, but also as high priest. The queen, too, took an important part in religious and other matters.

Just as the Hittites had borrowed their writing from Mesopotamia, so they also borrowed literary forms such as the writing of letters, treaties and laws. Mythological poetry was translated directly into Hittite from Akkadian and possibly from Hurrian. The Hattusas library seems to have been the creation of one of the later kings, probably Hattusilis III or Tudhaliyas IV. However, the Hittites did not only borrow, but also added to the tradition. The first recorded example of an early type of historical writing, in the form of yearly annals of the king, comes from Hatti.

It is clear from their achievements that the Hittites had good armies and disciplined soldiers. The king as commander-in-chief was supported by a bodyguard of courtiers and nobles. The Hittites made great use of chariots and were in fact among the earliest peoples to introduce the horse into the Near East. Their own cities were fortified with huge walls, and they were able to capture those of their enemies by siege-warfare. As victors they seem to have been generally merciful, governing their empire through a loose system of vassals bound to them by treaty. This, however, may have been a weakness, for the empire seems to have disintegrated very rapidly as a result of the rebellion of the western vassals.

The late Hittite states

The western and central areas of the Hittite Empire fell to the Phrygians, who had come from Thrace at the time of the great Aegean migrations of about 1200 BC. However the Hittites maintained themselves in the old south-eastern region, which split up into small city-states. To the east these were threatened by two great powers. In the Armenian mountains the kingdom of Urartu (the Old Testament Ararat) had appeared, created by a people related to the Hurrians of a previous age, and in northern Mesopotamia Assyria was once again expanding after a period of decline. These two powers constantly fought each other, not directly but through the Hittite states, which occupied an area in which both were concerned.

South of the Hittites were similar small city-states in Syria and Palestine, occupied by Aramaeans and Hebrews, who had settled there in the dark age after 1200 BC. In this precarious situation the Hittite states preserved a culture which had close links with that of the empire. The kings continued to use many of the ancient names, and Hattusilis, Mursilis, Suppiluliumas and Muwatallis reappear in garbled forms.

The same gods were worshipped, especially the storm god and personifications of the sun and moon. The kings usually contented themselves simply with the title of 'king' or even 'ruler', but occasional claims to be 'great king' suggest memories of their imperial past. They fortified their cities and built themselves palaces in the traditional style, taking particular care to adorn the gateways and entrances with sphinx-like beasts and scenes sculptured in relief.

The greatest of these states was probably Carchemish, on the crossing of the Euphrates, which carried on the tradition of being the seat of the Hittite king in Syria.

HITTITES, PHOENICIANS AND HEBREWS

Date	Hittite rulers	The Hittites and the outside world	Neighbouring countries	Phoenicians and Hebrews
1900	Anittas as Great King			
1800		Destruction of Kanesh		
1700	Hittite Old Kingdom (1700–1500 BC) Hattusilis I Mursilis I	Mursilis' raids in Babylonia		
1600			Kassites at Babylon	
	Telipinus		New Kingdom in Egypt	Hebrews in Egypt Trade between Byblos and Egypt
1500			Thuthmosis III	
	Hattusilis II	Height of Mitanni power	Amenophis II	Rivalry of Ugarit, Arvad, Byblos, Tyre and Sidon
			Amenophis III	
1400	Hittite Empire (1380–1200 BC) Suppiluliumas I (d. c. 1336) Arnuwandas II Mursilis II (d. c. 1310) Muwattallis (d. c. 1294)	Decline of Mitanni Pacification of Anatolia Conflict with Egypt	Amenophis IV Advance of Assyria Rameses II	Completion of the Phoenician alphabet

Date	Hittite rulers	The Hittites and the outside world	Neighbouring countries	Phoenicians and Hebrews
1300	Urhi Teshub Hattusilis III (d. c. 1265) Tudhaliyas IV (d. c. 1230) Arnuwandas III Suppiluliumas II	Kadesh War against Assyria Invasion of the peoples of the sea: fall of the Hittite Empire	Assyrians expelled by Babylon	Moses: establishment of the Hebrews in Palestine
1200	Small Hittite kingdoms remaining in Anatolia		Rameses III Assyria and Babylonia sacked by invaders	Destruction of Phoenician cities Period of the Judges Dominance of Tyre and Sidon
1100				Samuel Saul: war against the Philistines
1000	Late Hittite States (1000–700 BC) Hittite territories still surviving in Anatolia		Rebuilding of Assyrian power	Hiram of Tyre Division of Israel and Judah
900		Shalmaneser III subjects Hittites to tribute		
800		Tiglath-Pileser III reconquers Hittites		
700		Sargon destroys Hittite states		

Further up the Euphrates was the kingdom of Kummuh, and in the foothills of the Taurus mountains were the states of Melid and Gurgum. The state of Sam'al was an anomaly, being firmly Hittite by geography and tradition but ruled by an Aramaean dynasty which wrote Aramaic. Across the Taurus mountains, the land of Tabal included various of these late Hittite states at various times, and to the south of Tabal, the Hittite city of Tuwana continued an independent existence.

The amount of tribute and booty exacted from them by the Assyrians shows that these states possessed considerable wealth. However, the Assyrians did not find them easy subjects. Three Assyrian kings were particularly concerned with the Hittites. Shalmaneser III (858–824 BC) was the first to compel them to pay heavy and regular tribute, although he hardly penetrated across the Taurus to Tabal. His weaker successors left the Hittites in peace for a century. It was Tiglath-Pileser III (745–727 BC) who once more brought them under Assyrian control. The harshness of the tribute he imposed led to frequent Hittite revolts.

Sargon II (721–705 BC), who inherited the Hittite states governed by tributary kings, dealt with unrest in a ruthless Assyrian manner. After each revolt he would sack the cities, exterminate the royal house and deport the entire population, resettling the area with Assyrian colonists and placing it under an Assyrian governor. During his reign all the surviving Hittite states suffered this fate, and this was in effect the end of them. Thereafter occasional revolts were led by men who had Hittite names, but as a nation and a people the Hittites were dispersed, never to reappear upon the scene.

Below, relief showing a battle chariot from Carchemish, c. 850–700 BC. Archaeological Museum, Ankara, Turkey.

Opposite top right, head of Sargon II, found in his palace at Khorsabad. Museo Egizio di Torino.

Opposite top left, protective god on the Warrior Gate at Hattusas, which guarded the eastern entrance to the city, fourteenth century BC.

Opposite bottom right, bas-relief portraying two Hittite warriors, c. 900 BC. British Museum, London.

Opposite bottom left, hieroglyphic inscription in Hittite on a basalt slab from Carchemish, c. 750–700 BC. Archaeological Museum, Ankara, Turkey.

Chapter 4

The Might of Assyria

The natural division of modern Iraq into a northern district centred on the city of Mosul, and the southern plain with its capital at Baghdad, marks a difference which in earlier times was reflected in the political units of Assyria and Babylonia. Although Assyria's capital city, Assur, was far to the south on the Tigris, the agricultural nucleus of its empire lay in the fertile lands east of the river, and especially in the triangle formed by the Tigris and Upper Zab rivers.

In these lands, as also in the plain which stretches across to the west, furrowed by the waters of the Habur and Balih rivers, rainfall permits cultivation without irrigation, although additional and more dependable sources are always desirable to assist in times of drought. Crops, too, are different. The date palm will not ripen, but the milder climate allows a greater variety of fruit trees, and there is evidence that extensive vineyards existed in Assyrian times.

The origins of the city of Assur are lost in prehistory. The king lists compiled in later centuries describe the first rulers of Assyria as 'seventeen kings who lived in tents', and this tradition of a nomadic past is doubtless reliable, as far as it applies to the people known later as Assyrians. However, the city after which they are named was inhabited before these nomad sheikhs could have settled there and assumed political power. Long before Sargon of Agade conquered the lands up to the Mediterranean, Assur was the home of a people who seem to have been a northern outpost of Sumerian civilization. Although no records survive from this date, a building has been excavated in the lowest layers of the site which bears all the characteristics of an archaic Sumerian temple. Among the finds is a large group of statuary which is virtually indistinguishable from the statues from contemporary Sumer. The fact that similar statuary has recently been found at a shrine in the far north of Mesopotamia shows that there is still much to learn about the extent of Sumerian civilization.

Old Assyrian Assur

The first date at which it can be confidently said that Assyrians were living at Assur is about 2000 BC. The city was subject to the kings of the Akkadian Empire, and again came under the rule of the Ur Empire of the Third Dynasty, when Assur was the residence of a governor. It is not certain when the Assyrians themselves settled. Moreover, it is not clear where they came from or whether the settlement was a sudden or gradual process. The later Assyrians spoke a dialect of the Akkadian language known as Assyrian, which was quite distinct from the Babylonian dialect of their southern cousins, and which, despite the enormous cultural and literary pressure of Babylonian, retained in its own peculiar features until the final destruction of the Assyrian Empire.

When written documentation for the history of the city of Assur becomes available, in about 1900 BC, the inhabitants and their rulers are clearly Assyrian in the sense that they spoke this dialect. The picture which is given of these earliest Assyrians is very different from that of later times.

Following a tradition which dated back possibly to before the Akkadian conquest, the people of Assur lived in a small, tightly knit community, based on land holdings in or near the city, relying for their prosperity on trade. Concern for the Assyrian trader is attested in one of the earliest royal inscriptions, where the King of Assur describes how he had opened the markets of Babylonia to the merchants of his city. It seems that the kingship of Assur, although hereditary, did not confer on its holder any absolute powers such as were exercised by the kings of Agade.

Moreover, since there is no evidence as to whether the political boundaries extended beyond the immediate surroundings of Assur itself, it is impossible even to be sure if the later capital city of Assyria, Nineveh, was under the same government as Assur before the reign of Shamshi-Adad.

Information about these Assyrian merchants does not come from Assur, but from hundreds of miles away, at their trading colony at Kanesh. The business records and letters of these merchants have preserved invaluable information about their trade, presenting a picture of financial life which seems surprisingly modern. The chief items of trade were textiles and metals, expecially tin, brought from Assur and sold at a handsome profit in Anatolia. The mode of transport was by donkey caravan, and the traders might take three months over the northern journey, transacting business as they went from town to town across Mesopotamia.

Trade appears to have been in the hands of large wealthy families, the heads of which directed operations from Assur itself, while junior members organized the caravans, or acted as resident representatives at Kanesh. They looked after the family's business interests, arranged dealings with other merchants and saw to the distribution of goods to the other, smaller trading stations. The colony at Kanesh was vested with authority over the other Assyrian depots, and officials were chosen from among the leading merchants to act as instruments for the enforcement of justice. In a letter addressed to the colony, there is a request from the city of Assur for a contribution by Kanesh to help build a new wall round Assur—a reminder that Assur alone instigated and exercised this trade.

Amorite domination

The same movement which brought the dynasty of Hammurapi to power in Babylon affected the north as well. The Amorite usurper here was Shamshi-Adad, who apparently came from the town of Terqa on the middle Euphrates. After his conquest of the city of Assur itself, he extended his dominions to include the Amorite-ruled kingdom of Mari, where he installed one of his sons on the throne. He himself turned his attention to the north, and built a new capital in the Habur region.

At about the time of the accession of Hammurapi Shamshi-Adad's possessions stretched over most of northern Mesopotamia, and as such provided a pattern for the subsequent territorial expansion of Assyria. The archive of royal letters discovered at the palace at Mari disclose that Shamshi-Adad himself was in constant touch with Hammurapi in Babylon, and among the many letters referring to military campaigns mention is made of forces of up to 30,000 men. There is even some reason to think that Hammurapi himself at one time recognized Shamshi-Adad's sovereignty. However, the achievements of Shamshi-Adad did not survive him.

Soon after his death Mari was recaptured by the Amorite dynasty which had previously held it. It was not long before the conquering Hammurapi had received the submission of Shamshi-Adad's other son, Ishme-Dagan, who was ruling at Assur, and political circumstances combined to strangle the Anatolian trade.

The submission of Ishme-Dagan to Hammurapi was the prelude to a period of decline in Assyria which lasted for centuries. The dark ages which interrupt the history of the whole of the ancient world of the Near East began sooner in Assyria than anywhere else and lasted for a longer period. Almost the only source which relates to the history of this period is the list of the kings of Assur, which records an unbroken line of succession from father to son, but gives no clue to their strength or weakness.

For a considerable length of time these kings of Assur were no more than tributary vassals. An extensive archive of tablets from the town of Nuzi, near modern Kerkuk, shows that this region, in the foothills directly to the east of Assur, was part of the dominion of the great kings of Hurrian Mitanni, or Hanigalbat, whose capital lay in northern Mesopotamia; and Assur must

have formed part of this dominion. More-over, when Assur itself reappears in history, its art and language show clearly the influences of a long period of Hurrian overlordship.

Birth of the Assyrian state

Although the events which gave rise to the exchange of correspondence between Hittites, Hurrians and Egyptians affected Assyria only indirectly, two letters from this collection are significant. Assur-uballit, who was King of Assur in about 1350 BC, was sufficiently independent of the earlier Hurrian overlords to write on his own account to the pharaoh. In his second letter he treats the pharaoh as an equal, and refers to himself as 'great king'. This undoubtedly reflects the dwindling power of the Hurrians. They were no longer by this stage one of the great powers, but actually or virtually vassals of the Hittites, who were less concerned to recapture the territories which the Hurrians had lost than to keep them as a buffer state against the rising might of Assyria. It was inevitable that Assyria would expand its boundaries in areas that had recently been possessions of the Hurrian kings. Since Assur-uballit's two successors campaigned up in the mountains to the

Fresco, probably dating from the reign of Tiglath-Pileser III (745–737 BC), from the palace of the governor of Til Barsip, on the River Euphrates, depicting two official dignitaries. Aleppo Museum.

north and east, it must be presumed that he himself or his predecessors had regained the lands up the Tigris north of Assur, and especially the Tigris—Great Zab triangle.

From this time onwards the pattern of Assyrian history until the end, some seven hundred years later, achieves a rather monotonous regularity. Periods of conquest are followed by a succession of weak and transitory kings, until a powerful new king restores the country's fortunes and the conquests are repeated. Between 1350 and 625 BC Assyria extended its control over southwest Asia, as had Egypt several centuries earlier, and Babylon and to some

extent the Hittites. The three kings who followed Assur-uballit—Adad-nirari I. Shalmaneser I and Tukulti-Ninurta I—brought Assyria's power to its zenith in the second millennium BC.

The empire expanded mainly towards the Mediterranean, to the Hurrian kingdom of Hanigalbat, nominally under Hittite protection. However, both Adad-nirari and Shalmaneser were able to march over this territory as far as the Euphrates at Carchemish, and after its second conquest, the area was incorporated into the Assyrian Empire, governors were installed in the major cities, and the precedent set by Shamshi-Adad I was realized. There does not appear to have been any determined attempt by Hittites to reverse this state of affairs—a sure sign that Assyria's military might was internationally recognized. In a letter sent to Tukulti-Ninurta I on his accession, the Hittite king tried to dissuade him from an expedition into the hills to the north, which the Hittite clearly regarded as his own preserve. Yet the stable position to the west enabled Tukulti-Ninurta to ignore this warning, and he spent much time subduing the small Hurrian principalities. Among these was Uruatri, which was to become Assyria's powerful rival of the first millennium, Urartu.

Tukulti-Ninurta's proudest boast was his capture of Babylon, whose sovereignty Assyria seems to have acknowledged at an earlier date. Provoked by the Babylonian king over a border dispute, he defeated him and plundered Babylon itself. Although he ruled in Babylon for some time afterwards, it was not a successful conquest. Native opposition was too well organized and it may well be that the effort of administering Babylonia put too great a strain on the resources of the Assyrians.

Later in Tukulti-Ninurta's reign the Assyrian boundaries began to crumble again, and the murder of Tukulti-Ninurta in his newly built capital across the river from Assur was the prelude to another succession of weak, unstable kings. However, contact with Babylon reinvigorated Assyrian scribal traditions and literature.

The Aramaean threat

Already in the time of Shalmaneser I the desert nomads had been harassing the settled communities again, and for Tiglath-Pileser I they constituted a real menace. Assisted by a firm situation created by his father at home, this king was able in the early years of his reign to reconquer the lands to the north and west, penetrating as far as the Mediterranean. However, his own account of crossing the Euphrates twenty-eight times to inflict punitive raids on the Aramaeans shows his insecurity. A chronicle describes the misery and hunger at the end of his reign when Assyria was overrun

by these tribes. It is not known how long this unhappy situation lasted, but when Assyria recovered the first task of her kings was to crush the resistance of the Aramaean states.

The pattern of Assyrian aggression now repeated itself. First came the time of restoration of order and stability within the homeland, and then, under Adad-nirari II (911–889 BC), the boundaries were pushed out westwards to enclose those lands which Assyria felt to be its own. The centre of resistance was the Aramaean princedom whose capital was the town of Nisibis in the Anatolian foothills. Once Nisibis had been captured the north Mesopotamian plain as far west as the Habur reverted to Assyrian rule.

Tukulti-Ninurta II, Adad-nirari's successor, spent much energy consolidating Assyria's internal position. However, the nomads of the middle Euphrates were still a source of trouble, and he undertook a display of force. After marching south from Assur through desert regions where he and his troops suffered agonies of thirst, and delimiting the border with Babylonia, he crossed the Euphrates, along which he marched until he reached the confluence of the Habur. He then made his way north up this river as far as Nisibis and, after a raid into the mountains beyond, returned to Assyria.

Assur-nasir-pal II

Although, according to his own account, Assur-nasir-pal was a great conqueror, he did not in fact leave Assyria's boundaries greatly expanded. He did not try to impose his rule west of the Habur river, although he marched through the area and compelled its princes to pay tribute. Moreover, his march to the Mediterranean, acknowledged by gifts from distant Phoenician cities, was no more than a propaganda exercise, which also yielded valuable timber from the Amanus forests for his building schemes. In fact many of his campaigns were directed against the hill districts which ringed Assyria to the north and even here he merely consolidated and slightly expanded direct Assyrian rule. In the east and south he did no more than his predecessors, preferring to rely on the lethargy of the Babylonian kingship and the disunity of the mountain tribes.

However, Assur-nasir-pal was deeply concerned with the country's internal affairs, and he left very eloquent traces of his reign at home. In the first place he saw that the

Above, relief dating from the ninth century BC from Assur-nasir-pal's palace at Kalhu showing troops swimming across a river to attack a walled city. British Museum, London.

Left, relief from Nineveh showing Assur-bani-pal taking part in a hunt. British Museum, London.

Opposite right, statue of Assur-nasir-pal II from the palace at Kalhu. British Museum, London.

Opposite left, three Phoenician ivory figures found in an Assyrian palace; the Phoenicians (Phoenician territory was roughly equivalent to present-day Lebanon) were traders and seamen who held a virtual monopoly of commerce in western Asia and the western Mediterranean for several centuries after c. 1000 BC. Iraq Museum, Baghdad.

capital city, Assur, was badly situated. Lying far to the south, close to the Babylonian border and well downstream from the corn-growing centre of the country, it was not a convenient base for his campaigns, and so he moved his government to Kalhu, between the Tigris and Upper Zab rivers, where the age-old city of Nineveh also stood. The change showed imagination and insight.

Leaving Assur as religious capital of Assyria, he transformed Kalhu into a secular capital, supplying it with all suitable amenities. In an inscription commemorating the inauguration of his new palace, he tells how he dug a canal from the Upper Zab river, cutting through a hill at its highest point, and called it the Canal of Plenty, Patti-hegalli. He irrigated the meadows of the Tigris, and planted orchards beside it. He planted all kinds of fruits and vines, and established regular offerings for his lord, Assur, and for all the temples of his land. He adorned the palace itself with woods of various kinds, and to match the new importance of the town he built new temples to house its gods.

Secular and religious buildings alike benefited from an artistic innovation, the sculptured relief. Round the walls of the royal apartments stood slabs of lime-stone on which were carved—sometimes in superb detail—the exploits of the king in war or in the chase. Although these were only the first of a long series, the simple, vigorous dignity of their scenes was never recaptured by later artists. Great stone lions guarded a temple gateway, and the doorways of the palace, too, were flanked by gigantic guardians in the shape of winged bulls, which have stood as testimony to the grandeur and might of the Assyrian Empire.

Further conquests

When Assur-nasir-pal died he left his son, Shalmaneser III (859–824 BC), in command of a territory which now included most of the economically and strategically important land between the Tigris and the Euphrates. Assyria's borders had been pushed back far enough to keep the homeland between Tigris and Upper Zab free from hostile incursions by mountain tribes, and the system of provincial government established by his father allowed Shalmaneser to leave his northern and eastern borders in the capable hands of his provincial governors. Moreover, the experiences of the preceding twenty years had left Assyria's neighbours in no doubt that she was not lightly to be provoked.

In these circumstances Shalmaneser's chief concern was to gain control of the lucrative trade routes leading from Mesopotamia to Anatolia, and through the Phoenician coastal towns to the Mediterranean. Just as the Aramaean opposition to his predecessors had centred on the city of Nisibis, so now it was a king on the western borders who stubbornly resisted Shalmaneser's expansionist ambitions. Already in the reign of Assur-nasir-pal there was evidence of the presence of a strong, hostile state, which was known to the Assyrians as Bit-Adini. Its capital was Til Barsip, situated a little to the south of Carchemish on the Euphrates.

On the occasion of Assur-nasir-pal's march to the sea, its ruler, Ahuni, had in fact offered his submission, but there had been no question of conquest by Assyria, and, indeed, Shalmaneser needed three campaigns at the start of his reign to extend his control of the Euphrates. He made the old capital of Bit-Adini the chief town of an Assyrian province, naming it after himself 'Port Shalmaneser'. From this time the land between Euphrates and Tigris was never really out of Assyria's control.

Shalmaneser was not, however, content. To the south and west of the new Assyrian boundary lay a complex of Aramaean states, among them Israel and Judah, which had known a period of great power and prosperity in the preceding centuries when neither Egypt, Assyria nor any Anatolian

Above, detail of a stela showing King John of Israel paying tribute to Shalmaneser III. British Museum, London.

Left, detail from the bronze gates of Shalmaneser III at Balawat: above, Shalmaneser is shown watching his forces attacking a town; below, his archers are firing on a walled town, helped by a battering-ram. British Museum, London.

Opposite top, scenes of a military expedition from Shalmaneser's bronze gates at Balawat. British Museum, London.

Opposite bottom, Assyrian relief from Assur-nasir-pal II's palace at Kalhu showing two Phoenicians bringing tribute to the king. British Museum, London.

power had the strength to interfere in their affairs. They would not watch docilely while their country was overrun by another Assyrian conqueror.

It is no longer possible to guess the reasons why Shalmaneser chose to attack the Syrian states. Did he need control of the trade routes, or access to the cedar forests of Lebanon? Or was he simply drawn from one victory to another? In assessing his motives, the enormous strain which even a small campaign imposed on the resources of a country, whether in men, horses or materials, should not be forgotten.

When Shalmaneser turned his attention to Syria and Palestine he met with opposition far stronger than he could have expected. The ruler of Damascus was able to form a coalition which included his own former enemy in the south, Israel, and various neo-Hittite states from as far away as Cilicia. In 853 BC Shalmaneser launched a major campaign against Damascus, and at the Battle of Qarqar he met a large force to which Ahab of Israel had contributed 2,000 chariots and 10,000 infantry.

This battle proved indecisive, and it was not until the death of Ben-Hadad of Damascus, who seems to have kept the coalition alive, that Shalmaneser, having received conciliatory gifts from Israel and the Phoenician trading cities, was able to defeat his isolated successor, Hazael, in 851 BC. Damascus itself was not taken, and although he reigned another sixteen years, Shalmaneser gave little attention to the west.

Shalmaneser devoted some time to subduing the kingdoms on the upper reaches of the Euphrates and in the rich, metal-bearing Taurus Mountains. These campaigns may have been designed to check the growth of Assyria's northern rival, the kingdom of Urartu, which, despite three raids into its territory earlier in his reign, was fast becoming a threat, especially since Assyria depended on the northern mountains for its precious supplies of iron and copper. The inactivity of Shalmaneser's later years was partly due to his advancing age. He did, it is true, entrust campaigns, including two against Urartu, to his chief general, but discontent with his capacity to rule must have grown. In his last years he faced a revolt by one of his sons, which his chosen heir, Shamshi-Adad V, was able to suppress only after Shalmaneser had been assassinated.

Adad-nirari III

After Shamshi-Adad V had established his claim to his father's throne, and had reduced the rebel cities that still opposed him, he enjoyed a rather uneventful reign, characterized neither by great conquests nor by significant territorial losses. He must have died quite young, since, on his death, his son and heir, Adad-nirari III was still a minor, and for five years or so the country was under the regency of the king's mother, Sammuramat. Her character was forceful enough for her memory to be preserved until the days of Herodotus (484–428 BC), who knew her under the name of Semiramis.

Adad-nirari displayed great energy and as soon as he came of age he began the usual series of campaigns, designed no doubt chiefly to maintain Assyria's borders as they had been defined by Shalmaneser. He went several times up to the northeast to subdue the tribes of the region of Lake Urmia, and had some success in intimidating the mountain peoples of the Zagros.

His major efforts were, in fact, directed towards the west, where he was able to carry Shalmaneser's conquests one stage further. Beginning in 805 BC, he marched to the west, and in 801 BC he achieved the submission of Damascus. This seems to have removed the the core of the opposition to him, and he later received tribute and obeisance from the northern Hittite states, from the towns of the Phoenician seaboard, and, in the south, from the Philistines and Israel.

However, this achievement should not be overestimated. The area west of the Euphrates was never in fact incorporated into Assyria proper until the reign of Tiglath-Pileser III, and in spite of the wide area Adad-nirari claims to have reduced, he did not conquer it. Tribute was sent to buy off the Assyrian king and to dissuade him from plundering yet further afield, but at no stage was there any question of annexation. Even Damascus itself, although submissive, was never entered by the Assyrians. It is, moreover, doubtful if any formal treaty was concluded.

Although Adad-nirari's military achievements were less imposing than those of his two great predecessors, he should not be underrated. To administer a territory is a much more difficult undertaking than simply to march victoriously through it. Adad-nirari faced the problem of maintaining well-equipped divisions of Assyrian troops in places far distant from his capital, while retaining sufficiently large numbers at his immediate call for the yearly campaigns.

The military centre of the empire was Kalhu, the modern Nimrud. Under Shalmaneser the yearly succession of expeditions had become so regular that this king had built an enormous arsenal in one corner of the city, designed both to house the equipment and raw materials, and to serve as a marshalling ground for the army when it set out. Measuring about 400 square yards, this building, which has recently been excavated, is a powerful reminder of the material organization required by the Assyrian military machine.

Although the reign of Adad-nirari III is poorly covered by the usual historical annals, clay tablets have preserved for us a picture of how the machinery of administration functioned. On the assimilation of a territory to the empire, the first step was to install in a suitable centre a governor, who acted in all matters as the king's representative. At first, no doubt, his decisions were enforced with military backing, but slowly a civilian administration was built up.

One of the chief assets to Assyria in the acquisition of new territory was the manpower which this put at its disposal, and at the levy of troops for the yearly campaigns each of the governors would have been required to make his contribution. Each province was also expected to supply not only the needs of its own government by taxation, but also to furnish the central treasuries of Kalhu with goods of all kinds — woods, textiles, metals, foodstuffs and animals, especially horses for the army. Thus the governor of the province of Harran, west of the Habur river, was required on one occasion by Adad-nirari to collect six horses in each town or village of his province, and join the regular army at a fixed date for the yearly campaign.

As representative of the king, the governor had other responsibilities apart from military matters. A king was at all times the military, religious and judicial head of the country. He was personally responsible for interceding for his land and people with the national god, Assur. A letter from him to his governor conveys his instructions on how to avert a serious drought:

The king's word to Mannu-ki-mat-Assur: you and the people of your province are to hold a lamentation ceremony for three days before Adad [the weather god]. Pray; purify your land and your fields; make burnt offerings, and let them hold a purifying ritual wherever you have an enemy. So reconcile Adad. Let them do it at once.

Tiglath-Pileser III, Assyria's greatest ruler, changed the system of regional government, substituting smaller units which reduced the governor's power but enabled him to rule more effectively.

The achievements of Tiglath-Pileser III

As soon as Tiglath-Pileser III (745–727 BC) came to the throne he took upon himself the urgent task of restoring the country's fortunes.

The chief menace lay in the growing power of Urartu. While Assyria had suffered dissension at home the kings of Urartu had extended their power by conquest and alliance right down into Syria, thus flanking Assyria to the east and west. In his third year Tiglath-Pileser completely defeated the Urartian coalition in the west, and from

40

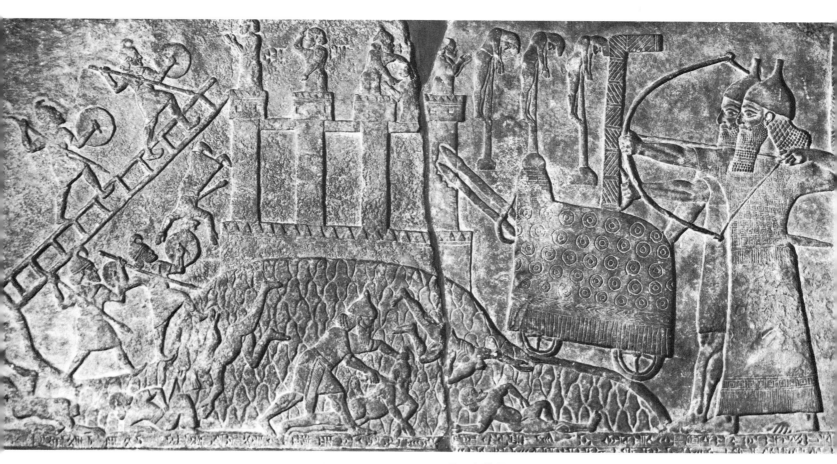

that time there was no interference from Urartu while he undertook the task of subjugating Syria. In 732 BC, having succeeded in isolating Damascus by over-running Israel and Phoenicia to the south, he was able to defeat Syria. Thus it was that the whole of the country as far south as Damascus became absorbed into the Assyrian Empire.

Tiglath-Pileser's exploits in the south were equally remarkable. At the time of his accession the nomadic Chaldean tribes were causing turmoil in Babylonia. He immediately marched south, and, after defeating the troublemakers, confirmed the reigning king on his throne at Babylon. Some ten years later the death of this king caused another revolt, and after dispossessing the Chaldean usurper, Tiglath-Pileser himself 'took the hands of the god Bel'—the symbolic action which conferred on him the kingship of Babylon; this was apparently the only way to secure peace and loyalty in Babylonia.

The Sargonid dynasty

In the century which followed the death of Tiglath-Pileser, Assyria awed the world with its apparently invincible might, and astounded it with the speed of its collapse. The four kings—Sargon II, Sennacherib, Esarhaddon and Assur-bani-pal—became well known to Egyptians, Jews, Elamites,

Above, relief from the palace at Kalhu showing Tiglath-Pileser attacking a city, probably Babylon. British Museum, London.

Left, ivory figure of a warrior from Kalhu. Iraq Museum, Baghdad.

Persians and even Greeks, as the far-distant rulers of the armies which oppressed them.

In 722 BC the capital of Israel, Samaria, was taken by the Assyrian armies after a siege which had been started by Shalmaneser V, Sargon's predecessor. This event allowed Sargon to ignore the west for a while, leaving Judah as the largest unconquered state. Trouble in Babylonia needed his attention, and he also had to deal with unrest among the tribes to the north and east. The events that followed made it clear that this unrest was due to the incitement of Urartu. Throughout the first millennium Assyria was always alert to the presence of a potential rival to the north. When Assyria was weak Urartu might encroach upon Assyria's sphere of influence, as happened before the reign of Tiglath-Pileser III. When Assyria was strong, Urartu was able to concentrate on extending its power elsewhere.

Centred on Lake Van, the dominion of the Urartian kings at times stretched west of the Euphrates, and the tribes of Lake Urmia and beyond generally acknowledged their suzerainty. To the north Urartian power reached well into the Caucasus. Although neither Assyria nor Urartu had designs on the other's homeland, especially since the

Above, figure of a winged bull with a human head from Sargon's palace at Khorsabad, eighth century BC; these bulls flanked the great doors of the palace. Musée du Louvre, Paris.

Left, capital decorated with the figure of a man-bull. Archaeological Museum, Tehran.

Opposite top right, a divine couple from Marash, eighth century BC; the god is carrying a bunch of grapes, the goddess a mirror (both symbols of divinity). Arts Council.

Opposite top left, a djinn, or spirit, from Khorsabad, eighth century BC. Musée du Louvre, Paris.

Opposite bottom, relief showing Tiglath-Pileser directing a military operation from his chariot.

mountain barrier which separated them made a direct military attack quite impracticable, their interests clashed in the east and the west. In the west Assyria under Shalmaneser V and Sargon had recently annexed two new provinces in the rich, metal-bearing Taurus regions, and in the east each country sought to promote its influence among the tribes of the Iranian plateau, especially the Mannaeans, whose fine horses they coveted.

In the year 714 BC Sargon set out northeastwards for the customary punitive expedition against these Iranian tribes, who had again unseated a king sympathetic to Assyria. He was met by a coalition which included not only the armies of the two strong chieftains who had instigated the tribal revolt, but the King of Urartu, Rusas, and his army. By thus lending his support to the Mannaeans, the Urartian king had made plain his hostility to Sargon's presence in this region. Sargon was unprepared to meet his most powerful opponent, but nonetheless attacked, and won the day. He decided to press home his advantage, making for the Urartian capital at Lake Van, and, although he did not attempt to take it, he ravaged the country round about, and left the land with a firm impression of Assyria's superiority.

Thereafter there was a truce between the two powers. Sargon kept a constant watch on the frontier, and many of the letters sent to him by his officials in the area—of whom his son, Sennacherib, was one—have survived. Spies reported on troop movements and events within Urartu, and a heavy defeat was inflicted on the Urartians by the Cimmerians. The latter were invaders from the Asian steppes, who later pressed into Asia Minor, and were kept out of Assyria only because of prompt action by Sargon in 705 BC.

In the battle which deflected the Cimmerian invaders Sargon was killed. Sennacherib had already seen service on the northern frontiers, organizing resistance against Urartu, and the kingship passed

smoothly into his hands. Sargon had built an entirely new capital north of Nineveh, with palaces and temples furnished with the most sumptuous decorations the empire could supply. It was not, however, a success, and Sennacherib decided to make Nineveh his capital. From then on Nineveh was the chief city of the empire, and its walls, still visible, have a circumference of nine miles —an 'exceeding great city of three days' journey' as later tradition in the Book of Jonah remembered it.

Assyria and the west

For many years the Euphrates had served as Assyria's western frontier and Tiglath-Pileser's action in incorporating lands beyond the empire was forced on him by the continuing unrest in the area. Now there was no such obvious boundary to Assyrian aggression. In the south the power of Elam and the Persian Gulf served as a check to Assyrian ambitions. In the north Urartu and the mountain regions of Anatolia formed psychological barriers at least.

However, westwards a chain of more or less vigorous states stretched right down to Egypt, and the conquest of one merely

involved Assyria in trouble with the next. The remaining states which lay between Assyria and Egypt faced a terrible dilemma: should they fear more the energy of Assyria or the nearness of Egypt? Hezekiah of Judah, the most powerful of the kings who had not yet submitted to Assyria, chose to ally himself with Egypt. However, as Sennacherib's ministers declared during the siege of Jerusalem by Assyria: 'Thou trustest upon the staff of this bruised reed, even upon Egypt; whereon if a man lean, it will go into his hand and pierce it: even so is Pharaoh king of Egypt to all that trust on him.'

Although Sennacherib did not take the city, the rest of Judah was overrun by the Assyrian army. However, after Sennacherib had turned homewards, Hezekiah chose a more prudent course, and sent an embassy to offer his submission. With the exception of the city of Tyre, secure in its island fortress, the whole of western Asia now acknowledged the supremacy of Assyria.

This, however, did not mean peace. There was still a strong power, Egypt, inciting unrest and disobedience, and after King Esarhaddon had twice come west to suppress revolts, he bypassed the city of Tyre which had intrigued with Egypt, and made straight for the Nile itself. After victories in

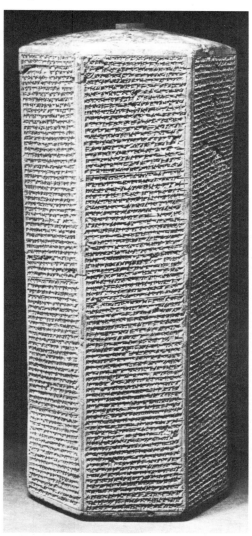

the Delta region in 674–673 BC, he gathered his forces for a final assault. In 671 BC he was able to defeat the pharaoh completely and occupy the city of Memphis. While on a further campaign to deal with the remainder of Upper Egypt, Esarhaddon fell sick and died, thus bringing the expedition to an end.

This was the time of Assyria's greatest expansion. The two great centres of civilization, Babylon and Egypt, were under its control, and all the nations of the world—even the Greeks—believed Assyria to be invincible. However, Egypt was a long way from Assyria, and, although Assur-bani-pal was able to reassert his authority in Egypt, he thought it easier to appoint local princes.

He found it necessary to undertake campaigns against Egypt in 667 and 663 BC, but he made no attempt to incorporate Egypt in the empire. When, some time after 658 BC the pharaoh Psammetichus expelled the Assyrian garrisons from Egypt, Assur-bani-pal does not seem to have attempted to restore his position. It is likely that the vast distance separating the two countries, the difficulty of imposing Assyrian rule on a country with its own civilization and his preoccupations elsewhere, convinced him that Egypt was not worth the trouble.

When Tiglath-Pileser took the hands of Bel, Assyria had finally allowed itself to be drawn into politics with its southern neighbour. This was to prove a tiresome problem. Although it had not been too difficult to reduce Chaldean opposition to Assyria at first, the activities of one Chaldean chief, Marduk-apla-iddina (the Merodach-Baladan of the Bible), changed the situation.

The latter managed to unite a number of the tribes under his authority, and, on the death of Shalmaneser V while campaigning in the west, he entered Babylon and claimed the kingship for himself. Sargon came south the next year to punish him, but was met by

was assigned to Assur-bani-pal. The succession was determined as he wished, but, although the brothers maintained outwardly friendly relations, they finally quarrelled.

About fifteen years after Esarhaddon's death Shamash-shum-ukin began to intrigue with Assyria's enemies—with Elam, the Chaldeans and other nomads, with Palestine and even with Egypt. However, although he offered the most stubborn resistance Assyria had encountered, in 648 BC Assur-bani-pal's troops entered the city of Babylon which had succumbed to famine after a two-year siege. Shamash-shum-ukin avoided capture by throwing himself into the flames of his burning palace. Assur-bani-pal took the throne and held it unchallenged until his death in 627 BC.

Assur-bani-pal's library at Nineveh was a lasting monument. He himself recorded how, as crown prince, he learnt besides horseriding and warfare, to read and write Akkadian and Sumerian in the cuneiform script, and even to solve mathematical problems. We must be grateful to him for his academic interests, because the library he collected forms the basis of modern knowledge of Mesopotamian science and literature. As is common in libraries, the works of reference are the bulkiest.

Following the Babylonians here, as in all branches of literature, the Assyrian scribes made huge compilations of omens, in which any event which might seem significant—for example, the behaviour of an animal—was given its interpretation by the priests. However, apart from this pseudo-science, much of value was recorded. In mathematics, astronomy and chemistry the Babylonians and Assyrians had made many discoveries since Sumerian times, and many of the texts of Assur-bani-pal's library bear witness to continued interest in these subjects.

The literary texts, which were copied by Assur-bani-pal's scribes, were of equal importance. These show a much greater dependence on the Sumerian traditions preserved by the Kassite scribes of Babylon. The Epic of Gilgamesh, the most famous work of Akkadian literature, is based on a number of the shorter Sumerian tales of Gilgamesh. The story of the flood, worked into the same Akkadian epic, is derived from the Sumerian original, entirely unconnected with Gilgamesh. Hymns, descriptions of rituals, prayers and incantations, lists of words, grammatical and legal compilations—all in constant use—owed their origin and their form to Sumerian, although written in Akkadian. Even the proverbs were derived not from the living language of contemporary Babylon or Assyria, but from Sumerian originals of more than a thousand years before. This parallels the use of Latin in the Middle Ages, when the debt extended far beyond the mere use of Latin as a scholarly language. Legends, history and, indeed, a whole way of thought were inherited from the earlier civilization.

a strong army from Merodach-Baladan's eastern ally, Elam, which halted his advance so effectively that Sargon was content to leave Babylonia under its rebel king until a more opportune moment. This came in 710 BC, when Sargon, meeting no serious opposition, magnanimously left Merodach-Baladan as chief of his own tribe and made himself King of Babylon.

His generous treatment of the enemy proved advantageous, and no further trouble came from Babylonia until his death. His successor, Sennacherib, kept military control of Babylonia, but did not take the hands of Bel, and thus in theory had no kingship of Babylon. This was claimed in 703 BC by Merodach-Baladan, who had now managed to secure the support of the Elamites, and even of Hezekiah of Judah.

However, Sennacherib was able to defeat him easily, and installed first a Babylonian puppet-king, and then one of his own sons, on the throne of Babylon. These attempts, too, foundered on the combined hostility of Elam and the Chaldean tribes, and in 689 BC, when Babylon fell after a long siege, Sennacherib's patience was exhausted, and he sacked the capital, carrying off the chief god, Bel, to Assyria. He himself assumed the title of King of Sumer and Akkad, and in his last years entrusted the government of the southern provinces to his son, Esarhaddon, whom he had designated as his successor. In 681 BC Esarhaddon succeeded to the throne after foiling the conspirators who had killed his father.

Esarhaddon and Assur-bani-pal

Although there were no major troubles in Babylonia during his reign, the experiences of the preceding two reigns left Esarhaddon well aware of the need for a satisfactory settlement there, and one which was compatible with Babylonian pride. He took very great care to ensure that after his death the empire would be well administered. His eldest son, Shamash-shum-ukin, was given the kingship of Babylon, while Assyria—and therefore the overlordship of Babylon—

The fall of Assyria

Records are lacking for the end of Assur-bani-pal's reign, and so it is impossible to judge how far Assyria's might had declined before his death. However, from that time, it faced revolt and aggression on all sides, and even the good generalship of its kings did not suffice to save it from new dangers. In 612 BC the king in Babylonia, Nabopolassar, and his ally, the Mede Cyaxares, were able to enlist the support of the Scythian army which had previously fought against them, and to launch their final attack on Nineveh. After three attempts the great capital of Assyria fell to its besiegers, and the 'burden of Nineveh' is described in the Old Testament by the prophet Nahum:

Thy shepherds slumber, O King of Assyria: Thy nobles shall dwell in the dust: thy people is scattered upon the mountains, and no man gathereth them. There is no healing of thy bruises; thy wound is grievous: All that hear the bruit of thee shall clap the hands over thee: For upon whom hath not thy wickedness passed continually?

The fall of Nineveh was irrevocable. A remnant of the Assyrian Empire held out for a time in the western city of Harran, but it was a hopeless cause. From now on events originated not in Assyria but in Babylonia, and Mesopotamia soon lost its special place in history. After the end of the First Dynasty power had passed to the Kassites, a people of mountain origin, who adopted the civilization of their subjects, and consciously fostered their ancient scribal traditions.

However, neither they nor any of the succeeding short-lived dynasties were the equal of Assyria in military strength. Although there were times in the second millennium BC when Assyria acknowledged the overlordship of Babylon, and although the two countries were in constant dispute over some of their border towns, Babylon seems always to have rejected the habit of military conquest which was so natural to Assyria.

Bordered on the east by the ancient state of Elam, on the south and west by the sea and desert, and on the north by Assyria itself, Babylon had few prospects of conquest. Yet the real reason for the difference between Assyria and Babylon is probably to be sought in the land itself. Babylonia was immensely fertile. Long established industries together with a highly developed commercial life greatly increased the country's

Above, tablet from Assur-bani-pal's library laying down moral precepts by which a king should govern. British Museum, London.

Left, ivory plaque depicting an Ethiopian and a lioness. British Museum, London.

Opposite top, relief from Assur-bani-pal's palace at Nineveh showing musicians and attendants waiting on the king in the palace gardens, mid-seventh century BC. British Museum, London.

Opposite bottom, boats on the River Tigris at Nineveh: detail from a series of reliefs showing the construction of Sennacherib's palace, c. 705 BC. British Museum, London.

prosperity. The power of the kings was not so great as in Assyria, and war inevitably meant increased trade disruption.

The guardians of ancient temples, possessing great land holdings, were just as anxious as influential merchant families to see that their prosperous activities were not curtailed by war. Although the kingship in Babylon changed hands frequently, the population as a whole was not concerned. When Babylon was under the Assyrian kings, the kingship was frequently wrested from them by local usurpers, of whom the most active were the Chaldeans.

When the Aramaeans, who were related to the Chaldeans, pushed into northern Mesopotamia, the Chaldeans themselves occupied the marshes in the south of Babylonia. They did not readily cooperate, and were hence both weak and difficult to control. They had no vested interest in peace, like the settled Babylonians further north, and they naturally took advantage of any disturbances to promote their own causes. The death of Assur-bani-pal provided just such an opportunity, and, after a struggle with his successors, which lasted several years, a Chaldean chief called Nabopolassar was able to claim the kingship of Babylon and win the allegiance of the

country. However not content with that, he assisted the Medes in the capture of Nineveh in 612 BC, and in 605 BC his son, Nebuchadnezzar, was able to rout the Egyptian army at Carchemish, thus destroying the last hopes of Assyria, with whom Egypt was in league. The Egyptians were chased by Nebuchadnezzar right down to their border, and he might well have followed them further, but for the news of his father's death. Hastening back to Babylon, he secured the throne, to which he had shown himself a worthy successor, and left his new conquests, Syria and Palestine, subdued.

Nebuchadnezzar

Nebuchadnezzar was in a remarkable position. Assyria had been effectively removed from the scene, Egypt was constrained within its borders and he was allied with the rising power of the Medes in the east. They held the lands to the north, and as time went on they advanced across the mountainous districts of Asia Minor to confront the Lydians, who were masters in the west, at the Halys river. There, after inconclusive fighting, the boundary was fixed, with the help of Babylonian arbitration, and each was now in a position to turn their efforts elsewhere.

With his northern and eastern borders guarded by the Median alliance, Nebuchadnezzar was free to deal with the southwest. Once more Judah, with encouragement from Egypt, defied the distant king in Mesopotamia. However, unlike Sennacherib, Nebuchadnezzar was in a position to punish rebels. In 597 BC Jerusalem was taken, its king Jehoiachin and some of its inhabitants deported to Babylonia, and a new king, Zedekiah, installed to maintain a Babylonian policy. However, national feeling was too much for him, and he too rebelled, only to bring down on his city a devastation

which was meant to be as final as that of Nineveh. In 586 BC city and temple were sacked and the population was carried off into exile in Babylonia.

Nebuchadnezzar's method of subjugation had already been tried by the Assyrians. They had found that if the native population were uprooted and replanted elsewhere, it lost much of the will to assert its independence. On the other hand, those brought in to replace them knew, in these strange surroundings, that their only chance of survival lay in obedience to the great king. It was not necessarily an inhuman process. From the correspondence of the Assyrian kings it can be seen that they were anxious to see their deportees well fed and clothed. The Jewish colonies in Babylonia flourished and ration lists found in Babylon show that King Jehoiachin, at least, was accorded dignified treatment.

Like the Assyrian kings, Nebuchadnezzar was not only a conqueror but a tireless builder. Although the Assyrian kings had not neglected the needs of Babylon, its destruction under Shamash-shum-ukin and the continual fighting over the city which had preceded Nabopolassar's final victory can hardly have left it in a state worthy of the capital of so great an empire. Nabopolassar himself began building schemes, but undoubtedly the most spectacular works were undertaken by his son. Nebuchadnezzar saw to it that Babylon was remembered in later years as the greatest city in the world.

About 100 years after him the Greek traveller and historian, Herodotus, saw the city under its Persian monarchs, and his comment, 'it is more splendid than any other city known to us', was an acknowledgment of Nebuchadnezzar's amazing achievements.

Not only the enigmatic 'hanging gardens', considered one of the seven wonders of the ancient world, but numerous temples, palaces, roads, walls, gates and even a bridge across the Euphrates, which ran

through the city, were among the works of this great king. The most spectacular of these monuments to survive is the Ishtar Gate, through which the Processional Way crosses the great walls. Designed in glazed bricks, yellow and white lions and dragons march against a blue background along the road leading to the massive, crenellated gate-towers, laid on foundations as deep as their walls are high.

Herodotus describes in great detail this seemingly impregnable wall, and other marvels like the bridge and the great temple of Marduk, or Bel, with its ziggurat. This stepped, pyramid-like structure—which must be the origin of the 'tower of Babel'—copied the Sumerian architecture of the Third Dynasty of Ur. It serves as another reminder that Nebuchadnezzar and his dynasty, who even used the archaic Sumerian script, were deeply conscious of their position as restorers of the glory of ancient Babylon and Sumer.

Nebuchadnezzar's successors were a disappointment. His own son, Amel-Marduk (562–560 BC) was weak, and was murdered in a palace conspiracy, being replaced by his brother-in-law, Nergalshar-usur (560–556 BC). The latter may have been more capable—he led an expedition to deal with a troublesome king as far away as Seleucia, west of Cilicia in Turkey—but he did not reign much longer. His son, Labashi-Marduk, was murdered within a year of his accession, his throne passing to the last ruler of independent Babylon, Nabu-naid, generally known as Nabonidus.

Nabonidus

Nabonidus is one of the most enigmatic figures of history. He was deeply religious and already an old man when he acceded, and his actions may well have given rise to the legends of madness which have been told

of Nebuchadnezzar. In the first year of his reign he was commanded in a dream to rebuild the temple of the moon god, Sin, at Harran, which had been left desolate since the city's capture by the Medes at the time of the final destruction of Assyria. Nabonidus, who was clearly no great warrior, objected that the Medes still held the city, but was assured that they and their allies were doomed. In fact, Nabonidus records: 'When the third year came, Marduk made his young servant, Cyrus, King of Anshan, rise against them, and he scattered the numerous Medes with his small army and captured Astyages, King of the Medes, and brought him in fetters into his land.'

Nabonidus fulfilled the task set him, but his attentions to the god Sin earned him the disfavour of the all-powerful priests of Marduk in Babylon, and later he himself stated that the gods no longer wished him to stay in the city, which was suffering plague and famine during his presence. He therefore retired to the city of Tema in central Arabia—always a stronghold of the worship of the moon god—and, leaving his son, Belshazzar, as his regent, lived there peacefully for ten years.

Cyrus

While Nabonidus was in retirement, important changes took place in the Near East. Cyrus, the founder of the Persian Empire, had inherited the Median possessions, and lost no time in enlarging them. Most ominously, the kingdom of Lydia, which had successfully defied the Medes, crumbled before him. In 547 BC he pursued them to the outskirts of their capital, Sardis, and after a siege, captured the city and their king, Croesus. With Asia Minor at his feet, and the sea his boundary in the west, he turned his attention to Babylon, and the old alliance between Babylon and Persia was now in jeopardy.

Above, the Ishtar Gate at Babylon built during the reign of Nebuchadnezzar II; the gates into Babylon were faced with glazed bricks in a variety of rich colours and decorated with heraldic animals. Staatliche Museum, Berlin.

Above left, the ruins of Babylon, all that remains of one of the most splendid cities of the ancient world.

Opposite right, seventh-century BC cylinder seal and its impression showing the goddess Ishtar, who carries a bow and arrow among other weapons, being worshipped by a lady with a mace. British Museum, London.

Opposite left, eighth-century BC ivory figure of a Nubian with oryx, monkey and leopard skin. British Museum, London.

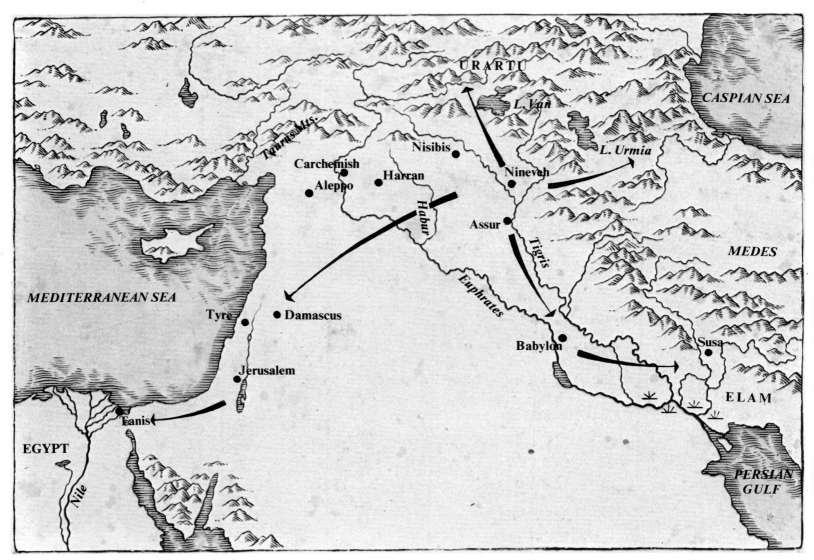

Cyrus' ambition was unbounded, and, employing the tactics he had used against the Medians and Lydians, he struck right at the heart of Babylonia. In 539 BC, when Nabonidus had returned to Babylon, Cyrus' army scattered a force sent to block its approach, and he met no further opposition to his advance. The bloodless capture of the city was accomplished so easily that historians are at a loss to explain it. There may be some truth in Herodotus' story that Cyrus diverted the Euphrates, allowing his troops to enter surreptitiously along the river bed, but this is not a complete explanation.

It is difficult to resist the conclusion that treachery had been used. After the conquest Cyrus did his best to blacken the memory of Nabonidus and to portray himself as a liberator, and it may be that priests within the city who resented the religious beliefs of Nabonidus arranged to betray the city. However, the events leave no doubt that the vigour of the neo-Babylonian empire had ebbed steadily since Nebuchadnezzar's death.

The Persian Empire was far greater than any previous one, and united countries whose names were strange to one another. In the west, the Persians followed the Assyrian example by ruling Egypt, and their empire stretched as far to the east of Babylon as to the west. Babylon itself still flourished. In Herodotus' day it supplied a third of the corn for the whole empire, and the Persian kings fostered Babylon's ancient traditions. However, the political importance of Mesopotamia had declined, and world history moved across the two rivers, the Tigris and the Euphrates, with little regard for their earlier glories.

Between 490 and 478 BC the Greeks weathered the storm of the Persian invasions. One of the decisive events of their history, and indeed of the Western world, for the Persians it was but a minor set-back; they had merely wanted to punish the insolent petty states which had dared to incite rebellion among their cities in western Anatolia. More serious for them was the revolt in Egypt, a potential source of great wealth. They could not, however, foresee Greece's future role.

Alexander and his successors

In 334 BC when Alexander the Great of Macedon defied the Persian Empire in the west—in lands where Greeks had dwelt long before Cyrus—he could not have known how far his action would take him. Two decisive battles, one in Syria, and one in the ancient Assyrian homeland, were enough to destroy completely the resistance of the Persian Empire. Alexander's conquests did not vanish with his mysterious death at Babylon. The Greeks maintained their hold on Babylon during the Seleucid dynasty founded by one of Alexander's generals. More important than conquest was cultural victory. The Greeks brought with them their own philosophy, science and literature, so that Babylon even lost its cherished claims to be the centre of learning of the ancient world.

The Seleucid dynasty lasted no longer than the Persian, and its empire was divided between the Romans and the Parthians. Rome was soon milking Asia Minor and Syria of their wealth, but was prevented from advancing further into Armenia and Persia by the vigorous opposition of the Parthian kings, and where Romans and Parthians met, along the Euphrates, the land was devastated by continual battles.

At Carrhae (Harran), the Parthians inflicted a crushing defeat on a Roman army. Although the Romans later managed to push their border eastwards into the lands of ancient Assyria, Parthia, with its Persian heritage, was an enemy which was always held in respect by Rome and never fell victim to Roman rapacity.

In time Parthians made way for Sassanians, who were opponents of the Byzantine emperors, and when they too succumbed to the might of Islam and the Abbasid caliphate made its capital at Baghdad, near ancient Babylon, the memories of Mesopotamia's earlier glories had faded beyond recall. Only in the nineteenth century were they revived by pioneering archaeologists.

For many years Assyrians and Babylonians alike were no more than the enemies of Israel mentioned in the Bible. However, modern discoveries have enabled a whole new civilization to be reconstructed, to which the Bible gives no clue, although the world of the Old Testament was itself a small part of this civilization. During more than two thousand years the rise and fall of successive empires can be followed. Throughout this period Mesopotamia is the centre of all learning, the source of all wealth and the ruler of the world.

Western civilization has two chief links with the ancient Near East: Greece and the Bible. It can be readily seen how Mesopotamia impinged on the Biblical world, and the discovery of a fragment of the Epic of Gilgamesh in the Palestinian city of Megiddo sheds some light on the channels by which the flood stories of ancient Sumer reached the author of the Book of Genesis. The influence on Greece is less tangible. In the second millennium BC, throughout the Near East—lands with which the Mycenaean Greeks traded— Akkadian was the language of diplomacy.

It was inevitable that culture and customs as well as language would permeate these lands. If Egyptian influence is more evident, other parts of the Near East also played their part in the genesis of Greece. Without the knowledge of astronomy, chemistry and mathematics which were the heritage of Egypt and Babylon, Greek philosophy would be unrecognizable. Moreover, Greek art in its formative stages was also subject to influences from the east.

However, perhaps the most valuable single asset a knowledge of Mesopotamia can offer is to provide a backcloth against which the original achievements of the Greeks stand out in greater relief than ever.

Opposite, map of the Near East at the time of the Assyrian kings.

ASSYRIA AND ITS NEIGHBOURS

Date	Assyrian rulers	Domestic and foreign history	Culture	Neighbouring countries	Date	Assyria and Babylon	Anatolia and Palestine	Iran	Egypt
1200		Invasion of the peoples of the sea		Dorian invasion of Greece	700	Sennacherib Esarhaddon		Dejoces Phraortes	Napatan rule Capture of
			Assur capital			Assur-bani-pal	Gyges King of	Cyrus I King of	Memphis
	Assurdan I	Assyrian incursions into Babylonia		Rameses III	650	Revolt of Babylon	Lydia Cimmerian invasions	Anshan	Sack of Thebes
1100									
	Tiglath-Pileser					Capture of Babylon Death of			Saite revival Psammeticus I expels
		Assyria attacked on all sides by Aramaeans and Gutians	Destruction of the first temples and palaces	Migration of Medes and Persians into Iran End of Middle Kingdom in Egypt		Assur-bani-pal Nabopolassar King of Babylon Destruction of	Lydians invent coinage	Cyaxares King of the Medes Alliance of Medes	the Assyrians Necho II
1000				Daniel	600	Nineveh Nebuchadnezzar	Jeremiah	and Babylonians	
			Palaces and bas-reliefs at Tell Halaf	Solomon			Siege of Jerusalem Ezekiel		
900	Adad-nirari II			Medes and Persians advance to Zagros		Brilliant Neo-Babylonian			
	Tukulti-Ninurta II Assur-nasir-pal II Shalmaneser III	Assyria the centre of an empire	Nineveh and Kalhu capitals			Empire	Destruction of Jerusalem Croesus King of Lydia	Astyages	Apries Amasis
800	Shamshi-Adad V		Babylonian cults spread into Assyria		550	Nabonidus	Cyrus annexes Lydia	Cyrus II deposes Astyages	Height of Saite power
	Adad-Nirari III Semiramis (regent)			Kingdom of Phrygia				Persian Empire	
700	Tiglath-Pileser III Sargon II	Further Assyrian conquests	Khorsabad Stele of Sargon	Kingdom of Lydia		Cyrus takes Babylon	End of Babylonian captivity	Cambyses	Psammeticus III Cambyses conquers Egypt
	Sennacherib	Invasion of Egypt Sack of Babylon	Nineveh again capital	Phraortes King of				Death of Cambyses	
	Esarhaddon		Flowering of sculpture	the Medes	500	Babylon annexed to Persian Empire			
	Assur-bani-pal	Assyria devastated by the Scythians						Darius I	
600		Destruction of Nineveh	Assur-bani-pal's library	Cyaxares King of the Medes and Persians					

Chapter 5

The Civilization of Egypt

Egypt's civilization developed in one of the largest arid desert areas in the world, larger than the whole of Europe. It could do so only because of the River Nile, which crosses an almost rainless desert from south to north carrying the waters of Lake Victoria more than 3,000 miles down to the Mediterranean Sea. In ancient times Egypt comprised just the last 700 miles, the stretch of river downstream from the First Cataract at Aswan. Along most of this distance the Nile has scoured a deep and wide gorge in the desert plateau, on the floor of which a thick layer of rich clay silt has built up. It is this which gave the Nile valley its astonishing fertility and has transformed what might have been a mere geological curiosity into a thickly populated agricultural country.

The Nile valley proper ends in the vicinity of Cairo. All that part of the valley lying to the north of Aswan, except for the last forty miles, formed the ancient kingdom of Shemau, or Upper Egypt as it is usually known. Today, however, this contains only about one-third of the total arable land in Egypt, for to the north the river flows out of the valley into a large bay in the coastline, now entirely choked with the same rich silt, to form a wide, flat delta, over which the river meanders in several branches. The two principal branches are the Damietta on the east and the Rosetta on the west. This delta, together with a short section of the valley,

formed the ancient kingdom of Ta-mehu, or Lower Egypt.

The cultivated lands of the Nile valley and delta today present a flat, unvarying landscape of intensively cultivated fields, crossed by irrigation and drainage canals, and studded with towns and villages half-hidden by groves of palm trees. The transition from fields to desert is abrupt and striking. Civilization visibly ends here, and on the east the desert plateau above the valley gradually rises to a jagged line of mountains bordering the Red Sea, while on the west it stretches, and empty, silent, wind-swept land of gravel and sand, for a distance of more than 3,000 miles to the Atlantic Ocean.

An agricultural society

The Nile receives two principal tributaries, the Blue Nile and the Atbara, both rising in the high, mountainous plateau of Ethiopa. The heavy summer rains in Ethiopia swell enormously the volume of water in these tributaries, enabling a greatly increased load of sediment to be carried, rich in minerals. Without the elaborate hydraulic controls which have been applied since the middle of the nineteenth century this surge of water is enough to flood the Nile valley and delta, forming a long, shallow lake, above which towns and villages emerge as islands, linked by causeways.

As the current is checked some of the silt settles on to the land and is left behind when the waters recede in October and November. If crops are then sown in the thick, wet mud, the warm, dry climate will have ripened them by March or April with little or no need for further watering. Then, after the harvest in summer, the ground dries and cracks, enabling aeration to take place, which prevents waterlogging and the excessive accumulation of salt. These three seasons formed the basic divisions of the ancient Egyptian's calendar: *Akhet* (inundation), *Peret* (growing) and *Shemu* (drought).

It is an ideal natural cycle but one that human ingenuity can still do much to improve. Banks can be built enclosing large basins where the farmer can allow the waters to remain for a period before releasing them. Water can be raised mechanically to irrigate areas above the normal reach of the flood or in summer, when the river is at its lowest, to irrigate the fields for a second crop. It is now very difficult to decide how far the ancient Egyptians improved on the natural cycle, and even more so to give dates to innovations.

When a river overflows its banks the coarsest and heaviest sediment is dropped first, leaving raised banks or levees along the sides of the channel. It is an irregular process since the course of a river is always slowly

changing and some levees are left behind as low mounds on the flood plain. In the Nile valley and delta these would have provided ideal sites for the first farming. The expansion of agriculture down on to the plain must have required a certain amount of drainage by digging canals, since levees tend to hold back the subsiding flood water.

It is, however, unlikely that the early prehistoric farmers had to face a thick, perennially swampy jungle. The only perennial swamps were probably confined to the very edge of the flood plains, alongside the desert, where the least amount of sediment was dropped during the inundation and the ground level was therefore at its lowest. The papyrus swamps which are so often depicted in ancient tomb paintings as the haunt of wild game and the hunting grounds of the rich must have been found here.

Mechanical irrigation aids become necessary only when the single annual crop no longer supplies enough food for the community. The only mechanical aid apparently known to the ancient Egyptians was the *shaduf*, a primitive and highly inefficient device still in limited use today. Its construction is of the simplest: a pivoted, horizontal pole with a counterweight at one end and a bucket of some sort suspended at the other. It is tempting to regard it as being of immemorial antiquity. Yet before the sixteenth century BC there is not a single illustration of the *shaduf* in the countless tomb paintings of agricultural work, stereotyped though many are, nor is there a reference in contemporary literature.

The earliest representations depict only the watering of gardens, not the irrigation of fields. This suggests that one crop a year, grown on the land watered by the natural yearly inundation, was normally sufficient for Egypt's economy, though a few texts seem to indicate a second crop, confined to banks and islands and watered by hand.

The crops grown were many and varied. Most important were barley and a kind of wheat called emmer, also flax for the manufacture of linen, and fruits and vegetables. There were sufficient pasture lands and supplies of fodder to support herds of cattle and flocks of sheep, goats and pigs, and ducks and geese. From the peripheral swamps and the river came waterfowl and fish. To neighbouring peoples Egypt must always have appeared immeasurably fertile and prosperous.

What archaeology reveals

The geography of Egypt has had a marked effect on its archaeological record. The dry sands have astonishing preservative qualities. The ancient Egyptians were doubtless aware of this and, like their modern successors, preferred to bury their dead on the sandy desert margins rather than in the

damp soil. Obviously where settlements were far from the desert, particularly in the delta, this was impracticable and the edge of the town had to suffice.

It was the custom to bury alongside the body articles of use or prized personal possessions which would be available to the dead man's spirit in the hereafter. There would often be provision for a regular service of offerings carried out by surviving relatives, and the chapels built for this contained commemorative and religious texts, and pictures of the happy life that the dead man hoped to live. As a result we have a considerable amount of information about the funerary beliefs and practices of the Egyptians, together with a vast accumulation of well preserved illustrative material which fills museums the world over.

Although this material contains a great deal that is relevant to the study of ancient Egyptian life, the coverage is very incomplete. A tomb painting may show craftsmen at work and the tomb itself may contain specimens of tools used, but we cannot learn from these where the work was carried out, the type of building involved, the numbers of men employed, or the exact processes used. Only the meticulous excavation of workshops, with a lucky find of documents relating to their use and administration, can yield all the answers.

Today the demand for agricultural land in Egypt is probably heavier than ever before. Yet nearly all towns and villages lie on the cultivable flood plain. There is no reason to believe that in ancient times the situation was at all different. Indeed, with internal

communications less well developed, the Nile, which was the chief means of transport, must have exerted an even stronger attraction in the location of important towns and cities. The natural levees must also have afforded the best sites for settlement in very early times. However, the annual deposition of Nile silt has meant a slow if irregular increase in the thickness of the arable soil, accompanied by a gradual horizontal spreading. In some places this soil has even buried the ancient cemeteries far underground, producing disconcerting gaps in archaeological knowledge. Most of the ancient cities, towns and villages have either been ploughed under fields, or lie beneath existing towns. In either case the practical difficulties of locating them and then arranging for excavation to take place render them virtually inaccessible. Even so, some town sites are still accessible.

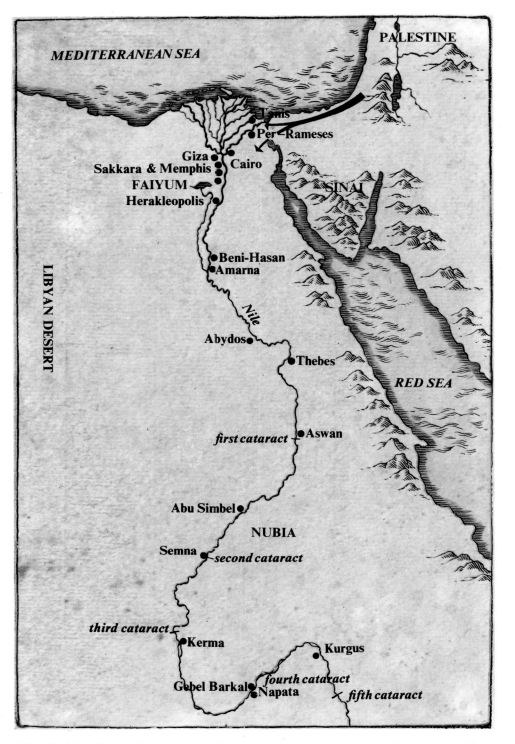

Egypt did not possess large towns and cities comparable to those of other ancient civilizations, and that in the prehistoric period, with no written records, the extent of urbanization is to be judged from the scanty traces of tiny, squalid hamlets excavated on the desert edge. It is still possible to see poverty-stricken settlements, but taken by themselves they offer no clue to the existence of the towns and cities of modern Egypt.

The same must be assumed for ancient times. There are huge gaps in our knowledge and our view of ancient Egyptian society must reflect this. Some of these gaps may be filled as further discoveries are brought to light. Others, unfortunately, may prove to be permanent.

Egyptian writing

Egyptian civilization was founded on writing: the ability to express graphically the sounds of speech. Considerable uncertainty exists over the precise affinities of the language spoken in ancient Egypt, although it does appear to have had links with the Semitic languages of western Asia. The system used to write the language, however, was a purely local one. It was basically phonetic. Most of the signs used, although depicting actual objects, such as birds or items of furniture, stood only for sounds.

As an essential step towards simplicity vowels were disregarded and only the consonants were written. For example, the word for 'a basket' contained two consonants, *n* followed by *b*; the picture of a basket could also be used to write any other words which contained these two consonants in this order, such as the words for 'lord, owner of', and the adjective 'all, every'. In terms of modern English it is equivalent to using a picture of a loaf, representing the consonants *l* and *f*, to write the words 'leaf', 'life', 'laugh' and 'aloof'. The context would normally indicate which of several possibilities was meant, but to assist the reader an additional symbol might be added indicating the general category to which the word belonged, such as a pair of legs walking to indicate a verb of motion, or a bound roll of papyrus to indicate something abstract.

In religious matters the Egyptians were acutely aware of the correctness of patterns laid down in the remote past, when the gods themselves had ruled the land. Perfection was complete conformity to the rules, whether in the design of a temple, the form of a text or the shape of a work of art. The same was true of the written signs, or hieroglyphs, which were used principally for monumental texts of a religious nature or in a religious setting. Thus until the very end of Egyptian civilization great care was taken to preserve the exact form of the signs. No stylization, with the accompanying loss of

Other limiting factors have however been at work. The organic refuse, called *sebakh*, which has accumulated in the sites of ancient towns, provides a valuable and ready source of fertilizer for the fields. Site after site has in the past been almost completely destroyed above ground level by peasants digging for *sebakh*. Furthermore, since cemeteries contain the best of the ancient Egyptians' possessions, often perfectly preserved and in conditions of easy recovery, most archaeological activity has been concentrated in this sector. The need to excavate town sites has met with continued indifference: they are often partly waterlogged and partly obliterated by diggers for *sebakh*,

and tend to produce large quantities of coarse household pottery fragments, matched by a dearth of the aesthetically pleasing. Yet these sites, offering the only hope of filling the huge gaps in our knowledge, are endangered by the needs of a rapidly expanding population.

The results of this pattern of work and preservation are easy to see. A fairly detailed history of the pyramids and of other kinds of tomb can be written, but the evidence for urban settlements is limited to a handful of sites from the desert edge, probably not typical and spread over a period of more than 3,000 years. It would, however, be misleading to believe that

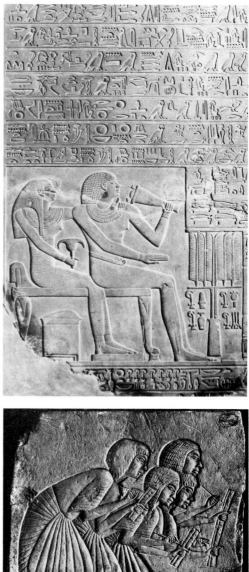

identity, was conceivable. Care was also taken in these texts to preserve a particular stage of the language which might be termed 'classical'. The success with which this process of deliberate fossilization was met contributes much to the overall impression of timeless continuity which ancient Egypt produces.

This artificiality had a relatively limited application, and it occupies a major place in our impression of ancient Egypt only because its products were designed to last for eternity. In business and administrative documents which the Egyptians seem to have produced in prodigious quantities, the hieroglyphic system was rapidly modified to a flowing, longhand form known as hieratic, for use with a rush pen and ink. The normal writing material was papyrus, a paper-like substance made from thin strips of the papyrus reed. It is normally preserved only when kept completely dry. Consequently most of the ancient archives kept in towns and cities on the cultivated flood plain have not survived, and only the minute selection which has bears witness to the detailed nature of Egyptian record keeping.

The general style of hieratic changed over the course of centuries, and eventually lost most of its resemblance to the parent hieroglyphic. The ultimate form, demotic, began to come into use somewhere in the seventh century BC. The form of the language of these everyday texts also changed considerably, although with a tendency to lag behind the spoken language. Eventually the system died out altogether, but the ancient language lingered on, written now in Greek letters, as the language of Christian or Coptic Egypt.

One final point needs to be made. Some of the hieroglyphs represented one consonant only. Here was the basis for an alphabetic script, employing only about twenty-four signs instead of the 700 or so normally in use. However, a simplification of this nature would have been anathema to the ancient Egyptians. Some ancient scholars did actually experiment with the system, but always towards greater complexity, using the basic principles on which the system had been created to produce new alternatives to accepted signs. These pedantic exercises are fortunately confined to certain religious texts, and had their greatest period of activity under the Ptolemies and the Romans. Simplicity could only detract from the sacred character of the hieroglyphic system. It is perhaps significant that an alphabetic script had to wait until Christianity arrived.

The discovery of ancient Egypt

Once the civilization of ancient Egypt had faded away and was overlaid first, by Christianity and then by Islam, its vestiges remained the object only of idle curiosity. Its rediscovery was a feature of western Romanticism of the eighteenth and nineteenth centuries. The chief stimulus was provided by the large team of scholars and engineers who formed part of the expedition with which Napoleon hoped to conquer Egypt in 1798. Their detailed description of the country included an extensive illustrated account of the ancient monuments.

In the nineteenth century the major western collections of Egyptian antiquities,

Above, fragment of an Eighteenth-Dynasty relief showing scribes at work. Archaeological Museum, Florence.

Top, Eleventh-Dynasty funerary stela: descriptive detail became one of the hall-marks of Middle Kingdom artistic style. Pushkin Museum, Moscow.

Above left, wall-painting of Apuy's house and garden from the Tomb of Apuy, Thebes, Nineteenth Dynasty. Metropolitan Museum of Art, New York.

Opposite, map of ancient Egypt and adjacent lands.

at last obtaining the proper equipment for tackling the excavation of difficult town sites on the flood plain. The information they can yield must greatly supplement our knowledge of ancient Egyptian society, to the point where we can reconstruct in some detail the overall shape of a major pre-Classical civilization.

The earliest surviving Egyptian records date from about 3200 BC and, by a fortunate coincidence, the ancient Egyptians themselves commonly began their enumeration of kings and dynasties at about the same point of time. It can, therefore, be said with some certainty that Egyptian history begins about 3200 BC. This date, like others in Egyptian history, has been calculated on the basis of ancient astronomical observations, combined with information derived from ancient lists of kings, and must be taken as a rough approximation. Prior to this the civilization of prehistoric Egypt can be defined and recorded only in terms of purely archaeological material arranged in a sequence of groups. Dates can be calculated only by scientific techniques, the most common using measurements of the proportion of radioactive carbon present in ancient organic material, such as charcoal or corn grains.

The history of ancient Egypt appears to be largely the history of its ruling families: their architectural achievements and military exploits occupy an unduly large proportion of modern history books. This is a consequence of the survival of a multiplicity of stone monuments designed to commemorate Egypt's rulers. The divine king was the most important element in Egyptian society. His deeds ensured the continued existence of world order, and recording them gave proof of his continued efficacy.

The monuments portray a timeless regulated world in which the king fraternizes confidently with the other gods, receives their blessings and ensures their well-being. He triumphs over his foes and receives the homage of his subjects. The smooth, unrippled surface of royal power extends from age to age, back to the rule of the gods.

Nevertheless, one should not be deceived by this attractive façade. The familiar features of absolute royal power—plots, usurpations, feuds and corruption—were present in ancient Egypt also, even though harsh realities like this had no place in a divinely ordered society.

The limitations inherent in the historical sources have been magnified by the passage of time. Only a tiny proportion of what was once available has survived, and this in a highly arbitrary and irregular way. The most important centres of documentation were the temples, particularly those in the capital, which served as repositories of important documents and records of successive kings.

In the Nile valley three cities functioned at different times as the capital. The site of the first, Memphis, is well known—fifteen

such as that at the British Museum, were established, often in a spirit of fierce national rivalry. Size as well as beauty played a considerable part in the selection. Treasure hunting has probably been endemic in Egypt since ancient times, but to the lust of gold was now added the possibility of a profitable trade in antiquities with western museums and collectors. At the same time serious attempts began to be made to record accurately the visible monumental remains and to copy inscriptions.

In the twentieth century there has been a gradual change of emphasis. The urge to collect has been somewhat diminished by the realization that a civilization cannot be described simply in terms of its more impressive monuments. A balanced view of society requires details of the minutiae of the daily life of people of all classes, and this can be gathered only by methodical and painstaking excavation and recording. The context in which an object is found has become as important as the object itself.

A golden statue, on its own, tells us little about anything except golden statues.

The framework into which all this material can be fitted has been provided by the decipherment of the ancient script and the subsequent analysis of its language. The initial clues were provided by a bilingual text, written in both Greek and in ancient Egyptian: the Rosetta Stone of the British Museum. The main credit for decipherment belongs to the French scholar, Jean Champollion, working on foundations laid by Åkerblad of Sweden and Thomas Young of England. As a result of over 150 years of study the main framework of Egyptian grammar is established with some certainty, and reasonably reliable translations can now be provided for most texts.

Yet the scope for further work remains enormous. As the techniques of archaeology grow more refined each year, so the amount of information which excavation can yield increases, not only in quantity but in variety also. Moreover, archaeologists are miles south of Cairo on the west bank of the Nile—but it has hardly been touched by excavation. The second, Amenemhet-ith-tawy, has never been located. Only in the third, Thebes, do the temples survive to any great extent. It is noticeable that when the centre of power is at Thebes, the number of sources increases considerably.

For the period of the Middle Kingdom (roughly the nineteenth and twentieth centuries BC), when the capital was at Amenemhet-ith-tawy, official documents are almost non-existent. Records are even more incomplete for the delta region, where destruction has been intense and excavation negligible. A connected history of the area hardly exists at all, and when ancient Egypt divides into its two component parts and civil war results, the conflict is seen only through the eyes of Upper Egypt. This is unfortunate since the delta had the closest contact with other civilizations.

Nevertheless, the 3000 years of Egyptian history have produced a formidable amount of documentation, and to reduce it to some order a system of classification has had to be adopted. The one universally accepted was created in the third century BC by an Egyptian priest, Manetho. Using a mass of documents no longer available he compiled a history of his country, and divided the kings into thirty dynasties. His work has unfortunately survived only in a number of inaccurate, abridged copies. The principal drawback to Manetho's work is that there are few means of checking the nature of the sources which he used. Sometimes they may have been contemporary with the events they describe, but at other times they seem to have been later traditions which had collected distortions, or simply folk tales. Nevertheless, convenience and familiarity have ensured the continued acceptance of Manetho's scheme.

Divine kingship

The King of Egypt was counted among the gods. For 3000 years the monuments proclaimed this even when the king was a distant foreign emperor and his role was essential for the survival of a safe, ordered society. He maintained the unity of the country by being at the same time king of both Upper and Lower Egypt, symbolizing this unity by wearing one or other of the crowns of the two kingdoms, or a double crown which combined the designs of both. The Biblical name 'Pharaoh' by which he is now commonly known is derived from a term for his palace, 'the great house', which was later used as a respectful circumlocution for the king himself. Every Egyptian temple preserved the fiction that the king alone made contact with the gods who dwelt within.

Although the scenes on the outer walls representing the king triumphing almost single-handedly over Egypt's enemies are often misinterpreted as a sign of vainglorious megalomania, they were intended to ensure, by the workings of sympathetic magic, that he would keep the country safe from foreign aggression.

One who slays the foreign bowmen without the blow of a club, who shoots the arrow without drawing the bowstring . . . The tongue of His Majesty restrains Nubia, his utterances cause the Asians to flee.
Lo, he is a place of refuge whose hand is not to be deflected.
Lo, he is a shelter who protects the fearful from his enemy.
Lo, he is a refreshing shade which is cool in summer.
Lo, he is a warm dry corner in the winter season.
Lo, he is a mountain which shuts off the tempest in the season when heaven rages.
(Hymns to King Senwosret III. Kahun Papyri. About 1850 BC.)

Theology placed the king firmly in the divine pantheon. He was an embodiment of the ancient falcon-god Horus, and he could claim parentage from some of the greatest of the gods, particularly the sun-god, Re, and later the Theban god Amon. Finally, at his death he was given a temple where he was worshipped like any other god. However, where the king differed from other gods was in appearing on earth in the form of a human being, ruling the lives of the people of Egypt. Some literary texts portray this human side of the king, who is depicted graciously pardoning a returned exile or finding amusement in being rowed up and down a lake by beautiful virgins clad only in fishnets. Particularly revealing, however, are two sets of instructions from a king to his son which illustrate the responsibilities and burdens of kingship:

Be a craftsman in speech that you may be strong. . .
Speech is more valorous than any fighting. No one can circumvent the skilful mind. Carry out justice while you remain on earth. Quiet the weeper, oppress not the widow, dispossess no man of the property of his father, interfere not with officials at their posts. Beware of punishing wrongfully. Trust not in length of years. A lifetime is regarded as [just] an hour. A man survives after death, his deeds are placed beside him in heaps. Existence yonder is truly for eternity, whoever disputes this is a fool. And as for him who reaches it without having done wrong, he shall exist there like a god, moving freely like the lords of eternity.
(Instruction for King Merikare. About 2020 BC)

The second instruction claims to be written by King Amenemhet I, about 1790 BC after an unsuccessful attempt at assassination. It is addressed to his son and heir, the future King Senwosret I:

Above and below, palette of King Narmer, a First-Dynasty monarch who ruled c. 3100 BC: palettes were among the first Egyptian records of actual events. Egyptian Museum, Cairo.

Opposite, the Rosetta Stone, c. 196 BC, discovered by a French military officer in 1799; its parallel inscriptions in three different scripts (the text is a decree in honour of Ptolemy V) provided the key to deciphering ancient Egyptian writing. British Museum, London.

Be wary of those subordinate to you lest something terrible happen to which no thought has been given. Approach them not in your loneliness, confide not in a brother, know not a friend, create no intimates for yourself. There is nothing to be gained by it ... It was he who ate my food that made mischief; the one to whom I had given my hands created terror.

Kingdoms of Upper and Lower Egypt

For much of the later prehistoric period Upper and Lower Egypt seem to have possessed different cultures, that of Lower Egypt appearing considerably more backward and impoverished than that of its southern neighbour. It is possible that this division into two cultural zones reflected the existence of two independent states.

However, towards the end of the prehistoric period Upper Egyptian culture spread northwards and evidence of this has been found in the eastern delta. The culture of Lower Egypt appears to have vanished without trace, the civilization of historic Egypt being a direct development of Upper Egyptian culture. One monument is of vital importance here. This is the Palermo Stone which once, before being broken and largely lost, summarized the events of every year of the reign of each king of the first five dynasties. However, at the very top it seems also to have listed the names of kings who ruled before the First Dynasty. In the little pictures of kings which accompany these names some wear only the crown of Lower Egypt, but at least seven wear the double crown. The unification thus clearly took

place before 3200 BC, Manetho's First Dynasty, and this may be linked with the final, northward spread of Upper Egyptian culture.

Manetho seems to have been drawing on traditions of kingship which first found expression in the thirteenth century BC. All the authorities start their enumeration of kings with Meni (Greek, *Menes*), except one which starts six kings later. Why did they ignore the evidence preserved on the much earlier Palermo Stone? In modern reconstructions Meni may occupy the beginning of the yearly enumeration, but he must still have been placed below, and thus, later than, the kings of the top row. It is possible that some legend had attached itself to Meni which made subsequent kings wish to be counted as his successors, or more likely, a political event of great importance had taken place in his reign, such as the founding of Memphis, which was attributed to Meni by the historian Herodotus.

It is also possible that the earliest documents had been lost, or had never in fact existed, since written records were not yet being kept. The Palermo Stone would have therefore recorded simply an oral tradition. It is difficult now to guess at the reasoning of which a tradition of legitimate kingship was reached. It seems clear, however, that the first Dynasty did not begin with the unification of Egypt.

The first period of greatness

The first two dynasties have been grouped together by historians as the Archaic Period, and the next four as the Old Kingdom. Although they lasted together about a

thousand years, they have left remarkably few historical data. There is, however, evidence that the continued existence of the union of the two Egypts was threatened. One of the earliest historical documents commemorates a victory of King Narmer over a rebellious prince of the delta, and similar monuments mark the close of the Second Dynasty about five centuries later.

The absence of records means that attention is chiefly drawn to physical achievements, especially the pyramid tombs of the kings. These begin at the start of the Third Dynasty, and reach their greatest dimensions in the Fourth at Giza. The capital seems to have been located at Memphis, and from the Second Dynasty onwards various suitable localities along a forty-five-mile stretch of the desert behind Memphis were selected for the royal tomb, around which a cemetery of courtiers and officials would grow. The most commonly chosen locality was at Sakkara, immediately west of Memphis, Giza lying approximately ten miles to the north. It is tempting to use them as an index of royal power, and to see the gigantic Giza group, which dominates the surrounding huddle of princely and ministerial tombs, as symbolizing the peak of royal might.

As the period progresses private tomb inscriptions begin to afford glimpses of the elaborate, centralized administration which gave the kings access to the resources and power which their monumental undertakings required. The tone of these inscriptions is one of total sycophantic service, which brings material rewards.

With the end of the Sixth Dynasty, about 2200 BC, the sequence of royal pyramids ceases, probably because they had become so small and roughly constructed as to escape discovery in the still only partially excavated necropolis at Sakkara. Manetho

Above, the sphinx at Memphis.

Above left, the Great Sphinx of Chephren, Fourth Dynasty.

Left, the grave of King Zoser, Third Dynasty, and, behind it, the Step Pyramid, built by Imhotep, who was later worshipped as a god.

Below, King Mycerinus, flanked by the goddess Hathor and a local deity, Fourth Dynasty. Egyptian Museum, Cairo.

Opposite above, the pyramids of Giza, Fourth Dynasty: in the front is the pyramid of King Mycerinus, flanked by small pyramids of three of his queens; behind is the pyramid of King Chephren and behind that the Great Pyramid of Cheops.

Opposite centre, flint knife with carved ivory handle, c. 2850 BC. Musée du Louvre, Paris.

Opposite bottom, ivory statuette of an Egyptian king wearing the crown of the Upper Kingdom, thought to date from the First Dynasty. British Museum, London.

took place seem to have resulted from the fact that for a time Egypt possessed two contemporary lines of kings, each claiming the divine kingship of the whole country.

After his Eighth Dynasty Manetho lists a Ninth and Tenth Dynasty, based at Herakleopolis, a city about fifty miles south of Memphis, although it is not certain whether they ruled from here rather than from Memphis. Their rule was challenged by princes of Thebes, as yet a relatively unimportant provincial city nearly 450 miles upstream from Memphis. Ruling from here with their own court and administration, they depicted themselves as divine rulers of all Egypt, although their power cannot have extended much further than Abydos, 100 miles downstream.

Within a space of probably less than fifty years a further palace revolution appears to have taken place at Thebes, and the succeeding dynasty, the Twelfth, established an entirely new capital city, named after the founder, Amenemhet - ith - tawy, '[King] Amenemhet seizes the two lands.' It seems to have been situated a short distance south of Memphis, but has never been discovered. This has unfortunately deprived historians of almost any historical documents of value, yet, as with the Old Kingdom, the material culture indicates that the two centuries of Twelfth Dynasty rule, called the Middle Kingdom, represents one of the most flourishing periods of Egyptian civilization.

One fascinating aspect of the Middle Kingdom is its secular literature. The range

lists a Seventh and an Eighth Dynasty of Memphis, but, without contemporary cemeteries, the kings are little more than simply names.

If the pyramids are taken as an index of royal power, why should the construction of pyramids have come to an end? It is very possible that continued building caused considerable strain on the economic system. Each pyramid formed a separate economic unit with its own administration and sources of wealth, established in perpetuity for the cult of the dead king. Over the centuries the wealth of these pyramids must have accumulated to become a significant proportion of the total wealth of the country, to which the living king presumably had little access. Conditions in the delta are quite unknown, but in Upper Egypt there are suggestions that from the twenty-fifth century onwards there was a degree of transference of power from the monarchy to local governors.

The first Theban revolt

The five centuries of the Old Kingdom were undoubtedly marked by violent struggles for power, although their echoes hardly reach the serene world of official monuments. To bridge the gap between the divine nature of the institution of kingship and reality in the person of the king must have required considerable rationalization on the part of the more thoughtful and educated members of society. However, the conflicts which now

was wide—from fantastic travellers' tales to homilies exhorting loyalty to the king. However, through some texts there runs a mood of scepticism and disquiet which accords ill with the confident, official façade of society. One recurrent theme is a despairing vision of an anarchic society in which every facet of ordered, civilized life is given a reverse, negative image. It finds its fullest expression in an elaborate literary composition, the *Admonitions of Ipuwer*, which probably belongs to the end of the period.

Truly, poor men have become owners of wealth, and he who could not provide [even] sandals for himself is now the possessor of riches.
Truly, the laws of the council-chamber are thrown out; truly, men walk on them in public places and poor men tear them up in the streets.
If only there were an end to mankind, with no conception, with no birth. Then would the earth cease from noise and tumult be no more.

In a similar vein is the discrediting of some of the great kings of the past. An example occurs in the Westcar Papyrus, in which a series of simple and amusing magicians' tales leads on to the story of the doom of the house of Khufu, builder of the Great Pyramid at Giza, whose dynasty was destined to be replaced by pious kings of the Fifth Dynasty. The legend of the impiety of Khufu's family took firm root and was repeated both by Herodotus and Manetho.

In another story, still popular in the seventh century BC, against a background of legal injustice, King Neferkare, probably the last king of the Sixth Dynasty, steals out of his palace each night to indulge a homosexual relationship with one of his generals. It can only be conjectured that the Theban revolt had brought home how fragile were

the basic assumptions on which their society rested, and forced them to consider how fragile were the defences against anarchy. This mood of pessimism affected the kingship itself and it is to this period that the *Instruction* of King Amenemhet belongs. It is also reflected in the expression of brooding weariness which characterizes the statues of the last kings.

The coming of the Hyksos

Contemporary records fail to show any historical break between the kings of the Twelfth and Thirteenth Dynasties; the change was presumably the result of a palace revolution. Yet the construction of royal tombs (still pyramids) follows exactly the same trend as at the end of the Old Kingdom. Upper Egypt appears still to have been ruled from the old capital of Amenemhet-ith-tawy, but there is no means of knowing if this was also true of Lower Egypt. One later king-list records at least sixty kings for the century or so of Thirteenth-Dynasty rule, allowing most of them extremely short reigns. Court intrigue was clearly at its most active. Significantly, one of the kings used as his official royal name simply his title, 'The General'.

Against this background an event of considerable importance was taking place. No doubt largely attracted by the wealth of the Middle Kingdom and the fertility of its countryside, people from Palestine began to drift southwards into Egypt. Some found their way into Upper Egyptian households as domestic servants. A few managed to make a successful career in the civil service, and presumably the Biblical story of Joseph's enslavement in Egypt belongs here. Eventually, in about 1680 BC, one of them

was able to claim for himself the kingship of Upper and Lower Egypt, and to found a dynasty of six kings, the Hyksos (meaning literally 'princes of foreign lands'), who were to rule for just over a century. They appear to have ruled from Avaris in the eastern delta.

Manetho recorded a tradition which said they overwhelmed Egypt with a barbarian invasion, but this seems to derive from the xenophobia which accompanied the second Theban revolt when the princes of Thebes again declared themselves kings of all Egypt, and carried out a successful civil war against the Hyksos. Monuments depict the Hyksos in the traditional guise of Egyptian Pharaohs, and in Upper Egypt at least there is no sign of an invasion or trace of an alien culture. However, until more is known of the archaeology of the delta the precise nature and scale of this movement must remain uncertain. Nevertheless, the Thebans found themselves fighting also against Egyptians serving the Hyksos during the war to expel the foreigners, and there is a record of at least one revolt subsequent to the Theban victory. This was clearly not a simple nationalist movement.

The period of expansion

The Thebans were faced with two enemies: the Hyksos to the north, whose territory may have included part of Palestine, and an African kingdom centred on the northern Sudan. The defeat of these two opponents carried the successful Upper Egyptian armies far beyond their earlier frontiers, and seems to have whetted an appetite for military conquest. Probably for the first time the Egyptians set out on regular military campaigns with the aim not merely of conquering and plundering, but also of establishing some rudimentary control over the conquered territories. In this way foreign aggression against Egypt could be prevented, and tribute regularly exacted. This increase in material wealth from abroad and the psychological effect of military success on a grand scale had a marked effect on Egyptian culture.

The new dynasty, Manetho's Eighteenth, was the beginning of the New Kingdom which was to be the third great period of cultural achievement. Thebes was retained as the capital, and the survival of many of its buildings meant that a mass of documentation has been made available on a scale hitherto lacking. The domestic quarters of Thebes on the east bank of the Nile, the palaces, government offices, mansions and slums have entirely disappeared under fields or under the modern town of Luxor. However, the temples, which must always have dominated the city, have survived remarkably intact.

The original local god of Thebes, Amon, now began to reap the reward for the dazzling success which he had brought to the Theban kings. A sizeable share of the spoils of conquest was bequeathed to him by grateful sovereigns, which provided for the erection of a complex of stone temples on a vast scale. These were to be continually enlarged and embellished during the next nine centuries. Across the river, another group of temples was constructed on the edge of the fields on a scale matching those on the east bank. Each provided for the cult of a dead king and was the centre of an economic unit with its own farms, villages and administration.

The royal tomb was no longer ostentatiously covered by a pyramid, but was hidden away in the remote Valley of the Kings, no doubt in the hopes of greater security against tomb robbery. In the hills and desert behind the royal mortuary temples a warren of private tombs proliferated, which included many for the courtiers and chief officials of the realm.

Despite the dominance of Thebes, however, Memphis was able to retain much of its former prestige; kings continued to reside there from time to time, and its naval dockyards witnessed the departure and return of the various expeditions bound for Palestine and Syria.

Contemporary documentation provides some evidence of the internal power politics of the age. The most obvious division of power was between the king and Amon, who not only in theory sired the kings and granted them their victories, but in practice sanctioned important decisions by means of oracles. The priests of Amon had at their disposal immense wealth, and at times were granted authority over all other priesthoods of Egypt. The official documents give no hint of whatever tensions must have arisen, and it was clearly not a straightforward rivalry since the king retained the right of appointment, and many former royal companions appear in the priesthood.

It is the events at the end of the Eighteenth Dynasty which give some indication of the conflicts which had preceded them. They centre on the person of King Akhenaton, who came to the throne when the Egyptian Empire was at the height of its power and splendour. The precise reasons for his actions are difficult to understand, but his main impulse seems to have been an attempt to alter the relationship between the king and the gods, and in particular to redress whatever imbalance had grown up between the king and Amon. He did this by fostering a version of the old solar cult, which excluded Amon altogether, and at the same time elevated the king to near equality with the sun-god, who was worshipped in the form of the sun's disc, the Aten.

Akhenaton's religion will be examined in a little more detail later on. For the moment it should be emphasized that there is no evidence for any direct foreign influence, or that it was intended to be a popular movement.

The first important practical application of Akhenaton's ideas seems to have been the construction of a large solar temple adjacent to the principal temple of Amon at Karnak in Thebes. It contained colossal statues of the king and its walls were covered with scenes showing him worshipping the sun-god, all conceived in the strange new style of art which Akhenaton had introduced, and which must have shocked those who considered the traditional artistic modes of expression as sacred and god-given. Thebes none the less remained the domain of Amon.

The logical step was to abandon it completely and this Akhenaton did around his fifth year as king, moving to a new capital built on virgin ground, the construction of which had probably begun shortly after his accession. It was called 'The horizon of the sun disc' (modern Amarna), and lay about 230 miles downstream from Thebes, straggling along the edge of the desert for about six miles. In the centre was the gigantic, symmetrically-planned palace linked by a bridge over the main street to a smaller private set of apartments, the main temple of the Aton (on a similarly vast scale), and the principal government offices. To the north and south stretched streets of spacious, bungalow-like mansions hemmed in by the houses of the poor, and at intervals separated by more palaces and temples. Once established here, Akhenaton began a campaign to destroy the very existence of Amon by methodically obliterating every mention of his name on monuments. In view of the immense magical significance attached to names in ancient times, this was an attack of the most serious kind.

Akhenaton reigned for sixteen years, but even before his death there is evidence that his policy had failed. A successor, Smenkhkare, was elevated to the position of co-regent with Akhenaton and sent to live at Thebes, married to the king's eldest surviving daughter. Both disappeared on Akhenaton's death. The real successor was another young man, Tutankhaten, who, after spending two or three years at Amarna, abandoned the city and the Aton cult.

He changed his name to Tutankhamun, and a restoration decree was set up in the temple of Amon at Karnak. He and his successor both reigned for a short time, and were followed by a series of military leaders who inaugurated the Nineteenth Dynasty. The name of Akhenaton was expunged from the official king-list. His city was abandoned

Above, two Eighteenth-Dynasty princesses of the Amarna period: the religious revolution of the Amarna era was accompanied by a marked change in artistic styles, and for the first time sculptors tried to reproduce individual characteristics. Schimmel Collection, New York.

Left, relief depicting Rameses II worshipping Amon.

Below centre, statue of Akhenaton from the temple of Aten, Eighteenth Dynasty, Amarna period.

Far left above, the funerary mask of Tutankhamun, Eighteenth Dynasty, made of beaten gold inlaid with coloured glass paste and semi-precious stones. Egyptian Museum, Cairo.

Far left below, seated statue of Queen Hatshepsut, Eighteenth Dynasty, from her funerary temple.

Opposite, Eighteenth-Dynasty statue from Karnak of Amenhotep III.

and seems to have remained empty and untouched for another fifty years until the great stone temples and palaces were completely demolished to provide cheap building material.

Hittite records from Anatolia show that on the death of an Egyptian king (almost certainly Tutankhamun) his widow, who must have been the young Ankhsenamen, wrote to the Hittite king asking for a son to be sent who should become her husband in preference to an Egyptian. The Hittite king, Suppiluliumas, who was at this time Egypt's chief enemy, delayed while making further enquiries. At last he sent one of his sons, who was however murdered before he had even reached Egypt. In retaliation the Hittites attacked and defeated an Egyptian force. Queen Ankhesenamen's name last appears in association with that of the next Egyptian king, an aging man of military background, which suggests that in the end she had to choose an Egyptian.

The resumption of the imperial age

Outwardly at least the Amarna period left little trace. Thebes remained the great religious capital where the kings were buried and where the additions to the temple of Amon, particularly the great Hypostyle Hall of Kings Seti I and Rameses II, were on an even larger scale than before. However, the military leaders who founded the new Nineteenth Dynasty were not Theban in origin, but appear to have come from the eastern delta. It was here that they built a new capital where, at least from the period of Rameses II, the third king of the dynasty, they resided for much of the time and where many of the great offices of state were situated. The city was called Per-Rameses, 'The house of Rameses', and was probably situated in the area of the modern towns of Kantir and Khatana, where remains of a palace and temples have been found over a wide area of cultivated land. This is almost certainly the Biblical Rameses, to the building of which the Israelites appear to have contributed. The king went south to Thebes probably only for the great religious festivals.

A dynastic change in about 1200 BC brought the Twentieth Dynasty to power. Its second king, Rameses III, was the last of the great Pharaohs to embellish Thebes with enduring monuments. In his reign, too, the Palestinian empire finally came to an end and his armies now had to fight on Egypt's own boundaries to keep back a hostile incursion from the north by land and sea. For the next fifty years the last eight kings, all called Rameses, must have confined their building projects (the chief means of measuring royal activity) to the delta. With the last king the line of royal tombs in the Valley of the Kings came to

Above, mother and child, Eighteenth Dynasty, Amarna period.

Top, pectoral (breast ornament) with solar and lunar emblems belonging to Tutankhamun, Eighteenth Dynasty. Egyptian Museum, Cairo.

Above left, the second mummiform coffin from the tomb of Tutankhamun, late Eighteenth Dynasty: this coffin contained the inner solid gold coffin in which rested the mummified body of the king. Egyptian Museum, Cairo.

Left, the young Tutankhamun, Eighteenth Dynasty. Egyptian Museum, Cairo.

Opposite, detail of the back of Tutankhamun's throne, Eighteenth Dynasty. Egyptian Museum, Cairo.

an end, marking the completion also of the New Kingdom, which had begun nearly five centuries earlier with the second Theban revolt.

Even before the death of the last Rameses the shift in the centre of power to the delta led to the division of the country, apparently peacefully, into two provinces. The Twenty-first Dynasty ruled in effect only Lower Egypt, and from a new capital, Tanis, in the far northeastern corner of the delta. In Upper Egypt power was vested in the office of high priest of Amon. Just before the end of the Twentieth Dynasty a ruthless struggle for the office of high priest appears to have taken place.

The incumbent, whose father had held the post before him, was expelled and his place taken by a military leader, Herihor, who founded what was in effect a dynasty of high priests controlling Upper Egypt, while the Twenty-first Dynasty ruled in the north. In Upper Egypt, this new arrangement was hailed as 'The Renaissance'.

During the New Kingdom colonies of Libyans sprang up in the western delta. Under the Nineteenth and Twentieth Dynasties military expeditions had been undertaken against them to prevent their further settlement in Egypt, and even at Thebes their presence was felt. Some adopted Egyptian culture, and even became priests in Egyptian temples, notably at Herakleopolis. Eventually, in about 945 BC, one of their leaders, Sheshonk I, declared himself king, and appears to have brought about the end of Upper Egyptian independence. It was probably he who began one of the last great additions to the Karnak temple. However, the kings of this Twenty-second Dynasty were merely the most successful of the Libyan chiefs, and towards the end of the dynasty Lower Egypt seems largely to have split up into provinces under the control of various Libyan chiefs. Their hold over Upper Egypt was also tenuous.

The son of one of the kings, who had been made high priest of Amon, was faced by rebellion at Thebes itself. Eventually Thebes produced a short-lived dynasty of its own, the Twenty-third, whose monuments did not extend outside the city. With the country divided, Egypt was a tempting prey for invasion.

Egypt's influence on Africa

Although Egypt lies across the land routes between Africa and western Asia, there was apparently no through-traffic in ancient times. The routes from both continents led to Egypt, but not beyond. Nevertheless, knowledge of some of the most important steps to settled, civilized life had managed to filter through from western Asia and to emerge and spread out over the African hinterland. These were the domestication of cereals and of certain animals, which enabled essentially hunting communities to become more settled and diversified. Knowledge of this sort, perhaps originating in the Kurdish foothills, had spread to Palestine by about 6500 BC, and thence to Egypt.

The earliest stages are badly documented in Egypt, probably because the communities were concentrated on the flood plain. The earliest settled communities which have left abundant remains are already at an advanced stage of development, out of which grew the civilization of Pharaonic Egypt. From Egypt knowledge spread in two directions: westward along the Mediterranean coast and southwards up the Nile valley into the Sudan.

One site near Khartoum has yielded evidence of a domesticated goat possibly as early as 4000 BC, and 1,000 years later sheep and oxen were being raised in Kenya, although in southern Africa these advances had to await the Iron Age of the first millennium AD. However, apart from this indirect transmission of ideas about agriculture, the effect of Egyptian civilization on Africa was small, and limited virtually to the north and central Sudan. Although geographically part of Africa, culturally Egypt belonged to western Asia.

Egypt and western Asia

The possibility that cultural influence spread from western Asia to Egypt during the late prehistoric period must be considered. In art experiments were taking place which were to lead to the development of the rules governing the Pharaonic art style. Cylinder seals of a Mesopotamian type from this period have been found in Egypt, together with other objects bearing pictures in an artistic style which seems to belong to southern Mesopotamia. It is also possible that a particular style of brick architecture, of which examples have survived from the First Dynasty onwards, may have derived from Mesopotamia.

Something more important than simple commercial exchange seems to have been involved, since, to judge from the distribution of Egyptian objects, Egyptian trade appears largely to have been limited to Palestine. However, the evidence for Mesopotamian influence does not amount to a foreign invasion, and if Mesopotamian craftsmen were living in Egypt, one cannot guess what sort of political arrangements made this feasible. However, there is also the possibility that the idea of writing phonetically, already practised in southern Mesopotamia at this period, was transmitted to Egypt.

The other great civilizations of the ancient Near East were separated from Egypt by Palestine, a land which supported a collection of city-states of varying degrees of independence and with little political cohesion. They seem rarely to have afforded a real military threat to Egypt and there is little evidence of Egyptian conquest and control until the Eighteenth Dynasty. At all times there must have been regular intercourse between the eastern delta and southern Palestine by way of the road which runs across northern Sinai, and some of the seaports on the Palestine coast played a vital role in trading with Egypt.

The most valuable commodity was timber from the cedar forests which clothed the hills of Lebanon, for Egypt was poor in good-quality timber. Byblos seems to have been the chief centre for this trade, and in the court of the princes of Byblos Egyptian culture became fashionable. Towards the end of the Twelfth Dynasty their tombs contained not only gifts from the Egyptian kings, but also locally made items of royal regalia in Egyptian style. They had scarab-shaped seals made bearing their names and their title, 'Prince of Byblos', written in Egyptian hieroglyphs. An Egyptian colony grew up there, served by a special temple devoted to the Egyptian goddess 'Hathor, Lady of Byblos'. A further source of wealth lay in the inhospitable southern part of the Sinai Peninsula. There diligent search by Egyptian expeditions located veins of turquoise and of copper ore. It was an arduous task, made more difficult by the threat of harassment from local tribesmen. The safety of the expeditions was entrusted to 'Hathor, Lady of the Turquoise', who was given a crude temple in a grotto at one of the main camping sites. Here leaders of successful expeditions left thanksgiving memorials before returning to Egypt.

Below, relief from Medinet Habu of Rameses III in action against Syrian forces, Twentieth Dynasty. Oriental Institute, University of Chicago.

Centre, detail of one of the columns in the great hypostyle at Karnak: the signs within the oval frame (known as a cartouche) are the names of kings.

Left, statue of Rameses II at Memphis, Nineteenth Dynasty.

Opposite right, the great hall of pillars of Kings Sethos I and Rameses II at Karnak, Eighteenth and Nineteenth Dynasties.

Opposite left, relief from the temple at Medinet Habu showing Rameses III hunting wild bulls, Twentieth Dynasty.

begun by the Hyksos, and furthered by the prisoners of war and hostages kept in Egypt. Unfamiliar-sounding foreign words passed into Egyptian speech. Egypt's impact on Palestine was, however, probably just as great, although more difficult to measure in view of the scarcity of written sources. It can be seen particularly clearly in art, notably in the very obvious Egyptian inspiration for the ivory carvings from Megiddo of the twelfth and thirteenth centuries BC, with their winged, human-headed sphinxes.

From time immemorial the eastern delta was subject to raids from tribesmen from just over the border, and in the early Twelfth Dynasty a fortress, 'The Walls of the Ruler', had been built to discourage such action. However, the success of the Hyksos rulers appears to have prompted the Thebans, who eventually expelled them, to far more vigorous action against Palestine.

The ensuing conquest aroused the suspicions of more powerful countries—at first Mitanni, across the River Euphrates, and later the Hittites in Asia Minor. Not only did they encourage rebellion in the Palestinian city-states but also supported them with military contingents. In retaliation against Mitanni the armies of the Eighteenth Dynasty campaigned as far as the Euphrates, and occasionally even crossed it. However, the area to which permanent claim was laid was mainly confined to Palestine.

Under the rudimentary system of control which the Egyptians set up the local princes were allowed to remain, as long as they took an oath of loyalty and agreed to measures such as the education in Egypt of their sons, who would eventually return to inherit their fathers' position. The limited amount of

evidence available suggests a possible division of the area into three provinces, each under the charge of an Egyptian official, but the chief burden of government probably still rested with the native princes. The purpose of this empire was simply to prevent a build-up of hostile forces on Egypt's borders. It also increasingly became a source of tribute. In fact the empire brought the Egyptians little peace. Palestine was held only by constant military campaigns or displays of force.

During Akhenaton's reign, when a crisis occurred in Egypt itself, most of the coast of Lebanon and Syria was lost, through the perfidy of the most powerful Syrian prince, who allied himself with the Hittites.

The acquisition of an empire inevitably had some effect on Egyptian culture. Commodities of foreign origin found their way into the country in far greater numbers than ever before. One notable aspect of this was the large-scale import of opium from Cyprus in specially made flasks. The tactics of the army were revolutionized by the adoption of new ideas from western Asia. Palestinian gods and goddesses achieved a limited popularity, a process no doubt

Warfare and diplomacy

Before the Eighteenth Dynasty, the equipment of the armies of Egypt was comparatively rudimentary. Consisting entirely of infantry, stiffened with mercenaries from the Nubian peoples living to the south, the Egyptian forces fought chiefly with spears, bows and flint- or bone-tipped arrows and wooden clubs, with perhaps an occasional copper or bronze battleaxe of simple design.

These weapons would no doubt have continued to be sufficient for dealing with recalcitrant Nubians, but the military adventures of the Eighteenth Dynasty and later required a much greater degree of sophistication to succeed against the armies of western Asia. In response to this a professional army, well organized and equipped, under professional officers led by the king himself, was formed. Weapons were improved and diversified, the Egyptians borrowing ideas extensively from their opponents. The horse-drawn chariot was introduced and was used in the Theban revolt against the Hyksos. The chariots were light, mobile fighting platforms, which probably prepared the way for the infantry by harrying and perhaps even charging the enemy.

However, war was not the only instrument of policy. A diplomacy as devious as any of later ages was practised. This is clearly shown by the chance preservation of diplomatic correspondence found at Amarna. The correspondence is written on little clay tablets in cuneiform, the official diplomatic language of the ancient Near East at this period. Most are letters from the supposedly loyal city-states of Palestine. They protest their loyalty to Pharaoh in beseeching, sycophantic terms and attempt to win favour by accusing their neighbours of treachery.

To these practical expressions of diplomacy the Egyptians added sympathetic magic, as shown in a group of objects, mostly dating from the Twelfth and perhaps Thirteenth Dynasties. They are either pottery vessels or statuettes of bound captives inscribed with lists of foreign peoples and their princes, identified by name and divided into three groups: Nubians, Asians and Libyans. At an appropriate ceremony it was intended that a formula would be recited over them and the pottery vessels broken, or the statuettes buried. By this means any hostile actions or thoughts would immediately be brought to nothing.

Egypt and Africa

South of Aswan, the first 250 miles of the Nile valley, called Lower Nubia, is a poor land agriculturally and has rarely supported a ruler of sufficient power seriously to threaten Egypt. Its value lay in mineral resources which the Egyptians exploited: gold, mined in the Red Sea hills and probably panned in riverine deposits, and copper.

The rich civilization of Egypt also provided an attractive market for exotic luxury goods from lands further to the south: ebony, ivory, incense, the skins of rare animals, and sometimes the animals themselves, such as giraffes. Even in the Old Kingdom military expeditions were sent as far as the Second Cataract, doubtless to ensure the safety of mining and quarrying expeditions, and at least one permanent Egyptian outpost was established near this limit. One of its purposes was probably to trade with caravans bringing these goods from the far south. Towards the end of the period its function appears to have been replaced by donkey caravans sent from Egypt to trade at a native town even further to the south.

In the Twelfth Dynasty the control of Lower Nubia was by a much more elaborately conceived military presence. A chain of impregnable, mud-brick fortresses was

Above, detail from a wall-painting in the tomb of Senmut, the architect of Queen Hatshepsut's temple at Dayir-el-Bahri, Eighteenth Dynasty: the tribute-bearers shown are carrying Minoan vases, an indication of Egypt's increasing consciousness and knowledge of other societies.

Opposite right, detail of a relief from the temple of Rameses II at Medinet Habu commemorating the king's second Libyan campaign, Twentieth, Dynasty.

Opposite left, statues from the rock-cut temple of Rameses II at Abu Simbel, Nineteenth Dynasty: the site of the temple is now beneath the waters of the new Aswan Dam.

erected between the First and Second Cataracts, and at Semna, at the southern end of the Second Cataract, a strict frontier control was brought into operation, with a special fortified trading zone under Egyptian surveillance. The reason for these precautions appears to have been the growth of potentially hostile native kingdoms to the south, their wealth perhaps initially derived from trade with Egypt. The climax came when the Egyptians withdrew and the Hyksos came to power. One powerful united kingdom of Kush seems to have taken control of Lower Nubia and to have established friendly diplomatic relations with the Hyksos, thus posing a threat to the ambitious Thebans squeezed between them.

The capital of this kingdom has been located at Kerma, south of the Third Cataract where these kings were buried in huge circular mounds, surrounded by sacrificed retainers, sometimes numbering hundreds. As at Byblos, contact with Egypt stimulated an interest in Egyptian fashions, and a hybrid culture developed. There were even Egyptians in the service of these kings. It was with the help of mercenary soldiers from Nubia that the Thebans finally expelled the Hyksos.

The Theban success against the Hyksos and the subsequent invasion of Palestine was matched in the south by a similar attack on the kingdom of Kush and an invasion which took the Egyptian armies to distant reaches of the Nile valley far beyond their earlier frontiers, down to Kurgus

beyond the Fourth Cataract. Again a rudimentary form of control was set up with a viceroy of Kush in overall charge. Some minor princes of Lower Nubia were allowed to remain in power, but the kingdom of Kush, after at least one rebellion, seems to have been finally destroyed.

The effect of conquest was that local cultures soon largely died out. For a time Egyptian culture seems to have been adopted wholesale, no doubt encouraged by the founding of Egyptian colonies with their own temples, such as that of Rameses II at Abu Simbel, rivalling the temples of Egypt itself. However, this culture disappeared leaving an archaeological gap which is presumably the sign of general impoverishment.

The decline in Egypt's ability to control a large empire after the Twentieth Dynasty must have meant a withdrawal from Nubia which was to prove permanent, but the records were silent about this. Nevertheless, the period of Egypt's greatest cultural influence in Africa was still to come, the result of a strange episode in history. One of the principal Egyptian cities of Nubia had been Napata, probably situated on the river bank near a prominent hill called Gebel Barkal. A sequence of tombs at a nearby cemetery, dating from a period after the Egyptian withdrawal, seems to have belonged to a line of native kings who now took over and whose culture owed relatively little to the period of Egyptian rule, although the temples of Amon at the foot of Gebel

Barkal must have been a constant reminder.

About 730 BC, one of these kings, Piankhi, adopting the titles and trappings of an Egyptian pharaoh, mounted an invasion against Egypt, now split up under the nominal rule of the Libyan Twenty-second Dynasty. The success of the invasion left this provincial Nubian ruler and his successors kings of all Egypt as well as of their own territory, a position which they held for about seventy years, forming Manetho's Twenty-fifth Dynasty.

Piankhi represented himself as a zealous observer of Egyptian religious practices, and was followed in this by his successors, under whom work was carried out on a number of temples in Egypt. Their tombs continued to be sited near Napata, but were now constructed as pyramids with the dead buried after the Egyptian fashion, although in Egypt no royal pyramids had been built for eight centuries. However, the most remarkable aspect of this period of Napatan rule was the beginning of a revival of art in Egypt, which was to continue under the succeeding dynasties, producing some of the finest works of sculpture ever made in Egypt.

The end of Twenty-fifth Dynasty rule came as a result of events outside Egypt. This was the period of Assyrian military expansion when Egypt was still a rich prize. In 671 BC the armies of Esarhaddon defeated the Egyptians, entered northern Egypt and annexed it. The Nubian kings made repeated attempts to regain complete control of the country but eventually, in 663 BC, the armies of Assur-bani-pal ascended the Nile and sacked the city of Thebes. The last Nubian king of Egypt fled back to Napata, but this was not the end of the Napatan kingdom. Its rulers continued to try to maintain a semblance of the court of distant Pharaonic Egypt, although gradually coming more and more under the influence of their own culture.

Eventually the site of the capital and the royal cemetery, still marked by pyramids, was moved further south to Meroe, 150 miles from Khartoum. Meroitic civilization continued into the fourth century AD as a vigorous native culture, still showing at the court level traces of its pretensions to Egyptian culture, although, through the absorption of local influences, its style

tended towards a heavy, richly ornamented, baroque Egyptian. Its most impressive monuments are its temples, dedicated to local gods, with inscriptions still written in hieroglyphs. Two features of this culture call for particular attention. Alone among ancient Egypt's African neighbours it was literate, having developed its own script which, unlike Egyptian, was alphabetic. It has been deciphered, but unfortunately its language cannot yet be translated. Secondly, probably by the middle of the first century BC, an iron-working industry was being carried on at Meroe, which lies in the vicinity of iron ore deposits. Most probably it was from here that knowledge of this technique spread into central and southern Africa.

The decline of Egypt

It is particularly difficult to give a balanced assessment of the last three centuries of ancient Egyptian history. The centre of political power and probably of cultural life as a whole was in the delta. Although the amount of documentation on daily life reaches formidable proportions, historical data are as scanty as ever. Egypt's importance in the Near East had declined considerably. Occasional forays into Palestine met only with defeat. The Assyrian invasion was followed in 525 BC by one mounted by the Persians, who held Egypt for a century and a quarter. Revolts against foreign rule took place, but without success.

The last fifty years of independence under Manetho's Twenty-ninth and Thirtieth Dynasties, between 404 and 343 BC, seem to have been possible only because of weakness in the Persian Empire. In 343 BC the Persians re-established their rule, but were themselves defeated shortly afterwards by Alexander the Great, who entered Egypt in triumph in 332 BC.

Deciding on a date for the end of ancient Egyptian history and civilization is inevitably an arbitrary matter. History is a continuous process; it is historians who create periods. Certain outward forms of an official or religious nature continued while Egypt was a Roman province. On the other hand, much of the culture which is commonly associated with the ancient Egypt of the Pharaohs had undergone profound changes centuries earlier. The date which conveniently serves as an end point is the defeat of the last native Egyptian ruler, Nekht-horheb, by the Persians in 343 BC.

In Upper Egypt Thebes remained the principal city. Its vast bewildering complex of temples included many which were now nearly a thousand years old—monuments to an imperial splendour that had long since departed. Even the kings of the Twenty-sixth Dynasty, who appear to have achieved some stature as rulers after the Assyrian withdrawal, made only negligible additions. The fact that Upper Egypt appears to have reverted slowly to provincialism may be partly responsible for the feeling of decline which the period induces. Nevertheless, the artistic works of the period belong not to the end of a great civilization, nor even to a tired academic revival, but represent a vigorous new approach, which in portrait sculpture created masterly studies.

This artistic revival came at a moment, when contacts between Egypt and Greece were being made. The Greeks who were being attracted to Egypt were mostly merchants and mercenary soldiers, but there were also some of a more scholarly frame of mind, who were deeply impressed by the great antiquity of Egyptian civilization, and particularly by the size and style of its monumental stone buildings and sculpture. It was in the contemplation of these that Greek artists seem to have felt the inspiration which was to produce the architecture and sculpture of Classical Greece.

Egyptian religion

Religion in ancient Egypt was not simply a matter of communication between men and remote gods. The entire world was the outward aspect of a complex divine order. It is not easy to make an intelligible survey of Egyptian religion. Apart from the fact that it is now impossible to enter into the state of mind of the ancient Egyptian, the documentation is as uneven as it is for Egyptian

history in general. It is, however, unwise to assume a static pattern of belief which changed little from period to period, although some support is given to this attitude by the stereotyped representations of gods seen in the formal setting of tomb and temple.

These are in fact little more than hieroglyphic adjuncts to the texts which invariably accompany them. Egyptian religion was a living thing. Until the very end of Pharaonic society the priests—the intellectuals of society—were engaged in the study of their religious texts, continually finding new strands in the complex skein of the divine world which surrounded Egypt.

The rigidity of Egyptian thought

The ancient Egyptians were a clever, gifted people, and it seems therefore surprising that, after several thousand years of constant speculation on the nature of the universe by the most intelligent members of society, they should have produced so little of any value.

The answer lies in the Egyptian's unquestioning acceptance of certain assumptions, on which all their reasoning was based. They assumed that the universe was governed by forces which were essentially personal, and thus subject to the same whims and irregularities of conduct as the human beings whom they were thought closely to resemble. This belief precluded natural, impersonal laws whose results could be predicted.

The representation of the universe painted on the ceiling in the tomb of Rameses VI about 1130 BC illustrates this view. The sky goddess, Nut, a naked woman with stars painted on her belly, bends over the earth. At one end the sun, held up by a winged beetle, is born from her womb. Four jackals who protect the eastern horizon stand in adoration: 'It is they who cause the sun-god to appear and who open the doors in the four gates of the eastern horizon of heaven.' From here the sun, now a hawk-headed man, sails in a boat across the heavenly river beneath Nut's body. Finally, in the evening, he is swallowed by the goddess while the king watches in adoration and thus 'causes the barge of the sun-god to return in peace'. In another part of the tomb the same sun-god is the focal point of a legend where he appears as an old man, angry at mankind whom he has created and who now plots rebellion against him. Imprisoned within this mental framework of a non-mechanical universe, accepting without question the validity of ancient documents, the Egyptians were doomed to pursue a course of thought which, while it grew broader and more elaborately patterned at every step, ultimately led nowhere.

If the Egyptians were conditioned to seeing natural phenomena in these terms how

did they set about building them up into the complex systems which represented divine reality? Their method was one which accepted metaphor as a valid process of argument. The sun crossed the sky slowly and steadily, a mode of travel which readily suggested voyaging on the Nile. For the ancient Egyptian this obvious metaphor was clear proof of how the sun-god actually travelled.

With this inclination towards vivid, concrete imagery the Egyptian then went on to give the boat its exact form, with two steering oars called 'Perception' and 'Command', supplied with a crew of other gods, including a pilot with sounding rod, and a troop of lesser divinities to haul the boat along from the bank. Hazards to navigation were described, suitably magnified to become attacks by terrible demons, who in turn needed to be repulsed by spells and by other friendly beings. In this way a whole system of mythology was carefully built up by the Egyptians from the acceptance of the initial metaphor.

The Egyptians were also eager to fit these individual revelations into a universal scheme. By a careful exegesis of the texts stored in temple archives which recorded the revelations of past ages, and by adding their own insights and explanations, they attempted to discover the mystic relationships which were assumed to exist between one god and another, and to interweave the various legends of which they formed part. In doing this they accepted the mystic nature of coincidence. Even similarity in sound between two words—a pun—indicated an underlying connection. This process, essentially a written and scholarly one, led them far in the direction of seeing every god simply as an aspect of every other god. It produced composite deities such as 'Osiris-Apis-Atum-Horus in one, the great

god', a Nineteenth-Dynasty designation for the sacred Apis bull of Sakkara. This might appear to be only one step away from belief in a single universal god. However, as with the sacred hieroglyphic script, simplicity held no attraction and complexity was considered a sign of profundity. Given the Egyptians' process of reasoning, what seem to be blatant contradictions were to them tokens of the mysterious, many-sided nature of the divine world and could be explained by the most elaborate and far-fetched interpretations.

The limit of simplicity and abstraction was reached with the Memphite theology, which may go as far back as the Old Kingdom. It describes the role of the Memphite god, Ptah, as the spiritual creator of the universe and the prime-mover of life:

He is in every body and in every mouth, of all gods, and of all mankind, of all beasts, of all creeping things, and of [everything] that lives, thinking and commanding whatever he wishes. . . . Indeed, all the divine order came into being through what [his] heart devised and what [his] tongue commanded.

The temples

The point of contact with the gods was in the temples of Egypt. Many of the gods and goddesses were associated with specific localities, often survivals from an early period when their patronage was limited to a specific village community. The priests attached to a local cult tended to provide their own particular interpretation of the divine scheme centred on their own temple and its deity. The process was aided by the fact that from an early date most deities had

to some extent been reduced to equal terms by being cast in human shape. Even if a god had originated as a sacred animal, his animal head was set on top of a human body.

Gods could therefore easily be arranged in patterns reflecting ancient Egyptian society, the most common being a triad of husband, wife and son. Thus a temple would serve not only the original god of the locality but others, who could be regarded as guests. Despite this parochialism there is normally no trace of hostility between one theological centre and another. Geographical diversity was merely a further element of the divine mystery.

The temple was primarily the home of the statue-images in which the gods dwelt. Its architecture to some extent reflected that of Egyptian upper-class mansions, with shady, colonnaded courts, and columned halls masking secluded private quarters at the rear. Unlike the houses of mortals, however, it was, wherever possible, built of stone to last for eternity. Its design also had to take into account the processions which played an important part in the ritual. Temples were usually built on one major axis facing the processional road which led down to a canal or the Nile, since some festivals entailed the visit of divine images to other temples. The stone walls of the temples were also used to record pictorial summaries of the main elements in the temple ritual, and on the outside sometimes scenes of the divine king triumphant over foreign foes.

All were given an existence of their own by a ceremony, the 'Opening of the Mouth', which was probably repeated annually. In this way the service of the gods and the safety of Egypt were ensured for eternity, even if human participation should cease. The design of the temple inevitably became the subject of symbolic association. The monumental gateway into the temple, which

ran between two high, oblong towers called pylons, became a representation of a mountainous horizon, with a central pass where the rising sun would first appear to light up the interior of the temple. The whole building was charged with divine energy, latent within the very fabric of its walls.

The temples provided the gods with dwellings suited to their superhuman nature, but, once present in the temples, they still needed regular attention to ensure their continued benevolence. This was achieved chiefly by a daily ritual, in essence a dramatization of daily human life. At dawn the doors of the sanctuary were opened, to the accompaniment of the chanting of a hymn of adoration. The priest entered, dressed the statue and purified it, and presented a selection of offerings of food and drink. At night a similar ritual was performed in reverse. Prayers, purification and food offerings were the main features of temple ritual, to which might be added music provided by the priestesses and the burning of incense.

In return the god was expected to behave in a reasonably benevolent manner. One king addresses the god Osiris:

And thou shalt double for me the long duration of the great reign of King Rameses, the great god. Certainly the benefactions which I have conferred on thy house . . . in the past four years are many compared to what King Rameses, the great god, conferred in his sixty-seven years . . . Besides thou art the one who hast said it with thine own mouth, and it cannot be upset.

In theory the king was the only person who communicated with the gods; he alone appears in the scenes of ritual on the temple walls. However, in practice this function had to be delegated to priests.

The sole qualification of a priest seems to have been ritual purity of the body while present in the temple, achieved mainly by bathing in ritually purified water. There was no special priestly class of society, and indeed, particularly in early periods, it appears to have been a task often performed by officials together with their other administrative duties, although it carried with it a specific title. The main task was serving the god, but there were other duties of a scholarly or administrative kind, although little is known about exact divisions of labour.

In addition to the study of documents in the archives there would also have been instruction for novices, and probably schools where the art of writing was taught, as well as the closely related discipline of line drawing. Each temple was at the centre of an economic unit which, in the case of a great state temple, could be one of the wealthiest in the land.

The wealth of the temples was measured in the fields and farms they possessed (in Egypt as well as in foreign provinces), in livestock and perhaps prisoners of war, and also in gifts of costly objects and materials from the king. The temple enclosure was filled with storehouses and granaries and the offices of administrators, and was surrounded by their houses. In later times the temples even played a part in internal trade, and the resources of materials and craftsmen which were in their possession must have meant that workshops and factories were also under their control.

All this wealth belonged to the god and the offerings which were presented to him were merely the tokens of the total produce of the god's estate. These offerings might then be presented to statues of other resident divinities, to the spirits of departed kings and to honoured private individuals represented by a statue. The estate's produce also paid for the priesthood and on occasions for other undertakings too, such as royal tomb construction. The temples were thus at the centre of the country's economic life.

The religion of Akhenaton

Egyptian religion also contained a political element. The success of the Theban princes was reflected on the divine plane by their god, Amon, becoming 'king of the gods'. The politics of the Theban kings of the Eighteenth Dynasty were intimately linked with him, and presumably with his priesthood. His statue became the oracle for ratifying major state decisions. It is characteristic of the times that the reaction to this took the form of a religious 'revolution'.

For inspiration Akhenaton drew heavily on concepts entirely native to Egypt. Sun worship was of great importance even in the Old Kingdom, and its growing popularity can be seen at Thebes during the Eighteenth Dynasty. Amon himself was identified with the old sun-god Re. Even the name Aton

was an old term for the sun's disc, though Akhenaton now depicted Aten as a disc, from which long rays that ended in hands emanated.

The most striking departure in Akhenaton's religion was its assault on the position of the great Theban god, Amon. The attack was not only destructive; it sought also to take over part of Amon's nature. Already in the Eighteenth Dynasty Amon, as Amon-Re, had been the subject of poetic compositions in which he appeared as the sole creator of life, whose daily presence in the sky as the sun-god, Re, brought happiness and life to all living things. The new hymn to the Aton develops the same themes, but with considerably more poetic inspiration. It is no reflection on Akhenaton's sincerity about his religion to say that all this was intended to achieve one end: a change in the relationship between the king and the principal god of the Egyptian state. Although the king is constantly shown worshipping his god there was a clear attempt to give them equality.

The Aton was given a set of titles as if it were a king and these titles often appear alongside those of Akhenaton as an object of worship. As if to emphasize this partnership the Aton celebrated festivals of a kind usually associated with kingship. This co-regency between king and god presumably restored the kingship to a more healthy status.

This improved status was reflected in the tombs of the courtiers, which were now filled with scenes, probably derived from the Aton temples, showing the king worshipping, riding through the city, rewarding loyal courtiers and sitting with his family. However, Aton religion had little appeal, or indeed, little relevance to the common people. Objects excavated from a workmen's village at Amarna belong only to time-honoured household cults.

Akhenaton's lack of attention to the affairs of empire is understandable in view of his domestic preoccupations. Pacifism was not part of his creed, as scenes of the king in the traditional pose of smiting captives are now known. The Amarna 'revolution' was about kingship. Its failure was presumably the result of the extreme measures which he took. Perhaps the non-Theban military leaders who eventually took over the kingship were better placed to combat whatever influences Akhenaton had been fighting.

The religion of the common people

The temples were not places of popular worship. Their sanctuaries could be entered only by the purified servants of the god. The gods, however, were not altogether remote from the people. Although the great state temples were staffed by high-ranking priests

and officials there must have been many small temples and shrines whose cult involved humbler people. In a village occupied by workmen at the necropolis at Thebes the priesthood of their patron god, the deified King Amenhotep I, was composed of certain of the workmen themselves.

However, even the exalted state gods were not locked away permanently in the depths of their giant temples. Festivals were held throughout the year, marked by public holidays, when a portable image of the god would be carried out of the temple for a procession to other shrines. These were occasions for public rejoicing and feasting and perhaps an opportunity to present a petition to the god who would signify his answer by transmitting movements through the bearers of his statue.

This practice of consulting a god's statue as an oracle, known from the Eighteenth Dynasty onwards, covered all aspects of life: 'Should I accept this bull?', 'Will I be blamed?', 'Will they mention me to the vizier?' Even Amon himself was not completely beyond the reach of someone like a Theban draughtsman who prayed in this fashion:

Thou art Amon, lord of the silent man, who comest at the voice of the poor man. I call thee when I am in distress and thou comest and rescuest me. . . . Though a servant is wont to do wrong, still the lord is wont to be merciful. The lord of Thebes does not spend a whole day angry. As for his anger, with the passing of a moment nought remains.

There were also cults for which the home was the most suitable shrine. The houses of

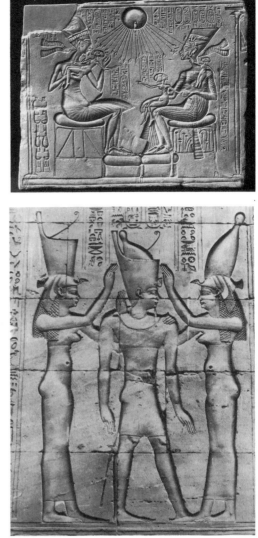

Above, wall-painting of a ritual voyage from the tomb of Meye, Dayir-el-Medina, end of the Eighteenth Dynasty. Turin Museum.

Left, statue of a scribe reading in front of the god Thoth, the inventor and patron of writing. Musée du Louvre, Paris.

Opposite top, informal portrait of Akhenaton, Nefertiti and three of their daughters beneath the rays of Aton: detail of an Eighteenth-Dynasty stele, Amarna period. Staatliche Museen zu Berlin.

Opposite centre, relief showing the coronation of Seti I: Buto, the goddess of Lower Egypt (on the left), and Nekhebet, the protectress of Upper Egypt, are crowning the king, Nineteenth Dynasty.

Opposite bottom, Sebek, the crocodile god, a relief from the temple at Ombos, erected as a sanctuary to Sebek and the falcon-headed Haroeris, the god of the sky, c. 145 BC.

the necropolis workmen at Thebes each contained a special shrine in the front room which, from paintings preserved on their walls, seems to have served particularly for a cult of an ugly little gnome called Bes, a friendly genie of the household. The houses also contained stone busts, possibly representing deceased members of the family, and little figurines of naked women—a few associated with children—perhaps used in rites to encourage fertility in wives.

However, below even this level of specific minor cults the Egyptians' lives were caught up in a web of superstition. A group of papryi from about the ninth century BC catalogues in some detail the hazards of life from which a person became exempt on possessing a copy, given as an oracle, from a god. Apart from various diseases, thunderbolts, the collapse of a wall, 'every evil eye', and 'every evil colour', an Egyptian needed protection from 'demons of a canal, from a demon of a well . . . from a demon of her father and her mother . . . from the magic of a Libyan, from the magic of all the people of Egypt'. Even the gods themselves might prove to be vindictive since protection was also required against 'every god and every goddess who assumes manifestations when they are not appeased', and, rather ominously, from 'the gods who seize someone instead of someone [else]'. Only constant

watchfulness, prayer, recitation of spells, and possession of charms could hope to keep a person safe in this jungle of hostile forces. One could even possess a calendar telling which part of every day of the year was lucky or unlucky.

It is to this world of evil spirits that much of Egyptian medicine belongs. Although evidence is occasionally found of a careful diagnosis of an illness, based on close observation, together with fairly rational suggestions for treatment, for most people this approach had little appeal. A course of treatment which grappled with the evil forces causing sickness was far more appropriate. Most medical treatises are a mixture of observation, of folk remedies employing substances like mouse oil and centipede fat, and of pure magic intended to persuade or frighten the possessing demon to leave the body of the ailing person. In the same treatise there might also be found recipes for removing fleas from the house and the preparation of a cream which, when smeared on the face 'transforms an old man into a youth. . . . Proved a million times'.

Life after death

The pattern of preservation of ancient remains in Egypt has favoured tombs and cemeteries at the expense of houses and towns. This tends to give a somewhat exaggerated idea of the importance which the preparation for death had among the ancient Egyptians, although funerals and tomb construction must have been a major item of family expenditure.

It was believed that a man's spirit lived on after death and that this existence was comparable with that on earth, with just the same requirements. These were met partly by burying household equipment in the grave, partly by magical substitutes (which might

extend to a complete environment for the deceased recorded in pictures showing the highlights of his earthly life), and partly by offering-ceremonies performed by surviving relatives, usually headed by the eldest son, which were basically similar to those performed in temples. In time this simple belief became caught up in mythological conceptions of the next world, particularly the identification of the deceased with the resurrected god, Osiris. The superstitious dangers which besieged the Egyptian during life also pursued him after death and required the recitation of spells, written on the coffin or on a roll of papyrus.

The dead were particularly vulnerable to the attentions of the living, who might rob the tomb of its contents, mutilate the pictures of the dead person in the hopes of destroying his heavenly happiness, and even destroy his body, carefully preserved as a home for his spirit either by artificial mummification or by the preservative qualities of dry sand.

The living even blamed the dead for causing trouble, and a number of letters have survived threatening them with legal proceedings before a company of gods. The significance of this was certainly not lost on the Egyptians: 'Cease not from following your desires until the day of death arrives. Those who have departed since the time of the god, they have not come back again. . . . They experience not the pleasure of their desires.'

Egyptian art

Although they depict scenes drawn from life, the majority of Egyptian illustrations are taken from tombs. They were therefore visible to only a few living people, and in some cases must have been sealed off altogether. The specialized function of art in

ancient Egypt must be realized for true assessment of its achievements.

In two-dimensional art (the representation on wall surfaces of scenes and inscriptions carved in stone and then painted, or just painted if carving were not possible) the Egyptians adhered to a uniform style for 3000 years. It was not the result of casual evolution. In prehistoric times art was disorderly in composition, and relatively crude in execution. However, in the last phase of the prehistoric period a school of artists and craftsmen of considerable talent appeared. They are known principally from a series of slate palettes carved with scenes in low relief. One of the last examples, from the beginning of the First Dynasty, was carved in the carefully measured style which was to characterize Pharaonic Egypt.

This is a style so scrupulously academic that it can only have been developed as the result of deliberate experimentation and careful thought. Some of the motifs show resemblances to the art of southern Mesopotamia although this was ultimately a source only for inspiration and not for copying. The appearance of this style of art apparently coincided with the appearance of the first carved hieroglyphic inscriptions. This may not be accidental, since hieroglyphs conform to the same rigid rules of artistic composition as do the scenes which they almost invariably accompany. Indeed the distinction between picture and text is a rather artificial one. The scenes on tomb and temple walls can often best be understood as greatly enlarged and complicated examples of a type of hieroglyphic sign—something which was added to words to make their meaning clearer. The relationship can be seen in the way in which the pictures are divided into scenes by horizontal lines, like rows of hieroglyphs.

Since Egyptian pictorial art normally had a religious context—summaries of rituals on

Above, zodiac at the temple of Denderah:
engraving after a first-century BC relief. Musée
du Louvre, Paris.

Top, plaster mask of an old woman, Eighteenth
Dynasty: this realistic portrayal is typical of the
lively style of the Amarna period. Staatliche
Museen zu Berlin.

Above left, the tomb of Nefertari, wife of
Rameses II, in the Valley of the Kings at Thebes,
Nineteenth Dynasty; the paintings depict the
presiding deities of the after-life.

Left, detail of a relief from the tomb of Rameses
III, Twentieth Dynasty.

Opposite right, King Tuthmosis III offers water
and fire to Amon-Ra: painting in the temple at
Dayir-el-Bahri, Eighteenth Dynasty. Egyptian
Museum, Cairo.

Opposite left, scene from the Nineteenth-Dynasty
Papyrus of Ani showing three goddesses guarding
Ani's tomb: on the left, Seker, the hawk-headed
god of the dead of the Memphis necropolis; on the
right, Hathor, emerging from the Libyan
mountains in the form of a cow; and, in front of
her, Taueret, the hippopotamus goddess. British
Museum, London.

temple walls, or pictures for the benefit of the dead—and was often the object of religious ritual, it was important to depict the subject matter as exactly as possible. Perspective drawing, which gives a photographic image, fails to do this since it introduces distortions which, although apparent to the human eye, are not actually present. Railway lines converging to a point on the horizon are after all only an optical illusion.

The Egyptians achieved their goal of objective truth in a more satisfactory way. Each component part of a scene was treated quite independently and depicted in its most characteristic, and therefore its truest, outline. No matter in what direction a figure might really be facing or moving, it would always be given the same shape. Relative size did not indicate distance from the viewer. A hare would be drawn much smaller than a donkey, but one donkey farther in the distance than another would still be the same size, which is quite logical since donkeys do not really increase in size as they draw nearer the person watching.

The same analytical attitude was to determine the shape of the individual parts of the scene. The characteristic shape of a bird is the profile of its body. However, the principal difference between a sparrow and a swallow is the shape of the tail feathers when seen from above. So the Egyptians drew the body in profile and added to it a top view of the tail feathers. In the case of the human figure this analysis went further.

The head was given its characteristic side view, the torso a front view, and the waist and legs a side view. The Egyptians' achievement was that they avoided carrying this approach to absurd conclusions. They drew the front view of an eye on the side of a face, but they refrained from adding the mouth in front view, although the hieroglyphic sign for mouth shows that a front view was thought the most characteristic.

Because of this restraint it is still possible to find pleasure in the skill the Egyptians showed in producing balanced compositions and for their scrupulously neat workmanship. Another result of this approach was to diminish the amount of action in a scene since violent contortion was not counted as typical of man or beast. The placid, frozen appearance which resulted was perfectly in keeping with the religious context.

In order to maintain the consistency of the style, which collected a sacred aura of its own, it was codified using a grid of squares. The human body for example, was eighteen squares tall with the shoulders, sixteen squares from the base. Students learnt draughtsmanship by copying models, and, although a whole scene in a tomb might need a preliminary grid drawn over the entire wall, constant practice made them exceptionally proficient in freehand drawing. Indeed, some of their practice pieces on rough flakes of limestone display a control of line and a freedom of expression which are outstanding by any standards.

However, the sacred nature and purpose of Egyptian art meant that a remarkably high standard of uniformity was achieved, with little room for individual experimentation. It may, however, be doubted whether artists were able to see any direction along which experimentation might proceed.

Akhenaton's innovations in religious practice were expressed very largely through art. One accidental effect of the capital's being at Thebes was the growth of a cemetery of courtiers' tombs hollowed in the Theban hills, where the rock was of too poor a quality for carving. Decoration was largely restricted to painting, and gradually the artists began to exploit the greater freedom which this medium offered, introducing a liveliness in the depiction of secondary figures which began to strain to the limit the framework of rules governing Egyptian art.

The period of Akhenaton's reign came as the climax to this movement. The principal monuments were undoubtedly the Aton temples, but these were subsequently demolished and the stones used in other temples. However, enough of these blocks have now been recovered to give an idea of the content of the scenes, which appear to

Above, stela depicting the Lady Ten-Chenat worshipping Re-Harakkte, the sovereign god of Egypt, Twenty-sixth Dynasty. Staatliche Museen zu Berlin.

Above left, Eighteenth-Dynasty tomb painting depicting a carpenter at work.

Left, fowling in the marshes: an Eighteenth-Dynasty tomb painting from Thebes. British Museum, London.

Opposite centre, cranes, as depicted on a Third-Dynasty relief. Staatliche Museen zu Berlin.

Opposite top left, wall-painting of Horus on a sacred boat from the tomb of Pashedu, Dayir-el-Medina, Twentieth Dynasty.

Opposite below, limestone tomb relief of fruit-gathering, late Twenty-fifth or early Twenty-sixth Dynasty.

have had much in common with the subject matter in courtiers' tombs at Amarna.

They illustrated the theme of the Aton as the universal giver of life. The manifold activities of life in Egypt were depicted with a freedom and pleasure in small detail which went even further than the products of the Theban tomb painters, although the style remained very recognizably Pharaonic. At the centre of all was the Aton stretching forth his rays towards elaborate representations of his temples and to figures of the king and royal family making offerings, praised by rows of obsequious courtiers. In the private tombs at least there were other scenes of the royal family eating or driving through the city.

The intimacy of these royal scenes is the most startling departure of all, and also the most difficult to explain. It may have been an attempt to make royalty an easier object for adulation. Yet the features of Akhenaton are a gross caricature of convention. The long hanging jaw with fat lips, wide effeminate hips and swollen belly—all seem a deliberate travesty of the accepted features of the divine king. It is possible that he actually suffered from some deforming disease, yet in the colossal statues from his early temple at Karnak these mannerisms produce an effect of inscrutable, non-human power bordering on the malevolent and suggest rather a deliberate attempt to achieve an expression of divine kingship which went beyond the clothing of a man in the crowns and robes normally signifying kingship. However, in the end these artistic innovations, like the Aton cult itself, proved a passing eccentricity, and were submerged without trace in history.

Egyptian statuary had a purpose even more limited than wall relief and painting. A statue was a home for a spirit: either a god in a temple or a king or private individual who would be able to receive offerings placed in front of them in a tomb, chapel or temple. Royal statues also had a limited application as architectural features in temples. Their form was based on specific formulae just as much as was two-dimensional art. They normally represent an idealized human form, youthful and confident, placidly waiting for the prayers and offerings which were their due. In some cases there are obvious attempts at portraiture, usually confined to the head, but this was not vital, for the identity of the statue lay in the owner's name carefully inscribed on it.

Statuary seems never to have been seen as a vehicle for recording emotion or action, except perhaps the little wooden models of domestic and agricultural activity which for a time were included in the burial equipment. Some of the most highly individual works of statuary, apart from those of Akhenaton's reign, belong to the last six centuries BC. The poses are as formal as before, but in the treatment of the head imagination has been given a wider scope to include the dignity of lined old age. Many show an amazing ability to render the detailed modelling of flesh and skull structure. Some seem intended to depict the brutality of temporal power.

The production of what are now regarded as works of art was a major industry designed to please the gods and the dead. Little, however, seems to have been done for the living. The art of wall decoration appears to have had a very limited application in domestic architecture. The courtiers' houses at Amarna had ceilings painted with bright patterns and gay friezes at the top of the walls containing fruit and flower patterns, but this was probably a luxury that few could afford. The houses of the necropolis workmen at Thebes were whitewashed except for small scenes of largely religious content painted around the household shrine. Only in the royal places are there traces of decoration to match the art of tombs and temples. The best preserved are from Amarna, with scenes of animal and bird life in the marshes, free from interference from god or man.

The Egyptians applied their artistic talents to objects of daily use: furniture, jewellery, cosmetic equipment and even weapons. They mostly show the same carefully controlled outlines, symmetry and formalism found in religious art. It may have been this which inhibited the development of ceramics, the one art which relies most heavily on abstraction. The Egyptians produced great quantities of pottery, but it remained an unsophisticated utilitarian product, quite devoid of decoration.

Above, funeral stela dating from the Twenty-fifth or Twenty-sixth Dynasty: the deceased woman is worshipping the sun god Re-Harakhte-Aton, who is carrying a crook and flail; the sun disc surmounts his falcon head. Musée du Louvre, Paris.

Left, cosmetic jar dating from the Eighteenth Dynasty. Musée du Louvre, Paris.

Opposite top, portraits dating from the Eighteenth Dynasty, Amarna period. Cairo Museum.

Opposite bottom, portrait of Akmer, mother of Queen Hatshepsut, from the queen's tomb, Eighteenth Dynasty.

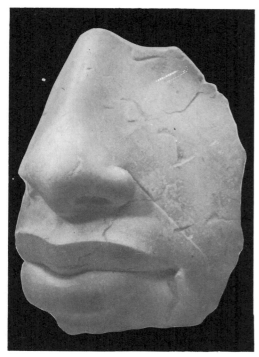

Egyptian society

The basic unit of society was a family of husband and wife who set up their own independent household on marriage. Although there was no prohibition against a man possessing more than one wife, in practice monogamy seems to have been the rule. This is understandable in view of the serious nature of the written contract which secured the wife's property rights. Husband and wife contributed to the formation of a joint property for the establishment of an independent household. Either party could end the contract with a divorce, in which case the wife's share was restored to her, although adultery was punished by repudiation.

However, in all cases provision was made for children of the marriage. A defaulting husband could also be liable for the payment of maintenance to the divorced wife. Even within the marriage the wife could arrange for the ultimate disposal of her own share of the joint property. One old woman left a will disinheriting her ungrateful children who failed to look after her.

It is not known whether marriages were celebrated with something more than a legal agreement or to what extent they were arranged solely by parents, although among the lower classes this was probably usual.

However, a number of texts from the Nineteenth and Twentieth Dynasties have survived containing collections of songs or poems which deal with romantic life in terms which are instantly familiar. Some make extravagant comparisons with the beloved and others deal with the pains of unrequited love. In a few suggestive double meanings can be detected, as when a maiden invites her lover to share with her the pleasures of bird-snaring in the fields. One description of love-sickness is particularly poignant. (It should be noted that the Egyptians used the words 'brother' and 'sister' as common terms of endearment.)

Seven [days] to yesterday I have not seen the sister.
Sickness has invaded me, my limbs have grown heavy.
I am forgetful of myself.
If the master physicians come to me, my heart has no comfort in their remedies.
The magicians: there is no escape through them, my sickness is not recognized.
Telling me 'Here she is' is what revives me, her name is what raises me up.
The entering and leaving of her messengers is what revives my spirits.
Of more benefit to me is the sister than all remedies.
She is more to me than the entire pharmacopoeia.
My recovery is her entering from without.
When I see her I am well.
When he opens her eyes my body grows young.
When she speaks I am strong.
When I embrace her she drives evil from me.
But she has been gone from me for seven days.

Above, painted relief from the tomb of Queen Hatshepsut, Dayir-el-Bahri, Eighteenth Dynasty. Cairo Museum.

Left, fragment of a head, Eighteenth Dynasty, Amarna period. Metropolitan Museum of Art, New York.

Opposite top, limestone relief of Amen Moser and his wife Depet, late Eighteenth Dynasty. Musée du Louvre, Paris.

Opposite bottom right, granite statue of Sesostris III found at Dayir-el-Bahri, Twelfth Dynasty. Fitzwilliam Museum, Cambridge.

Opposite bottom centre, statue, of painted limestone, of Nofret, Fourth Dynasty: Nofret, who is wearing a colourful necklace and headband, was the wife of Rahotep, a high priest and army commander; the figure comes from Rahotep's tomb at Medun. Egyptian Museum, Cairo.

Opposite bottom left, sculpture in relief from Queen Hatshepsut's temple, Eighteenth Dynasty.

Education

For Egyptian children the key to a successful career was literacy. There is no evidence showing how a child gained admittance to the scribal schools, though personal connections were no doubt important. However, once there, pupils learnt how to write their language by copying out passages from classical literary texts. They often apparently learned the texts and then copied from memory, even at the beginning when what they wrote was unintelligible to them.

Copying from dictation also had a part in their training. These schoolboy exercises, often full of every kind of error, are sometimes the only source for some lost literary work. The pupils also copied models of the kinds of text they might be expected later to compose—letters, official reports, lists of royal titles, and praises of the king. They might also find themselves copying enthusiastic compliments to their teacher (doubtless good practice for the future). Constant reminders on the need for diligence and on the penalties of idleness were included for good measure:

I am told that you have abandoned writing and that you cavort about in pleasures. You go from street to street, the smell of beer everywhere you loiter. Beer makes one cease from being a man. . . . You have been taught to sing to the pipe, to chant to the flute. . . . But you sit in the house surrounded by harlots.

The ape brought from Kush understands words; lions can be trained, horses can be tamed. But as for you, no one like you can be discovered amongst the whole of mankind.

A boy's ear is on his back; he listens when it is beaten.

I give you a hundred blows and you ignore them all. You appear to me to be like a beaten ass that recovers in a day. You appear to me to be like a jabbering Nubian brought in with the tribute.

The rewards were carefully spelt out:

Be a scribe. It saves you from toil, it protects you from all manner of work. It spares you from bearing hoe and mattock.

Be a scribe. Your limbs will be sleek, your hands will grow soft. You will go forth in white attire, honoured with courtiers saluting you.

Compare other professions:

The potter is smeared with dirt like one whose folk have died. His hands and his feet are filled with clay. He is like one from the swamp. . . . The carpenter in the shipyard carries the timber and stacks it. If he should render yesterday's quota today, woe to his limbs! But the scribe, he it is who reckons up the labour of all of them.

Once he was trained as a scribe, there was no high office to which an Egyptian could not aspire, no matter how humble his beginnings, though it may be assumed that the right connections as well as the possession of ability aided promotion. The administration seems to have had an insatiable appetite for paper-work and the scribe could enter a wide variety of employments. There was financial administration—keeping accounts of agricultural produce for estate owners or making the assessments for the complicated taxation system. The temples and the army had their own scribes too: religious texts and official records had to be prepared; distant fortresses in foreign lands sent back the most detailed despatches. The legal system made its own enormous demands. The standard procedure for legal hearings or for registering a property deal or marriage settlement was a declaration made before senior officials, perhaps accompanied by an oath, which was then copied down in writing, signed by witnesses and deposited in an archive. If the matter related to a previous settlement of some kind, the original document was looked up and copied down as a preamble. It is very apparent that the sheer bulk of accumulated documents must have been enormous.

Many of these tasks required some specialized knowledge, and suitable books of instruction were compiled. Among them were treatises on mathematics which provide a valuable insight not only into the state of Egyptian mathematics, but also into the mental attitude of the Egyptians. They had evolved, probably entirely by trial and error, a set of solutions to the various problems of arithmetic and geometry which their accounting and building projects presented. The treatises simply list the problems one by one, giving a separate method of solution for each. It seems never to have occurred to the Egyptians that behind these solutions might lie theoretical generalizations which could be applied universally.

This is understandable since, with abstract thought, the Egyptians immediately entered

Above, wall-painting depicting a banquet. British Museum, London.

Left, Nineteenth-Dynasty wall-painting of an acrobat in performance.

Opposite right, detail of a wall-painting from the tomb of Itet at Medium showing geese in a marsh, Fourth Dynasty; there are six in all, three walking to the right, three to the left. Cairo Museum.

Opposite left, statue of King Chephren, Fourth Dynasty: the king's throne has lion legs, and a maned lion surmounts them; above Chephren's brow the erect forepart of the divine serpent, symbol of royal power, is visible. Egyptian Museum, Cairo.

a world of personal, non-mechanical forces where mathematics was irrelevant. Nevertheless, they were able to devise methods for computing the areas of triangles, trapezoids, rectangles and circles, and also the volumes of cylinders, cubes and truncated pyramids. This knowledge was important for calculating such things as the amount of corn in grain bins, areas of fields for taxation purposes and amounts of stone for various stages in building pyramids. It is, however, characteristic of the Egyptians that, although they employed methods which involved a very close approximation to π, they remained unaware that such an abstraction existed. They could also handle the most complicated fractions, but either they could not conceive or did not see the need to develop a special system to express fractions whose numerator was not 1. Thus, if an Egyptian wished to multiply $\frac{1}{11}$ by 2, his answer would have been not $\frac{2}{11}$ but $\frac{1}{6}+\frac{1}{66}$. He would also probably have had to make use of one of the various sets of tables which had been specially developed for just this particular purpose.

The man who used the solutions in a mathematical treatise was not regarded as a mathematician or a specialist, but simply as a scribe performing a particular task. One composition included in the syllabus of some scribal schools—a satirical letter to an army scribe showing up his ignorance—indicates the peak of attainment to which a scribe should aspire: the ability to deal with any practical problem. In addition to knowing the ancient classics chapter and verse, the scribe should be able to calculate the distribution of rations to soldiers, estimate the number of bricks needed for a construction ramp, get together a team to fetch an obelisk from a quarry, supervise the erection of a colossus using exactly the right number of men needed to complete the task in the six hours between meals, and organize a foreign military expedition. The letter ends with a colourful lesson in Palestinian military geography. The interest of the Egyptians in acquiring an encyclopedic knowledge of places and names is also exemplified in long lists of words grouped into various categories, such as classes of people and occupations, types of building, parts of an ox, and extensive lists of place names in Egypt, the purpose being 'to clear the mind, to instruct the ignorant, to know everything that exists'. The compiler of the longest list known was a scribe of sacred books in a temple scriptorium.

Precepts and rules of etiquette

The term 'instructions' was used by the Egyptians for collections of edifying statements. These included pithy sayings about life in general, some with a definite moral content and some simply rules of etiquette.

They were directed at the official who wished to be just in his dealings, and successful in his career. They formed part of the syllabus of scribal schools:

If you are one to whom petition is made, be patient in listening to the speech of the petitioner. . . . A petitioner loves attention to his words more than the fulfilment of that about which he came.

Be not arrogant on account of your knowledge. . . . Good words are more hidden than green jasper, [yet] are found amongst maidservants over the millstones.

Justice is great, its value enduring. It has not been disturbed since the days of him who created it. He who transgresses the laws is punished.

If you are sitting at the table of someone greater than yourself, accept what he gives when it is placed before your nose. You should stare at what is in front of you. Do not pierce him with many stares. . . . Let your face be cast down until he addresses you, speak when he does address you. . . . laugh when he laughs. It will be well pleasing in his heart.

If you desire to prolong friendship in a house into which you have admittance as a son, as a brother, or as a friend, wherever you enter beware of approaching the women. . . . One is made a fool by limbs of faience as she stands looking like carnelian. A fleeting moment, the likeness of a dream, [then] death overtakes you through having known her!

If you are a man of status, establish your household. You must love your wife with passion, fill her belly, clothe her back. Scented oil is the prescription for her body. Please her heart for as long as you live. She is a fertile field for her lord. . . . Keep her

from control, be firm with her. Her eye can be a storm wind when it looks. Soothe her heart with what accrues to you: this is how to keep her in your house.
(Instruction of the vizier, Ptah-hetep. Fifth Dynasty. About 2450 BC)

The frank materialism of this collection of sayings, doubtless the cause of its popularity, is noticeably absent from a much later composition, the *Instruction of Amenemope*. Extant copies appear to date from the Twenty-first or Twenty-second Dynasties. The tone is far more philosophical and far humbler. The contrast between the confidence of the former and the resigned humility of the latter is a reflection of the moods of the two very different periods in which they were composed.

Of more profit is poverty from the hand of god than riches in a storehouse.
Of more profit is bread when the heart is joyful than riches with sorrow.
If you find a large debt against a poor man, divide it into three parts.
Forgive two, let one remain. You will find that it is like the paths of life.
Do not spend the night fearful of the morrow.
[Even] at dawn what will the morrow be like? A man cannot know what the morrow is like.
Do not speak falsely with men: the abomination of god.
God desires respect for the humble more than the honouring of the exalted.
Laugh not at a blind man nor taunt a dwarf, nor injure the affairs of the lame.

Above, Queen Tiy, chief wife of Amenhotep III, Eighteenth Dynasty: the queen was not of royal descent, being the daughter of a priest. Staatliche Museen zu Berlin.

Left, ebony and ivory chair dating from the New Kingdom (post 1580 BC). Musée du Louvre, Paris.

Opposite top, detail of the lid of a chest from the tomb of Tutankhamun, Eighteenth Dynasty. Egyptian Museum, Cairo.

Opposite bottom, fresco depicting a kingfisher in a papyrus thicket from the palace of Tell-el-Amarna, Nineteenth Dynasty.

Above, gold cup given to Undebunded, an army commander, Twenty-first Dynasty. Rogers Fund, Metropolitan Museum of Art, New York.

Left, ebony state chair made in the form of a folding stool decorated with religious symbols, among them the sun god Aton. Griffith Institute, Ashmolean Museum, Oxford.

Taunt not a man possessed of god, nor laugh at him when he goes astray.
Man is but clay and straw; god is his builder, tearing down and building up every day.
He makes a thousand poor men as he wishes, he makes a thousand overseers in [just] an hour of his life.

Even Ptah-hetep's precepts reflect a code of social responsibility whose ultimate authority was a divine, eternally established justice, regarded as a tangible part of the universe. On pages 57–58 a passage was quoted on the responsibilities of kingship where a like theme was expressed and where a man was regarded as answerable after death for his transgressions. The theme of judgement after death became a standard part of magical papyri buried in tombs during and after the Eighteenth Dynasty, but was given a decidedly amoral twist. The purpose of these papyri, the so-called 'Book of the Dead', was to arm a person with magical spells sufficient to overcome all obstacles in the underworld. One of these was judgement in which the heart was weighed against a feather. A fearsome beast waited to consume anyone whose heart tipped the balance. To avoid this fate a spell was included to prevent the heart from giving an unsatisfactory performance.

There was also a text which contained a complete denial of forty-two specified sins. However, even the behaviour of gods could not be relied upon; and it is certain that thoughts of ultimate retribution must have disturbed the conscience of many an official.

Memorandum concerning their theft of five robes and ten plain garments, total fifteen, from the temple of Anukis, Lady of Aswan. The treasury scribe, Mentu-herkhepshef, who held the office of mayor of Elephantine, cross-examined them. He found that they had been in their possession, but they had sold them to Amenrekhy, an artisan from the 'Place of Truth', for a price. This same mayor accepted bribes from them and released them.
(Turin Indictment Papyrus. About 1140 BC)

Literature

The Egyptians found time for literature whose purpose was simply to entertain and the fragments which have survived reveal a richly variegated tradition of story-telling. In many cases the stories have a message to impart, which would have increased the appreciation of the readers or listeners. One story tells of a sailor, shipwrecked on a magic island, where he is befriended by a giant, melancholy serpent. Another relates the adventures of a prince, predestined by fate to die through the agency of a crocodile, a snake, or a dog, and who sets off to seek his fortune abroad. Reaching a land beyond the Euphrates he wins a contest for the hand of a beautiful princess. She it is who saves him from the snake, but as the episode with the crocodile is reached the papyrus breaks off leaving the ending to be guessed. In some stories an allegorical meaning is very obvious. One relates a dispute between two brothers, Truth and Falsehood, in which Truth is blinded. He is, however, vindicated by his son, who secures in turn the blinding of Falsehood.

Although the texts are lost numerous illustrations survive from animal fables in which animals take the part of humans. Whatever instructure message they contained, it was heavily laced with satire. One is a very obvious burlesque of the standard temple scene showing the victorious king attacking an enemy fortress in his chariot, but here the chariot contains a mouse, and the fortress is manned by cats.

Commerce

The documents and monuments which have survived give the impression of a simple division of society between the considerable body of literate men running the country for the divine king, and the illiterate peasantry who, though forming the bulk of the population, have survived only through their occasional appearance on the monuments of their superiors. One class of people is noticeably absent: merchants and shop-keepers who made an independent living through private trading. Superficially the explanation seems simple. At the level of day-to-day subsistence simple barter sufficed. From the Nineteenth and Twentieth Dynasties there is considerable information about relative values, which could also be expressed absolutely in terms of gold, silver, copper, or corn units. Thus, one wooden adze handle could be exchanged for one jar of beer plus a goat-skin, which were together worth the same in copper units as the handle.

At the other end of the scale the import of foreign produce, both through trade and by direct exploitation, such as mining in Sinai or Nubia, appears to have been a royal monopoly, or at least surviving records commemorate only missions sent out by the king. In the case of mining expeditions it is easy to accept the evidence at its face value since these expeditions were of a semi-military nature. It is also clear that the temples engaged in internal trade since the resources they owned were so many and varied, and there are explicit references from the period following the Eighteenth Dynasty to traders attached to particular temples.

Private biographical inscriptions from tombs and lists of titles held in the administration relate almost exclusively to tasks performed for the king and the gods. Other more personal activities were quite inappropriate. However, it seems clear that private commercial activity flourished, from

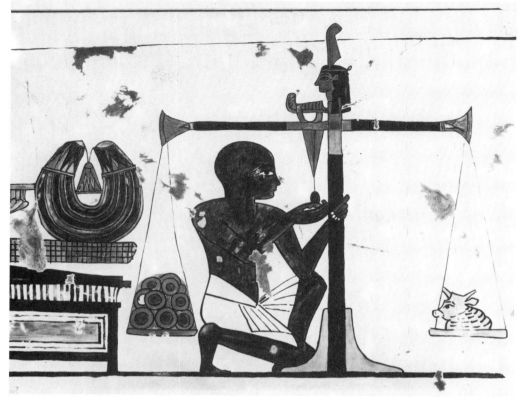

occasional references in secular literature from the post-Eighteenth Dynasty period to traders and even to Nile freighters in the charge of private individuals. One scribal exercise of the Nineteenth Dynasty, a letter of praise apparently addressed to the teacher, even refers to private ownership of vessels trading abroad: 'Your ship has arrived from Syria laden with all manner of good things.' Once again we are made aware that the basic structure of Egyptian society is not necessarily reflected accurately in the principal written sources.

Personal liberty

The status of the literate administrative class is fairly clear: their rights as individuals and as property owners were carefully guarded by laws. Within the limitations of ancient societies they were free men. The great landed estates of the king, of the temples and of the senior officials and nobility possessed large numbers of dependents over whom their owner or employer had a considerable amount of control. One example comes from a text listing ninety-five dependents in an Upper Egyptian household of the Thirteenth Dynasty. Two thirds were women and more than half were Asians. The men were employed as house-boys, field hands, brewers, cooks, tutors and sandal-makers, the women as makers of cloth (at least twenty of them), household storekeepers, gardeners and hairdressers.

The list is part of a legal document recording successive transfers of ownership. At first these servants belonged to an official

Above, wall-painting depicting weighing scales. British Museum, London.

Opposite top, relief from Tell-el-Amarna depicting a princess kissing a child, Eighteenth Dynasty, Amarna period. Brooklyn Museum.

Opposite bottom, Eleventh-Dynasty papyrus inscribed with a romance and bearing the names Thothmes III and Autef. British Museum, London.

whose disgrace had led to the confiscation of his property. They were then passed to another official, who first had to petition the king for them, and then made them over to his wife by a deed of gift. From the point of view of ownership their status is clear: they are listed alongside movable property, fields and a house. Little is known, however, of the degree of authority which their owner had over them. From the period following the Eighteenth Dynasty, for example, it is known that servants could own and dispose of their own property, including land. Perhaps it was just a person's labour that was owned. Naturally under a generous owner a servant could do well. In one instance a servant girl's daughter was allowed to marry the owner's brother, becoming a free woman and, with her husband, an heir to the owner's estate.

People in a similar condition, permanently attached to temples and royal establishments, their numbers continually swollen by prisoners of war, formed a permanent pool of labour for the construction of monuments, often aided by army contingents. In this capacity they were fed and housed. What is probably a town of builders and permanent workers belonging to the pyramid of a Twelfth Dynasty king at Lahun has survived in a fairly intact state. It was carefully planned and composed of rectangular units. There were large mansions for administrators, and for labourers row upon row of terrace houses, small but far from cramped.

However, if this labour force proved insufficient for building or agricultural work, the government had authority to conscript people from many walks of life to labour without reward for a specific period. While engaged on this work they might live in a government labour camp. Absconding carried with it the penalty of permanent servitude for the guilty man, his family and descendants. For work on large monuments it is possible that forced labour was confined to the summer when agricultural work was at a minimum. One advantage of being a scribe was to avoid this fate. Yet so unpopular was it that fear of it pursued all classes beyond the grave and led to the burial in the tomb of little magical figures equipped with tools, who could labour on the owner's behalf.

Dayir-el-Medina

Fortunately, considerable documentation is available about one group of workmen permanently in the employ of the king, although as skilled craftsmen they appear to have had unusually high status. Their relative freedom is itself an illustration of how misleading it can be to generalize too broadly about Egyptian society. These were the men who excavated and decorated the royal tombs in the Valley of the Kings at

Thebes and must have included craftsmen of the highest ability. Their village has survived remarkably intact in a little valley behind the mortuary temple of Rameses III and is now known as Dayir-el-Medina. It was occupied from early in the Eighteenth Dynasty until the end of the Twentieth, when the royal necropolis was abandoned a span of about four centuries.

It was composed of identical houses on either side of a street, with later additions around its edges. The houses were quite comfortable: a front reception room containing the household shrine, a main living-room, its roof supported by a painted wooden column, two rooms behind this, and then a small yard. Outside the village were a communal water cistern, chapels for the various deities and the tombs of the villagers rising in terraces up the sides of the valley. The tombs show the affluence of the villagers. They are often quite large with their own chapel and pyramid, decorated inside, and some contained fairly rich sets of burial equipment. The site has also yielded innumerable scraps of pottery and limestone used as a cheap substitute for papyrus in recording the daily events and dealings of the inhabitants. From these a remarkably

complete account of their life can be reconstructed.

On average the work force consisted of about sixty men organized into two gangs. Each was in the charge of a foreman assisted by a deputy, and the inevitable scribe kept a close watch on everything: on the progress of the work, on the number and weight of copper tools issued to workmen, and on the absentees. They worked for nine days at a stretch, sleeping in little huts in front of the tomb they were preparing. They returned to their village, which lay on the other side of a high ridge, only on their free day, or on the holidays which the principal religious festivals provided. Their work was regularly inspected by the vizier, their ultimate superior, or by one of his deputies.

In return for this work they were paid a regular monthly wage in kind, drawn largely from the revenues collected by the great mortuary temples at Thebes, such as that of Rameses II. The basic payment was made in grain, emmer for bread, and barley for beer, although both could be bartered for other articles. They were also supplied with quantities of fish, firewood, vegetables, oil and cloth, and with irregular bonuses of luxuries such as wine and meat, and beer

Below painted wooden statuette of a maidservant, Middle kingdom.

Left, bronze figure of a cat, c. 600 BC. British Museum, London.

Opposite, votive plaque depicting a woman thought to be Cleopatra as a goddess, Ptolemaic period. Schindler Collection, New York.

Egypt's legacy

In the year 30 BC Queen Cleopatra of Egypt committed suicide. A major threat to the newly emergent Roman empire had gone, and with it a last opportunity for Egypt itself to become yet again the centre of an empire. Far to the north, on the misty perimeter of the known world, Celtic Britain was still in its last century of independence before the final Roman conquest of AD 43. So much that is basic in our own inheritance had not begun to take shape. Yet Cleopatra was the heiress to a civilization which stretched back into antiquity for a period longer by a thousand years than the period which separates Cleopatra from ourselves. Fourteen centuries before her birth the Egyptian Empire had reached its maximum extent, but even to the Egyptians of this period the early pyramid builders were legendary figures from a remoter past. Their great monuments were an invitation to the curious to scribble their names on walls, which had already been standing for 1,000 years.

The Greeks and Romans entered a civilized world which was already old. They did not invent from nothing the ideas and patterns of life on which our own civilization is built. Complex, literate societies with rich, well-organized resources, supporting artists and scholars who had long traditions of experiment and intellectual enquiry, were the main feature of the ancient Near East. They had already progressed far from man's primitive beginnings. The Greeks and Romans inherited the achievements of this world; their own achievement is that they were able to break out of the intellectual inhibitions which seemed inbred in their predecessors. Egypt formed a major part of this fertile matrix, and the remarkable continuity and homogeneity of its culture have made it one of the easiest to study.

imported from Asia. The amount of payment varied with status, the scribe, for example, receiving half the rations of the foreman, and often less than the workmen themselves. Some of the workmen's needs were also met by dependents: a potter, water-carriers, washermen, fishermen and slave girls for grinding corn.

They were allowed to exercise considerable control over their own affairs. Petty crime was judged and punished by a council drawn from members of the village, and their various religious cults, including the dead king. Amenhotep I, who acted as an oracle for even trivial decisions, were served by priests selected from among their own number.

Their relative independence is made clear from a papyrus dating from the reign of Rameses III. On successive occasions the workmen demonstrated against the non-payment of their wages by leaving their work and sitting down (on at least one occasion with their families) behind the various mortuary temples which provided their wages. Their object in doing this seems to have been to bring their plight to the attention of senior officials such as the mayor of Thebes or the vizier.

This little community is a reminder that ancient Egypt possessed a complex society of living human beings whose lives were by no means characterized by the ponderous monuments of their rulers.

Above, the falcon of the god Horus in the temple of Horus at Edfu, Ptolemaic period.

EGYPT FROM 4000 BC TO ROMAN TIMES

Date	Pharaonic dynasties	Domestic history	External history	Culture
Fourth millennium BC	Prehistoric monarchy	Two kingdoms: Upper and Lower Egypt		
3300		Unification of Egypt? Kings of top row of Palermo Stone	Cultural influence from Sumer and Elam felt in Egypt	Prehistoric cultures Copper in use in Upper Egypt
3200	ARCHAIC PERIOD (3200–2700) 1st Dynasty	Later king lists commence with Menes Rebellion in delta	Trade relations with Byblos already established Armies reach 2nd Cataract	First written records, Narmer Palette First monumental brick architecture
	2nd Dynasty	Civil war?		
2700	OLD KINGDOM (2700–2150) 3rd Dynasty Djoser		First recorded expedition to Sinai mines	Step Pyramid of Djoser at Sakkara
2600	4th Dynasty			
	Sneferu Khufu (Cheops) Khafra (Chephren) Menkaura			First true pyramid Pyramids and Sphinx at Giza
2500	(Mycerinus)		Egyptian copper-smelting town in Nubia (Buhen)	
2400	5th Dynasty	Growth of provincial autonomy in Upper Egypt		Tombs of Ti, Ptahhetep, Akhethetep and Mereruka at Sakkara
2300	6th Dynasty		Trade caravans to southern Nubia	
2200	Pepi I and II			Pyramid texts
	FIRST INTERMEDIATE PERIOD (2150–1991) 7th and 8th Dynasties			
2100				
	9th/10th Dynasty of Herakleopolis 11th Dynasty of Thebes	First Theban revolt ended by about 2030		Tombs of kings and nobility at Thebes
2000				
	MIDDLE KINGDOM (1991–1786) 12th Dynasty Amenemhet I Senwosret I	Thebans masters of Egypt New capital of Amenemhet-ith-tawy founded	Renewed activity at Sinai mines, renewed relations with Byblos	First preserved literary texts First widespread use of bronze Painted tombs at Beni Hasan Revival of pyramid building in brick
1900	Amenemhet II Senwosret II Senwosret III		Nubian fortress chain constructed Egyptian influence at Byblos particularly marked	Probable land reclamation in Faiyum
1800	Amenemhet III Amenemhet IV			
	SECOND INTERMEDIATE PERIOD (1786–1575) 13th Dynasty	Upper Egypt at least still ruled from Amenemhet-ith-tawy	Palestine probably under Hyksos rule	
1700				
	Dynasty of six Hyksos kings	Egypt ruled from Avaris in eastern delta		
1600	17th Dynasty Thebes	Second Theban revolt ended	Kingdom of Kush	Small royal tombs at Thebes
	NEW KINGDOM (1575–1087) 18th Dynasty Ahmose Amenhotep I Tuthmosis I	Avaris captured Capital at Thebes	Hyksos pursued into Palestine	
			Boundary inscriptions at Euphrates and in Nubia	First tomb in Valley of the Kings
1500	Tuthmosis II Queen Hatshepsut Tuthmosis III	Illegal seizure of power	Palestine and Syria administered as an empire	Dayir-el-Bahri temple
1400	Amenhotep III Amenhotep IV (Akhenaton)	Religious revolutions New capital built at Amarna	Loss of northern part of the empire	Luxor temple, colossi of Memnon Artistic revolution
	Tutankhamen Aye Horemheb	Cult of Amen restored		Tomb in Valley of the Kings preserved intact

Date	Pharaonic dynasties	Domestic history	External history	Culture
1300	19th Dynasty Seti I Rameses II	Capital at Per-Rameses in eastern delta	Battle of Kadesh Egyptian-Hittite treaty; Israelite Exodus? Libyan invasion crushed	Temple at Abydos Enormous building programme: Hypostyle Hall at Karnak, Abu Simbel temple, Ramesseum at Thebes
1200	Merenptah			
	20th Dynasty Rameses III	Death from harem conspiracy; Tomb robbery trials at Thebes	Defeat of invasion by Peoples of the Sea and by Libyans; Egyptian Empire fades away	Medinet Habu temple Last tombs in Valley of the Kings
1100				
	21st Dynasty (1087–945)	Kings rule from Tanis in eastern delta Effective rule of Upper Egypt in hands of High Priests of Amen		Royal tombs at Tanis
1000				
900	22nd Dynasty (945–730) Sheshonk I	Libyan kings Period ends in anarchy 23rd Dynasty at Thebes	Sheshonk I (Shishak) attacks Jerusalem in 930	Royal tombs at Tanis
800				
700	25th Dynasty (730–656) Piankhy Taharka	Invaders from Napata in the Sudan Rebellions against Assyrian occupation	Esarhaddon of Assyria invades in 671 Assur-bani-pal of Assyria invades in 667	Artistic revival begins Pyramid tombs at Napata
600	26th Dynasty (664–525) Psemtek Neko II Psemtek Wahibre Ahmose II	Capital at Sais in delta	Circumnavigation of Africa	First demotic texts Greek trading colony established at Naukratis
500	27th Dynasty (525–404) Cambyses Darius Xerxes Artaxerxes I	Egypt a Persian province	Cambyses of Persia invades in 525	Nile-Red Sea canal completed Herodotus visits Egypt Jewish colony at Elephantine
400	28th and 29th Dynasties (404–380) 30th Dynasty (380–343) Nekhtnebef Nekhthorheb	Egyptian kings		
	'31st Dynasty' (343–332)	Egypt again a Persian province	Artaxerxes III of Persia invades	
300 200 100	Ptolemaic period	Capital at Alexandria Death of Cleopatra VII in 30	Alexander Battle of Actium	Manetho Greek language widely adopted Last Pharaonic temples built
	Egypt a Roman province			

Part II

THE TRIUMPH OF THE GREEKS

Introduction

The world of the Ancient Greeks was geographically a small one. From the island of Ithaca in the west, traditionally the home of Odysseus, to one of the little eastern towns or islets that claimed to be Homer's birthplace (possibly Smyrna on the coast of Turkey, or nearby Khios) the total distance was a trifling three or four hundred miles. Of course there were colonies or more casual settlements very much further away: Greek cities along the shores of the Black Sea or southern Italy and recognizably Greek things at Marseilles or in the Libyan coastlands.

Greek craftsmen were to be found even further afield. The Persian king, Darius, who first invaded Europe, and his son, Xerxes, who burnt the Acropolis of Athens, were at the same time using a Greek as their master-of-works 2,000 miles further east at the great palace of Persepolis, then under construction. When, a century and a half later, the conquering Alexander entered Persia on his way to that same wealthy capital, he was confronted by a crowd of forlorn Greek craftsmen who besought his protection. Good Greek inscriptions of the third century BC, combining a significant mixture of Delphic and oriental wisdom, have been found in recent years at Kandahar and at Aï Khanum beside the Oxus, both in modern Afghanistan. All these, however, represent chance extensions of the small, compact Greek homeland in what is today known geographically as Greece and the fringe of Asia Minor.

Yet it is important not to belittle the Greek world of the fifth century BC in comparison with the swarming, closely-knit world of the present. In terms of space-time, Moscow is today nearer to Washington than ancient Athens was to Sparta. Theoretically, China could today invade Europe in a fraction of the time that it took Darius to move his vast army across the Bosporus. In terms of population, it may be claimed that the Eurasia of today holds a hundred human beings for every one of twenty-five centuries ago. However, proportionately, the Greek world was already essentially a mansize world, and many of the problems with which it was confronted were not so very different from those which still face us.

At the same time it was, of course, a simpler world. The Parthenon was a very great building, trimmed and elaborated by all manner of sensitive calculation and adornment. Nevertheless, for all its perfection, its problems were aesthetically and technologically rudimentary compared with those of the cathedrals of Saint Sophia or Chartres. The Parthenon's famous frieze, carved as marble may never be carved again, is utterly untroubled by the intellectual or emotional stresses and individualities which were to challenge the sculptors of later and, in a sense, more adult ages. Its function, which it fulfilled to perfection, was to express repetitively a geometrically exquisite human type of action.

Under Roman influence this aesthetic simplicity evolved into more diverse and individual shapes. The Hellenistic era of Greece itself—roughly the third and second

centuries BC—was already moving fast in that direction.

The balanced perfection of fifth-century Athens had in turn grown out of successive and sometimes erratic and experimental phases. The word 'balanced' is a term which may be applied to the age of Phidias just as it may be applied nearly 2,000 years later to that of Raphael. These were ages when purpose and expression were for a moment so closely in accord as almost to conceal the effort and genius which went to the making of them.

The Minoan and Mycenaean civilizations of the second millennium BC, and, to a much greater extent, the Greek dark age, which appears to isolate the Mycenaean achievement from that of classical Greece, are full of manifest trial and error. Partly for that reason they move the spectator to an extent which perfection of achievement sometimes fails to do. Those immense, heroic bulls of Minoan Crete, tossing featherweight acrobats hither and thither like toys, have often a wilful emphasis that bridges time and is almost nearer to us than the cultivated naturalism of the Phidian reliefs. Some of the geometric creations of the dark age even have a curiously modern nuance. Then at last, about the end of the eighth century BC, we detect the beginning of the systematic, organic growth, which was to flower in the mighty achievement of the Athenian Acropolis and has continued to develop almost unbroken ever since.

In spite of our full awareness of the problem, the dark age still escapes our understanding. It is still substantially a sudden night, followed by a no less sudden dawn. When, after three or four centuries, Greece awoke once more, it was immediately articulate, full of intelligent curiosity and not forgetful of some of its old thoughts, especially of its inherited oral poetry. But it had an essentially new outlook and new problems. Above all, it was now maturely literate in a new way.

In about 750 BC Greek contacts with Phoenicia abruptly provided Greek thought with a new dimension—a sensitive alphabet which, after minor adaptation, served the mobile minds of the Hellenic world as it still serves the major part of the civilized world today. With this essential aid, Greek thinking of all kinds made a tremendous leap forward.

Already, before the end of the eighth century BC, an Attic vase had a hexameter scratched upon it prior to burial in the Kerameikes at Athens. The verse concerns someone 'who now performs the most gracefully of all dancers', and the pot may well have been a prize won in characteristically Greek skill. This is one of the earliest alphabetic Greek inscriptions left to us. It marks the threshold of the classical age and, in a sense, the threshold of our own.

All else seems to have stemmed from the gift of literacy, partly because records thenceforth begin to achieve precision, but also partly because a new means of interchange and new knowledge were now made available to an intelligent people with unprecedented speed. All at once, everything came alive.

During the seventh century BC the Greek sculptors, hitherto unambitious, began for the first time to make large statues of gods and heroes and even of ordinary people. Thenceforth, a steady progression, accelerating as time went by, led on to the climactic attainments of the fifth century BC. Parallel with this, the enquiring Greek mind began to combine philosophical speculation with mathematics and astronomy and, ultimately, biology. It produced the 'physical' schools of thought which were initially centred on Ionia, and particularly Miletus, a great city which was to become traditionally associated with orderly town-planning and civic discipline.

In this experimental era of politics it was Ionia again which first displayed the uses and abuses of centralized rule (technically 'tyranny') under Asian inspiration. Mainland Greece caught the infection for a while, but derived more solid worth from appointed and constitutional lawgivers, thus adding Solon to the great names of history. It is no less important that Solon's laws were inscribed upon wooden turntables set up in a hall at Athens for all to see—much as the visitor to Gortyna in central Crete can still see the Greek laws of a somewhat later date exhibited openly upon the walls of a public building.

There was nothing secretive about the Greek way of life. It was truly a life of the marketplace and the theatre. Its weaknesses, ranging from hasty and often unintelligent demagogy to moments of near-autocracy, are obvious enough. They have, however, been the weakness of democracy through the ages. It is the essential modernity of Greek thought that constantly recurs to us as we listen to Greek poets, philosophers and historians, or look upon the splendid fragments of Greek visual art.

On page 98, bronze head of Aphrodite by Praxiteles, fourth century BC.

Opposite, gold death-mask found in the royal grave circle at Mycenae by the German archaeologist Heinrich Schliemann and thought to have belonged to an Achaean king of the fifteenth century BC; Schliemann believed it was Agamemnon's mask and on its discovery cabled dramatically to the King of Greece, 'I have gazed on the face of Agamemnon'. National Archaeological Museum, Athens.

Chapter 6

The Birth of Greece

One of the finest statues in the National Museum at Athens is a life-size bronze of the god Poseidon, a powerful figure, his trident poised menacingly above his shoulder. The severity and strength of this statue reflect the awe in which the Greeks held the god of the sea, and the importance of the sea in their lives.

It was no accident that placed Poseidon, the brother of Zeus, second in the hierarchy of the gods. The sea pervaded the whole of Greek life: it was a source of food and an arena for battles, but, above all, the highway linking distant towns, colonies and trading posts. A history of Greece, therefore, is not only a history of mainland Greece and its inhabitants, but to a certain extent a history of all the peoples whose countries border the Mediterranean basin and beyond, especially the Persians. The Greek world extended from as far west as the coast of Spain to the northern shores of the Black Sea in the east. The neighbours of the Greeks ranged from the Etruscans in Italy to the wild Scythians in the plains of southern Russia.

The Greeks had an interesting name for their neighbours. Whether they were referring to the Great King of Persia in his palace at Susa, or a humble Egyptian flute player, they called them all *barbaroi*, or barbarians. There were no insulting overtones to this name; it merely meant that these people did not speak Greek, but instead languages which to Greek ears sounded confused and unintelligible, like the baaing of sheep. This highlights the second great unifying force among the Greeks—their language. In spite of variations of dialect, two Greeks from the opposite ends of the Mediterranean could understand each other as easily as a Scotsman and a Welshman today.

Hand in hand with this unity of language went a unity of culture. When the Syracusans destroyed the Athenian expedition to Sicily in 413 BC some of the Athenian prisoners were saved by cultured Syracusans from their fate in the stone quarries because of their ability to recite the plays of Euripides, the Athenian playwright.

The third factor which was a hallmark of Greek life and stamped them as different from other people was their religion. Zeus and the gods, who lived on Mount Olympus, were worshipped throughout the Greek world: corporately, with great magnificence and ceremony by cities in the state religion, and privately by individuals. Different gods might be more favoured in different cities, and local cults to minor deities might flourish in isolation, but these differences were not so important.

The Greek ideal

The language, culture and religion of the Greeks are important not only because, with the sea, they formed the sinews of their society, but also because it was the achievements of the Greeks in this respect which had the greatest influence on the formation of our society. They were the expression of what is loosely termed the Greek ideal. It is, however, very easy to be lured into accepting an idealized and romantic view of the cultural achievements of Greece. Western European society owes a great deal to the Greeks. From Greece came the seeds of modern democracy, philosophy, medicine, science, architecture, tragedy and epic poetry.

The danger, however, is that in our enthusiasm to grasp our 'classical heritage', we will overlook the far from ideal conditions in which these arts and sciences were

produced and so our critical appreciation of them will be dulled. Not all Athenians were as interested in philosophy as Plato. Socrates, Plato's master, was executed because his teaching was thought too revolutionary. Aristotle, Plato's pupil and the great mentor of philosophers in the Middle Ages, was forced to flee Athens to escape a similar fate.

In the tragedies of Aeschylus and Sophocles one can admire the almost religious respect for the individual as a person, yet it was standard Greek practice to massacre all the male inhabitants of a captured town. Knowledge of such facts

Left, head of Poseidon found on the island of Mylos. National Archaeological Museum, Athens.

Opposite top, amphora depicting Zeus, the goddess Leto and their twins Artemis and Apollo. British Museum, London.

Opposite bottom, Poseidon hurling his trident; the statue was found off Cape Artemision and is one of the few original Greek bronzes that have survived. National Archaeological Museum, Athens.

helps us to appreciate better the cultural heritage of Greece. This is all to the good, but there is an even more dangerous pitfall. This is to allow enthusiasm for Greek culture to colour our view of historical and political events.

In the fifth century BC Athens was the most cultivated and civilized city in Greece, yet at the same time ruled over an extensive empire. The question here is whether Athens' rule was welcomed by its subjects or not. The instinctive reaction to such a question is that a city which built the Parthenon and produced writers such as Sophocles must have exercised a benign and enlightened authority over its subjects. Yet it is very likely that the majority of Greeks living under Athenian rule regarded it as repressive and burdensome. There was ample justification for this attitude, for Athens was as self-interested and rapacious as any other imperial power. The idealism of a few savants never filtered down to a colonial administration which continued to be rigorous.

In studying Greek culture there is one final pitfall to be avoided. Because many ideas of the Greeks are current nowadays, especially in philosophy and politics, there is a strong temptation to think that their society was similar to ours in other ways. This was not so. For example, during the seventh century BC in Greece, there arose rulers in the cities called tyrants who overthrew the ruling aristocrats. Nowadays the word 'tyrant' conjures up the cruelty and treachery of a Borgia. Yet if we think of the Greek tyrants as being necessarily cruel and treacherous, we will get a completely false picture of them. For the Greeks, the word 'tyrant', which they borrowed from the Lydians, was completely neutral and merely meant a ruler.

Greek history must be reconstructed without preconception, and with patience and a certain toughness of mind. Nowhere have these qualities been demonstrated better than in the part archaeology has played in piecing together the period from 2000 to 800 BC. The discovery of the civilizations of Crete and Mycenae is almost entirely a result of the work done by archaeologists, and in particular one man.

Archaeology and history

Before 1870 a Greek historian would have had very little to say about the years 2000 to 800 BC (known as the pre-Hellenic period). He would have stated that Homer in the *Iliad* wrote of a heroic war fought at Troy by a confederation of Greek states under the command of Agamemnon, King of Mycenae. Agamemnon was acting on behalf of his brother, Menelaus, whose wife, Helen, had been abducted by a Trojan prince called Paris. The historian might have added that

Homer called these people the Achaeans and that the Greeks after 800 BC, who called themselves Hellenes, regarded the Achaeans as their ancestors and the *Iliad* as a factual account of their early history.

However, he would not have been able to say any more about the Achaeans: exactly when they lived, what their houses, pots and pans, chariots and weapons were like, and, indeed, whether they even existed or the Trojan war ever took place. He would have explained that the *Iliad* could not be taken as a record of historical fact because there was no evidence, written or archaeological, to support it. Consequently, the Achaeans had to remain shadowy, legendary figures without historical substance.

One man, a German, Heinrich Schliemann, did not accept this orthodox, scholarly view. He was neither an orthodox nor a scholarly man, but a self-made millionaire with an overriding passion for Homer. As a young grocer's apprentice in the town of Fürstenburg, he would listen entranced to a drunken vagabond who used to stand outside his master's shop reciting Homer's verses. From this time Schliemann became increasingly steeped in the *Iliad* and *Odyssey*. Like the ancient Greeks, he seriously believed that the *Iliad* was a factual account of a real war fought by historical people. In 1868, having acquired a large fortune in a short space of time, he set off for Greece to verify this belief.

His aim was to discover the remains of Troy, using the *Iliad* itself as a reference map. Arriving in Turkey with his Greek wife, Sophie, whom he regarded as a latter-day Helen, and using the *Iliad* as other tourists used a Baedeker guide book, Schliemann picked a prospective site for Troy at a place on the Asian coast of the Dardanelles called the mound of Hissarlik. Hissarlik was in fact the site of Troy.

Schliemann discovered beneath the top layer of the mound the remains of not one town but seven, each built on the ruins of the other. On the second layer from the bottom he found a town whose walls were made of huge Cyclopean stones, and which showed traces of having been burnt. This town, he maintained, was Priam's Troy, burnt by Agamemnon and the Achaeans. It was in the walls of this town that Schliemann made his most dramatic discovery. Hidden in a niche in the wall was a hoard of golden jewellery: necklaces, brooches and clasps. Schliemann had found not only Priam's town but Priam's treasure, which had been worn as a dowry by Helen herself.

Later archaeologists showed that the town and treasure, which Schliemann attributed to Priam, were in fact considerably older. This, however, was not important. The discovery of Troy was a triumph both for Schliemann, and, more important, for Homer. His poetry was now raised from the rank of myth to that of history. Agamemnon and

his companions had existed. Their palaces and treasures, like those of Priam, were waiting to be excavated.

Homer relates that Agamemnon, the son of Atreus, was 'king of Mycenae, rich in gold'. In his play *The Agamemnon* Aeschylus, the fifth-century Athenian dramatist, tells how on his return from Troy, Agamemnon was murdered in his bath by his wife, Clytemnestra, and her lover, Aegisthus, who had been regent of Mycenae in his absence. The drama of his homecoming (rivalled only by that of Odysseus), the use of the Homeric epithet 'rich in gold' and the indications that Mycenae was an important centre of Achaean civilization, drew Schliemann in 1876 to the Argolid to excavate Mycenae. Unlike Troy its position was already known.

Clearly visible from a distance on the side of the mountains at Mycenae was a vast wall pierced by the famous lion gate. The problem which had vexed archaeologists before Schliemann was the exact position of the royal tombs, including that of Agamemnon. Pausanias, who wrote a travelogue on the Mediterranean in the second century BC, described the tombs when he visited Mycenae. Until Schliemann took up the task of locating them it had always been supposed that they lay outside the walls of Mycenae.

With his usual disregard for the generally accepted hypothesis Schliemann re-read Pausanias and decided that the tombs were

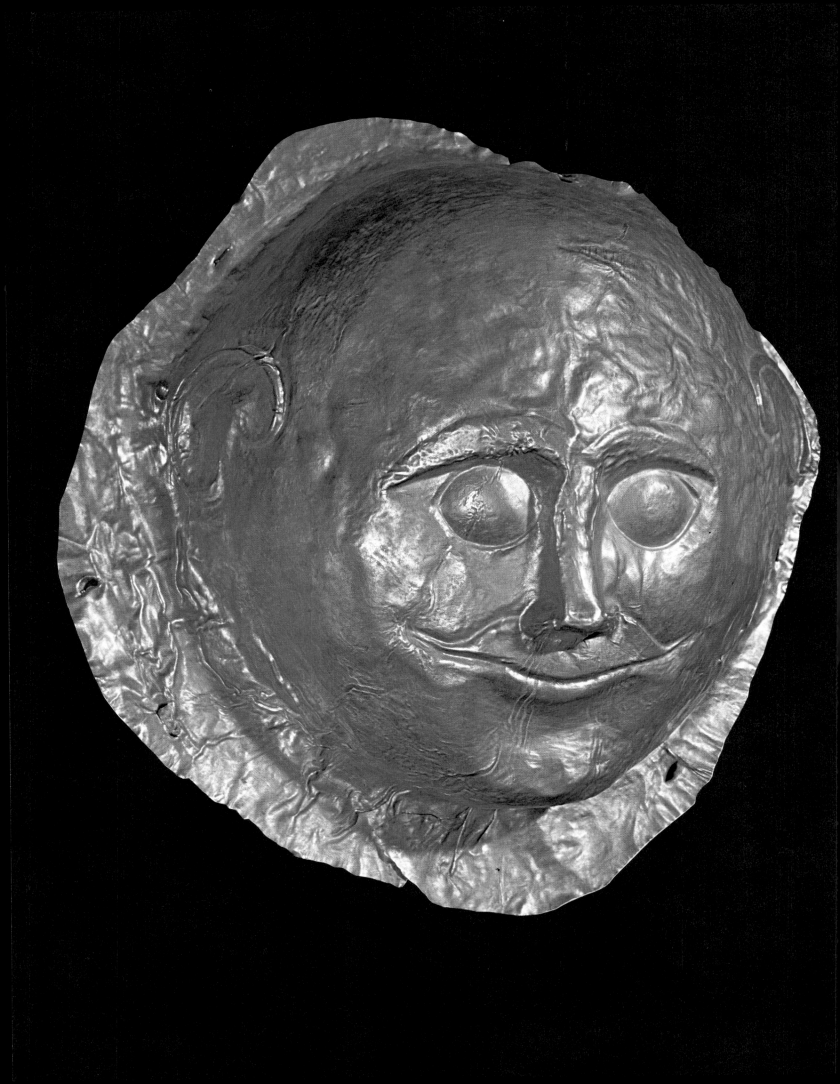

inside the walls. The first discovery he made was not the tombs but the agora of Mycenae —a circle of stone seats where the public councils were held. Schliemann continued to dig, convinced that the tombs lay beneath the agora. Once again he was right and made a sensational discovery. He found eighteen tombs, mere shafts sunk into the ground. Within them, however, lay the bodies of the kings of Mycenae, their wives and children, their faces covered with golden funerary masks, and surrounded by swords and daggers, bowls, goblets, diadems and bracelets—all made of gold.

This was a treasure which both in quantity and the intricacy of the metalwork surpassed that of Priam. The damascened swords, in particular, inlaid with scenes of hunting parties, lions, birds and other animals, indicated the existence of a rich and relatively sophisticated society. Homer's claim for Mycenae as being 'rich in gold' had been more than substantiated. Once again Schliemann, in his enthusiasm, dated these tombs incorrectly, being convinced that they were those of Agamemnon and Atreus. In fact they antedated the reign of Agamemnon by more than a hundred years. However, as with Schliemann's mistake at Troy, this is a trifle compared with the importance of his achievement.

His archaeological flair and faith in Homer had shown the way to the discovery of a whole new era in Greek history. He lacked the training to make the correct deductions from his finds, but others who followed him consolidated and continued the work he had so brilliantly begun.

The missing link

Schliemann died in 1890, six years after excavating the town of Tiryns in the Argolid, where he found the ruins of a megaron (the king's palace), similar to the palace of Odysseus described by Homer in the *Odyssey*. During the following decade his successors brought to light a Mycenaean civilization which was found to extend over the whole of the Aegean. At Athens, Pylos, Cyprus and Sparta the same kind of pottery, decorated with flowers and stylized figures, was found. In 1890 the dates of Mycenaean civilization were fixed between 1400 and 1000 BC, through the findings of Mycenaean vases which had been used by the Egyptians between the reigns of Amenophis III and Rameses VI (1400–1050 BC). Yet as more Mycenaean sites were excavated and a clearer picture was built up of Achaean society, it became increasingly clear to archaeologists that the lack of a traceable development in Mycenaean art pointed to the existence of a foreign culture which had exerted a strong influence on Mycenaean craftsmen, and from which much of their art

Above, stela depicting a chariot found at Mycenae. National Museum, Athens.

Opposite, gold mask from Mycenae, sixteenth century BC. National Museum, Athens.

Crete

At Phaestos, Mallia, Ayra, Triadha and, above all, Knossos (before 1900 merely names on the map of Crete), Evans and the archaeologists who followed in his footsteps discovered the remains of a brilliant civilization which they called Minoan.

This was a far older civilization than that of Mycenae, stretching back to the third millennium BC. Here among the ruins of Knossos the full development of the art and architecture of a civilization could be traced, from the first painting of ceramics around 3000 BC, to the sophisticated frescoes which decorated the walls of Knossos at the height of its power between 1570 and 1400 BC. However, the unearthed remains of Knossos and the other Cretan palaces not only provide a catalogue of Minoan art, but are also an open history book which records the rise and fall of the Minoans and their contacts with the other great Bronze Age civilizations of the eastern Mediterranean.

Minoan power was based on control of the sea. Unlike Mycenae, Knossos had no walls to repel a besieging army, since it was supposed that an enemy would be defeated at sea before ever reaching Crete. The rise of Minoan sea power dates from 2000 BC. It was then that the Minoans began to open up the trade route from Crete to the east. Sailing via Rhodes and Cyprus their seamen reached the Phoenician ports of Byblos and Ugarit on the Levantine coast. There they came into contact with two great empires: the empire of Egypt, recently unified under the Theban pharaohs, and the Semitic empire of Mesopotamia whose capital was Babylon. It is difficult to say which of these two states had the greater influence on Crete.

Too much emphasis is usually placed on the contacts between Crete and Egypt at the expense of Asia. It is true that there were strong links between Crete and Egypt: Egyptian scarabs and statues were found in Crete and Cretan ceramics were discovered at Fayoum and d'Abydos. An Egyptian document of the Twelfth Dynasty, *The Adventure of Sinuhe*, mentions the 'folk of

had been derived. For instance, on the walls of the megaron at Tiryns Schliemann had found a fresco which showed, against a blue background, a man gracefully lifting himself up on the horns of a charging bull. This fresco seemed foreign in origin not only because of the colours and style used by the artist but also because of the activity depicted. There is no mention of wrestling or dancing with bulls in Homer, where they appear only as sacrificial victims.

By the turn of the century an increasing amount of evidence pointed to the island of Crete as the centre of a powerful, and as yet undiscovered, civilization. Thucydides, the Athenian historian, had stated that the first thalassocracy ('control of the sea') had been held by Minos, the King of Crete. This claim was supported by the Athenian legend of Theseus and the Minotaur. The background of this legend was that every seven years Athens was forced to pay Minos, as an indemnity for the murder of his son, a tribute of seven girls and seven boys who

were fed to the Minotaur (a monster, half a man and half bull) which lived in a labyrinth on Crete. Theseus, helped by the amorous daughter of Minos, Ariadne, killed the Minotaur and freed Athens from the necessity of paying this distasteful tribute. This legend probably concealed a shift in the power structure of the Aegean—perhaps the breaking of the thalassocracy of Crete mentioned by Thucydides.

Various finds in Crete in 1900 also lent support to the theory that Crete had been a centre of civilization before Mycenae flourished. Fragments of pre-Mycenaean pottery decorated with vividly coloured floral designs had been found in a cave on Mount Ida, and, most significant of all, a British archaeologist, Arthur Evans, had found a series of stones carved with a type of primitive writing. Encouraged by these signs, Evans began in 1900 to excavate the site of Knossos—the place which Schliemann had foretold, before his death, would reveal the missing link in pre-Hellenic history.

Left, vase found at Phaestos, one of a set of vessels used at royal banquets. Archaeological Museum, Heraklion.

Opposite left, the massive stone walls of the palace at Tiryns, thirteenth century BC, and, right, detail of processional frieze from the interior of the palace.

the sea'—certainly a reference to the Minoans. Yet it was from the Phoenicians that the Minoans borrowed their linear writing and the architecture of the first palaces built on Crete (2000–1750 BC) at Knossos, Phaistos and Mallia is strongly influenced by the architecture of such Babylonian palaces as Mari. The fact that these palaces were built indicates a consolidation and centralization of political power by the aristocratic families, which culminated at the time of the second palaces in the supremacy of Knossos and its ruler Minos. Models for this political development were provided by both the Egyptian and Mesopotamian empires where similar processes had recently taken place.

At some time about 1750 BC the first Cretan palaces were destroyed by an earthquake. This disaster led to a shift in the balance of power among the Cretan cities. The rise of Knossos and the thalassocracy of Minos date from this period. Between 1750 and 1400 BC Minoan civilization was at its apogee.

Throughout the Aegean, on the mainland of Greece, in the Cyclades and among the islands of Asia Minor as far north as Samos, the Cretan navies bartered and traded. It is unlikely, however, that their commercial and political predominance extended beyond Cyprus to the Phoenician ports, and there must have been a state of uneasy coexistence in this area. At home the Minoan aristocracy, rich with the revenue from their trade, led a life of leisure and civilized ease, patrons of the skilled craftsmen who have bequeathed us the wonders of Minoan art.

Before examining the religious and social life of Knossos it is important to know why the Minoans prospered and flourished at this particular time in Bronze Age history.

Two important factors favoured the rise of Crete: the fact that it is an island, and its particular position in the Mediterranean. Living on an island which was strategically placed in the centre of the eastern basin of the Mediterranean between Greece and Asia and in an age when navigation at sea

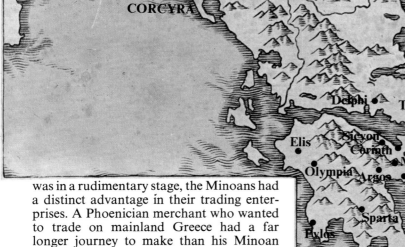

was in a rudimentary stage, the Minoans had a distinct advantage in their trading enterprises. A Phoenician merchant who wanted to trade on mainland Greece had a far longer journey to make than his Minoan counterpart, and was therefore less inclined to take the risk.

After the decline of Knossos Crete became one of the main pirate centres of the Mediterranean; the corsairs who used it were fully aware of the advantages of a central base for their operations. Yet a trader needs not only a well-placed base but a safe one. The mainland of Greece had been invaded at the beginning of the second millennium by waves of Indo-Europeans, the ancestors of Homer's Achaeans. Crete, however, escaped this invasion and, indeed, probably profited from the weak state of the Greek cities. The intervening sea and the superiority of Minoan seamanship over that of the land-loving newcomers allowed Crete to remain for 600 years outside the turmoil in mainland Greece.

Knossos

There are some striking parallels between the court of Minos and that of Louis XIV of France. At both Knossos and Versailles a palace of great beauty housed a resident court of aristocrats who passed their time in pursuit of the social graces and appreciation of the arts. At both courts the status of women was high and they played a prominent part in the life of the court—surely a mark of real civilization. Although it would be misleading to pursue this analogy too far, it is useful as a rough yardstick with which to measure the worth of Minoan culture.

Knossos lies in the north of Crete, in the gently sloping valley of the Kyrtaios, three miles inland from the port of Herakleion. To the traveller arriving from the sea it must have presented a magnificent spectacle. The

town houses of merchants and aristocrats covered an area of about two square miles. From these houses paved roads ran up to the palace itself, which with its five storeys of open balconies, tapering columns and fresco-covered walls rose up and dominated the town beneath.

The palace was built round a large central court. From this ran a network of corridors linking storerooms, offices, kitchens and workshops. This ground floor, and the first storey which was similar to it, must have given rise to the legend of the labyrinth. They were probably built on the remains of the first palace (destroyed about 1750 BC) and they lacked the light and spaciousness of the upper storeys. Here the members of a vast bureaucratic machine responsible for the running of a palace and the empire it controlled hurried and scurried about their errands.

The upper storeys of the palace provided a complete contrast to the busy maze below them. They housed the state apartments, the throne room of Minos and the domestic quarters—all built in a light and fantastic style. Where possible tapering columns were substituted for walls, and the rooms were full of light, opening out on to balconies and with wells of light sunk through the flat roofs. This architectural style, perhaps one of the most remarkable in antiquity, was completely original and in no way imitated Egyptian or Asian architecture. In fact Egyptian palaces built after Knossos seem to have derived certain elements from Crete.

The Minoans obviously loved nature, lightness and fantasy. This can be seen not only in the architecture of their palaces but in many of the frescoes with which they decorated them. Such subjects as a school of flying fish gambolling in the sea, or a cat, painted in a warm ochre, stealthily stalking an unsuspecting pheasant are quite typical.

These many frescoes of animals tell us what appealed to the Minoans, but luckily there are many more which show us the Minoans themselves. The royal apartments at Knossos were reached by an impressive ceremonial staircase which bypassed the administrative quarters and ran up the outside of the palace from the courtyard on the west side of the palace. In the corridor which led to the staircase a great number of miniature frescoes illustrating the ceremonial life of the court were discovered. In all of them the figures are painted in two dimensions, silhouettes standing against bright yellow and blue backgrounds. There are a man in a tight-waisted, russet tunic carrying a large drinking horn in a religious procession, ladies of the court seated in front of a crowd watching some spectacle (perhaps a display of bull-leaping) and other women dancing before a crowd seated under olive trees.

In all these frescoes women predominate, hence the assumption that they played an important part in Minoan life. These charming creatures have very pale skins and wear wasp-waisted skirts which fall in flounces to

the ground. Their bodices are close-fitting and plunge to the waist, leaving their breasts exposed, and their hair is elaborately dressed in curls and ringlets which they let fall down over their shoulders. This predominance of women, hinted at by the frescoes, seems to be confirmed by what little is known of Cretan religion.

As in many Asian communities the chief deity seems to have been a mother goddess of fertility. The most remarkable representation of her is a statue in faience from Knossos which shows her dressed as a Cretan woman holding up two snakes, the children of the earth. Her consort was probably the Minotaur itself, the bull-god. The representation of a god as a bull was not confined to Crete. Similar bull-gods were worshipped among the Elamites and Sumerians, for whom the bull was a symbol of strength and energy. The frescoes of bull-leaping now take on a new aspect.

It seems likely that they were not merely athletic displays but a religious ceremony in honour of the god, and the boys and girls sent to Minos as tribute by Athens were possibly destined as bull-leapers. Minos himself (the name was a dynastic one held by all Cretan kings, as was Pharaoh by the Egyptian kings) was probably the chief priest of this religion, or may even have been regarded as an incarnation of the god.

Nevertheless, whether their kings were gods or not, the Minoan Empire fell. In 1400 BC the palace of Knossos was destroyed and burnt, possibly as the result of a violent earthquake or a Mycenaean invasion. Although Crete's artistic and religious tradition was perpetuated on the mainland of Greece, a great and original civilization had

disappeared. The thalassocracy of the Aegean passed from Knossos to the Mycenaeans.

The myth of Mycenae

The term 'Mycenaean' has been applied to the remains of settlements which stretch from the south of the Peloponnese through Attica into northern Boeotia. It can be rightly said that a unity of culture existed in the main centres of civilization in Greece between 1600 and 1200 BC. However, it is often suggested that this unity of culture presupposes a corresponding political unity. The leadership of Agamemnon in the *Iliad* and references in Hittite manuscripts to 'the King of the Achaeans' are invoked to show that the Achaeans were joined together in some kind of federal framework under the rule of the King of Mycenae. There are, however, strong objections to such a view.

The testimony of Homer has been severely shaken by the decipherment of the Linear B tablets from Pylos. These present a very different social picture to the one drawn in the *Iliad*, and show that many of the Mycenaean elements which Homer (who composed his poetry in about 900 BC) is supposed to have reported were in fact unknown to him. The most that can be said is that the names of Mycenaean kings and heroes survived in the epic tradition. With the argument in favour of a Mycenaean king of the Achaeans thus refuted, it is difficult to maintain the view that cultural unity implies political unity.

As far as the Hittite manuscripts are concerned there is no evidence to suggest that the statement 'the King of the Achaeans' referred to the King of Mycenae. The king in question could have been any minor prince giving himself airs at a foreign court. 'Mycenaean' must therefore be regarded as a neutral word—a useful term with which to designate a certain period of history. Nevertheless, if little information is available about the political relations between Mycenaean cities, this gap in our knowledge is compensated for by what is known about their foreign affairs and the glimpses afforded into the internal administration of their cities.

In about 1400 BC the warlike Mycenaeans invaded Crete and usurped Minoan control of the sea. They took over Cretan markets in the east and established new ones in the western basin of the Mediterranean where Mycenaean pottery has been found. As well as pottery the Mycenaean merchants (like the Minoans) probably carried wool and fabrics which they bartered for metals, since Greece is poor in mineral wealth.

On the mainland of Greece the quality of Mycenaean life can be judged from the remains found by archaeologists. Mycenaean pottery and metalwork are of a high standard and, both before and after the fall of Knossos, were strongly influenced by Minoan art. However, in both style and subject-matter the art of the Mycenaeans was an adaptation and not a straight copy.

Their craftsmen added plain geometric patterns to the floral, naturalistic designs from Crete, and the subjects they treated were more robust and manly, such as war-parties and hunting scenes. This artistic independence suggests that the Mycenaean cities retained their autonomy and never submitted to direct political control from Knossos. Even before 1400 BC, therefore, the Mycenaean kings were both rich and powerful (the golden treasure from shaft-tombs at Mycenae is dated about 1600 BC), and one would expect them to have lived in palaces which reflected their rank and power.

The remains of megarons at Pylos and Tiryns amply fulfil such expectations. The megaron was usually found in the centre of a conglomeration of lesser buildings (bedrooms, offices, storerooms, etc.) and had the dual function of a throne room and banquet-

ing hall. Entry to the megaron was through a portico of columns and then into a small antechamber which led directly into the main hall. This was a long rectangular room with small windows (if any), whose roof was supported by four large columns. In the centre of these columns was a hearth. The king's throne was placed against the furthest wall, perhaps on a raised dais. The walls of the megaron were painted with frescoes (Cretan in their inspiration) showing scenes of battles and warriors.

From these richly decorated but, by comparison with the palace at Knossos, rather stolid halls the Mycenaean kings exercised, through a complex of intrusive bureaucracy, a strong, centralized control over their subjects. The scribes and clerks who formed this bureaucracy used a primitive script called Linear B, which they wrote on wet clay tablets with a stylus.

When the palaces of Knossos and Pylos were burnt, in 1400 BC and 1200 BC respectively, large numbers of these tablets were baked in the conflagration and thus survived to the present day. Ironically, these tablets were never meant to be permanent records, but simply temporary memoranda. The permanent records (which were possibly written on papyrus) proved less durable and were burnt.

In 1952 the Linear B script was deciphered by an Englishman, Michael Ventris, and the language used by the Mycenaeans was found to be a type of primitive Greek—containing, unfortunately, many words which had been lost to classical Greek. Nevertheless, enough could be deciphered to present a picture of a society ruled by a strict hierarchical system (with the king at the apex of the pyramid), and in which interference in the private life of the citizen existed on a scale that would have been quite unconceivable to a Greek of the classical period.

What is most remarkable about the records from Pylos is the passion for detail. Exact inventories are made of such items as weapons, herds, furniture and regiments of soldiers. Even broken chariot wheels are minutely described before being put aside. However, a more general picture also emerges from the tablets. The palace at Pylos obviously played a central role in economic and social life. A large proportion of the population depended on it for food and employment. There are lists itemizing servants and the amount of food they were given. Other lists show the quantity of

CRETE AND MYCENAE FROM THEIR ORIGINS TO THE DORIAN INVASIONS

Date	Crete	The Peloponnese	Egypt and Mesopotamia	Date	Crete	The Peloponnese	Egypt and Mesopotamia
3000	Early Minoan period Painted pottery	Early Helladic culture	Cuneiform writing 3rd Dynasty at Memphis	1800	First destruction of palaces at Knossos, Phaistos, Mallia		
2500	Copper working		Great pyramids 1st Dynasty of Ur		Peak of Minoan civilization		Hammurapi
2400		Neolithic civilization of Dimini	Sargon of Agade	1600	Late Minoan period	Emergence of Mycenae Late Helladic culture	Kassites at Babylon Egyptian New Kingdom
2200	Middle Minoan period	Middle Helladic culture	Gudea of Lagash	1400	Destruction of palace at Knossos	High point of Mycenae	Hittite Empire
2000	First Cretan palaces	Indo-European infiltration into Greece	Egyptian Middle Kingdom	1200	Destruction of palace at Pylos	Dorian invasions	Invasion by the peoples of the sea
	Cretan hegemony in the Aegean						

bronze allocated to the local smiths, and a third group which are, unfortunately, not totally decipherable tell of dues paid to the palace and hint at the system of land tenure, this, too, being probably controlled by the palace.

This centralization was imitated from the advanced administrative systems of Asia and Egypt, and possibly transmitted to Greece through the Minoans. No remnants, however, of such a bureaucracy are to be found in the classical era, and the system, its scribes and the writing they used were completely wiped out when the main centres of Mycenaean civilization were destroyed at the end of the thirteenth century BC.

The dark age

The Dorian Greeks of the classical period explained the arrival of their ancestors in the Peloponnese by a legend which told how the three sons of Heracles inherited this area from their heroic father, took possession of it and established the kingdoms of Argos, Sparta and Messenia. This simplification of history into legend in an illiterate age is generally supposed to conceal events such as the destruction of the palaces of the Mycenaean Greeks, and the forcible possession of their lands by the Dorians, Greek-

speaking tribes from the northwestern highlands. What really happened seems to be somewhat more complicated.

At the end of the thirteenth century BC the Mycenaean cities were anxious and on the defensive. A wall was built across the Corinthian isthmus and the fortifications at Tiryns and Mycenae were strengthened. Shortly afterwards the blow fell. The Mycenaean civilization was overthrown: its palaces were burnt and its kings killed in battle. Those who survived this wave of destruction were seafaring migrants from coast of the Peloponnese or to the haven of Attica, which had either repulsed the invaders or had been bypassed by them.

It seems unlikely that these invaders were the Dorians. Although Mycenaean power had received a body-blow from which it never recovered, some refugees nevertheless crept back to the ruins of their palaces and settlements and continued to live in them for more than 100 years. Those most likely to have been responsible for this wave of destruction were seafaring migrants from the east who, during the same period, destroyed the Hittite empire in Anatolia and were repulsed with difficulty from Egypt by the Pharaohs.

The sub-Mycenaean culture which continued to support itself in western Greece after these migrants had plundered and

Below, vase of the geometric style: the effect is achieved by variations on simple ornamental themes. National Museum, Athens.

Left, vase depicting a scene from Greek mythology in which Menelaus and Hector fight over the body of Euphorbus. British Museum, London.

Opposite, tablet written in Linear B script. Archaeological Museum, Heraklion.

passed on was swept away or assimilated by the Dorians in about 1100 BC. At this time methods of burial changed and sub-Mycenaean pottery was replaced by proto-geometric vases, decorated, as their name suggests, with simple geometric designs. The Dorians probably infiltrated Attica (protogeometric pottery and cist-tombs have been found there), but were themselves assimilated by the Ionian-speaking inhabitants, who were not as weak as those in the west. This was one pattern of conquest and not a very successful one.

In Laconia and Thessaly the Dorians remained a ruling minority, having subdued the original inhabitants. In the Argolid they completely swallowed up the Ionian-speaking people, who disappeared without trace. Arcadia, a rough, mountainous tract in the Peloponnese, successfully resisted the invaders, and remained independent and a thorn in Sparta's flesh far into the classical period.

However, not all the Mycenaean Greeks were content either to settle down under their conquerors or fight them to the death. Many took refuge in Attica, and from there moved on, usually under Athenian leadership, to colonize the islands off the west coast of Asia Minor. These colonies flourished and grew into the famous cities of Ionia which were to play such an important part in subsequent Greek history.

Art and poetry

The period from the twelfth to the end of the ninth century BC is rightly called the dark age. Apart from the probable pattern of the Dorian invasion sketched out previously, little is known about this period. It must have been a time of friction and adjustment between new and old states. The violence of its beginnings prevented any continuity of civilization and there was a sharp decline from the standard of living achieved by the Mycenaeans. However, in spite of the general darkness there were two glimmers of progress: the evolution of protogeometric pottery into the geometric style and the continuity of epic poetry.

The difference between protogeometric and geometric pottery (the main centres of which were Corinth and Athens) consisted in the use of a lighter shade of colour for the designs of geometric pottery, which became more intricate and stood out more clearly against their dark backgrounds. Human figures, at first stilted and brittle, and later becoming more lifelike and supple, were also added with increasing frequency and effect. The chief significance of this development in pottery was that the geometric designs showed distinct eastern influences. After 200 years the Greeks were becoming aware of the world around them and enlarging their horizons.

During those 200 years they had not only kept alive the art of pottery but poetry as well. The *Iliad* and the *Odyssey* bear the distinctive stamp of a brilliant exponent of an oral epic tradition. It is not known who Homer was, whether he was the first man to write down epic poems, or whether he sang them like his predecessors. The Greeks, who revered the *Iliad* and *Odyssey* as educational and morally improving works, thought that Homer was a blind bard who lived on the island of Khios in Ionia. There seems no reason to dispute this traditional view, and it can be further stated that he lived at some time during the ninth century BC. The rest is a subject of controversy.

It is, however, obvious that the *Iliad* and *Odyssey* are the final flowering of a sophisticated method of composition. In epic poetry the singer was able to compose very long poems on set themes by using stock phrases. His ability was judged by his arrangement of episodes and by the skill with which he manipulated the set phrases and vocabulary. This technique enabled long passages of poetry to be passed on orally to each successive generation, various details of everyday life being kept or dropped and new ones being added. It is, therefore, difficult to say to which periods the social details in Homer's poems should be assigned.

They do not present a picture of Mycenaean life, but rather glimpses of Greek society at different stages of development throughout the dark age. Even the Trojan expedition is no longer accepted as a definite historical fact. There may have been an expedition from Mycenae to the Troad

Left, detail from the seventh-century BC Chigi Vase from Corinth showing Trojans and Achaeans in battle. Villa Giulia, Rome.

Left, detail from the seventh-century BC Chigi Vase from Corinth showing Trojans and Achaeans in battle. Villa Giulia, Rome.

Opposite, fresco from Knossos, called 'la Parisienne' because of its resemblance to the Parisian ladies of Impressionist paintings, sixteenth to fifteenth centuries BC. Archaeological Museum, Heraklion.

about 1200 BC—the last desperate enterprise of a doomed society—but it is more likely that Homer was here commemorating a campaign conducted by the first Ionian colonists. Whichever theory is accepted, the war was certainly never conducted on the heroic scale described in the *Iliad*. Troy was far too small to have held all the Trojans and their allies who appear in the *Iliad*.

This relegation of Homer to the frontiers of legend does not detract from the value and interest of his poetry, whose main aim is to entertain, and which ranks as the first great contribution to European literature.

The city-state

When light dawned on Greek history once more (officially in 776 BC when the first Olympic games took place) the country consisted of a number of small, fiercely independent city-states ruled by oligarchies of aristocrats. In the dangerous conditions of the dark age a political idea which was to dominate and influence the rest of Greek history had been forged: loyalty to the city-state (the *polis*). The small, mountainous and, therefore, isolating valleys of Greece are often cited to explain the growth of this idea. Geographical seclusion may have helped, but when the Greeks began settling in colonies on the plains there was no weakening of their allegiance to the city.

The main reason for the growth of polity (and hence of politics) was that during the dark age a man stood little chance of survival unless he supported his fellow citizens. Beyond the city the Greeks could not envisage with enthusiasm any larger and more permanent political framework to which to give their support. National unity (pan-Hellenism) was, for the most part, a negligible and theoretical issue, except when revived temporarily by danger from abroad, or in the less important spheres of religion and athletics. A complete break was made with the wide perspectives of pre-Hellenic history. From now on the history of Greece was the story of political change and development within the city, and the often stormy relations between different cities.

SPARTA, ATHENS AND THE BIRTH OF ROME

Date	Sparta	Athens	Etruria, Rome	Outside world	Date	Sparta	Athens	Etruria, Rome	Outside world
800	The Dorians settle in Laconia. Foundation of Sparta		The Etruscans in Tuscany. Legendary foundation of Rome	Kingdom of Phrygia	650	Second Messenian War	Dracon's laws	Etruscans influence Roman buildings	Byzantium founded. Cyaxares of Media destroys Nineveh
750	War against Argos. First Messenian War		Greek colonization in Naples and Sicily	Kingdom of Lydia. Sargon II	600	Pythian Games at Delphi. Peloponnesian League established by Sparta	Solon's judicial and constitutional reforms. Tyranny of Peisistratus		Nebuchadnezzar. Cyrus founds Persian Empire
700	Constitution of Sparta. Period of wealth and culture. Revolt of the Helots	Attica unified under Athenian leadership	Etruscan rule in Rome	Sennacherib. Assur-bani-pal	550	Corinth joins Sparta		Tarquin the Proud expelled by Romans	Cambyses, son of Cyrus, conquers Egypt
					500		Reforms of Cleisthenes	Roman Republic	

Chapter 7

Lawgivers and Tyrants

The Bacchiads at Corinth, the Eupatrids in Attica, the Hippeis in Euboea: these were only three of the aristocratic factions in power throughout Greece at the beginning of the eighth century BC. The kings had all but disappeared. At Argos they remained longer than elsewhere. Pheidon, the King of Argos in the seventh century BC, who is credited with the invention of a system of measures, fought successfully against Sparta. The Spartans retained throughout their history a system whereby two kings ruled jointly. They acted as commanders in battle and had special privileges, but their powers were severely limited by the council of ephors (or magistrates). However, with the exception of Argos and Sparta the monarchies had been absorbed by aristocratic oligarchies in all the other Greek states.

The process by which the Greek monarchs were ousted from their positions of supreme power is difficult to trace exactly since it happened in the illiterate period of the dark age. There is, however, some evidence from Athens and Sparta which gives an idea of what took place. The first step in the process would have been the curtailing of the king's power in politics by groups of aristocrats who thought that they, too, had a right to take part in the city's government. At this point a king was in the same position as the kings at Sparta: only his power as chief policymaker had been curtailed. The Spartan kings managed to stop the process at this stage but others were not so fortunate.

The king was now left with his position of permanent high priest in charge of religious ceremonies, but not for long. In most states the next step was to deprive him of office. His priestly duties were shared out among his fellow aristocrats in the form of an annual magistrateship, to which anyone from a suitable family could be elected. At Athens a magistrate who was elected annually to be in charge of sacrifices and all religious ceremonies was called 'the king'. The fact that the Athenian aristocrats kept and used their king's titles implies that they did not overthrow him in a wave of violence and hatred but merely demanded and got a wider distribution of power and privileges.

The details of what happened probably differed from city to city, and some kings may have held on to their power more obstinately than others. However, in Greece the word 'king' left no legacy of hatred. This was in marked contrast to the Romans who ejected their kings forcibly and for whom the word 'king' was anathema. From all the evidence available it appears that in Greece the transition to aristocratic government— the first step towards democracy—was relatively painless.

The rule of the best

The word aristocrat comes from two Greek words: *aristos* meaning 'best' and *kratein* 'to rule'. The aristocrat ruled because he was the best man. However, he was not the best man because he was kinder or wiser than anyone else (this concept of 'good' was quite foreign to the Greeks), but because he was richer. In an agricultural community like Greece this meant that he owned more land than his neighbours.

However, the small freeholder living in Thebes or Athens in the eighth century BC would probably not have seen an aristocrat's power in terms of the amount of land he owned, but would have judged him on the effects of his wealth. For him the aristocrat was the best man and entitled to rule because he could afford the weapons and equipment which were needed to defend the city. As the descendant of a hero he knew the proper rituals for a burial or sacrifice. If there was trouble between neighbours the aristocrat would (for a price) judge the quarrel, and his decision would be accepted because of his influence in the district. If the weather was bad he could lend grain to tide one over a lean period. In addition to these useful functions the aristocrat cut a better figure in the neighbourhood than anyone else: his house was bigger, he bred hounds and hunted, he could afford to pay for a band to entertain his guests and he entered chariots for the Olympic Games.

Few Greeks questioned the authority of the aristocrat which rested on the effect of such outward signs of wealth and on the traditional acceptance of the aristocrat's role in society. However, there were more formal ties which bound early Greek society together and also kept the aristocrat in his traditional leading position. These ties are usually conveniently grouped together under the heading of the 'clan system'. The Greek clan system was based on vertical divisions, a pattern reproduced more recently in the Scottish clans.

The support of his herdsman was in the last analysis more important to a Greek aristocrat than the esteem of a fellow aristocrat from another city. The Greek word for a clan was *genos*. The *genos* was made up of several families (*oikiae*), some rich and some poor, who all claimed descent from a common ancestor, usually a hero, but, in the case of a particularly distinguished clan, a god. The head of the most important family was the head of the clan. So far, the clan system, based as it was on kinship, is a relatively simple concept and quite easy to understand (Mediterranean families still have a strong sense of kinship). In the dangerous days of the dark age it was an obvious course for families related to one another to stick together for defence, however much they varied in social standing.

The next division in the social hierarchy was the phratry, which meant an association or brotherhood, and was made up of several clans grouped together. The last and largest unit was the tribe, which was composed of several phratries. Dorian communities were divided into three tribes and the Ionian into four.

At first sight these divisions—*genos*, phratry, tribe—may seem to be no more than convenient classifications for the various distinctions and relationships which spring naturally from a sense of kinship. However, the existence of the phratry seems to disprove such a view. The phratry was a far later division than the immemorial ones of clan and tribe. Moreover, by comparison with them it was an artificial one, and seems to be the result of the first conscious attempt by the Greeks to give formal recognition to a division in society not based on kinship.

The phratry probably did not figure very largely in the life of the small farmer, who was orientated towards the traditional ties of the *genos*. The head of his clan, with whom he was immediately concerned, might well not be the head of his phratry. Nonetheless, membership of a phratry gave him a civil status which was important in times of war. If he had a dispute with a neighbour it would be the phratry to which he would turn. Above all, membership of the phratry put him in an enviable 'official', position by comparison with a slave or foreigner who did not belong to one.

It would be wrong to say that to belong to a phratry was a mark of citizenship, since at this time the concept of citizenship did

not exist, but as a rough analogy it may help to understand the importance of phratries. The development of the phratry was the first slow step towards a society regulated by man-made institutions and laws. However, Greece was a conservative agricultural community and the development of an institution like the phratry did not correspond to any improvement in social justice. The aristocrat's control of affairs was not impaired by the phratry. Rather it was strengthened by it, since the phratry provided him with a convenient following which he could use for his own personal ends. In his capacity of justice of the peace the aristocrat controlled the phratry and, as will be seen, this justice remained a very rough and ready affair.

The unwritten law

At some time in the middle of the eighth century BC a Greek at Cyme in Asia Minor, who made his living by trading and carrying freight from port to port, went bankrupt. Abandoning trade for farming, he crossed the Aegean and settled on a small farm in the fertile plain of Boeotia. When he died he left the farm to be divided between his two sons, Perses and Hesiod. Perses was not content with his share, quarrelled with Hesiod over the division of the land and got a decision (by bribery) in his favour from the local aristocrat. He was no farmer, however, and his portion of the family land went to rack and ruin.

Hesiod was a poet of great ability who had already written a poem, *The Theogony*, on the gods of Greece, and in an attempt to put some life into his brother he wrote a long tract in hexameters on the duties of a farmer called *The Works and Days*. This famous poem describes the life of a small farmer in

the eighth century BC, when even the man with reasonable property could be ruined by a spate of bad weather, and hunger was often a painful reality.

Perhaps the most interesting section of the poem is Hesiod's account of his dispute with his brother and his views on the justice handed out by the Boeotian aristocrats. Hesiod had no illusions about them. They were corruptible and greedy ('gift-hungry'), and would bend their judgement in favour of the highest bidder. Nor was there any redress

against this corruption. The aristocrat was justice of the peace, assize judge and president of the court of appeal. The peasant before the aristocrat, Hesiod declared, was like the nightingale in the power of a hawk. 'There is no point in complaining, my good bird', says the hawk, 'I am stronger than you, and for all your sweet singing you cannot prevent me from doing what I like.'

However, in the face of this injustice Hesiod did not clamour for a programme of popular reform or a codified law with protection against discrimination. Instead he took comfort from the idea that there was a higher justice than that of the aristocrat—the justice of Zeus, who would one day give these corrupt judges their deserts. This was small consolation for a man who had had half his farm taken away from him but it shows that in the eighth century BC the ordinary Greek was not yet so desperate and disillusioned with the traditional system that he was prepared to do anything about it other than grumble. As long as the law was not fixed and written down, the aristocrat could bend it to suit his purpose, and, as long as the peasant felt there was an unbridgeable gap between himself and the aristocrat, then he would not question his ability to do this and get away with it.

How wide this gap was between aristocrats and the remainder of the population can also be seen in *The Iliad*. Although Homer's heroes are larger-than-life aristocrats, they are often made to express social attitudes which were certainly current in Homer's

Colonization

day and which after the eighth century BC lost their force only gradually. (It was not until 462 BC that the traditional aristocrats' council at Athens, the Areopagus, had its powers completely curtailed by Pericles and Ephialtes.) In the second book of *The Iliad* Odysseus summons a council on behalf of Agamemnon, courteously asking his fellow aristocrats to attend, but driving in the rest with his stick. At the council a man called Thersites dares to get up and criticize Agamemnon. Odysseus gives him a thrashing with his stick, Thersites retires in tears and everyone else roars with laughter.

The importance of this scene is that Odysseus felt confident that everyone would approve of his behaviour. Obviously it was unthinkable that a non-aristocrat should put forward an opinion. The aristocrat's assumption was that because a man was different from them he should not have any say in government. The gap between the classes was never closed in the sense that the aristocrat could reconcile his interests and way of life with those of a baker. It was, however, bridged to the extent that the aristocrat lost his position in the community as the one man capable of doing things and getting things done.

The seventh century BC in Greece was an age of unrest and political change: tyrannies at Corinth, Megaron and Sicyon, the reforms of Lycurgus at Sparta, and the laws of Dracon and the reforms of Solon at Athens. In many Greek cities the ruling aristocrats were either overthrown or forced to make real political concessions to the members of what could be conveniently called a rising middle class. This was not a middle class in any modern sense of the term, but a loosely defined class of small farmers. This group was beginning to challenge the unformulated, traditional power of the aristocrats. The Hesiods of the seventh century BC had acquired a new confidence and importance that made the old state of affairs intolerable. Two vitally important factors contributed to this rise of the previously humble farmer: the increase in wealth resulting from colonization, and the development of hoplite fighting.

Greek colonization took place in two waves: in the early eighth century BC, when colonies were founded mainly in Sicily and southern Italy, and towards the end of the seventh century BC when the Greeks turned their attention to the shores of the Black Sea. The reasons why a city sent out its inhabitants to found a colony varied, but the chief motive seems always to have been to relieve overcrowding at home.

After the dark age, when Greece settled down to a more peaceful way of life, there was a sharp rise in population. This was certainly not dramatic by present-day standards of population increase, but, seen in

Above, bronze figure of a jockey made in the second century BC; it was found in the sea off Cape Artemisium. National Museum, Athens.

Left, Statue of the goddess Minerva. Vatican Museum, Rome.

Opposite, bell krater with the figure of Alcmene on the pyre: the vase is signed by the artist Python. British Museum, London.

relation to the land which provided the only means of livelihood, it takes on serious proportions. The addition to a small farmer's family of one or two sons above the usual number meant that there was not enough family land to support all the male members of the family. Since there were few alternative occupations to that of farmer, to escape living on the threshold of starvation the younger sons would go abroad. The departure of the colonists meant a rise in the standard of living among those who stayed behind. There were fewer mouths to feed and the land no longer had to be divided up into small, uneconomical plots.

Obviously there were other reasons besides overpopulation for the increase of colonization. The earliest known Greek colony, Almina, at the mouth of the

Orontes, was no more than a trading post, and Cumae, in Etruria, was founded to exploit the mineral wealth of the region. It would, however, be wrong to think of colonies as trading-posts controlled by the mother city. They were independent cities which often, as in the case of Syracuse and Corinth, equalled or even excelled their mother-city. Relations between the two cities were usually friendly, but sometimes not. The earliest Greek naval battle, the historian Thucydides tells us, was in 664 BC between Corinth and its colony Corcyra.

Most colonists settled down to an agricultural existence similar to the one they had left behind them, but the mere fact of their venturing abroad opened up trade routes which the few craftsmen, and farmers with a surplus of olive oil, were not slow to exploit.

Similarly, in any shipment of surplus grain being exported to Greece, an agricultural colony would include spices, pottery and jewellery obtained from its barbarian neighbours. There is no doubt that there was increase of trade throughout the Aegean as a result of colonization, but foreign trade as such was never regarded as an economic activity to be pursued purely for its own sake. It was an adjunct to everyday trade, and there were no people who could be called businessmen as such.

However, in spite of the casual nature of trade between the colonies and Greece, there was enough of it to have a real effect on the Greek standard of living and on the way of thinking of the ordinary Greek. Strange designs in jewellery and pottery appeared in the markets throughout Greece,

ARCHAIC GREECE

Date	The Greek world	Culture	Egypt and Asia Minor	Date	The Greek world	Culture	Egypt and Asia Minor
1200	Dorian invasions Dorians in Crete		End of the Hittite Empire Rameses III	800	Greek colonies in Sicily and southern Italy Spartan conquest of Messenia	First Olympic Games	Growth of Assyria
1100	First Greek colonization The Achaeans settle on the coast of Asia Minor	Evolution of geometric pottery	David King of Israel	700	Tyrannies at Corinth, Megaron, Sicyon Second Messenian War	Sappho Hesiod's *Works and Days* Laws of Dracon	Sargon II Zenith of Assyrian Empire Destruction of Nineveh
1000	Ionian confederation		Solomon King of Israel Phoenician expansion	600	Greek colonies near Black Sea Increasing militarism in Sparta Solon appointed *archon* at Athens	Milesian school of Philisophy Thales, Anaximander, Anaximenes	Persian conquest: Cyrus' empire incorporates Greek cities in Asia Minor
900	The Greeks adopt the Phoenician alphabet The Spartans settle in Laconia	Homer's *Iliad* and *Odyssey*	First prophets: Elijah and Elisha Kingdom of Phrygia	500	Peisistratus tyrant at Athens Cleisthenes establishes the demes in Athens	Heraclitus Pythagoras	Darius usurps Persian throne

and ships' captains brought back tales from the east of revolt against the established order—tales such as that of Gyges who killed the King of Lydia and took both his throne and his wife. Horizons were being opened up, and the depressed classes were beginning to see that there was more to life than heavy toil in the fields.

The rise of the hoplite

In the *Iliad* battles took the form of individual duels between the heroes on each side. The remainder of the Greek army played a very minor role, hovering on the sidelines, slinging stones and shouting encouragement to its champions. When a hero fell or was wounded they would close in to strip him of his armour, like jackals attacking a dying lion. Infantry tactics remained at this rudimentary stage because only aristocrats could afford armour, spears and swords. The rest had to make do with daggers and stones from the battlefield. It was not until the end of the eighth century BC that this inefficient method of fighting was changed and its place taken by the hoplite citizen army fighting in a regular line. The reason for the change was that, with the increase in wealth among the middle classes, a considerable number of farmers could afford the necessary armour

for proper infantry engagements. Tactics were modified to accommodate and make the best use of this increase in manpower.

The hoplite, equipped with a shield on his left arm, wearing armour and holding a thrusting spear in his right hand, was drawn up in ranks eight-deep, the shield of each man overlapping that of the man next to him. The aim of a battle now was to break the enemy's line by the weight of the charge. Whichever line of hoplites wavered first usually lost the battle since the right flank of a hoplite in a broken line was no longer protected by the shield of the man next to him—a fatal disadvantage.

Once a city's defending force had been defeated the victors could sweep through the surrounding farmland and destroy the crops. Discipline was essential to successful hoplite fighting, especially the ability to regroup and deploy as a single unit. The hoplite in most Greek cities had a short period of training from the age of eighteen to twenty, and this aspect of war was generally left to luck and the commonsense of the hoplite.

The Spartans were not so slap-dash. Their disciplined drill was famous, and Thucydides tells us that they had a proper chain of orders and hoped that they would be heard above the din of battle. This improvement in military technique had important repercussions on the political structure of the cities. The safety of the city and its food

Above, bronze figure known as the Delphic Charioteer, c. 470 BC. Delphi Museum.

Top, hoplites and chariots as depicted on a relief from a funeral stela, c. 450 BC. National Museum, Athens.

121

supply now depended on the fighting qualities of the ordinary farmer and no longer on those of a handful of aristocrats. In return for these services the hoplite wanted to play a part in the government of the city, and was no longer satisfied with the concentration of power in the hands of a few. The changes which resulted from this unrest and discontent took different forms in different cities. The first city to be affected by the new mood was Sparta.

The Spartan revolution

Sparta was by far the most unusual state in Greece. Founded by Dorians in the valley of the Eurotas in the southern Peloponnese, it was the most extreme example of a Dorian community which did not assimilate or wipe out the original inhabitants in its area but kept them in a state of subjection. In Thessaly the members of such a depressed class were called the *penestai* ('the poor ones') and at Sicyon the *konipodes* ('the dusty feet'). At Sparta they were known as helots. The existence of the helots, who far outnumbered the Spartans, had a decisive and permanent effect on their society, an effect which became even more marked after the Messenian Wars when the number of helots was vastly increased.

Yet even before these wars the Spartans, unlike other Dorian communities, never relaxed their original Dorian habits. Their men ate in common public eating houses, not at home, and the education of their children was carried out on a tribal basis. Since, for these reasons, they were an extremely close-knit and conservative society, political and social differences were settled among them without the great upheavals and repercussions which shook other Greek states. However, apart from these small but significant differences, before the beginning of the seventh century BC Sparta did not differ greatly from other cities in Greece. There were the same small farmers such as Hesiod in Boeotia and aristocrats sufficiently wealthy to live the good life and influence the course of public affairs.

Like other cities Sparta seems to have been faced in the eighth century BC with the problem of overpopulation. However, the course Sparta took to solve this problem was completely different from that adopted by other cities, and the results were important and far-reaching. Instead of embarking on a programme of colonization (they were notorious landlubbers), the Spartans solved their problem by annexing (*c.* 735–715 BC) the fertile lands of the Messenians, their neighbours in the western Peloponnese and reducing the Messenians to the status of helots. The conquest of Messenia was the most momentous event in Spartan history. Overnight the Spartans had acquired the

wealth which other cities took many years to obtain by trade and colonization and, most important of all, they had injected a large and extremely hostile element into the helot population.

As a result they were faced with two distinct problems. The first was social and economic: how to distribute this new wealth and how to stabilize the effect of the political demands which would come in its wake. The second problem was how to keep the helots in their place. About 675 BC, as the result of social unrest, possibly exacerbated by tension between the kings and aristocrats, the Spartans acquired a constitution. From that time onwards a regular citizen body of Spartans, numbering 9,000 and called the 'equals', was recognized. It was divided up into administrative units called *obai*, which were based on residential areas not kinship. This citizen body was to meet in assembly at regular intervals and could vote by acclamation on proposals put before it by the *gerousia*. The *gerousia* was a council of elders (its members had to be over sixty years of age) which had existed before 675 BC. It was now pruned to thirty members, among whom were the two Spartan kings.

Not mentioned in the documents on the constitution were the *ephors*, an aristocratic panel of five members set up shortly before 675 BC to act as a brake on the kings' powers. The *ephors* had wide executive authority, and the real direction of the state was provided by a triumvirate of the *gerousia*, the kings and the *ephors*. Yet in spite of these realities of power and the conservative and inflexible nature of Spartan government when compared with the volatile political life of Athens under democracy, the establishment of a constitution at Sparta was a revolutionary event. For the first time in Greek history the members of a state had been given formal rights of citizenship which were not based on membership of a tribe or phratry. Furthermore, these men now had

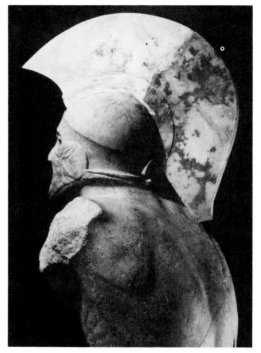

the right of voicing their opinion and grievances in an assembly which was obliged to meet regularly by law, and not according to the whim of an aristocratic clique.

After the year 675 BC Sparta still remained a conservative, oligarchic state, but a step had been taken which was to have momentous repercussions throughout Greece: rule by tradition had been abandoned and had been replaced by rule by law.

Helots and Spartiates

It is hard to find a historical parallel which illustrates the relationship between the Spartans and the helots: a minority group living in its own country as though it were an invading army, keeping itself in a state of

permanent military readiness, reducing family life to a minimum to avoid any weakening of morale and subjecting its children to an inhumanly tough education— all in order to keep down the major part of the population. The helots posed a permanent threat to the small body of Spartans whose land they cultivated. Every year the *ephors* declared war on the helots—a formality which allowed any Spartan to kill a helot without subsequently having to stand trial. On one occasion the Spartans offered their freedom to any helots who had performed outstanding services in war. The 2,000 helots who were singled out for this honour were killed. The Spartans also possessed a type of secret police, the *Crypteia*, which consisted of groups of Spartan youths who hid in the countryside by day, and at night murdered helots whom they considered to be dangerous.

The Spartans enjoyed one enormous advantage over their hostile slaves: they were the toughest and best trained soldiers in the Greek world. Since the helots did all the work on the land, the Spartans had the leisure to devote themselves to full-time military training. This training started early.

At the age of seven the Spartan boy was taken away from his mother and his education became the responsibility of the state. From the age of fourteen to twenty Spartan youths were divided into groups, under the supervision of an older boy, and went

Above, detail from the Vix krater—a large bowl used to mix wine and water—depicting hoplites and warriors in chariots, c. 520 BC. Archaeological Museum, Chatillon-sur-Seine.

Left, early marble kouros *figure known as 'the Calf-Bearer' and found on the Acropolis. Acropolis Museum, Athens.*

Opposite top, frieze from the funerary monument of the Nereids at Xanthus depicting eight hoplites advancing in line, early fourth century BC. British Museum, London.

Opposite bottom, statue of Leonidas, King of Sparta and commander of the Greek troops at the Battle of Thermopylae (in which he was killed) during the Persian Wars, 480 BC. Sparta Museum.

through a form of vigorous paramilitary training. They were given little clothing or food, and were often compelled to undergo savage endurance tests. One test was to make them hide in the countryside and live solely on what they could steal. If they were caught they were beaten. At the end of this training, if they passed all the initiation tests, the young men became fully-fledged Spartiates, living in barracks and eating in common messes. If the young Spartan married he could not set up house with his bride, but continued to live in his barracks, and could visit her only in secret. Spartan women themselves were extremely tough and amazed visitors from other cities by doing gymnastics with the men.

As Sparta became more and more militaristic after the seventh century BC there was a corresponding rise in the austerity of its life. Sparta became a cultural wilderness. This decline was, however, more gradual

than is generally supposed, and it was not until the end of the sixth century BC that the city became notorious for its philistinism. Respectable pottery and bronze figures were still being produced by Laconian craftsmen well into the middle of the sixth century BC. However, by the time of the Peloponnesian War, Aristophanes' Athenian audiences were roaring with laughter at the idea of Alcibiades, their high-living general, gloomily eating black broth in his self-imposed exile at Sparta.

Unattractive as its dour, conservative society may seem, Sparta was admired as a model society by many Greeks from other cities. What men such as Plato liked in Sparta was the subordination of the individual's will to a set of rigid rules, and also the fact that the Spartans were 'gentlemen' who kept the lower orders in their place. Today, such qualities seem to be of dubious value, and Athens with its bustling, rumbustious democracy and cultural achievements has far more appeal than Sparta. However, even though Sparta's only bequest to us has been the words 'spartan' and 'laconic', it would be wrong to dismiss Sparta lightly. The Spartans, with the Athenians, were the protagonists in Greek politics for more than 400 years.

Tyranny

In about 680 BC, Gyges, an aristocrat at the court of Candaules, the King of Lydia, killed his master and set himself up to rule in his place. Five years later the Spartans carried through their peaceable revolution. At Argos, as Aristotle relates, Pheidon, the king, reasserted his control over the aristocrats by enlisting the help of the hoplite class. Throughout the Greek-speaking world clever men were beginning to discover the rudiments of political theory and were using this new-found knowledge to overthrow the long-established aristocratic oligarchies. The lower classes, who had benefited from colonization and had acquired a new independence of mind, were intolerant of the old order. Therefore they did not oppose, and indeed often helped, these political adventurers in their bids for power. Their reward for such help was that they got a new man to judge their lawsuits who, even if he turned out to be a bad man, was rarely worse than their former judges. Moreover, they were often given grants of land from the estates of the dispossessed aristocrats.

To describe these men who seized power from the aristocrats and who were neither kings nor magistrates, the Greeks borrowed a Lydian word, *tyrannos*, which meant 'ruler'. At Megara, Sicyon, Corinth and Mytilene tyrants seized power. In each city the issues which the tyrant exploited to gain power were different, but the background (an aristocratic candidate for power and an acquiescent hoplite class) was the same. The

most typical tyrant is perhaps Cypselus, who in 657 BC seized power at Corinth.

Placed at the head of the Saronic and Corinthian gulfs and controlling the isthmus road from the Peloponnese to the rest of Greece, Corinth was the one city in Greece where trade played as important a part in the economy of the city as agriculture. Corinthian pottery was eagerly sought after throughout the Mediterranean and its fame was only eventually eclipsed by the famous red vases of Attica. Corinth was the mother-city of colonies in the east and west, the most famous of which was Syracuse in Sicily. The rulers of this prosperous state were the Bacchiads, one of the aristocratic clans at Corinth. They formed a closed, narrowly based oligarchic faction, passing on the magistracies among themselves and not permitting a Bacchiad (male or female) to marry anyone outside the clan.

As far as is known they only once allowed an exception to this rule and this caused their downfall. Labda, the mother of Cypselus, was a Bacchiad, but because she was lame she was allowed to marry a man called Aëtion who was an outsider. When Cypselus was born, so his story goes, the Bacchiads, on the strength of a warning oracle from Delphi, tried to murder him, but his mother hid him in a chest (*cypselon* in Greek) and he was saved.

The details of his career between then and his bid for power are not certain. He may have gone into exile from Corinth, which was too dangerous for him, and have spent some time in the Peloponnese, where he became friendly with Pheidon of Argos. Some time before 657 BC he seems to have returned to Corinth and to have gained a certain amount of popularity while serving as a hoplite officer under the Bacchiads. In 657 BC, with the help of Pheidon, the encouragement of the priests at Delphi and the support of some of the Corinthians, he expelled the Bacchiads, many of whom fled to Sparta, and set himself up as tyrant.

He ruled Corinth successfully for thirty-two years, and was undoubtedly a popular ruler, for we are told that he did not need a bodyguard. However, revolutions start because people have specific grievances and it is necessary to look for something more precise than the rise of political consciousness among the hoplites and a vague desire for justice to account for Cypselus' support at Corinth. The Bacchiads, it must be supposed, for want of evidence to the contrary, were no better or worse than the aristocrats in other Greek states where revolution did not take place. Yet all oligarchs are resented by those whom they rule, and it can be assumed that the Bacchiads were disliked for individual acts of arrogance by enough potters and independent farmers for Cypselus to be able to gain the support of the hoplites. Moreover, Pheidon, Cypselus' ally in the venture, was an established champion of hoplite rights, and the Corinthian hoplites, rightly or wrongly, must have thought that Cypselus sympathized with his political views.

However, the later history of Corinth (the city was always an oligarchy after the end of the tyranny) does not suggest that the Corinthian hoplite was a rabid revolutionary. It is therefore necessary to look further for the main grievance which brought Cypselus to power. His chief support must have come from the Corinthian aristocrats who did not belong to the Bacchiad clan.

These were men with a real grievance. The equals of the Bacchiads in lineage, wealth and education, they had been consistently excluded from the direction of the city's affairs by the selfishness of a small faction. Cypselus needed their help in running the city, and they must have calculated that having him as tyrant was a price worth paying for a say in its government.

The error the Bacchiads had made was to rule alone. Cypselus pinpointed this and exploited it. Like all tyrants he was not really interested in justice, except in so far as attention to it helped his cause. The paradox of tyranny was, however, that in the pursuit of absolute power the tyrant indirectly encouraged the growth of democracy.

Solon

Political unrest at Athens developed later than in other Greek states. In 630 BC a young aristocrat, Cylon, seized the acropolis with some armed followers in an attempt to become tyrant, but he and his men were killed—unfortunately after they had taken refuge in a temple and had been promised their lives. This act of sacrilege was blamed on the magistrate responsible, an Alcmaeonid, one of the most colourful and politically active clans at Athens. The Alcmaeonids were hounded from the city.

Above, sixth-century BC bowl from Corinth. Musée du Louvre, Paris.

Opposite top, head of Apollo found in the stadium at Olympia. Olympia Museum, Greece.

Opposite bottom, bronze figure of a warrior. Wadsworth Atheneum, Hartford.

Ten years later, in 620 BC, a code of law was drawn up by Dracon which was memorable for the severity of its penalties. Dracon's code does not seem to have alleviated Athen's troubles: rather it aggravated them, for the traditional injustices which existed in Attic society were now made explicit and clear for all to see.

By the year 594 BC discontent had reached fever pitch, and at this point the Athenians very wisely appointed Solon as archon, or chief magistrate, with full powers to resolve the crisis. Athens was faced with two problems.

The first was that among the lower classes there were many men who were in debt to the *eupatrids*, the aristocratic class. If a man failed to pay his debt he forfeited the security he had given to his creditor—which was himself. The luckless debtor became the slave of his creditor and as such was probably sold abroad.

The second problem was that of the *hektemoroi*. These were small farmers who owed a sixth of their produce to an aristocrat. No satisfactory reasons for such an arrangement have ever been advanced. This form of payment may have been a kind of protection money which had its origins in the dark age, or possibly an aristocrat may have preferred to keep a defaulting debtor as a *hektemoros* and so derive a steady income from him rather than sell him as a slave and make an immediate profit. However, it seems most probable that the *hektemoros* was paying the aristocrat a traditional insurance for a dubious protection which he no longer needed.

Nevertheless, the problems of debt and the *hektemoros* were of long standing, and it is reasonable to suppose that the crisis in 594 BC was precipitated by something more immediate—possibly an agricultural crisis. It may have been that Athens, which never took part in the eighth-century wars of colonization, was now beginning to build up an export trade in olive oil to the Black Sea from where it was starting to import corn. Athens had fought a war with Mytilene in 600 BC for control of the city of Sigeon in the Troad. Many farmers may have borrowed capital in order to plant olive trees and, because the olive does not produce fruit for several years, may not have had quick enough returns on their investment for their creditors' liking. This seems to be the most plausible of the various theories about an agricultural crisis which are invoked to explain the appointment of Solon as archon.

However, it is not really necessary to look beyond the obvious fact that the debtors and *hektemoroi*, especially after Dracon's laws had made their position painfully obvious, no longer accepted their ignominious inferiority. Solon's solution was simple and direct: he abolished the *hektemoroi* system and the lending of money on the surety of a man's person. That the Eupatrids accepted (with a great deal of grumbling) this radical solution is an indication of how serious was

the discontent among the lower classes before his reforms.

The depressed farmers of Attica were not the only people at variance with the Eupatrids. The aristocrats were divided among themselves. Those who farmed the less fertile land of the southwestern and eastern coasts of Attica had always been less well off, and therefore less influential, than the great Eupatrid families who had their estates on the rich soil of the central plain. However, the increase in olive growing had made many of these outlying aristocrats as rich as the families on the plain. Moreover, they were no longer willing, in an age of increasing political reorganization, to tolerate the traditional superiority of their neighbours.

Solon's main support was from among loosely-knit groups of these new rich, eager for a more equitable distribution of power and influence, and official recognition of their wealth and talents. The Alcmaeonids, who had been exiled after the scandal of Cylon's murder, supported Solon and returned to their estates in the southwest. The family of Peisistratus (the future tyrant), who came from the east, also gave him their support. Solon himself had restored his family fortune by trade and so had divorced himself from the traditional aristocracy of landowners on the plain. In his poems he castigates the injustice of the great families and warns them that their day is over. Had Solon been dishonest and inclined to

violence the Eupatrid families might have had an excuse for entrenching themselves in a reactionary position, and Athens would have suffered a civil war. Solon was, however, neither dishonest nor violent, committed though he was to a partisan policy. His obvious wisdom and abhorrence of violence disarmed the Eupatrids and they could do nothing when he brought forward constitutional reforms which rocked their power to its foundations.

Solon established four classes of citizen (outside the phratry system), which were for the first time based on an assessment of wealth. Depending on how much a man produced on his farm, he belonged to the class of *pentakosioimediminoi*, *hippeis* (cavalry), *zengitai* (hoplites), or *thetes* (commoners). Of these classes only that of the *pentakosioimediminoi*, who had to produce 500 bushels of wheat or oil, was entirely new.

The relevance of establishing classes based on wealth becomes clear. It is seen that Solon opened all public offices to all the members of the *pentakosioimediminoi*. The avenue to power for the new rich was now open. However, the reactionaries still controlled the ancient assembly of the Areopagus which was composed of ex-magistrates. It was to counteract the influence of this body that Solon established a council of 400, for which all the classes except the *thetes* were eligible. This council decided what public business should be transacted, conducted the election of magistrates and acted as a court of appeal against magistrates' decisions. Most important of all, the council had to meet on specific dates. Thus, the rule by tradition from the Olympian heights of the Areopagus was ended.

In retrospect, Solon may seem to be a great democratic reformer. No judgement would have surprised him more. It never occurred to him to give political power to the *demos* (the common people). His aim was to liberate the lower classes from their most crushing economic burdens, and to resolve the political injustices which were plaguing relations among the aristocrats. It was Athens' good fortune that, in the process of accomplishing this second task, he set up the constitutional framework within which democracy was later to develop.

No inkling of such a development can have occurred to Solon as the year 594 BC drew to a close. His aristocratic opponents, defeated on one front, were far from finished. They still controlled the phratries, and they still managed the local religious cult centres and could exploit the influence this gave them over the pious farmers. His reforms had put right some grave injustices, but they had also clarified the political issues and were indirectly responsible for the period of fierce party quarrels which followed.

Peisistratus

In 546 BC Peisistratus, an exiled politician, landed in Attica with an army of supporters and Thracian mercenaries, defeated his enemies at the Battle of Pallene and made himself tyrant of Athens. It was his third bid for power. He ruled Attica firmly and well for the next eighteen years until his death in 528 BC when he was succeeded by his son, Hippias.

The period of nearly fifty years between Solon's reforms and Peisistratus' final bid for power present a confused picture. It is hard to trace in any detail the disturbances which led a great number of Athenians to accept a tyranny. The main difficulty seems to have been that Solon's reforms, essentially moderate though they were, had not brought harmony to Athens. In short, they had failed. Just as Dracon's law code had made the misery of the *hektemoroi* explicit, so the measures Solon had taken aggravated the factional interests which existed among the aristocrats.

Three distinct parties had emerged from the loose-knit groups of the period before Solon. They gave themselves names which denoted their regional basis. There were 'the men of the plain' (reactionary Eupatrids who had suffered most from Solon), 'the men of the coast' (the party led by the Alcmaeonid clan) and 'the men beyond the hills' (the party of Peisistratus from the east coast). Economic disparity may have split the former supporters of Solon. The reasons

for the hostility of 'the men of the plain' to the other two parties is not hard to find. They had still not accepted the arrival of the upstarts, and did their best to prevent them from exercising their newly won power.

The office of archon (chief magistrate) proved to be a continual source of strife. In the lists of archons for this period we twice see the entry *anarchia*, meaning that no candidate was acceptable to all the parties for a particular year, and accordingly no archon was elected. In 582 BC the archon Damasias attempted to hold on to his office for an extra year and had to be removed from it by force.

In addition to such inter-party bickering, it is possible to guess at other difficulties which were upsetting the stability of Athenian society. Athens' fortunes were prospering: its potters were exporting their wares further afield and the change to olive growing was now paying dividends. At a time of economic expansion, however, not everyone shared in the general prosperity and their bad luck was emphasized by the good fortune of others.

Numbers of such discontented men may have lived in the east, the poorest part of Attica, which was the stronghold of Peisistratus. These men would have been eager for a change, especially one brought about by their own party leader. Those who were profiting from the economic boom would have wanted political changes to match their new wealth. Moreover, for the greater part of these men, who were born after 594 BC Solon's political system would have lost its revolutionary appeal, and would merely appear to be a system set up by the authorities in order to frustrate their political aspirations.

A tyranny, with its opportunities for easy promotion, may have seemed to many Athenians a pleasant prospect. It was against such a background of political instability and economic evolution that Peisistratus came to power.

He proved to be a benevolent, enlightened and strong ruler. During the thirty-six years of his family's rule Athens grew more prosperous than ever before. From the constitutional point of view his rule was also of great importance, for there is no doubt that as tyrant he unknowingly made a major contribution to the establishment of full democracy at Athens. The one aim which seemed to underlie every action he took was to break the influence of the aristocrats over the *demos*. That he was successful in this was probably Peisistratus' greatest achievement. He made the ordinary Athenian aware that he was not only the dependant of the head of his phratry, but also the citizen of a state, and that allegiance to that state was more important than allegiance to any aristocrat, however wealthy or proud.

How did Peisistratus effect this revolution in political attitudes? To begin with he drew the teeth of the aristocratic parties. Many aristocrats had gone into exile after the

Two Attic vases, c. 540 BC, depicting, above, the olive harvest and, opposite, a warship. British Museum, London.

Battle of Pallene, and those who remained were kept quiet by the threat of Peisistratus' Thracian mercenaries, paid for with the revenues from his silver mines in Thrace. Peisistratus, however, went further than this and persuaded many aristocrats to support him openly. He did this with the lure of marriage pacts and judicious appointments to the major magistracies, which he kept within his patronage. However, the public support of the aristocrat was not enough. Peisistratus also had to check the private, local influence of the aristocrat when he was safe on his estate. He accomplished this by taking upon himself all the functions which aristocrats had previously performed for the peasants. By centralizing all public administration and works he made the aristocrat, as a public figure, redundant.

Before the period of tyranny the aristocrat had acted as the local justice of the peace. Peisistratus now removed this function from him, by appointing his own judges who travelled round the countryside hearing the peasants' cases. Before Solon's reforms, and probably afterwards, the Attic peasant had depended on his local aristocrat for help in any capital projects he undertook on his farm. Now he no longer needed this help. Peisistratus instituted a ten percent tax on all land and used the proceeds to subsidize the poorer farmers—in particular to encourage the growth of olives.

Besides taking such direct measures, Peisistratus undermined the prestige of the aristocrats by other, more oblique, methods.

Before his rule any cultural stimulus at Athens had been provided by individual, rich families. Peisistratus set out to show that state patronage could achieve more spectacular results. He encouraged the pottery trade, and it was under his rule that Athenian potters first began to make the red-figure vases which were to give Athens the monopoly in luxury pottery throughout the Aegean. He also paid for an extensive public building programme which resulted in a new council chamber and a fine temple to Athena. Such projects were beyond the purse of any single Eupatrid, and the lesson cannot have been lost on the Athenians.

However, Peisistratus' most important step was to challenge the aristocrats on the issue of religion. Throughout Attica there were many small local centres in honour of various gods. These centres were controlled by different aristocratic families, and the traditional priesthoods they held enhanced their authority with the *demos*.

To counterbalance this authority Peisistratus built up into a national event the recently established festival of the Panathenaea, and instituted a new festival on a similar scale in honour of Dionysius, called the Dionysia. The festival of the Dionysia, where poets performed their works in honour of the god, became the cradle of Greek tragedy. In particular, Peisistratus encouraged performances of Homer's poems, and he may have been responsible for having the *Iliad* and the *Odyssey* written down for the first time—a

move which saved them for posterity.

In the sphere of formal politics Peisistratus was content to let Solon's council continue its functions and, indeed, from the evidence of the new council chamber he had built, he seems actually to have encouraged the participation of the common people in public affairs. There were two good reasons for such a policy. A politically active *demos* was unlikely to tolerate a recurrence of aristocratic feuding. Moreover, Peisistratus had no quarrel with the people. Dangerous opposition could come only from the aristocrats. As long as he kept his nominees in high office Peisistratus was safe. The *demos* and their council were a side issue in the game of power politics in which Peisistratus had appointed himself referee. Nevertheless, under the protection of the tyranny the concept of participation by the people in the city's affairs took root and flourished—with momentous results for the future of Athens and the Greek world.

Peisistratus died in 528 BC and his son, Hippias, succeeded him. For twelve years Hippias ruled Athens uneventfully, his only act of any note being the introduction of a four-drachma silver coin, distinctively minted with the head of Athena on the obverse side, and the owl of Athena on the reverse. Coinage had been introduced to Greece from Lydia early in the sixth century BC and had been gradually adopted by all the Greek cities, except Sparta, which hung on obdurately to its currency of iron bars. At first Aeginetan 'turtles' were the most popular coins, but Hippias' 'owls' were soon as widely used, especially in the eastern Mediterranean. However, apart from this one achievement, which impressed early Greek historians, Hippias does not seem to have been as successful a ruler as his father. Opposition to his rule was mounting and in 514 BC his brother Hipparchus was murdered. Hippias responded with a series of harsh and repressive measures against real or imagined opponents. Rather than saving the tyranny this policy hastened its downfall. In 510 BC Hippias and his supporters were driven from Athens by a Spartan army, which was brought in by the exiled Alcmaeonids. Thus, the first and only tyranny ended.

Whatever theoretical reservations may be made about absolute rule, the tyranny of the Peisistratids was beneficial to Athens. With the exception of jealous, power-hungry aristocrats all the Athenians were grateful for it. Peisistratus by his policies laid the foundations of the future power of Athens and that bold and imaginative form of government—democracy.

Cleisthenes

The aristocrats who returned to Athens in 510 BC under the protection of Spartan arms, and those who had lain low at Athens during the long years of the tyranny, immediately resumed their inter-party strife —the traditional political activity they had

Above, medallion, dating from c. 565 BC, depicting King Arkesilas of Cyrene (now part of modern Libya) watching silphium being weighed and despatched; the Greeks used the plant for both culinary and medicinal purposes. Cabinet des Medailles, Paris.

Above left and opposite right, two ten-drachma coins minted in Athens c. 486 BC: the images are of the head of Athena and the owl of Athena. British Museum, London.

Opposite left, funeral monument of the soldier Aristion, 510–500 BC: the figure is life-size and stands on a marble slab. National Museum, Athens.

been forced to drop. Herodotus tells us that there were two parties at Athens which dominated events after the expulsion of Hippas. The one was run by Cleisthenes, the Alcmaeonid, and the other by Isaporas, a Eupatrid. The issues over which they disagreed can, however, only be guessed at.

By 508 BC Isaporas' party was in the ascendant, for he was elected archon for this year. At this point Cleisthenes took a remarkable step. By one of the great ironies of history he put through the assembly, under the unwilling chairmanship of Isaporas, a series of radical proposals that completely altered the administrative and political life of Athens, and which were specifically designed to wrest the political ascendancy from Isaporas and his supporters and give it to the people—and to himself.

As Herodotus laconically says: 'He took the people into partnership.' In reply to Cleistenes' bold countermove Isaporas called in the Spartans, but Cleisthenes with the support of the people threw them out of Attica. Obviously Cleisthenes must have offered the ordinary Athenian an extremely tempting reward to make him stand up to the Spartans. In fact, he offered the *demos* an end to aristocratic control of politics, and in its place a political system within which they would be free to conduct their own affairs on an equal basis. He did this by substituting for the phratry system, which was based on kinship, a system of citizen classification which was based on locality. Where a man lived, not to whom he was related, now determined his civic status.

Cleisthenes divided Attica up into demes, roughly the equivalent of a borough, parish or ward. These basic units, which represented real areas of Attica and the city of Athens, were combined into artificial groups called *trittyes*. One curious point about the composition of these was that often a *trittyes* included a deme which was situated far away from the other demes with which it was grouped. The significance of this becomes clear when Cleisthenes' motives for his reforms are examined. From the *trittyes* Cleisthenes composed ten new tribes in place of the four which had existed previously. A Cleisthenic tribe consisted, we are told, of one *trittyes* from the coast, one from the plain and one from the city.

The increased number of tribes resulted in certain relatively unimportant changes: there were now ten military commanders in time of war instead of four, and the council numbered 500 instead of 400. However, the establishment of the deme in the place of the phratry was of great political importance. Demes kept records of all births and deaths, and the citizens they registered were regarded as equals. They had their own constitutions, elected leaders called *demarchs*, and put up candidates for election by lot to the council.

Here was a political unit within which the ambitious Athenian could prove himself politically without interference from the local aristocrat. The details of the deme-*trittyes* tribe system devised by Cleisthenes were complicated, and much remains obscure. However, what is certain is that the demes by breaking once and for all the influence of the aristocrat on local politics, formed the basis for the future Athenian democracy. By establishing the demes Cleisthenes completed a slow process which had been started by Solon and fostered by Peisistratus—rule by the people.

It is difficult to know whether he was an idealistic reformer, or whether he was playing party politics, as Herodotus suggests, and using the aspirations of the people to further his own ends. There is no sure answer to these questions, but the curious unit of the *trittyes* may provide a clue. Recent research into Cleisthenes' reforms seems to indicate that by not always building up the *trittyes* from demes which lay next to each other he was undermining the support his aristocratic opponents received from the people who attended the religious cult centres controlled by the aristocrats. Cleisthenes changed their congregations and the Eupatrids now found themselves trying to influence people with whom they had no traditional connections.

The Alcmaeonids, on the other hand, made sure that they themselves suffered from no such disadvantage. There is not enough evidence available to show whether Cleisthenes arranged the distribution of demes within the *trittyes* in favour of the Alcmaeonids. However, whether he was a cynic or an idealist, Cleisthenes had brought about the beginning of real democracy at Athens. The political battles of the sixth-century aristocrats against tyrants and the people against aristocrats now gave way to the larger, clearly-defined battles which occupied fifth-century Greece: Sparta against Athens and Greece against Persia.

Chapter 8

The Persian Menace

In 545 BC Cyrus, the founder of the Persian Empire, defeated Croesus, King of Lydia, and incorporated his extensive territories into his new empire. As a result of this victory the Persians came into contact for the first time with Croesus' neighbours, the Greeks, who lived in the Ionian colonies of the eastern Aegean. For the next 200 years, until Alexander sacked the Persian capitol of Persepolis, relations between the Greek cities and the Achaemenid kings dominated the political history of Greece and Asia Minor.

The early story of the Persians and Greeks—their various battles, alliances and acts of treachery towards each other—is made all the more fascinating and vivid because of the account given of it in the *Histories* of Herodotus of Halicarnassus. The *Histories* do not, however, deal only with the Persian-Greek wars. Their title in Greek literally means 'The Inquiries', and this is what they are. Herodotus inquired

into everything and thought almost everything worth writing about. He talks of pygmies and gold-bearing ants, discusses whether the earth is flat or round, recounts legends and scurrilous anecdotes, and provides a wealth of detail about the everyday habits of the people of the numerous countries he visited, in particular Egypt and Persia.

Another Greek before Herodotus, Hecataeus of Miletus, had written about the things he saw around him, compiling notebooks on geography and genealogy, and Herodotus was, to some extent, writing in the same tradition as his fellow Ionian— as a geographer and sociologist. However, Herodotus differs from Hecataeus in his inclusion of political narrative in his histories. Living a generation after the second Persian war, he saw the importance of the ideological and military clash between Persia and Greece, and he took the unprecedented step of recording and commenting on the struggle between the two peoples. This was his great achievement, and justifies his claim to be regarded as the father of history.

Polybius, a later Greek historian, observed in the introduction to his *Universal History* that no man should write history who had not had experience of public life, and who had not also made every effort to get firsthand knowledge of what he was writing about. Herodotus certainly measured up to these standards. As a young man in Halicarnassus he had been exiled by the tyrant Lygdamis, and had then returned with his fellow exiles to depose the tyrant. He subsequently left Halicarnassus and spent

Above, head from an Achaemenid royal statue, sixth century BC. Musée du Louvre, Paris.

Opposite, vase depicting a merchant vessel and a warship, 540 BC. British Museum, London.

The tomb of Cyrus II at Pasargadae, sixth century BC.

many years visiting various parts of the Persian Empire and the countries of the eastern Mediterranean. Thus, when Herodotus speaks about the bricks of Babylon or the height of the pyramids, we know that he is speaking of something he has seen himself. Herodotus is also an impartial if irreverent historian. He is extremely authoritative about Athens, a city where he lived under the patronage of the Alcmaeonids for several years, and which honoured him for his literary achievements.

As an Ionian who had been born on the fringes of the Persian Empire and had travelled extensively through it, he had an encyclopedic knowledge of Persian history and habits. Unlike most Greeks, who hated the Persians without understanding them, Herodotus did understand them and viewed their different way of life sympathetically. If he includes an occasional implausible story in his narrative, he always makes it clear that he is reporting only what he has heard, and the reader is under no obligation to believe him. Herodotus can be infuriating, especially for the strict moralist, when he delightedly recounts the unimportant exploits of some Greek or Egyptian rogue, or the sexual customs of the Scythians, at the same time omitting important historical details. However, without him we should know far less about the history of the fifth century BC than we do.

From Cyrus to Darius

By the middle of the sixth century BC, after the confusion which surrounded the fall of the Hittite and Assyrian Empires, four powers had emerged as the dominant forces in the ancient Near East: Media, Lydia, Chaedaea and Egypt. Among the vassal kings of Astyages, the Median king, was Cyrus, the Achaemenid, who ruled over the Persians—Iranians in origin like the Medes. Astyages lived a luxurious life in his capital Ecbatana. Median rule was strongly resented by the Persians who, on the high mountain plateau of Parsu, had maintained the austere, tough way of life of their Iranian ancestors. In the person of Cyrus they had a strong leader who translated their discontent into action. In 550 BC Cyrus made an alliance with the Babylonians and rose in open revolt against Astyages. He quickly defeated the Medes with the help of Astyages' treacherous general, Harpagus, and Ecbatana fell to the Persians.

Cyrus, however, was not content to rule only the Medes and Persians. Croesus, the King of Lydia, had moved into Median territory during Cyrus' campaign against Astyages to claim some disputed lands beyond the river Halys. Cyrus used this move as a pretext to invade Lydia. After an indecisive campaign in 547 BC Croesus retired to his capital, Sardis, for the winter. To his surprise Cyrus did not retire to winter quarters, as Croesus had expected,

but advanced towards Sardis. In the battle which took place before Sardis the Lydian cavalry, Croesus' main weapon, were stampeded by the smell of the Persian camels, and Croesus' capital fell to the Persians.

The Ionian Greeks, who lived along the Lydian coast and on the adjacent islands, had always enjoyed good relations with the Lydian kings, giving them nominal allegiance but never paying them taxes. They now sent letters to Cyrus asking that this satisfactory state of affairs should be maintained.

He declared them rebels against Persian rule and marched against them. One by one the mainland cities—Cnidus, Magnesia, Phocaea—fell to the Persian armies, and the island states were bribed or terrorized into submission. In this short campaign the Persians consolidated the northwestern frontier of their new empire and in the process learnt two important lessons about the Greeks. First, in times of danger they could be certain the Greeks would not unite among themselves, and secondly, their loyalty could easily be bought. These were lessons that the Persians later put to good advantage.

Cyrus now turned his attention to Babylon. After the strong rule of Nebuchadnezzar Babylon had been plagued by a succession of weak kings and palace intrigues. The support of the priests for the ruling house

had been alienated, the fertile plains surrounding the city had been neglected, and the peasants were hungry and discontented. Jewish prophets in the city were already foretelling its capture by the Persians. They were not proved wrong. After a short campaign in the wild regions of Bactria and Sogdiana, from where he drew welcome reinforcements for his army, Cyrus marched against Babylon. Since the Babylonians had broken their alliance with Cyrus when he invaded Lydia and had given their support to Croesus, Cyrus had a ready-made quarrel with them to justify his invasion.

There was little opposition to the Persians. After losing two brief battles on the Tigris, Nabu-Naid, the King of Babylon, fled and all serious resistance subsequently collapsed. Cyrus' general, Gobryas, the future satrap of Babylonia, entered the city in 539 BC and received an enthusiastic welcome from the population.

One result of Cyrus' successful Babylonian campaign was to prove most dangerous for the Greeks. The Syrian cities of Tyre and Sidon, after waiting for a victor to emerge from the contest between Cyrus and Nabu-Naid, submitted to the Persians and put their fleets at Cyrus' disposal. The Persians now controlled the whole of the eastern Mediterranean seaboard and, with the help of their Phoenician allies, could reach the Ionian islands and the Greek mainland.

However, future developments in this direction were not to worry Cyrus. The great conqueror who had acquired for his people a vast empire in the space of twenty years was killed in 530 BC during a frontier skirmish against the Massegetae, a nomadic tribe led by a woman. Cyrus' son Cambyses succeeded him as king and ruled for eight years. The whole of his short reign was spent in conquering Egypt—a task which he had successfully carried out by 522 BC.

Thus, the last threat to Persian domination of the East was disposed of. Herodotus portrays Cambyses as a cruel tyrant who rode roughshod over the Egyptians' religious sensibilities by killing the sacred bull of Apis, but such an act seems quite contrary to the usual Persian policy of religious toleration, and the story is probably a piece of later Greek propaganda. Cambyses was returning from Egypt and had reached Canaan when he heard that his brother, Smerdis, had recovered and proclaimed himself king. According to Herodotus Cambyses committed suicide when he heard this news, but it seems more likely that he was killed by someone in his retinue who favoured Smerdis. The story Herodotus got hold of would appear to have been a fabrication put out later to cover up the traces of the murder.

Whatever the truth about Cambyses' death, Smerdis himself did not remain king for long. Darius, the son of Hystaspes, who had been Cyrus' satrap of Parthia, was a young man of twenty-eight in 522 BC. He was a member of a collateral branch of the Persian royal house, and he had gone with Cambyses to Egypt as his personal spear-bearer. On Cambyses' death, Darius moved against Smerdis, killed him and proclaimed himself king. The ancient Greek authorities —Herodotus, Xenophon and Ctesias—all tell conflicting stories of how Darius usurped the Persian throne. Darius himself, in the official Persian account—the inspiration of Behistun—seems to have been guilty of simplifying his difficulties.

The details will probably always remain in dispute, but the general picture is clear. When Cambyses died revolts broke out in various parts of the empire as the individual satraps set themselves up as claimants to the Achaemenid throne. Darius was only one of several contestants and it took him two years of hard fighting before he could safely claim that he was the sole ruler.

He now turned to the task of reconstruction, and showed himself to be an outstanding legislator and administrator. During his reign Achaemenid power and wealth grew to unprecedented heights and the first clashes between the mainland Greeks and Persians took place. It is worth examining in some detail the colossus against which the Greeks pitted themselves.

The subject races

In the opening chorus of Aeschylus' prize-winning play, the *Persae*, which was produced at Athens in 472 BC eight years after the Battle of Salamix, the Persian elders, left behind by Xerxes as his regents, give a long catalogue of the Persian troops who have marched to conquer Greece. One by one they list the contingents which have been gathered together from all quarters of the far-flung empire, and recount the names of their aristocratic generals: Artaphernes, Mesabazus and Astaspes. In this fine chorus Aeschylus is indulging in patriotic self-congratulation, for most of his audience must have consisted of the very men who had fought and defeated this impressive army at Salamis and Plataea. At the same time, however, he is stating a simple historical fact: the Persian Empire was vast and made up of very diverse peoples. Indeed, the Greeks who fought them were probably not aware of quite how large were Persian resources of manpower and money.

The Persian Empire stretched from Libya in the west to the borders of India in the East, and from the northern shores of the Black Sea to the southern tip of Arabia. Within this huge area (approximately 5,000,000 square miles) lived a teeming mass of people who differed widely in religion and social customs. There were primitive marsh dwellers from Egypt, complacent money-lenders from Babylon, spice merchants from Arabia, Phoenician sailors, Jewish mercenaries and Ionian philosophers.

All these disparate groups paid allegiance to one man—the Great King. It would have been impossible to rule these vast numbers through a system of centralized government, and the Achaemenids never tried to do so. They adopted from the Assyrians the system of dividing up their empire into independently administered provinces.

At the height of their power there were twenty-nine such provinces, which were called satrapies. Each satrapy was ruled by a satrap, the title meaning 'protector of the kingdom'. Officially the satraps were provincial governors responsible to the Great King for what they did, but in practise they enjoyed the status of independent monarchs, surrounded by courtiers, devising and carrying out their own foreign policies (sometimes in conflict with one another), and with the power of life and death over their subjects.

There were, however, certain checks designed to prevent a satrap from becoming dangerously independent. The satrap's secretary, his chief financial officer and the commander of the main garrison within his satrapy, were all under the direct control of the king. They were appointed by the king, and were answerable only to him for their actions. Moreover, the satrapy and its affairs were inspected by officials sent by the king, who were known as the 'king's eyes'. A satrap had two main tasks: in time of war he had to levy troops for the king and lead them himself; in peacetime he had to see that the king's laws were obeyed and that the people paid their taxes. Each satrapy was assessed according to its wealth, and had to pay its tax at the beginning of the year.

The amounts involved were enormous. It is not surprising, therefore, that the Persians could afford to dictate, to a great extent, the course of events in Greek politics, by paying out an endless stream of bribes. However, these vast riches had inherent disadvantages. A theory has been put forward that the Persian Empire fell easily to Alexander the Great because it was overtaxed and there is no doubt that high taxes caused much suffering and discontent among the subject peoples of the Persian Empire.

The root of the trouble lay in what was done with the taxes once they had been collected. When the gold and silver tribute arrived at Persepolis, it was melted down into ingots and stored in the king's treasury indefinitely. By not putting it back into circulation the Persian kings caused widespread deflation which got worse as less and less gold and silver was left in the empire outside their treasury. When a farmer's taxes were due and he had no money with which to pay them, he was compelled to go to a money-lender and mortgage his land and slaves. The rate of interest at which he borrowed money was often as high as forty percent and so it was virtually impossible for him to regain possession of his land. By the time of Artaxerxes' reign revolts in the satrapies against overtaxation and its pernicious consequences were frequent, and there can be no doubt that it was this aspect of the Achaemenid administration which was its gravest defect.

Palaces and armies

The Persian army against which the Greeks fought twice in ten years was a microcosm of the Persian Empire. The only first-rate troops in the Persian army were 'the Immortals' and the cavalry, which was made up of the Iranian aristocracy. The Persian soldiers, most of whom came straight from their farms when they were needed, were badly armed and trained. Their function was to crush the enemy with the sheer weight of their numbers. When they were sent into battle against the heavily armoured hoplites, they were cut down in their hundreds.

Above, relief from the royal palace at Susa of two crowned sphinxes, 404–358 BC; they are seated under a winged disc, symbol of Ahura Mazda (wise lord), god of ancient Iran. Musée du Louvre, Paris.

Left, the ruins of the palace at the festival city of Persepolis from the porch of Xerxes.

Opposite, details from the processional reliefs at Persepolis, built by Darius I as a monument to his own power; the city was destroyed by Alexander the Great in 331 BC. Ny Carlsberg Glypthotek, Copenhagen.

The 'Immortals', so called because their strength was always kept up to 10,000, were a hand-picked regiment of heavy infantry. In peacetime they acted as the king's palace guards. They were armed with spears, bows and shields. The amount of empty wine bottles found in their barrack rooms at Susa confirms Herodotus' information that they were given special privileges, even being allowed to bring with them when campaigning their own personal food train, their concubines and servants. They were recruited exclusively from among the Medes, Persians and Elamites, and competition to join their ranks was always fierce. They can be seen mounting guard in the glazed reliefs from the palace at Susa; their hair is filleted with bands, their quivers decorated with tassels and they stand rigidly to attention with their spears in front of them.

Just as 'the Immortals' were set apart from the rest of the Persian army, so the Achaemenids and their fellow Iranian aristocrats ruled over their subjects from their various palaces in a state of isolated glory. Cyrus had three palaces: Pasargadae (his original home), Ecbatana and Babylon. Darius was responsible for building two more—Susa and Persepolis. The latter—the most luxurious—was begun by Darius in a valley near Pasargadae and completed by Xerxes, and remains the best preserved. When Alexander sacked and burnt the palace, following a drunken banquet, the greater part of it, which was built of cedar wood, was destroyed.

However, the monumental gateways, terraces and staircases, which were of stone, survived, together with the clay tablets of the royal archives which were baked hard by the flames. Abandoned by Greeks and Persians, these remains were left undisturbed for the first curious travellers to discover more than 1,000 years later. The most impressive of the monumental remains at Persepolis is the Apadana ('the hall of columns'), which stands at the northern end of the palace. Access to the hall was through terraced stairways. On these stairways are carved the beautiful reliefs which have made the building so famous.

The figures on these reliefs—Persian noblemen, guards from the 'Immortals' and tribute bearers from every satrapy mounting the stairs with their New Year offerings for the Great King—are not as elastic as those relief figures executed by Greek craftsmen, but their very rigidity and the arrogance of their posture convey a perfect picture of the grandeur and ceremony of the Achaemenid court. At the banquet to which these stone guests are advancing the King would eat apart from them. When he appeared before them, they had to prostrate themselves on the ground, at the same time keeping their hands inside their sleeves to avert any suspicion of an attempt at assassination. If a guest walked, even by accident, on the rug before the king's throne, he was executed.

It is not surprising that the Greeks reacted strongly against Persian luxury when it went hand in hand with such cruelty and servility. To them the Achaemenid kings were despots and they preferred to lead a simple life and be free, rather than abase themselves before one man and be pampered. The root of

all Greek hostility to the Persians lay in this simple ideological difference. However, Greco-Persian disputes usually presented themselves in more concrete terms: the Athenians fought at Marathon to defend their city against an invader. It would not have mattered whether the invader was a Persian, an Egyptian or a Gaul. Nevertheless, behind these obvious motives there was always the ideological division which gave added fire to Greek resistance.

Basically, the Greeks were politically far more advanced than the Persians. After 400 years of slow, painful development they wanted the freedom to make decisions for themselves, even if these decisions seemed wrong or misguided or were not accepted by their fellow Greeks. They did not want to have government thrust upon them by one distant, all-powerful man. It seemed better to die than to find themselves depicted carrying tribute up the staircase of the Apadana of the Great King. The Ionian revolt of 499 BC was the first instance of the Greek resistance to tyranny.

The first philosophers

In the seventh century BC an ideological division between Greek autonomy and Persian absolutism could never have existed, for the simple reason that the Greeks at that time did not have the ability to make abstract generalizations and thus establish political principles. By the fifth century BC, however, conceptual thinking had been born and tempered into a serviceable weapon by men from that very part of the Greek world which Persia was to rule—Ionia. The first Greek philosophers—Thales, Anaximander and Pythagoras—known as the pre-Socratics, were almost exclusively Ionians. They were not concerned with the usual subjects of

philosophy (morality, ethics and epistemology) but with the formulation of mathematical, physical and astronomical laws.

Living in the eastern Mediterranean they had access to, and were able to immerse themselves in, the accumulated knowledge of the Babylonian and Egyptian astronomers and mathematicians, whose achievements were considerable. Men such as Thales of Miletus could study under Egyptian teachers and amaze their fellow Greeks with the application of their knowledge. For example, Thales predicted accurately the year of a solar eclipse, but the real credit for this must go to the eastern astrologers who collected the data on which he based his prediction.

Pythagoras was the first Greek to recognize that the morning and evening stars were identical, although this had been known to the Babylonians for 1,500 years. The originality of these first Greek philosophers lay in their attempts to try to arrange the knowledge they had obtained from the East into universal theories, and to establish principles which covered all their facts and at the same time explained them.

Thus Pythagoras, knowing that Egyptian engineers had constructed a triangle with sides in the ratio 3:4:5 in order to make a right-angle, formulated his theory of the square on the hypotenuse, which enabled him to construct a right-angled triangle of any size. This desire to formulate general principles led Thales to ask the question which later occupied the attention of nearly all the pre-Socratics: what was the basic substance of the universe? In short, what was the nature of matter or being? Among the Greeks the men who came nearest to a correct answer were Leucippus and Democritus who formulated a rudimentary atomic theory. Their theory, however, was only one among many. Some philosophers stated that the basic substance of the universe was

water, others fire, air, and earth. Some declared that matter was always changing, others that it was static.

It is not surprising that the pre-Socratics were wrong in many of the answers they suggested. In all their investigations they were hampered by their lack of a scientific vocabulary, and their disinclination to verify their theories by practical experiments. Their great contribution was in the realm of pure thought. By asking the questions they did and then attempting to answer them in their heads, they developed, for the first time an ability to think in general, abstract terms.

This was a development of tremendous importance, and perhaps the greatest achievement of the Greek race. Its application resulted in the discovery of history by Herodotus and of medicine by Hippocrates of Cos. In particular, the myths which men had previously used to explain all the frightening aspects of their world could now be demolished. To the Greeks the myth of the Persian monarchy, shrouded in its pomp and ceremony, was not acceptable.

The colonies in revolt

The city which took the lead in the revolt of the Ionian cities against Darius in 499 BC was Miletus. In 511 BC Darius had removed the tyrant of Miletus, the devious Histiaeus, to an honourable exile at Susa. His place was taken by his son-in-law Anaxagorus—an equally devious man. Anaxagoras was the prime mover of the revolt. Whether he thought that the suspicious gaze of Artaphernes, the satrap of Sardis, rested on him, and he wanted to stir up trouble for its own sake, or whether he was a disinterested patriot is not known. However, it was he who called the Ionians together for a

Above, soldiers carrying spears, a stairway relief from Persepolis.

Above left, the ruins of Persepolis.

Opposite below, relief from Persepolis depicting a lion attacking a bull.

Opposite, relief from a stairway at Persepolis of two columns of soldiers in procession.

council, and who played on their grievances until they rebelled.

The reason for the discontent of the Ionians was they that they were ruled by puppet tyrants appointed by the Persians. They felt that they had developed beyond such a form of government which was only for the unthinking masses. Hence, when the revolt broke out the first step the Ionians took was to kill or expel their tyrants. Aristagoras had taken the precaution of resigning as tyrant of Miletus. The other grievances of the Ionians can only be guessed at.

In 514 BC Darius had attacked the European Scythians who lived on the northern shores of the Black Sea. During this campaign the Samians and Milesians had been forcibly enlisted into the Persian army to build and guard the bridges needed for Darius' advance over the Bosporus and Ister. They must have resented this interruption in their lives, and at the same time they must have realized, for the first time, what their potential fighting strength was when they were united. Though Darius was forced to retreat from the Scythian plains, he left Persian troops in occupation of the coast.

The presence of Persians in this area would not have been welcomed by the Milesians. Before this intrusion they had enjoyed a monopoly of trade with the Scythian nomads who wanted luxury goods such as golden goblets and bowls from the Greeks for use in their macabre burial ceremonies. Other Ionian cities had apparently been losing their markets to Phoenician traders. Discontent among the merchants, who were usually tolerant of Persian rule as

THE FORMATION OF THE PERSIAN EMPIRE

Date	Achaemenid rulers	Persian conquests	Greece and Rome	Date	Achaemenid rulers	Persian conquests	Greece and Rome
550	Cyrus II deposes Astyages Foundation of the Persian Empire	Assyria Sardis and Lydia	Rome under Etruscan rule	510		Thrace, Aegean Islands, northern India	Roman Republic
		Babylon		500		Revolt of the Ionians First Persian War	
540		Eastern Iran					
			Peisistratus	490			
530	Cambyses succeeds Cyrus	Egypt			Death of Darius		
			Cleisthenes	480			
	Darius I						
520		General uprising in the Empire Darius suppresses the revolt					
			Fall of the Pisistratids				

long as it did not interfere with their business, was fanned into a flame by the land-owning aristocrats, who were always hostile to Persia.

Before making any open move against Artaphernes the Ionians tried to enlist the help of their countrymen on the mainland. Anaxagoras headed a diplomatic mission sent to find allies. The Ionians did not lack arguments to persuade the Greeks to join them. In 512 BC Darius had invaded Thrace and Macedonia, and had brought them under Persian rule. It must have been obvious to the Greeks that this campaign was only the first stage of a Persian scheme which aimed at conquering the whole of Greece, and thus finally solving the problem of the Greek frontier.

To make an early stand in Ionia, on Persia's own doorstep, seemed good political sense. Unfortunately the Greeks paid attention only to their immediate, short-term interests, and Anaxagoras' arguments went unheeded. Only the Euboeans and the Athenians agreed to send small contingents consisting of five and twenty ships respectively. Athens answered this appeal because Miletus was a daughter-city, and because Artaphernes was championing Hippias, the deposed tyrant, in his plans to return to Athens. Sparta, the strongest military power and the head of the loose alliance of Dorian states called the Peloponnesian League, refused to send help.

Herodotus relates that when Anaxagoras was trying to bribe Cleomenes, the progressive Spartan king, to change his mind, it was the latter's young daughter who spoke up as her father wavered, and warned him against the stranger who offered him gold. Thus Spartan education and conservatism triumphed, and Anaxagoras left empty-handed. In fact, Cleomenes may well have wanted to help the Ionians, but did not feel sure that he could win over the Spartans and their allies to his point of view, and did not care to risk his prestige and authority in trying to do so.

The Ionian revolt began well. Landing at Ephesus, the allied army, which included the Athenians, marched inland, besieged Artaphernes inside the citadel at Sardis, and burnt the surrounding town. However, they were not able to hold their position and retreated to Ephesus where they were defeated by Persian levies from beyond the river Halys. After this foray, which had met with mixed success, the Athenians, hearing that war had broken out between Athens and Aegina (possibly fostered by the Persians), abandoned the allies and sailed for home. The place of the Athenians was soon taken, however, by Greeks from the Hellespont, the Bosporus and Caria, whose previous hesitations about resorting to rebellion had been dispelled by the news of the destruction of Sardis. Most important of all, the Greek towns in Cyprus, under the leadership of the brother of the deposed tyrant of Salamis, joined the rebels.

The Ionians immediately sailed to Cyprus and defeated the Persian fleet which was

patrolling the coast. They did not, however, prevent a Persian army being ferried over from Cilicia. The Persians soon reached Salamis and began to besiege it. The Ionians refused to land their troops, and during a hard-fought battle before Salamis some of the Cypriots defected, and the town, which was the centre of resistance on the island, fell to the Persians. When they had received this news the Ionians sailed away, and Cyprus was soon under Persian control once more.

The tide of events now began to turn against the Ionians. While the allied fleet had been away in Cyprus Persian troops had been active in the North. One by one the cities of the Hellespont were captured, and the Carians were defeated in two pitched battles. Clazomenae and Cyme fell, and Anaxagoras, in despair, fled to Thrace, where he was soon killed. The Persians closed in inexorably on Miletus, the ringleader of the revolt. Late in 494 BC the city was captured and razed to the ground. The men were killed, and the women and children taken as slaves to Susa. With Miletus gone, the remaining, isolated cities and islands which were still under arms fell one by one, and the Ionian revolt ended in a wave of savage Persian reprisals.

The Persians had possessed an overwhelming advantage in their inexhaustible supplies of manpower and their consequent ability to open a front wherever they liked. However, the real reason for the failure of the Ionians was lack of unity. They had formed a federation and had minted coins to commemorate it, but in the last resort they saved their own skins. The Persians were able to divide them by the use of bribes and then pick them off individually. Undoubtedly the first round in the fight between Persia and Greece had been won by Darius.

The continuation of the struggle could not be long delayed. Darius had been so incensed by the burning of Sardis by the Athenians that, according to Herodotus, a slave was given the sole duty of intoning to the king every day, 'master remember the Athenians!' By burning Sardis the Athenians had in fact presented Darius with a pretext for attacking mainland Greece: an unjustified invasion of his territory would have to be punished. Preparations for this punishment could now go forward.

The first invasion

Although the Persians punished the Ionian cities severely, they did try to remedy one of the political grievances which had caused the revolt. Instead of reinstating tyrants as before 499 BC, Darius instructed his son-in-law, Mardonius, who had been appointed commander of the Persian armies in the west in 492 BC, to allow the Ionians to establish democracies in their cities. No doubt Darius hoped that this concession to the Greeks in the east would win him support among the democrats of the mainland. In fact, he severely underestimated the antipathy of the ordinary Greek towards the Persians. Although some states, notably Aegina, submitted to Darius, when Persian envoys arrived at Athens and Sparta demanding earth and water they were thrown down wells and told they could find what they were looking for there. In the face of Persian aggression the Greeks, for the first and only time in their history, managed to bury their political differences, and presented a united front to the enemy.

The Persians did not become completely aware of this solidarity until after Marathon. Hoping to weaken the morale of the Greeks and give Persian sympathizers in Greece time to do their work, Mardonius began a

slow advance towards northern Greece through Macedonia, protected by a large Persian fleet offshore. The expedition was not a success. In a storm off Mount Athos, 300 ships and 20,000 sailors were lost. Moreover, Mardonius' army was severely mauled by the Brygi, a Phrygian tribe, who lay in the path of the Persian advance. Mardonius withdrew to Persia, and was relieved of his command.

Darius put Datis, a Median general, and Artaphernes, Darius' nephew, in command of a new army and changed his tactics. His plan was to send his fleet across the Aegean,

hopping from island to island, and to attack Athens and Euboea directly. Until the Persians reached Euboea all went well. Landing on the island they besieged Eretria, which was betrayed to them after a week. The Persians razed the city, burnt the temples and deported the population.

This harsh treatment was a gross blunder. Any Athenians who had been thinking of 'medising' (collaborating with the Persians) quickly saw where their best interests lay. It was, therefore, an extremely angry and united citizen army that met the Persians when they attempted to land on the east coast of Attica at Marathon. The Athenians fought at Marathon alone apart from the help provided by 1,000 Plataeans. The Spartans, to whom they had sent requests for help, could not for religious reasons leave Sparta before the full moon, and they arrived at Athens after the battle. It is not certain whether this was a ploy by the Spartans to await the outcome of the struggle between Persia and Athens or a genuine excuse, but the latter is more likely.

Demaratus, the pro-Persian Spartan king, had been expelled from Sparta by Cleomenes and, during the second invasion, it was the Spartans who led the Greeks against the invaders. It was unfortunate for the Spartans that their religious conservatism prevented them from taking part in the battle, for the Athenians gained enormous prestige by this victory, and from that time forward were rivals to Sparta for the military leadership of Greece.

The Battle of Marathon itself was a simple affair, although there was some trouble among the ten Athenian generals before Miltiades, the most able, took command. The plain of Marathon runs gently up from the sea to some low hills. It was in these hills that Miltiades drew up his hoplites. When the Persian army had landed the Athenians charged them at the run. The Persian centre resisted the impetus of this charge and even managed to break through the Greek ranks, but their success was short-lived. The hoplites on the left and right wings smashed through the Persian wings and, swinging round, they caught the Persian centre in a pincer movement from the sides and rear.

The Persian army fled to its ships, and in the ensuing rout seven of them were burnt and destroyed by the Greeks. Athenian casualties were surprisingly light. Only 192 men were killed; the Persians lost 6,000. Yet in spite of this resounding, but unexpected, victory, the Athenians could not rest. As the Persians withdrew from the shore, a signal was flashed to them off a polished shield from the hills to the south. The message was clear: Athens was undefended. The Persians had only to sail to the Piraeus and the city was theirs. Fortunately, the Athenians also saw the signal, and immediately marched back to the city. When the Persian fleet, after rounding Cape Sunium hove to off Piraeus, they saw the victorious Athenians waiting for them. Datis realized that this particular piece of treachery had failed, and after a few days he sailed back to Persia. The first Persian invasion had been repulsed.

There remains the great question: who flashed the shield? Traditionally the Alcmaeonids were blamed, but this does not seem likely. The most probable culprits were supporters of the ex-tyrant, Hippias, who was in Datis' retinue and was counting on being reinstated as tyrant once the city fell. The Alcmaeonids, who had driven him out in 510 BC, had the most to fear from him, and therefore cannot have been eager for a Persian victory. Their name was probably linked much later with the incident as a piece of propaganda designed to discredit Pericles, whose father had married an Alcmaeonid girl.

This alleged sympathy between Greek democrats and the Persians during the early period of the Persian wars has been overemphasized, and is made all the more improbable by later events. The victory at Marathon gave Greece a breathing space. Athens, at least, prepared for the second blow which it knew must come.

Below, sculpted head of a griffin from Persepolis.

Left, limestone head of a king, thought to be Darius.

Opposite top, rock relief commemorating one of Darius' victories, sixth century BC.

Opposite bottom, relief showing Darius as a 'superman' fighting a monster.

Themistocles

The ten years which elapsed between the first and second Persian invasions were dominated at Athens by the rise to power of one man, who eclipsed the political power of the Alcmaeonids and, single-handed, laid the foundations of Athen's future empire. This man was Themistocles. The historian Plutarch says that Themistocles was a raffish aristocrat (*i.e.*, a poor one) from southern Attica, who had the common touch, and was popular with ordinary people. Thucydides paints a more finely drawn and complimentary portrait.

According to him Themistocles was quick-witted, farsighted and deep-thinking a man who could produce an intelligent solution to any problem that was put to him. It is extraordinary that Thucydides, who is the most reserved of historians, should devote a whole chapter to a single man (as he does to Themistocles), but when he writes of him in these terms one can be sure that he is talking about a genius.

Before Marathon, Themistocles was a relatively unknown politician. However, in 490 BC he had had the good sense to side with Miltiades in the quarrel as to who should have overall command of the Athenian army during the campaign. After Marathon, Miltiades was supreme at Athens, and much of his glory and prestige was reflected on to Themistocles, who had supported him. When Miltiades died shortly afterwards, discredited after leading a disastrous expedition to Paros, Themistocles was one of the main contenders for his position. The political fight Themistocles now entered was very different from the battles of the days before Cleisthenes. Party politics as they had been conducted then no longer existed. Since Cleisthenes' reforms and, especially after Marathon, when the people finally proved their worth, there was, effectively, only one party at Athens—the *demos*. The main political issues centred on foreign policy; what should Athens' attitude to Persia be? Themistocles saw that the first Persian invasion was only a temporary setback for Darius, and that it would be followed by a second one. He therefore devoted all his efforts to urging hostility towards Persia and building up Athenian military strength.

This was a policy which incidentally, but fortunately for Themistocles, reflected the general feeling among the ordinary Athenians, who stood to win nothing from Persian rule. Domestic politics, for want of any clear-cut social or constitutional issues, consisted of the efforts of the various politicians to woo and win the support of the *demos*. Success in this depended very much on a man's foreign policy. The main opponents of Themistocles—Megacles, Aristides (nicknamed 'the just') and Xanthippus (Pericles' father)—were all men who belonged to, or were linked by marriage with, the Alcmaeonid clan. Since the Alcmaeonids, whether justly or unjustly, were suspected of being pro-Persian, Themistocles held an advantage over these men.

In 483 BC a rich vein of silver was discovered in the city mines at Laurium. Themistocles defeated a proposal by Aristides that this windfall should be divided as a bounty among the population, and persuaded the Athenians to use it to build a fleet of 200 ships. This was a notable political victory, which had far-reaching consequences. In the first place, Themistocles' popularity increased among the *thetes*—the labourers who not only did most of the work involved in the building of these ships, but

also, because they were the most numerous and to row a ship requires no armour, provided the great bulk of the sailors who manned them. From then on the *thetes* played an important part in the Athenian military machine (previously a privilege held by the hoplite classes and above).

It seems certain that they repaid Themistocles, the man responsible for their new status, with their support in the assembly. The building of an Athenian fleet at the suggestion of Themistocles marked the beginning of Athens' rise to power and prosperity. It was this fleet which played the decisive role in defeating the Persians at Salamis, and on which the power of the Athenian Empire was later based.

The suggestion has been put forward that the sudden creation of a fleet manned mainly by the *thetes* resulted in immediate demands by them for more political power. However, this was certainly not true when the fleet was first built. The *thetes* as such never constituted a political pressure group with radical democratic tendencies. However, the fact that Themistocles did gain popular support is confirmed by the action he proceeded to take against his political rivals. One of Cleisthenes' reforms had been the institution of ostracism, which was a kind of impeachment. By this procedure the Athenians could, once a year, send any politician into exile for ten years. The assembly had to vote, first, that an ostracism

should take place. After that the citizens voted against the man they wanted to see go by scratching his name on a potsherd (*ostrakon*). There were usually two candidates for this dubious honour, and the man who received the most votes had to leave the city, though no special opprobrium was attached to his name.

It was claimed that Cleisthenes devised this procedure to avoid a recurrence of tyranny, but this does not seem likely, as a real tyrant would have rode roughshod over any such system. Ostracism was used, in practise, as a means of resolving a deadlock in policy between two men, and as a way of avoiding civil strife—the dread of all Greek cities. The long delay between its being put on the statute books by Cleisthenes in 508 BC and its first use in 487 BC suggests a lack of confidence on the part of the *demos*. After Marathon and the building of the fleet, this lack of confidence had been dispelled. The *demos* had saved the city and it was the decisive force in the city's politics.

Themistocles obviously felt sure that the people would support him in challenging the Alcmaeonids to a series of trials by ostracism. In a short space of time Megacles, Aristides, and Xanthippus were ostracized. Themistocles was left the dominent figure at Athens. Although he himself was ostracized in 474 BC he was to use his period of power to good effect, both for Athens and for the rest of Greece.

Xerxes invades

In 486 BC Darius died at the age of sixty-four, his ambition to conquer Greece in person unfulfilled. He was succeeded by his son Xerxes. The new King of Kings was a young man eager to prove himself in war, and it did not require much persuasion from his experienced general, Mardonius, to make him decide to continue with his father's projected invasion. Luckily for the Greeks, just before Darius' death the satrapy of Egypt had rebelled in protest against the imposition of a new batch of taxes designed to pay for the forthcoming war against Greece.

It was not until 484 BC that order was restored, and Xerxes could safely turn to Greece. This time the Persians intended to make no mistakes, and they planned a slow parallel advance down from the north by the army and the fleet. To avoid a repetition of the naval disaster off Mount Athos, they spent three years digging a canal through the narrow promontory, so that their fleet could bypass the dangerous headland.

In 480 BC, after a delay of six years, Xerxes finally gathered his army together at Troy and gave the order for them to march over the Hellespont into Europe on a bridge of boats. Several Greek stories about Xerxes and his army need be discounted. First, it is highly unlikely that the Persian army numbered more than 1,000,000 men, as Herodotus reports. The real figure is more likely to have been about 180,000—three divisions of the Persian armed forces. It was only natural, once the invasion had failed, for the Greeks to exaggerate Persian numbers. Similarly, the story of Xerxes lashing the sea to punish Poseidon, after his first bridge across the Hellespont had been broken up by a storm, is most improbable.

Once they were safe, the Greeks depicted Xerxes as a sacrilegious enemy of heaven who was finally punished by the gods. In the *Persae* Aeschylus dwells on the destruction of Greek temples by the Persians and the terrible price they paid for this sacrilege. The implicit and satisfying corollary of such religious propaganda was that the Greeks were the favourites of the gods. The blacker they depicted Xerxes, the purer they became. For a true portrait of Xerxes it is necessary to turn to Persian records, and these show that in his youth, before he became enmeshed in the stifling suspicions of harem intrigues, he was a vigorous and successful king. In 480 BC, however, as he marched through Macedonia surrounded by his 'immortals', he was heading for his first and only serious military defeat.

The Greeks, as the menace from the north loomed near, met at the Isthmus of Corinth under the leadership of Sparta to discuss their strategy. The situation appeared to be very unfavourable to the Greeks. All the cities of Thessaly and Boeotia, including powerful Thebes, had already submitted to the Persians. The Athenians, who had received a typically cryptic message from the oracle at Delphi to 'trust themselves to the wooden walls', had retired (following the interpretation and advice of Themistocles) to the island of Salamis in their newly built ships. The members of the Peloponnesian League, who formed the most composite and most powerful group among the allies, wanted, for both selfish and strategic reasons, to make a stand at the Isthmus of Corinth—the gateway to the Peloponnese. The Aeginetans, Megarians and Athenians, whose cities were on the northern side of the isthmus and would have been left defenceless, were naturally opposed to this. A respite was gained when the Spartans agreed, since the defences at the isthmus were not completed, to send forward a force under King Leonidas to Thessaly to delay the Persian advance.

The first clashes of the war were glorious but inconclusive. In Phocia, at the narrow and virtually impregnable pass of Thermopylae, Leonidas and his Spartans were betrayed and forced to face heavy Persian attacks from the front and the rear. They were killed to a man after inflicting serious losses on the Persians which were quite out of proportion to their numbers. The allied fleet (which was predominantly Athenian) attacked the Persians off Cape Artemisium in an inconclusive naval engagement, which was broken off by bad weather. The allied ships, hearing that the pass at Thermopylae had been forced, retired to Salamis. The Persian army and fleet moved on to sack Athens.

The Battle of Salamis nearly did not take place. The Spartans and the other Peloponnesians were eager to retire to the isthmus. They were prevented from doing this and, through the ingenuity and good sense of Themistocles, were forced to fight at Salamis. He realized that the Persian fleet had to be destroyed. As long as it was abroad in force the Persian army could be ferried past the isthmus and could attack the allied army in the rear, as had happened at Thermopylae. He also realized that this would be the last chance to face the Persians at sea with a full allied fleet. Once the Peloponnesians retired the precarious Greek unity would dissolve, and the Persians would pick the cities off one by one. In addition, the narrowness of the straits between Salamis and the Attic coast, where the allied fleet lay at anchor, would force the light Persian ships to bunch together (at the expense of manoeuvrability) and this would favour the heavier Greek ships.

By 21 September the Persian fleet was lying off the eastern exit from the straits. During that night the Peloponnesian admirals were deliberating whether to slip away through the channel to the west (which was still not guarded by the Persians), when Themistocles made his decisive move and left them with no choice. Posing as a traitor and counting on Xerxes' desire to force a quick and spectacular victory, he sent a message to the king telling him that the Greeks were about to sail away. Xerxes swallowed the bait. An Egyptian squadron was immediately sent to block the western channel and the trap was sprung to the satisfaction of Themistocles. The Greeks now had to fight their way out of the straits.

The next morning Xerxes stationed himself on a hill above the Bay of Salamis to watch his fleet move in and destroy the Greeks. He was disappointed. The Greeks fought with the desperation of trapped men and, as Themistocles had calculated, the Persian ships crowded into the straits and were battered to pieces by their heavier opponents. Although the Ionians—Persia's allies—broke through the Spartan squadron, the Athenians and Aeginetans shattered the Persian line and the invading fleet was routed. The Persians lost 200 ships and the allies only forty. Moreover, a contingent of Persian troops which had been put on to the islet of Psyttelia in the middle of the straits, to pick off Greek survivors, was wiped out by Aristides and a hoplite force, before the horrified gaze of Xerxes.

Perhaps the most important result of Salamis was its effect on Xerxes, who completely lost his head. His first move was to execute several Phoenician captains on a charge of cowardice. The surviving Phoenician and Egyptian ships promptly sailed away. Even at this juncture Xerxes need not have retreated. He still had his army intact, and time and dissensions among the Greeks would have worked in his favour. He was, however, dispirited and felt cheated of his personal victory. Moreover, he was terrified that the Greek fleet would sail to the Hellespont and destroy his bridge—a course of action from which, in fact, Themistocles had great difficulty in dissuading the allies. He therefore retired by land to Sardis, taking two infantry divisions with him. Mardonius was left with one division to winter in friendly Boeotia and to complete the conquest—if he could.

Mardonius had at his disposal an army of good-quality Iranian troops who still outnumbered the allied armies. His supplies were secured by a Persian army in Thrace under Artabazus and another in Ionia commanded by Tigranes. The Peloponnesians had retired to their cities after Salamis and there was a good chance that their natural dilatoriness would keep them there, thus isolating Athens and causing a fatal division between the allies.

At the beginning of 479 BC, in an effort to cause such a split. Mardonius offered terms to the Athenians: the status of an independent ally and generous reparation for the damage done to their property. The offer was rejected. In reply, Mardonius invaded Attica, and the Athenians withdrew once again to Salamis. From this position of strength Mardonius repeated his terms, and again the Athenians refused to treat with him. One unfortunate man who suggested discussing the terms was stoned to death

together with his family. Such an action suggests growing weakness and hysteria rather than solidarity. The situation was now desperate. The Spartans were procrastinating as usual and seemed unlikely to leave the Peloponnese. While Mardonius' overtures were being rejected, an Athenian embassy was in the Peloponnese desperately trying to persuade the Spartans to march against Mardonius. Finally, the efforts of a Tegean embassy, and the threat from the Athenians that Athens would accept Mardonius' terms, persuaded the Spartans to act. Under the regent Pausanias, their army set out for Boeotia.

This news convinced Mardonius that further diplomatic activity was useless and, after ravaging Attica, he withdrew to his camp near Thebes. The allied army under the supreme command of Pausanias moved slowly north through Attica, and finally came into contact with the Persians outside the town of Plataea in Boeotia. After an initial skirmish in which the Persian cavalry commander, Matistius, was killed, the two armies took up their lines and remained facing on the lower slopes of Mount Cithaeron. Neither wanted to attack, since the omens on both sides predicted victory for the army which remained on the defensive.

That evening the allied generals decided to retire from their position, since their troops lacked food and water, and the Persian cavalry were cutting off the supply trains attempting to get through the passes. During the night the great bulk of the allies began to withdraw, but they did this in such confusion and so slowly, that by dawn they were still not far from their original positions. The Spartans, however, at the instigation of an unruly captain, had not moved.

When Mardonius saw them isolated before him and beginning to turn and move off, he threw caution to the winds and sent in his troops at the run without even bothering to draw them up properly. The lightly-armed Persian troops failed to break the Spartan ranks, and they were checked and held. News that a battle had brokem out quickly reached the allies and they started back to help the Spartans.

The Athenians were delayed by contingents of Ionian Greeks, and the Megarians were turned away by Theban cavalry. By the time the Corinthians and Athenians reached the Spartans the Persian line had been broken. Mardonius was dead, and the surviving Persians had withdrawn in confusion to their stockaded camp. This did not long resist the combined onslaught of the allies and the last Persian invaders were massacred. This was a great victory, won almost single-handed by the Spartans. It did much to restore Spartan prestige, which had recently been eclipsed by the Athenians' exploits at Marathon and Salamis.

Immediately after the battle, while their troops were still looting the Persian baggage train, the allied generals met, at Aristides'

suggestion to organize the future of their alliance. This was ratified, as was Spartan leadership, and it was decided to carry the war into Ionia and remove for good the threat of a Persian attack. This task the Hellenic League, as the new organization was known, was to perform successfully, but not under Spartan leadership.

The Delian League

Even before Plataea and the subsequent formation of the Hellenic League, the Greeks had struck in Ionia. At Cape Mycale on Samos, in 479 BC, an allied fleet, with the help of dissident Ionians, attacked the beached Persian fleet, destroyed it, and then proceeded to annihilate the Persian division under Tigranes, which had been guarding the fleet. This victory was perhaps more important than Plataea. It was certainly the decisive blow which persuaded Artabazus to withdraw his troops from Thrace rather than advance into Greece and take up Mardonius' uncompleted task.

The Persians had lost two of their best divisions, in two years and a great many ships and their crews. The allied navies now moved into the Ionian Sea to press their advantage. In 478 BC Pausanias, the victor of Plataea, was sent to take command of the league forces in the area. In the one year he spent in the east Pausanias was apparently extremely successful. He liberated the Greek cities of Cyprus, and captured the strategically important town of Byzantium. The islands of Khios, Lesbos and Samos, and the towns of Miletus, Abydos, and Cyzicus all regained their independence.

Unable to check the Greeks militarily, the Persians turned to diplomacy and bribery, with more succes. In spite of his ability as a general, Pausanias demonstrated all too well the vulnerability of the Spartans abroad to the lures of luxury and power. He entered into negotiation with Xerxes. In return for a royal bride and the tyrantship of Greece, he promised to betray the Greeks to Xerxes. How in fact, given the balance of military power, he would have carried this out is uncertain. The Persians can scarcely have still hoped for this, and were probably aiming to cause divisions among the Greeks by playing on Pausanias' ambitions.

Whatever the motives of the Persians, Pausanias had entered upon a course of action that was fatal both for himself and for Sparta's chances of retaining the leadership of the league. After the capture of Byzantium, Pausanias began to adopt Persian dress and habits. The suspicions of the other Greeks were aroused, and soon letters were intercepted which proved that he had been negotiating with the Persians.

Pausanias was denounced and recalled to Sparta where he brought about his death by his continued political machinations.

The exposure of his treachery destroyed all Spartan credit with the Ionians.

As well as this important loss of trust, Sparta had other difficulties to face. It was basically a land power, unsuited to the naval warfare in the east. Moreover, it was embroiled with its allies in the Peloponnese and so unwilling to keep a large number of its troops tied up in Ionia. It was not altogether reluctant, therefore, to allow Athens to usurp its position as leader of the league.

Athens, in fact, did more than this. On the invitation of the Ionians it formed an entirely new league, without Sparta, which was called the Delian League. The Hellenic League became no more than a name, and Sparta abandoned Ionia as a possible sphere of interest for the next sixty years. The Delian League, which began as a defensive alliance, forced into being by Spartan insularity, was in a few short years transformed into an Athenian empire.

Chapter 9

The Glory of Athens

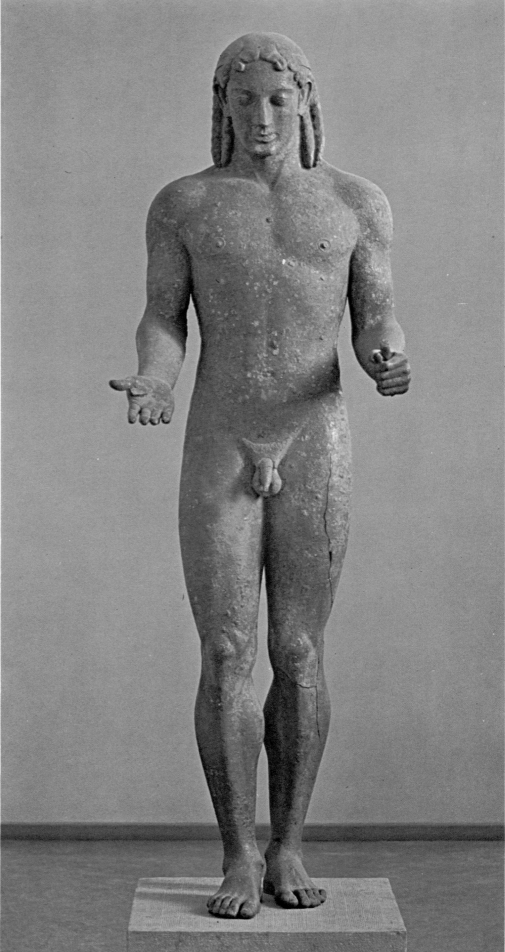

The Greek historian Polybius wrote in his *History* (second century BC) that the Romans acquired an empire in spite of themselves. This was a judgement he had borrowed from Thucydides who was referring to the Athenian Empire. In both cases there is a certain amount of truth in such an opinion. To understand how the Delian League was transformed into an Athenian empire the nature of the league in its early days must be examined in some detail.

The league was set up, under the presidency of Aristides, as an offensive and defensive alliance, all of whose members were equal and autonomous. Its aim was to prosecute the war against Persia in order to liberate the Ionians still under Persian control and to indemnify the Greeks for the damage they had suffered. The war which the armies embarked upon was, because of the geography of Ionia, essentially a naval one. The preponderant naval strength of Athens made it unnecessary for all the members of the League to provide ships and fight in person. Many states, instead, contributed money, according to their resources, to finance the fleets of Athens and the more powerful allies who fought on their behalf. This money was collected by officers of the league called Hellenic treasurers, who were exclusively Athenian. Thus, from the very beginning, the Athenians had executive control of the league in both military and financial matters.

Gradually, as the threat from Persia was reduced, and especially after the Athenian victory at Eurymedon in 469 BC, more and more states contributed money instead of

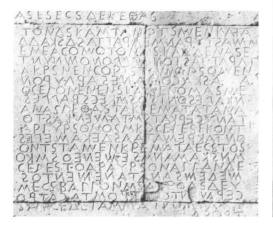

ships. The financial and moral hold of the Athenians over their allies therefore tightened, and their influence hardened into authority. States which were dissatisfied with Athenian control of the league and tried to leave it were treated as rebels and punished, on the pretext that they were threatening the collective safety of their allies. As early as 470 BC, Naxos revolted and was brought forcibly back into the fold. Thasos in 465 BC and Samos in 440 BC followed suit and suffered the same fate.

Athenian colonists

The revolt of Naxos saw the beginning of *cleruchies*, an Athenian practice which was to cause much resentment among the allies, and which was intended to keep Athens' subjects (for this is what in effect the allies were becoming) loyal to the league. The *cleruchies* were plots of land which were confiscated and then given to Athenian settlers to farm. The settlers (*cleruchoi*) kept their Athenian citizenship and acted as a focal point of pro-Athenian feeling in their adopted land. They were colonists in the worst tradition. In addition to such clumsy methods of political control, the threat of the Athenian navy ensured that the allied states were ruled by democracies and that local oligarchies were kept in check.

Friends of the Athenians were allowed to bring their lawsuits to be heard at Athens, and occasionally this privilege was granted to a whole town as a special mark of favour. The change in Athens' position from 'first among equals' to that of ruler of an empire took place gradually and almost imperceptibly. Certainly, there was a good deal of calculation on the part of the Athenians, but the allies played into their hands by opting out of their military duties. This gave the Athenians a questionable, but very real, moral right to dictate the course of events.

In 449 BC peace was concluded between the Delian League and Persia, but the league, its ostensible aim fulfilled, was not disbanded. The last shreds of pretence were removed and the Athenian Empire became an official reality. Athens in 449 BC, grown rich on the allies' tribute, its food supply from southern Russia guaranteed by its fleet and the long walls which linked the city with the port of Piraeus was, with Sparta, the major power in Greece. This was a remarkable change in a city which, in 490 BC, had been able to send only twenty ships to help the Ionians. Taken by itself the growth of Athenian power between 490 and 449 BC seemed inevitable, but political events at Athens itself during this period present a more varied appearance.

Themistocles, the founder of Athenian power, had fallen, Cimon, the aristocratic champion of the league in its early days, had been ostracized, and Perciles, the prophet of pure imperialism, had cut his political teeth. The issues which divided these politicians rarely touched on the increasing exploitation of the allies by Athens. They were concerned rather with the question of how radical democracy could become and, above all, with Athens' relations with Sparta.

Sparta or Persia

Politics at Athens after 479 BC, as immediately before the Persian war, revolved round the subject of foreign politics. Opinion was roughly divided into two main groups. On one side there were the radical democrats under Themistocles who believed that the threat from Persia had been decisively removed, and that Spartan jealousy presented a greater danger for the future. On the other side there were the conservatives under Cimon, Miltiades' son, who were in favour of friendship with aristocratic Sparta, and who believed that Athens' energy should be devoted to destroying Persian power completely.

Themistocles and his supporters had only a limited success with their policy at first. Immediately after Plataea the Spartans suggested to the Athenians that they should not rebuild their city walls, on the pretext that in the event of another Persian invasion the enemy would have no secure base from which to operate.Themistocles still had enough prestige as the architect of victory at Salamis to persuade the Athenians to disregard such a suggestion. While the whole population of Athens worked feverishly to build up the walls, Themistocles headed a delegation to Sparta, and bought vital time by a series of clever delaying tactics. When news reached him that the walls were high enough to be defended he left Sparta, having told the Spartans that Athens was now quite capable of taking its own decisions, and that the best alliances were those in which there was parity of power among the allies. The Spartans were furious at being duped, although they did not show it at the time, and the first seeds of future hostility towards Athens were sown.

Themistocles did not survive this diplomatic triumph for long. Cimon's prestige as the succesful commander of the Delian League's fleet against Persia was growing. In 474 BC he and his supporters managed to get Themistocles ostracized. Themistocles went to Argos, the traditional enemy of Sparta, where he formed anti-Spartan feeling among the Arcadians and helots. This was too much for the Spartans. In 470 BC they brought trumped-up charges of pro-Persian treachery against Themistocles, and these were readily believed at Athens where Cimon, Sparta's champion, was approaching the height of his power. Themistocles was proscribed and hounded out of Greece. He fled to Persia where, ironically, he finished his days as the trusted

counsellor of the Great King. The personal defeat of Themistocles was not in the long run fatal to his policies. His place was taken by two politicians of equal calibre. Ephalites and Pericles. However, the democrats did not regain the ascendancy until 462 BC.

In 469 BC Cimon imposed a crushing defeat on the Persians at Eurymedon. This victory, though it greatly increased his popularity, in effect cut away the main plank of his party's policies—the need for a strong anti-Persian policy. However, this did not become apparent immediately, and for the next four years he was the master of Athens. Then, in 465 BC Cimon suffered a serious defeat at the hand of the Thracians while trying to found an Athenian colony, and his popularity began to wane. Two years later Pericles felt strong enough to prosecute him in the courts for corruption. Though the prosecution was unsuccessful, the fact that it took place is a clear indication that the tide was turning against the conservatives.

Cimon's political ruin was completed by the Spartans themselves. In 462 BC Cimon persuaded the Athenians to send an army to help the Spartans who were fighting a rebellion of helots entrenched at Ithome. Suddenly, and with no apparent justification, the Spartans told the Athenians that their help was no longer needed. Thucydides says that the Spartans feared Athenian unorthodoxy, and were also apprehensive that the Athenians might sponsor further revolutions in the Peloponnese.

Neither Cimon nor his party survived the damage done by this public repudiation of their policies. Ephialtes and Pericles immediately brought forward reforms that drastically curtailed the powers of the Areopagus, until then the highest court at Athens, and the stronghold of Athenian conservatism. The court was left with only the right to try cases of homicide and certain religious issues. The remainder of its important supervisory and advisory powers were transferred to the Council of Five Hundred. The last real vestige of aristocratic, non-constitutional power at Athens had been removed.

Cimon himself was ostracized the following year, and Ephialtes was murdered by the conservatives as a futile and bitter reaction to their defeat. Thucydides, the son of Melesias, took Cimon's place and caused Perciels a certain amount of trouble in the Council. However, although he was a clever tactician, introducing the practice of party whips, he was not of the stature of Cimon, still less Pericles, and in 443 BC he too was ostracized. For the next fifteen years Pericles, the consistent opponent of Sparta, the champion of imperialism abroad and of radical democracy at home, was the supreme politician at Athens.

Pericles

Pericles controlled Athenian affairs absolutely for the last fifteen years of his life by being elected each year as one of the ten city generals, the *strategoi*.

After 486 BC, when archons were no longer elected but selected by lot, the *strategoi* were the only elected executive officers at Athens. Not even the most dedicated democrat thought it reasonable to trust the serious matter of war to a lottery, and thus possibly to a novice. Though Pericles was a competent soldier, it was more by virtue of the moral influence he exerted over the Athenians that he was elected each year to this important office.

Pericles had a lofty vision of Athens' role in Greek society, to which was allied a strong sense of the practicable. Since he was also a master of public relations (depending a great deal on the technique of personal reticence and the infrequent public statement) he brought a style to Athenian politics which the Athenians found irresistible.

Pericles' idealism, however, did not prevent him from being an astute and hard-hitting politician. He was the supreme exponent of a political formula which to modern eyes seems extremely unusual: democratic imperialism. He saw that the Athenian Empire depended on its navy, which was manned by the *demos*. The political strength of the *demos* was, therefore, his main concern.

The year before he helped to curb the powers of the Areopagus, he was responsible for a reform which made Athenian justice truly democratic: pay for jurors at the rate of two obols a day was instituted. This measure, which was unique in Greece, meant that even the poorest citizen could take part

in the city's judicial processes. Ultimate power was now given to the people.

Between 460 and 445 BC Athens was engaged in a sporadic war against the Peloponnesians, which was apparently based on the false military and political assumptions that the city was strong enough to expand its rule over the mainland of Greece, and that Sparta would not, or could not, prevent such an expansion, Pericles must take much of the blame for this policy, which proved to be completely unsuccessful.

Although during the course of the war Athens gained control of Boethius, Megara, Achaea in the northern Peloponnese, and the island of Aegina, the Athenians were not strong enough to hold these territories. Athenian armies were twice defeated in

pitched battles at Tanagra and Coronea. When finally the Spartans invaded Attica in 446 BC the Athenians abandoned the policy of expansion on land, renounced their claims to the territories they had won and concluded a thirty-year truce with the Spartans.

The peace lasted for only fifteen years. During this time Pericles not only consolidated and strengthened the Athenian naval empire to such an extent that he finally drove the fearful Spartans to war again, but also created a truly imperial capital—a cultural centre whose achievements represent the best in Greek art, literature and philosophy.

The Parthenon

The greatest memorials to Periclean Athens are the magnificent temple of Athena, the

Parthenon, and the gateway to the temple, the Propylaea, whose remains still crown the Acropolis at Athens. The temples of victory and the Erechtheum, which stand beside them, were built later, after Pericles death. The morality of paying for these buildings from the funds of the Delian League (as Pericles did) may be questioned, but scruples become irrelevant when the Parthenon is seen in all its splendour. Apart from their intrinsic beauty, works of art such as the Parthenon and its sculptures (the Elgin marbles) represent perhaps the best surviving examples of early classical architecture and architectural sculpture. Pericles did not commission his craftsmen to erect a large but ordinary temple which would merely recall the past with its inevitable overtones of conservatism. He got them to build a temple which incorporated the latest modern

styles in architecture and decoration and which would be a suitable symbol of the brash new Athenian Empire.

The term 'classical' is used here to define a distinct period in the history of Greek art, which started at the beginning of the fifth century BC when, for the first time, artists managed to represent the human figure in anatomical detail as a moving object. Before the classical revolution in sculpture, Greek artists had always worked on set themes and within the context of certain artistic conventions. The archaic sculptors, as they are called, almost invariably made statues of boys and girls called *koroi*. These were stylized and stiff pieces of work: the expressions on their faces are smiling, blank and introspective, and there is no hint of movement about the limbs. Although at Athens and in Ionia attempts at anatomical differentiation were made in the sixth century BC, and the Ionians, in particular, became skilled at showing the folds of dresses on their sculptures, the art of portraying the human figure as it really was eluded the archaic sculptors.

The first successful attempts to break free from the four-square, upright image of the *koroi* and to depict living and moving people in natural poses were made in architectural sculpture: the carving of figures, in high or low relief, on to slabs of marble, which were fixed under the eaves of temples to provide a continuous, decorative frieze.

This new realism in showing human movement continued to be developed on friezes and funeral stele. Because the artist was working in relief the problems of balance did not occur, Greek sculptors were encouraged to begin experimenting with the new style on proper, free-standing statues, and the classical style became established. Unfortunately, since a marble statue of the human body in a moving pose was difficult

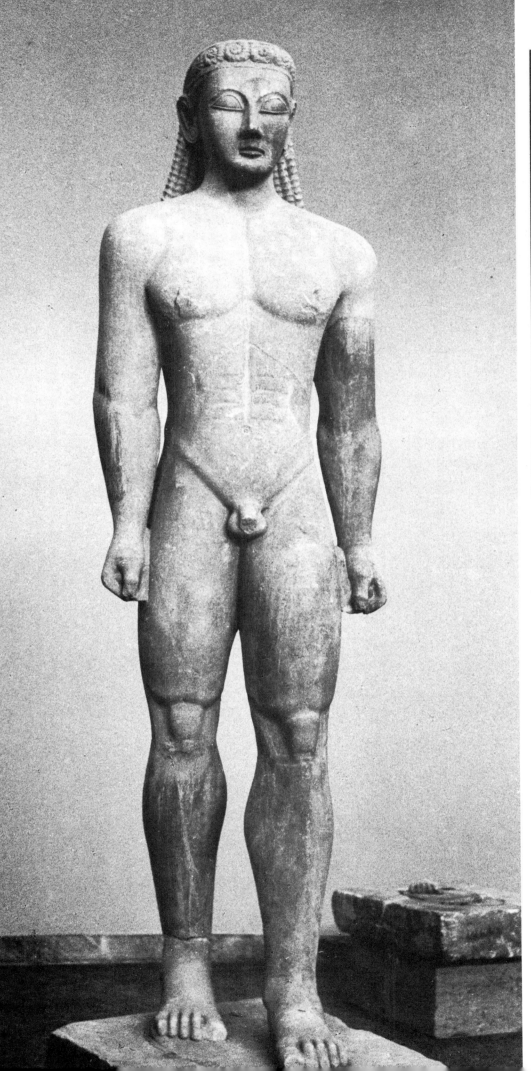

Above, statue of Athene Parthenos, the goddess Athena, whose chief temple was the Parthenon. National Museum, Athens.

Left, marble kouros, c. 600 BC, found at Cape Sunion, Attica: the figure has been put together from fragments and its left arm is a modern reconstruction. National Museum, Athens.

Opposite right, marble kore dating from 525–500 BC. Acropolis Museum, Athens.

Opposite left, bronze head of a warrior, found on the Acropolis, c. 530 BC. National Museum, Athens.

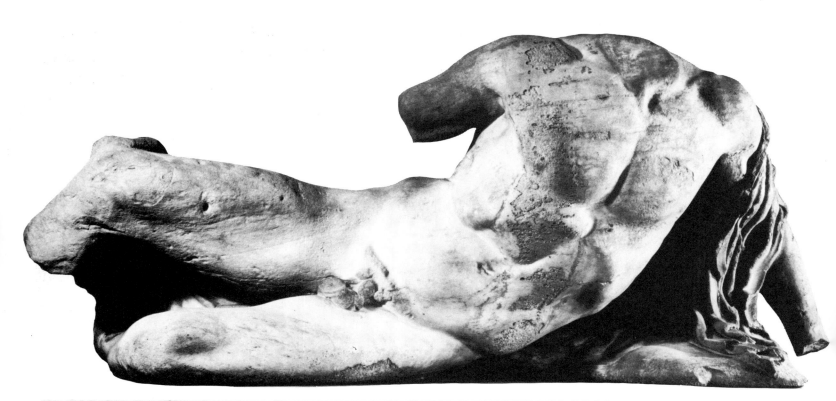

to balance (unlike the upright *koroi*), the sculptors of the classical school made the majority of their works in bronze, which were hollow and therefore could be weighted to make them stand up. Later these bronze statues were melted down. It is for this reason that there exist today a number of copies of Greek statues made by Roman collectors, but only a very few original Greek statues of the classical period. This scarcity gives the friezes of the Parthenon their great interest and value.

Who made these beautiful friezes? Records of pay to the craftsmen who decorated the temple of the Erechtheum show that the usual method was for a master-sculptor (probably Phidias in the case of the Parthenon) to elaborate a design for the frieze. Teams of lesser craftsmen would do the actual work in accordance

with his instructions. These unknown craftsmen executed for the Parthenon a beautiful
but for their times extremely unorthodox
frieze. Conventionally, the themes depicted
on friezes were mythical or religious, showing only the figures of gods and heroes. For
example, the frieze on the temple of Zeus at
Olympia shows the twelve labours of
Heracles. However, Pericles' Parthenon was
not only in honour of Athena but also of the
Athenians, and so ordinary Athenians—
mere mortals—are included on the Parthenon frieze.

The theme Phidias chose to represent was
the procession which took place at the time
of the Great Panathenaic festival, when a
specially woven robe was brought by the
Athenians to clothe the sacred olivewood
statue of Athena. The frieze shows the
Athenians in procession: young horsemen,
men walking or stooping to tie up their
sandals and maidens bearing the sacred
robe. All the figures are extremely rich in
detail and movement, but the frieze is not
an actual representation of the event—a
photograph in stone. The faces are all ideally
handsome, and some of the men are naked
which, in reality, they would not have been.

The building which bore this fascinating
and unorthodox frieze was no ordinary
temple. Designed by Iktinus and Callicrates
in the simple Doric style, it was much longer
than an ordinary temple, but it does not
appear cumbersome or overpowering. This
was avoided by introducing various small
subtle modifications into its design: the
columns are more slender than usual and
the metopes are smaller as well. The apparently straight lines of the floor of the
colonnade are in fact imperceptibly curved.
The result of these changes is that the
Parthenon has an apprent lightness which
belies its size. Inside the temple was a forty-
foot statue of Athena made in gold and
ivory by Phidias. The Propylaea, the beautiful double porch leading to the Parthenon,
was similarly built in the Doric style, but
again avoided any semblance of rigidity by
having the two porches linked by a hall of
columns in the lighter Ionic style.

For the Athenians the Parthenon was
primarily of religious, not architectural
interest. Yet the temple, although the house
of a very fearsome goddess, was not isolated
as it is today, but was surrounded by a
conglomeration of statues, minor temples,
and public inscriptions. It was the focal
point of a busy part of the city. The Greeks
made religion an integral part of their everyday lives, and did not believe in mock piety.
They had a practical, commonsense attitude
towards the gods, and thus contrived to make
their reverence for them the mainspring and
inspiration for most of their activities. In
architecture the Parthenon was the product
of this attitude, in literature, tragedy.

Tragedy

The connection between tragedy and religion
is even closer than in the case of sculpture.
Greek tragedy was developed from the odes
sung by choruses in honour of the god
Dionysius. Plutarch tells us that a certain
Thespis first introduced an actor who
commented in colloquial verse on the lyrical
choruses, and ushered in the performance
with a prologue. Although Thespis was
gently reproved by Solon for this innovation, the first step in the gradual development of tragedy had been taken.

A second actor was introduced by Aeschylus (525–456 BC), the first of the three great tragedians, and later Sophocles introduced a third. The small number of actors employed in a play was responsible for several conventions peculiar to tragedy: no violence was ever shown on the stage, but all actions such as murders, battles and the sacking of cities were reported by a messenger. Also, because each actor had to play several parts, they wore masks to show their changes of identity. This precluded the conveying of emotion by changes of expression and so all the drama had to be in the words they spoke.

Plots as we know them in modern drama were noticeably lacking in Greek tragedy. The stories the tragedians dealt with were drawn from the heroic legends, which were already well known to their audiences. The poet's skill was judged by the beauty of his lyrics and the nobility of the moral and metaphysical conclusions he drew from his material. Integral parts of a tragedy (which we no longer possess) were the music to which the choruses sang their lyrics, and the dances they performed. All these were the responsiblity of the poet. To be a tragedian

entailed being a composer and choreo-grapher as well as a playwright.

By the end of the sixth century BC tragedy had become an accepted literary genre at Athens and received powerful support from the city. Each year at the festival Dionysius three poets were chosen to compete for the tragic prize. For this they had to produce three tragedies and a shorter, satirical play in a lighter vein. The expenses of the chorus were paid for by a rich citizen. The performance of this duty was considered a great honour. Such a system produced a large number of plays, yet of the several thousand tragedies pro-duced at Athens a bare handful have survived to the present day.

There are seven written by Aeschylus, seven by Sophocles and nineteen by Euri-pides. However, these few remaining plays allow a fairly clear picture of tragedy to be built. Sometimes the tragedians concerned themselves with topical matters, as when Phrynicus, the shadowy but impressive pre-decessor of Aeschylus, dealt with the sack of Miletus by the Persians in 494 BC or when Aeschylus himself wrote of the tragedy of Xerxes' invasion in the *Persae*. Again,

Aeschylus in the final play of the Oresteia trilogy, the *Eumenides*, makes the matricide Orestes, who is being pursued by the daemonic Furies, come to Athens where he is acquitted by the Areopagus, convened for the first time on this occasion by Athena. *The Eumenides*, first performed in 457 BC, is a curious and often baffling concoction of old and new, but it is clear that Aeschylus in his tortuous way is urging the Athenians to accept the constitutional implications of the reforms of the Areopagus carried through by Ephialtes and Pericles in 462 BC.

The tragedians, however, even when they were dealing with topical issues, never strayed far from their central themes: the implacable imperatives of the blood feud, the gulf between men and gods, and the terrible justice of Zeus which is visited on the man who dares, in his pride, to bridge that gulf. These harsh realities, which take such a toll in human suffering, and the nobility shown by men when in their grip are the subjects of tragedy. One of the most frequent sequences is that of *Ate—Hubris—Nemesis*. *Ate* is blindness sent by the gods to make a man commit an act of *hubris*. This is false pride which leads him to an insolent and

Above, the theatre at Delphi, with seats for an audience of 15,000: originally built in the fourth century BC of white marble, it was restored in grey limestone by the Romans.

Opposite top, metope from the Parthenon depict-ing a battle between the Lapiths and Centaurs, c. 440–432 BC. British Museum, London.

Opposite bottom, aerial view of the Acropolis from the southeast: the Parthenon is the main building in the centre and slightly to the left; the Erechtheum can be seen on the centre right and the Propylaea, the entrance way to the citadel, at the far end; the restored Odeum of Herodes Atticus lies below the Propylaea to the left.

and Orestes his father. The Delphic motto 'know thyself', at first sight no more than a helpful platitude, becomes a grim warning in the light of such chilling events.

Sophocles (496–405 BC) is the second great tragedian. His plays are more muted than those of the stern and grandiloquent Aeschylus and show a greater compassion for human suffering, especially in the the *Philoctetes* and *Antigone*. However, the themes are the same: the power of divine retribution and man's helplessness before the gods and his fate.

The Athenians did not consider Euripides (480–406 BC) as good a poet as Sophocles or Aeschylus. Though the gods are never totally absent from his plays, he concentrated far more on human passion as the cause for tragic actions, and in delineating this he is surpassed. Such plays as the *Medea* and the *Bacchae* are as moving as any in Greek tragedy. His style, however, which was heavily influenced by the rhetoric of the sophists, is often brittle and artificial and is not as pure as that of Sophocles.

Euripides is often regarded as being in some way almost a 'modern', psychological playwright, who is somehow intrinsically different from Sophocles and Aeschylus. This is not so, Euripides, like the other two tragedians, wrote in a heroic context. He employed the same tragic conventions of three actors, choruses and speeches by messengers. Where he differed was in the emphasis he placed on the relations between men and gods, and the literary style he used. Indeed, some critics tend to read into Greek tragedy modern ideas which could never have occurred to their authors, seeing in Antigone's opposition to Creon in Sophocles' *Antigone*, for example, an apologia for civil disobedience. Sophocles, who was a general and a friend of Pericles, would have been either shocked or amused at such an interpretation. In the *Antigone* he simply took as his subject a family curse and the Greek custom that the dead must be buried.

Aristophanes

Old comedy, which flourished at Athens in the last half of the fifth century BC, has come down to us in the plays of Aristophanes, who provides a complete contrast to the high-minded philosophy of the tragedians. The comic poet was able to say what he liked. He could attack prominent public men quite slanderously, bring the gods down to earth and make fools of them, and send Socrates up into the heavens in a basket and make a fool of him. All this was interspersed with the most obscene buffoonery.

Aristophanes (446–385 BC) was a rich Athenian (only the rich had the leisure to be poets). His plays span the period of time from the middle of the Peloponnesian War to its

end. After the death of Pericles in 429 BC the quality of Athenian leadership fell sharply. Cleon the demagogue, the brilliant but irresponsible Alcibiades, the cautious Nicias and Theramenes ('the trimmer'), one of the leaders of the brief oligarchic revolution in 411 BC—these were the men who took Pericles' place. Democracy, especially after the Sicilian disaster in 414 BC, began to falter and lost much of its confidence and impetus.

In his plays Aristophanes reflects many of the doubts and fears of the common people at this time, for comedy, unlike tragedy was concerned primarily with contemporary events. Aristophanes' plots are virtually non-existent. He takes a topical event and weaves a fantasy about it, creating a series of comic scenes which barely hang together. Halfway through a comic play a speech, called the *parabasis*, was made by the chorus leader, in which the poet quite seriously proffered his advice to the city on contemporary affairs.

The picture of Aristophanes which his *parabases* provide is that of a moderate, kindly man. He had a marked distaste for the war and felt strongly for the peasants who suffered most from it. Nevertheless,

unforgiveable sin. Then *nemesis*, divine retribution, comes to him in some horrible form.

In Aeschylus' *Agamemnon* the leader of the Achaeans returns triumphantly from Troy to Argos, where his adulterous wife is waiting eagerly to avenge her daughter Iphegenia whom Agamemnon sacrificed ten years before to obtain a fair wind for Troy. To bring about his downfall Clytemnestra tempts Agamemnon to an act of *hubris*: she asks him to enter his palace on a red carpet. *Ate* descends on him and he agrees to her requests. He enters the palace and meets his *nemesis* by being murdered by Clytemnestra in his bath.

In the *Libation Bearers*, the next play in the trilogy, Orestes, his son, avenges his father by killing Clytemnestra and her adulterous lover Aegisthus. He goes mad when he realizes what he has done and flees, demented, from Argos pursued by the Furies. The *Eumenides* puts an end to the bloodshed and breaks the tragic sequence, but the introduction of the Areopagus is really an arbitrary and unjustifiable decision on the part of Aeschylus. The tragedy of the divine law and the dictates of honour in a heroic society, as shown in the plays, is that the protagonists all had some justification for their acts and, indeed, were compelled to do what they did. Agamemnon was ordered by the goddess Artemis to kill Iphegenia; Clytemnestra had to avenge her daughter

Aristophanes could be vitriolic when he wanted to be. In particular, he ridicules Cleon mercilessly in the *Acharmians* and the *Knights*, depicting him as a low-born tanner, all because Cleon had brought a slanderous suit against him questioning his citizenship. The great merit of old comedy was that there was something in it for everyone: every class of person at Athens is paraded and made fun of—even Aristophanes' fellow poets. Again and again Aristophanes took lines from Euripides and ruined them by putting them into ludicrous contexts. This joke reached its climax when he staged a burlesque literary competition between Euripides and Aeschylus in the *Frogs* (495 BC), as a parting

jibe at Euripides, who had died during the same year.

The political content of Aristophanes' plays must always be accepted with caution. Comic convention forced him to look at politics from the point of view of the ordinary man. This is not always of much value, but he was a keen social commentator. His slaves, farmers and grumpy old jurors have the stamp of authenticity, and they compel us to turn our attention away from public men and events to the ordinary Athenian, his city and the everyday life he led.

Thetes, slaves and metics

The *demos* of fifth-century Athens has been subjected, in the past, to some very curious analysis. The most common misconception has been that the *thetes* lived mainly in or around the port of Piraeus and that they depended on the flow of maritime trade for their livelihood. They thus constituted a type of urban proletariat, whose every whim was pandered to by the politicians—at the expense of the more honest, hard-working farming.

Such a picture is very misleading. The only class of people at Athens who were engaged solely in trade were foreign residents, called *metics* (those who had changed

Above, aerial view of the theatre at Epidaurus built by Polycleitus the Younger in the mid-fourth century BC: it had—and still has—superb acoustics and could seat up to 14,000 spectators, each of whom had an excellent view.

Left, a first-century BC mask of comedy found in Stoa of Attalos, Athens.

Opposite top right, bust of Sophocles, author of some 120 plays, of which seven tragedies have survived. British Museum, London.

Opposite bottom, clay plaque from Locri of men riding in a chariot.

Opposite top left, bronze statuette of Athene Promachos, the protectress of Athens and the patroness of urban arts and handicrafts, especially spinning and weaving, early sixth century BC. National Museum, Athens.

their home). The *metics* had to remain traders for the simple reason that, since they were not allowed to acquire Athenian citizenship, they could not buy property and thus could never become farmers. However, they were in no sense a depressed class. Although, as foreigners, they were debarred from taking part in political life and when they went to law had to be represented by an Athenian in court, many of them developed a strong attachment for their foster city. Some 3,000 of them served loyally in the Athenian army during the Peloponnesian War.

The *metics* did not enjoy a complete monopoly in trade, and a certain proportion of *thetes* were masons, potters and small shopkeepers. The minute volume of trade, however, which actually took place at Athens suggests very strongly that the majority of the *thetes* followed the traditional Athenian occupation of farming. The thetic farmer from Marathon or Eleusis would only take up his oar in periods of war. The rest of the time he had nothing to do with Piraeus or the sea.

The whole question of trade in Greece has been bedevilled by modern economic theory and the presumption that ancient Athens was in some way similar to the modern city and port of Piraeus. In fact, trade in Greece never rose above the level of a cottage industry. The country was so poor that there was little that the Greeks could offer in large quantities to the foreigners they traded with. The Attic farmer, when he had a bumper crop of olives, might ship his surplus oil to the Crimea, but in the small boats then available this was a dangerous venture and never became a regular practice. Athenian pottery was exported as a luxury, but even at the height of the industry's development it has been estimated that there were no more than 150 potters working at Athens. Indeed, to even talk of an industry, with its connotations of mass production, is misleading. The masons who contracted to decorate the Erechtheum were individual artisans working for themselves, perhaps helped by a slave or two, and this state of affairs existed in pottery and all other trades.

The nearest thing to mass production is the case of the *metic*, Cephalus, a Syracusan and a friend of Plato, who had a workshop in which 120 slaves manufactured shields. Again, Demosthenes, the orator, mentions that on his father's estate there were twenty slaves employed in making beds, and another thirty who were cutlers making knives. These are the largest manufacturing units we hear of at Athens.

Perhaps the most profitable area of trade was slavery. Slavery was a universal and unquestioned institution in the ancient world. The slave population of Athens has been estimated at about 80,000, and even the poorest farmers could afford at least one. Slaves came to Athens from the east, from Thrace and Phrygia and, of course, from those Greek cities which had had the misfortune to be defeated in war. A common practice among rich Athenians was to hire out slaves to do work for other, less prosperous citizens. Nicias, the Athenian general who was defeated at Syracuse, is said to have owned 1,000 such slaves.

The life of a slave at Athens depended largely on the skills he possessed and the character of the master by whom he was bought. The majority of slaves performed domestic and agricultural work on their master's farms, and often, as in the case of Eumaeus, the swineherd in the *Odyssey*, they were treated well and became friends of the family. Some skilled slaves were allowed by their masters to live on their own with their families and carry on a trade. These slaves, to all intents and purposes, lived like free men. For this privilege they had of course to pay their masters a percentage of their takings. Manumission existed at Athens, though there is no evidence that it was an extensive practice, and there was certainly never a large class of freedom as later at Rome.

On the debit side there is the undoubted fact that many slaves were treated brutally and callously. A frequent joke in Aristophane's plays is the beating a slave received as a matter of course whenever he did something wrong, and the life of the slaves who worked the silver mines at Laurium must have been very unpleasant. At the end of the Peloponnesian War, when the Spartans were occupying the fort of Decelea in Attica, Thucydides relates that 20,000 slaves fled to them from Athens.

Slavery was a brutal system, but it is hard to see how the Greek's could have done away with it (if such a notion ever occurred to them) without disorganizing their whole economy and way of life. Their land was so poor that to rise above subsistence level and to obtain even a modicum of leisure they had to have an extremely cheap system of labour. Slavery was their answer to this problem. The small Athenian farmer probably worked just as hard as his few slaves. It was the rich, who could afford large numbers of slaves, who benefited most. Slaves enabled Plato to spend his time talking philosophy, Aeschylus to write his plays and, most important of all, Pericles to indulge in politics. Although Athens was theoretically a total democracy, only the very rich had the time and inclination to conduct a full-time political career.

Above, view of the tholos, part of the sanctuary of Athena Pronaea at Delphi, fourth century BC.

Opposite right, white-ground lekythos *by the Achilles Painter, c. 440 BC, depicting a woman handing a soldier his helmet. British Museum, London.*

Opposite top centre, white-ground vase in the style of the Achilles painter: vases like this, known as lekythoi, *were common grave-offerings in fifth-century BC Athens. Museum of Fine Arts, Boston.*

Opposite bottom centre, detail of a late sixth-century BC vase by the Andokides painter depicting Heracles coaxing Cerberus, the two-headed watchdog of Hades. Musée du Louvre, Paris.

Opposite left, drinking cup from Vulci, Etruria, depicting Achilles tending the wounds of his friend Patroclus, c. 500 BC. Antikenmuseum, Staatliche Museen zu Berlin.

159

The democratic process

Dissatisfaction with modern democratic forms of governement sometimes gives rise to a strong nostalgia for the older models of democracy (the Swiss city-states of the eighteenth century, Athens in the fifth century BC) and a tendency to set them up as the perfect models of total democracy. The truth about Athens lies somewhere between such an ideal and the modern monolithic state.

Athens was, of course, a total democracy. In theory every Athenian citizen could vote in the Assembly, sit on the juries and put himself up for election by lot to the Council. Such a state of affairs, however, was made possible only because of the small size of Attica and the correspondingly small number of citizens. Athenian women were debarred from politics and the citizens eligible to play a part in the city's affairs probably never numbered more than 80,000.

The danger that an increase in the number of male citizens would cripple the democratic system was avoided by a measure, introduced by Pericles in 451 BC, by which a man had to prove that both his mother and father were Athenians in order to be accounted an Athenian citizen. This was a difficult qualification and one which the great Themistocles himself would have failed, but it was effective in curbing the franchise. Yet even 80,000 was a large number of men to accommodate in a system based on direct citizen participation. In practice, however, there was never any congestion. The wage of two, and later three,

obols which was paid to jurors and members of the Council of Five Hundred was not enough to justify the small thetic farmer's abandoning his farm for public business. Politics were for the rich or the very dedicated.

Apart from economic obstacles there was the problem of proximity to Athens. Those Athenians who lived in the outlying districts of Attica, (with the exception of the very rich or politically zealous) would have been discouraged by the inconvenience of a long journey from playing a great part in the city's political life. An important debate in the assembly, such as that in 415 BC on whether to invade Sicily, might bring in the poorer citizens, but this was the exception rather than the rule.

Nevertheless, the fact that all Athenians did not, in practice, actively participate in politics should not obscure the very real liberties which were incorporated into their democracy. Their dependence on selection by lot and the rotation of offices among the citizens may seem to smack of amateurism, as indeed, it did then to certain well-born critics of the democracy. But the achievements of Athens belie such a judgement, and in a time of no technology, when specialization was unknown, such amateurism was perhaps a strength rather than a failing.

Athenian democracy was based on faith in the ability of the ordinary man to take responsibility and in his common sense. The way in which the assemblies and courts of Athens functioned illustrates how this faith

was put into practice. The most important body at Athens was the Assembly. Since the Athenians made no distinction between legislative and judical powers the Assembly voted on measures put before it, but could also sit in judgement on public officials who were charged with incompetence. It was in the Assembly that the politicians put forward their views and swayed public policy. The chairmanship of the Assembly, an important position, was not a permanent appointment, but was filled by rota from among the members of the Council. Occasionally the inexperience of the chairman resulted in blunders, as when the six victorious generals at Arginusae (406 BC) were jointly condemned for failing to pick up survivors. However, the Athenians thought such lapses preferable to the prospect of one expert (and perhaps a politically ambitious one) dominating the Assembly for a year.

The Council of Five Hundred, which prepared motions for the Assembly, and which Solon had seen as the main check on that body, did not influence the Council's decisions as greatly as might have been expected. The Assembly often altered its proposals and tacked on emendations of its own. In practice the Council's main function was administrative, dealing in committees with public accounts for festivals, public buildings and the navy. Yet, even in this specialized atmosphere a class of profession bureaucrats like the imperial freedmen at Rome never appeared at Athens. This was because councillors were chosen by lot, and no man could serve on the Council more than twice in his lifetime.

In the field of litigation the Athenian's faith in the ordinary man's ability is most clearly seen. The law seems never to have attracted the intellectual energies and imagination of the Greeks as it did those of the Romans and, in the absence of a detailed code of civil and criminal law, a specialized class of advocates was never formed in Greece. The courts of Athens were an off-shoot of Solon's old court of appeal, the Heliaea. When, in 487 BC, archons were chosen by lottery the Heliaea became a court of primary jurisdiction.

The number of jurors, called dicasts, who served on the Heliaea was 6,000. They were split into groups of 500 and sat on panels which were called dicasteries. The dicasteries were the courts of Athens. Before an Athenian took a civil case to be heard in court he had to submit it to a panel of arbitrators composed of elder citizens. If he disagreed with the verdict given by the arbitrators he would then appear before a dicastery to dispute it. Each court, with its jury of 500 (and sometimes more in particularly important cases), was presided over by a magistrate, but unlike an English judge he gave no opinion on the cases before the court. His only function was to see that the case was tried in the proper conventional manner.

The two litigants conducted their own case and laid down the law to the dicasts according to their personal views. Verdicts were reached by a majority vote, and a split vote resulted in an acquittal. The lack of procedural rules and legal precedents meant that in effect an Athenian trial was the public

airing of a personal quarrel, and the emotional overtones of such an exercise were never played down. Litigants would cast aspersions on their opponents' private life, ancestry and civil status, and they would introduce their weeping families into court in the hope of influencing the jurors. Such dramatic antics emphasize the central fact of Athenian justice: acquittal lay in eloquence. Since professional advocates were not allowed into the courts, a man who distrusted his own rhetorical powers would often have a speech written for him before his trial, and professional speech writers, such as Lysias, were a thriving class.

A more sinister group of people associated with the Athenian courts were the sycophants whose heyday was in the fourth century BC. Since there was no equivalent of police prosecutions or a public prosecutor at Athens, the responsibility for prosecuting rested with the injured party, or a third party who acted on his behalf. The sycophants were men who abused this privilege enabling a third party to bring a prosecution. They would approach rich men and threaten them with a court case (usually over some matter of public policy) and then allow themselves to be bought off.

However, apart from such abuses, the Athenians' system of law seems to have functioned satisfactorily. The lack of a unified code of law never appears to have worried the Athenians and there were obvious advantages in having such large juries since the cost of bribing them was prohibitive. The democratic nature of the Athenian courts was unique in Greece. Yet it is as well not to forget that it was the tribute of Athens' allies which paid the jurors. Some of the Athenians' subjects had the right to appear in Athenian courts, but certainly not all. This raises the question of how just and, therefore, how popular was the Athenian Empire.

Athenian imperialism

The Athenians took a great interest in the justice and morality of their empire. Thucydides, though never explicitly stating his own view, does not conceal in his *History* the extent to which the Athenians' subjects (especially during the Peloponnesian War) resented their rule. In 416 BC Athens sacked the pro-Spartan island of Melos which had refused to join the Athenian League. Thucydides makes this incident the occasion for a debate between the Melians and Athenians on the morality of the empire. During this debate the Athenians admit quite freely that their empire is based on self-interest, and that many of their subjects are embittered against them.

The theme of self-interest is echoed again by both Pericles and Alcibiades. It is not surprising that the Athenians, having an empire should, for selfish reasons, want to keep it, but that they should feel compelled to justify this selfishness, as they did by pointing to the weakness of human nature, is certainly remarkable.

There is no doubt that the main benefit Athens received from its empire was a financial one. At the beginning of the Peloponnesian war, Pericles made public the city's resources in order to bolster the citizens' confidence. Their reserves stood at 6,000 talents of silver, and had been as high as 9,100. Their annual income from the allies came to 600 talents. It is hardly surprising that the Athenians were unwilling to relinquish their rule.

But what did the allies who sent this large amount of money each year to the Athenian treasury get in return? An Athenian apologist could have made out a strong case to show that the allies did gain considerable benefits from Athenian rule. They enjoyed democratic constitutions; Athenian magistrates presided in their courts; certain of them on occasions had the right to bring their lawsuits to be heard in Athens; and, above all, the Athenian navy protected their merchant ships and their cities.

To draw up such a simple profit and loss account, however, does not properly answer the question of whether the Athenian Empire was popular. The attitudes of the different political and social groups in the allied cities must also be taken into account. When the important city of Mytilene revolted against Athenian rule, the parts played in this revolt by the different classes at Mytilene throw a great deal of light on this vexed question. The men who instigated the revolt were oligarchs who favoured Sparta. However, they were few in number, and it is doubtful whether they could have resisted a year-long Athenian siege, as they did, without the support of the *demos*.

The siege ended when the people, desperate for food, threatened to hand the city over to the Athenians, and the oligarchs, hoping to gain some political advantage, surrendered the city themselves. Now Thucydides insists that it was the desperation caused by hunger which made the *demos* threaten to treat with the Athenians and not any overriding political sympathy with their former masters. The events at Mytilene would seem to confirm the obvious and natural view that in any city allied to Athens those men who believed in oligarchy were hostile to Athens (because Athenian rule prevented them from exercising power), whereas the poorer classes were basically indifferent but could be swayed by a temporary wave of patriotism. The most sensible conclusion is that the Athenians received their support from those people who were politically active, but were excluded from the ranks of the oligarchs. To discover the exact size of these different groups would obviously be impossible and so the question of how popular Athenian rule was can never be conclusively answered.

For the Samian or Lesbian who threw in his lot with the Athenians and for whom democracy provided the only opportunity to be active in politics, Athenian rule must have seemed an excellent state of affairs. But to his richer neighbour, who had to provide a large portion of the tribute paid to Athens and who resented the imposed egalitarianism of a democracy dictated by Athens, Sparta, where gentlemen ruled and the lower classes knew their place in society, must have seemed infinitely desirable. The ordinary man, as so often in history, probably concerned himself with other things.

The Peloponnesian War

The Peloponnesian War, which broke out in 431 BC and lasted until 404 BC (apart from one short interval provided by the Peace of Nicias in 421 BC), was a monumental struggle for power between Athens and Sparta, and their respective allies. Thucydides leaves us in no doubt as to why the war broke out. In the first chapter of his *History* he states that the real reason for the war was the Spartans' fear of the growing power of the Athenians. The Spartans, just as much as the Athenians, were imperialists, anxious to safeguard their sphere of interest.

In the years immediately preceding 431 BC there were several incidents which indicated that Athens was prepared to encroach on Spartan preserves. The Spartans decided that a stand had to be made and went to war. The statement that the Spartans were as imperialistic as Athens may seem surprising and needs some explanation. It is certainly true that nowhere in ancient or modern histories are the words 'The Spartan Empire' used. Today we speak of the Spartan League and the Greeks themselves said 'the Spartans and their allies'.

Nevertheless, the Spartan League, in spite of appearances, was very much an empire, in which the members had oligarchic governments in accordance with Spartan ideology, which supported Spartan policies. Spartan officers were attached to allied armies as 'military supervisors', and rebellious allies were brought back into the fold by force of arms, as in the case of Elis in 402 BC.

Sparta's avoidance of the stigma of 'imperialist' was mainly because of the nature of its league, which made it more sensible for the Spartans to allow their allies a certain degree of apparent autonomy. Since their league was a land-based one, as opposed to the Athenian seaborne league, it was against the interests of the Spartans (because of their small numbers) to disarm their allies. Moreover, since hoplites paid for their own armour and met all other expenses themselves, they had no need to exact tribute from their allies. Thus Sparta enjoyed the advantages of an empire without being plagued, as the Athenians were, by its disadvantages.

As imperialists, although not openly, the Spartans were sensitive to any disruption of the balance of power. The strongest justification the Spartans had for their view that Athens was set on expansion were the notorious Megarian decrees. These decrees, which were passed at the instigation of Pericles, forbade Megarian ships to trade at Athens or in any ports in the Athenian Empire. Apart from the obvious conclusion that these sanctions constituted an unfriendly act against a member of the Spartan League, Pericles' political objective in formulating the decrees has always remained a matter of debate. Perhaps the most plausible explanation is that he hoped to force the Megarians back into the alliance with Athens which they had abandoned at the end of the first Peloponnesian War. If this had happened, the Spartans and other Peloponnesians would have been placed in a most awkward strategic position. Athens already controlled the Gulf of Corinth. If it could in addition control the isthmus from Megara the Peloponnesians would find themselves completely isolated and cut off from their allies in Boeotia.

If this was Pericles' intention, as seems likely to judge by his obduracy in keeping the decrees in force, the violence of the Peloponnesians' reaction against them can

readily be understood. Two additional incidents which brought Corinth, one of Sparta's strongest and most influential allies, and Athens into direct military conflict increased Sparta's suspicions. The first of these involved the city of Epidamnus, a colony of Corcyra (modern Corfu), and Corinth. Corcyra was itself a colony of Corinth but an extremely powerful and disrespectful one. When civil war broke out in Epidamnus between oligarchs and democrats, appeals were made to Corcyra and Corinth in their capacity as mother cities, and they were both dragged into the quarrel —unfortunately on opposite sides. The Corcyreans were now threatened by Corinth and, since they had previously remained studiously aloof from power politics, they found themselves without allies, and so went to Athens to seek an alliance. Their plea was sympathetically received, since the Corcyrean navy of 200 triremes was a strong incentive to friendship, and Athens entered into an alliance with Corcyra.

As a result of this alliance the Athenians fought against the Corinthians in a series of naval engagements. Apart from the hostility this caused at Corinth, the alliance of the two most powerful naval cities in Greece was extremely worrying to the Spartans, and made them even more prone to listen favourably to those of their allies who were already advocating war against Athens.

The final incident, which led to a meeting of the Spartan League and a vote for war, again involved Athens and Corinth and concerned the town of Potidaea. The incident was an extension of the existing Athenian-Corinthian quarrel. Potidaea was a Corinthian colony in Thrace, but also a member of the Athenian Empire. When ordered to pull down their walls by the Athenians, who feared that their Corinthian sympathies after Epidamnus might lead them to revolt, the Potidaeans refused, and after a period of unsuccessful negotiations at Athens, quite predictably revolted. Corinthian and Athenian forces hurried to Thrace and once again met in battle. The Corinthians were defeated and retired. The Athenians then sat down to besiege Potidaea, which they eventually took after long and costly manoeuvres.

It would be wrong to consider these confrontations between Athens and Corinth over Epidamnus and Potidaea as evidence of a deep-seated plot on the part of the Athenians to weaken Corinth, because they wanted to capture Corinth's markets in the western Mediterranean and Adriatic. This view is often put forward, with the corollary that Sparta went to war to defend Corinthian commercial interests, but there is little supporting evidence for such a theory. These incidents, as Thucydides points out, were pretexts, not causes, for the war. It was to check Athens' aggressive expansionism, which they saw would be quite indiscriminate in its objectives, that the Spartans went to war. Whether they were completely justified

165

in holding this view is not certain, but it took twenty-five years of long-drawn-out and bloody warfare for them to prove this point to their satisfaction.

Athens and Sparta in conflict

The fight between Sparta and Athens in the Peloponnesian War has been compared to a fight between an elephant and a whale. Pericles, who laid down the strategy Athens should follow, saw quite clearly that his country would quickly lose the war in a series of pitched battles against the formidable Spartan army. Therefore, each year when the Spartans marched into Attica to burn the corn, the Athenians retired behind their city walls and offered no resistance. Of course they could afford to do this only because they did not depend on their home-grown grain for survival. The bulk of Athens' corn came from the plains of what is now southern Russia, and this vital supply line was safeguarded by the powerful Athenian fleet, and the Long Walls which linked the Piraeus with Athens. Unless the Spartans managed to storm the Long Walls or gain mastery of the sea they had little chance of defeating Athens.

The inadequacy of Greek methods of siege warfare made an attempted siege of the Long Walls totally impracticable, and it was not until 405 BC that Sparta had gained sufficient confidence to defeat Athens at sea. The annual invasion of Attica by the Spartans certainly had little military value and was probably carried out to keep up appearances. The Athenians, for their part, could not hope to threaten Sparta on land, and the naval raiding expeditions led by Pericles round the Peloponnesian coast in the early years of the war were designed to keep morale high rather than to effect any definite military aim.

Thus from the beginning of the war a strategic stalemate existed between the two sides—provided the Athenians followed Pericles' advice and avoided a pitched battle. These strategic considerations explain why the war dragged on for so long, although it must not be forgotten that the 'open season' for war in the ancient world only lasted from spring until early autumn. For the remainder of the year both sides attended to their farms.

It would, however, be wrong to imagine the Peloponnesian War as a kind of make-believe conflict between two inert giants. The pages of Thucydides' *History* are a catalogue of desperate fights and ruthless intrigues, as each probed the other's weak spots in an attempt to break the deadlock. On both sides civil wars raged with great ferocity as democrats (pro-Athenian) and oligarchs (pro-Spartan) sought to change or maintain their cities' political allegiances. Naturally, the Athenians and Spartans tried to check or exploit such differences,

thus exacerbating the dissensions and causing more bloodshed. In this particular sphere Brasidas, an energetic and far-sighted Spartan general, was the most successful. Between the years 424 and 422 BC he won over many of Athens' allies in Thrace. He was remarkable in that he did this more by the trust he inspired and the reasonableness of the terms he offered than by the threat or use of force.

Unluckily for Sparta he was killed in 422 BC in a battle between Spartans and Athenians outside the key Athenian colony of Amphipolis. Cleon, the Athenian commander, who was also killed at Amphipolis, was another outstanding figure in the war. When Pericles had died in 429 BC, Cleon, who was the son of a successful businessman, took his place as the unofficial leader of Athens. He was reviled by his opponents as a low-born boor and a demagogue (he raised the pay of jurors from two to three obols a day) and Thucydides does not disguise his dislike for him. In Aristophanes' plays Cleon is constantly being lampooned as a corrupt moneygrabber. Nevertheless, it must be remembered that both Thucydides and Aristophanes had personal grounds for disliking Cleon, and recent research has shown Cleon to have been a competent politician.

It was not only in politics that Cleon distinguished himself. He also deserves much of the credit for Athens' principal military victory in the war. In 425 BC an Athenian fleet on the way to Sicily, under the command of the experienced and imaginative Demosthenes, occupied a small, rocky headland called Pylos, on the Messenian coast, only forty-five miles from Sparta. The Spartan force which went to dislodge these impudent invaders was repulsed. Athenian naval reinforcements arrived and sank the supporting Spartan fleet, thus trapping 400 Spartiates on the small island of Sphacteria, which lay just off Pylos.

The Spartans sent ambassadors to Athens and offered to end the war in return for a safe passage for these troops. Cleon persuaded the Athenians to reject the Spartan offer, and clamoured for the capture of the Spartiates on Sphacteria. He would do the job himself, he insisted, if no one else would. To his intense mortification his moderate opponents, anxious to discredit him, took him up on this rash offer. They forced him, struggling and protesting, into the generalship and sent him off to Pylos in command of reinforcements. Cleon, who had had no previous military experience, enjoyed a beginner's luck. The Athenians (mainly directed by Demosthenes) landed on Sphacteria and by skilful use of light infantry, which harried the cumbersome Spartans, compelled them to surrender.

The victory at Pylos marked the height of Athens' and Cleon's fortunes during the war. Cleon's moment of glory after Pylos, however, was brief. His military pretensions received a fatal setback at Amphipolis,

three years later, when he lost his life and the battle.

His death left the stage clear for the rise of an even more picturesque and brilliant figure—Alcibiades. Rich, young, and aristocratic, a protégé of the famous Pericles, Alcibiades was an extremely able and personable politician. If he had restrained his ambition, he could well have won the war for Athens. More than anyone Alcibiades had a genius for arousing men's enthusiasm; but he misdirected the Athenians' energies towards reckless policies which were designed to further his own selfish interests and not those of the city as a whole.

In 421 BC an armistice was agreed on between Athens and Sparta. It has been called the Peace of Nicias, after the moderate Athenian general who was its main champion at Athens. Like its namesake the peace was ineffective. Apart from the Spartan setback at Pylos (and they now had the captured Spartiates back from Athens), there had not been a sufficiently important change in the status quo to make the Peace effective. Alcibiades for one regarded it as a mere formality. His first attempt at diplomacy on the grand scale, an alliance between Athens and Argos, Sparta's traditional enemy, which had hitherto been neutral, was decisively checked by Sparta at Mantinea in 418 BC. There Sparta defeated a combined Athenian and Argive army in one of the few hoplite battles of the war.

The Sicilian expedition

Three years after Mantinea, Alcibiades hit on another plan, and proceeded to make preparations for the Sicilian expedition, which was to prove the greatest disaster in the history of the Athenian Empire. The rich island of Sicily had been mainly colonized by Dorians, and their towns, among which the maritime city of Syracuse was the strongest, had been actively in favour of Sparta and its allies during the war, sending important supplies of wood and grain to the Peloponnese. With the ostensible aim of cutting off these supplies and helping the Ionian cities in Sicily against their aggressive Dorian neighbours, the Athenians voted (after a long debate) to send a vast invasion to Sicily.

Thucydides states quite clearly what Alcibiades' motives were in intiating and carrying through the proposal for the invasion of Sicily. He wanted to conquer all Sicily and then move against Carthage, thus gaining for Athens a new empire in the west—an empire in which he would be the leading figure. Nicias, who was put in command of the expedition with Alcibiades, was a very cautious man who had spoken against the expedition and had attacked Alcibiades personally in the debate. He

hoped the Athenians would make a show of strength, frighten the Sicilians into a stricter neutrality and then return home.

Thus, with a high command divided in its aims (Lamachus, the third general, tended towards Alcibiades' views), and also divided by personal ill feeling, the Athenian force of 100 triremes set sail for Sicily in 415 BC. Alcibiades did not stay long enough in Sicily to see the wreck of his hopes. Summoned back to Athens to face a charge of sacrilege (he and some drunken friends were supposed to have defaced a large number of the statues of Hermes which stood outside most Athenian houses), he preferred not to trust himself to the justice of his political enemies and defected to Sparta.

In spite of Alcibiades' absence, the Athenians remained in Sicily. After some delays they settled down to besiege Syracuse, the focal point of Sicilian resistance. The Syracusans, under their inspiring leader Hermocrates, and with the help of a Spartan military adviser, Gylippus, fought far more bravely and skilfully than the Athenians had thought they would. An attempt to surround the city with a wall and thus slowly starve it into submission was foiled by a Syracusan counter-wall. The Athenians were pinned down to the seashore by Syracusan cavalry operating in the hinterland, and there, surrounded by unhealthy marshes, their ranks were steadily thinned by fevers.

In a report to the Athenians' Assembly in 414 BC Nicias himself complained that he was ill and asked to be relieved of his command. His request was refused and instead fresh reinforcements under Demosthenes were sent out. Many of these troops were squandered in a costly night

engagement on the heights above Syracuse and they did little to alleviate the situation. The moment their encircling wall was stopped, the Athenians became the besieged and the Syracusans were now even attacking them by sea. Finally, the Athenian fleet, which was blockaded in the great harbour, was defeated by the Syracusans who had carefully strengthened their ships' prows to help them in a battle in a confined space.

Thucydides' description of the reactions of the Athenian troops watching this final struggle in the great harbour (most of them from their sickbeds on the shore) is one of the most dramatic in history. The battle was a desperately fought affair, but eventually the Syracusans broke the Athenian line and drove their opponents back to shore.

This victory was decisive. The Athenians were now stranded in Sicily and were in danger of being wiped out. Nicias immediately struck camp and led the 40,000 survivors of his army away from Syracuse, intending to march towards the friendly Sicilian cities in the west. The Athenians never escaped. The Syracusans and their allies harried them mercilessly on the march with their light troops and also their cavalry of which the Athenians had virtually none. First Demosthenes, and then Nicias (after a near massacre of his thirst-crazed troops at the river Assinarus) surrendered.

Nicias and Demosthenes were put to death and the bulk of their troops were put to work as slaves. Only a few Athenians managed to reach Athens to announce the complete destruction of the Sicilian invasion force. The Sicilian disaster was the turning point in the Peloponnesian War. It is, however, a measure of the resilience of the Athenians that, even after this crushing blow, they continued to fight for a further nine years.

Perhaps the most damaging aspect of the whole affair was the naval defeat of the Athenians, which meant that the Spartans and their allies now had the confidence to challenge the Athenians at sea. The main theatre of war became the Ionian sea in the east, where the Spartans, with the financial help of the Persians, who had scented a winning side and wanted to back it, tried to cut off Athens' grain supply from the plains of southern Russia.

At home, Athens itself for the first time in the war was under constant pressure from the Spartan garrison which had occupied the fort of Decelea to the north of the city, and which harried the countryside all the year round. In 406 BC the Athenians defeated the Spartans in the naval Battle of Arginusae. but the value of this victory was immediately nullified by the Persians' making good the Spartan losses.

The strain of war was also beginning to tell on the political life of Athens. In 411 BC, while the fleet was away in the east, an oligarchy was set up at Athens (the Four Hundred and subsequently the Five Thousand). Although this oligarchy lasted only a

Two fifth-century BC statues of Athena in mourning, left, and, below, flying her owl. Acropolis Museum, Athens, and Metropolitan Museum of Art, New York.

year, it was a sign that Athenians were beginning to lose confidence both in their city's aims and in its political system.

Finally, in 405 BC, the Spartan admiral Lysander delivered the final blow when he caught the Athenians unawares on the beach at Aegospotami and destroyed their last fleet. The Athenians, faced with starvation, surrendered and the war came to an end. The long walls dismantled to the strains of music by flute players and an extreme oligarchy ('The Thirty') was imposed by the Spartans on the city. Although democracy was restored soon after, and Athenian power revived for a short time before Philip of Macedon's victory over Greece, the Athenian Empire, as conceived by Pericles, ended in 404 BC.

Philosophy and politics

Historians who set out to write the obituary of the Athenian Empire must ask themselves the question: why did the Athenian Empire fall? Was there in fact an inherent flaw in the democratic system which led to Athens' losing the Peloponnesian War? More often than not an answer is given which goes along these lines. After the death of Pericles the Athenian people were corrupted by the demagogues (such as Cleon and Cleophon) who were pursuing their own selfish ends, and so 'the people', won over to their views, passed the resolutions which ruined Athens. The Athenian people, therefore, and the demagogues were to blame. Such an explanation is grossly unfair to the Athenians and the majority of their leaders. Moreover, this view is implicitly contradicted by Athen's most famous philosopher, Plato, who was no friend of democracy.

Plato was born in 429 BC, the year of Pericles' death, and was brought up in oligarchic circles. An aristocrat, he devoted himself to philosophy, and in particular to the philosophy of one man, Socrates. Socrates became Plato's master and is commemorated by Plato in his dialogues as one of the best and most lovable men.

A stonemason by profession, Socrates was not concerned with the traditional mathematical and physical problems of Greek philosophy but with man himself. He carried out his investigations by the technique of inching towards the truth through a series of questions and answers. These, which Plato recorded and expanded in his works, dealt with such problems as: How should the good man behave? What is the good life? What does the word 'good' actually mean?

From such simple but important questions it is natural to go on to ask (having decided who is the good and just man): what type of society is the most conducive to justice? Thus Socrates and Plato played a vital part in directing philosophy into the

areas of research which it is still examining today: morals, logic, epistemology, and political science.

In his investigations in political science Plato turned to existing states for models on which to work. When he examined Athens he found much to criticize, in particular the amateurism which allowed men with no special training to fill important political posts. In his blueprint for an ideal state, the *Republic*, which examines the nature of justice, Plato argues strongly for a small, highly trained elite who should rule the city. Yet, though he was on oligarch both by conviction and upbringing, Plato was also a constitutionalist who saw the necessity of having laws which all obeyed. And it is when discussing the observance of laws in his dialogue, the *Georgias*, that Plato gives a strong indication as to why Athens failed.

In the *Georgias* Socrates is debating with an old and respected sophist, Georgias, the relative merits and demerits of rhetoric. The sophists were teachers who, for large sums of money, taught their pupils methods of argument and rhetorical techniques which would bring them success in public life. Plato objected to them strongly because of the moral relativism they propagated. This allowed people to ignore the absolute moral

standards he believed in, and set up self-interest in the place of justice as a respectable criterion for men in public life.

A young man, Callicles, who has studied with the sophists, defends his belief that the clever politician can disregard the laws of his city and use his rhetorical skill to pursue his own selfish ends. Callicles is severely reprimanded by Socrates who gives him a strong warning against the dangers which come from holding such a view. Plato's implied criticism of Athens is obvious.

It was men like Alcibiades, not Cleon, who were responsible for Athens' fate. Alcibiades pressed home his plan for the invasion of Sicily to further his own ends, and thus lost sight of justice. Once he had done that, he and the unfortunate Athenians who were duped by him, were lost. Aeschylus would have seen the situation in terms of *hubris* and *nemesis*, but his analysis would have been basically the same as Plato's.

It is hard not to agree with this view. Although democracy faltered temporarily after the Sicilian disaster (there was a brief period of oligarchic rule in 411–410 BC) democracy soon reasserted itself. Neither the democratic system nor the ordinary Athenians on whom it depended were to blame for the country's misfortunes, but

those ambitious individuals who thought they could use democracy as a means to their own self-aggrandizement.

The decline of the cities

The Peloponnesian War exhausted the Greek cities and destroyed a great empire, but unfortunately taught the Greeks no political lessons. The seventy years between the end of the war and the Battle of Chaeronea in 338 BC, when Philip of Macedon smashed the Athenian-Theban alliance and gained control of the Greek cities, read as a depressingly familiar catalogue of battles, treaties and alliances—symptoms of the endemic instability which plagued the Greek cities.

In the place of the defeated Athenians, the Spartans assumed the role of principal political villains. Their inveterate desire for power dragged them into quarrels with Persia in the east, and with Athens, Argos and Thebes at home. Unable to meet the exigencies of naval warfare in the east, the Spartans ceded the Ionian cities to Persia by the Peace of Antalcidas (387 BC).

In Greece the Spartans' military skill maintained their hegemony for thirty years, but this was broken for a decade by the Thebans, who defeated them at the Battle of Leuctra. However, in 362 BC, at Mantinea, Sparta avenged the insult of Leuctra, and Epaminondas, the driving force behind Thebes' revival, was killed. Thus the status quo was re-established. The power of Athens had revived to some extent, and in 371 BC it formed a second naval confederacy. But, though the Athenians made conscious efforts to avoid the worst abuses of their first league, relations between them and their allies gradually deteriorated, culminating in the Social War (357–355 BC).

This period of Greek history may appear trivial in retrospect, since the bickering cities were soon to fall to the power of Macedon. However, one factor which affected the history of this period is of great importance—the rise of the mercenary. The incessant wars of the fifth and early fourth centuries BC had produced throughout the Greek world large numbers of political exiles and free-booting, stateless soldiers. Many of these men entered the services of Persian satraps and the Greek cities soon found it convenient to follow their example and employ mercenaries. Slowly but surely

Above, Attic kylix, or drinking-cup, depicting a young man chasing a hare, c. 500 BC. British Museum, London.

Top, relief depicting Socrates with some of his pupils. British Museum, London.

Opposite, Socrates (before 469–399 BC), one of classical Greece's—and indeed the world's—most important thinkers: his ideas made him unpopular in democratic Athens, and in 399 he was tried and condemned to death; he ignored an opportunity to escape and died after drinking a draught of hemlock. British Museum, London.

the citizen army lost its importance, and money became more desirable than patriotism.

This need for money explains the continuing influence of Persia in Greek politics. The military calibre of mercenary troops was amply proved by the famous March of the Ten Thousand in 401 BC. In 401 BC Cyrus, the brother of the new Persian king, Artaxerxes II, rose in rebellion with an army which included some 13,000 Greek mercenaries. His bid for the Achaemenid throne failed when he was defeated at Cunaxa, near Babylon, losing his life in the battle.

Cyrus' rashness and the weakness of his native troops lost him Cunaxa, but his Greek mercenaries escaped from the battle virtually unscathed. When their generals were captured by Persian treachery the soldiers elected new leaders and decided to fight their way out of the hostile Persian Empire. In spite of continual harassment they achieved the amazing feat of marching through Mesopotamia and Armenia to the friendly Greek cities on the shores of the Black Sea. The story of their exploits was written down by one of their officers, Xenophon, the Athenian, in his famous work the *Anabasis*.

Even if Xenophon had not recorded the March of the Ten Thousand it would have remained a memorable and important event, for it revealed to the Greeks the military weakness of the Persian Empire. Was the Great King really so powerful when he could not prevent 10,000 men from escaping from the very heart of his dominions? Xenophon and his comrades had given the Greek world a clear and unmistakable answer to this question. However, nearly seventy years were to elapse before this information was acted upon, and then not by the Greeks but by the Macedonians.

GREECE IN THE FIFTH AND FOURTH CENTURIES BC

Date	Greece	Culture	Outside world and Rome
500	Revolt of the Ionians Persians capture Miletus Athenian victory at Marathon	Phrynichus: *The Capture of Miletus*	The Etruscans lose Latium
490	Growth of Athenian power Themistocles rebuilds Athenian fleet Spartans defeated at Thermopylae	Herodotus: *Histories*	Struggles of the Plebians at Rome Xerxes becomes Great King of Persia
480	Persians defeated at Salamis Spartan victory at Plateaa Construction of the Long Walls Themistocles ostracized	Pausanias weakens Sparta's reputation Aeschylus: *The Persians*	Victory of Syracuse at Himera Rome wages war against Veii, the Sabines and the Volsci
470	Death of Aristides Delian League founded	Birth of Socrates Phidias decorates the Parthenon Sophocles	Golden Age of Philosophy in China (Confucius)
460	Athenian victory at Aegina Spartan victory at Tanagra Death of Cimon	Aeschylus: *Oresteia* First plays at Euripides	Laws of the Twelve Tables at Rome
450	Peace between Delian League and Persia Athenian expansion over the Peloponnese Pericles *strategus* Thirty Years' Peace		

Date	Greece	Culture	Outside world and Rome
440	Peloponnesian War	Euripides: *Medea*	Rome wages war against the Volsci
430	Death of Pericles Cleon victorious at Sphacteria Peace of Nicias	Aristophanes: *Knights, Peace*	
420	Alcibiades: Sicilian expedition Disaster in Sicily	Euripides: *The Trojans*	
410	Lysander of Sparta Surrender of Athens; fall of Athenian Empire	Thucydides Aristophanes: *Frogs* Sophocles: *Oedipus Coloneus*	Dionysius the Elder of Syracuse
400	March of the Ten Thousand Spartan hegemony	Xenephon's *Anabasis* Death of Socrates Plato's first Dialogues	Rome takes Veii
390	Sparta's war against Persia Peace of Antalcidas	Birth of Aristotle	Rome taken by the Gauls
380	Liberation of Thebes Spartans defeated at Leuctra	Plato's Academy	
370	Theban hegemony	Praxiteles Plato at Syracuse	

Chapter 10

Alexander the Great

Before the fourth century BC Macedonia, lying between Thrace and Thessaly, had never been considered as a force to be reckoned with by the more powerful Greek states. Its tough mountaineers had never been recruited to any more useful purpose than to fight in the perpetual feuds which racked its noble families and kept the country weak. The man who finally welded the Macedonians into a cohesive nation was Philip II, the father of Alexander the Great, who was probably as great a man as his more famous son. A ruthless politician and a brilliant general, he achieved the hitherto impossible task of uniting Macedonia by pursuing an aggressive, nationalistic foreign policy.

Both in diplomacy and in open warfare Philip easily surpassed the Greeks. On the diplomatic front he enjoyed an enormous advantage. The Greeks regarded the Macedonians as their inferiors. In one of his speeches Demosthenes, the orator reminds his Athenian audience who the Macedonians are—a worthless pack of barbarians who do not even make competent slaves. This unreasonable sense of superiority proved the undoing of the Greek cities. They did not take the threat from Philip seriously until it was too late.

To reinforce his diplomatic subterfuges Philip created a formidable military machine. Before his reign the Macedonian peasant levies had been tough but undisciplined troops supporting their aristocratic masters (who fought as cavalry), rather in the manner of the mob in the Homeric army. Because they could not afford the heavy armour worn by the more prosperous Greek hoplites, Philip armed them with a new defensive weapon—a fourteen-foot-long pike. Then he drilled them into hardened, well-disciplined regiments of infantry, the phalanxes, which were to be the backbone of the Macedonian army. Their function was to hold the enemy's infantry line with their long pikes until the mounted aristocrats could charge in a body at one point in the line and break it. Then the rout would begin. The Greek cities, who refused or were unable to adapt their traditional methods of fighting, were helpless before such tactics.

Philip, who succeeded to the Macedonian throne in 359 BC, soon began a policy of expansion. To secure his rear and to gain valuable mineral resources, he first annexed the wild kingdom of Thrace to the east.

This brought him to the borders of the Persian Empire, a fact which was later of great importance. In 348 BC he destroyed the Chalcidian League, and at last the Greek cities began to realize the threat that he represented. At Athens, Demosthenes denounced Philip in a series of brilliant speeches, but the Athenians' actions never matched his oratory. Inexorably Philip's territories grew, as did his influence over the Greek cities.

In 338 BC Athens and Thebes overcame their traditional hatred of each other to join in an alliance against Philip. This last hope

of saving Greece from the Macedonian threat was smashed at the Battle of Chaeronea when Philip defeated the allied army. In command of the Macedonian cavalry on the left wing was the eighteen-year-old Alexander, and it was the charge of his cavalry which decided the battle.

Philip was too clever a politician to attempt to hold down the conquered Greek cities by directly occupying them. Instead, he formed them into the League of Corinth, which was responsible for the control of Greek internal affairs and, although nominally autonomous, was subservient to his wishes. He was the commander-in-chief of its forces, and the decision to take military action on behalf of the league lay with him. A year after its formation Philip asked for (and naturally received) the support of the League for a projected invasion of Persia. As a pretext for this attack, Philip announced that Persia was going to be invaded because of the injuries inflicted by Xerxes on the Greeks 150 years before. Since the Athenians had made this one of the reasons for the formation of their empire, more immediate and realistic motives should be sought.

It has often been supposed that Philip was acting upon a plan put forward by the aged Athenian philosopher, Isocrates, who saw a crusade against Persia as a convenient method of uniting the feuding Greek cities. But the main brunt of the invasion fell on the Macedonian troops and this could have done little to unite the Greek cities. Philip's chief motive for the invasion was probably that he wanted to annex Asia Minor in order to secure his Thracian border.

Philip never led his troops into battle however, for in 336 BC he was murdered at Pella, his capital. Alexander succeeded him and inherited his plan, which he made the basis of his brief but brilliant career.

The early years

Alexander came to the throne as a young man of twenty. He died in 324 BC. In the twelve years of his reign he conquered the greatest empire the ancient world had ever known and created a reputation as one of the foremost military geniuses in history.

Throughout his career the influence of his parents, two equally strong but incompatible people, can be traced. His father, Philip, bequeathed to him a fine army and a blueprint for a glorious career as well as his own outstanding military talents and force of character. His mother, Olympias, was responsible for less obvious but no less important traits in his character. She was an Epirote princess, and her uncle, Arrybus, the King of Epirus, had been more than glad to marry off his tempestuous niece to the powerful neighbouring king of Macedonia.

Olympias was a superstitious and passionate woman who exerted a strong influence on Alexander. She continually reminded her young son that he was the descendant of Achilles through his maternal

line, and of Perseus through his paternal line. The belief that he was descended from two of the most famous heroes in Greek mythology acted on Alexander as a continual spur to action and the importance of this belief must never be discounted when assessing the motives for his achievements.

Perhaps the most famous stage of Alexander's boyhood was the period from 343 to 340 BC when he had as his tutor the famous philosopher Aristotle. Much has been made of the relationship between these two. Aristotle, as a pupil of Plato's Academy, cannot have been slow to foist on his pupil his rather conservative political views, but they seem to have made little impression. Aristotle believed in the racial superiority of the Greeks, yet Alexander in the course of his conquests came to treat the Persians, if not as equals, yet as men to be respected.

The only lasting impression Aristotle seems to have made on his famous pupil was in literature and science, for Alexander was an ardent student of Homer and at the end of his campaigns sent his admiral, Nearchus, down the Persian Gulf on a voyage of scientific discovery. No doubt Alexander received from Aristotle the education befitting a young Greek of high birth, but he could still revert to the brutal excesses of a Macedonian. This side of his character and the influence of his mother far outweighed any civilizing effect Aristotle may have had.

Alexander succeeded to the throne in an atmosphere of intrigue and confusion. Many Macedonian nobles believed Olympias herself to have been behind the assassination of Philip, who had divorced her in 337 BC, an insult she found almost impossible to bear. Philip had been a notorious womanizer and Alexander had shared his mother's hatred of him for many years before his death. The hostility that Olympias inspired among many of the Macedonian nobles both because of her dominating ways and because of her Epirote nationality reflected on Alexander and made his claim to the throne far from secure. However, the prompt murder of rival claimants and the weighty support of two of Philip's most experienced and powerful generals, Antipater and Parmenion, was decisive, and the first crisis of Alexander's career was averted.

First successes

One of Alexander's most important characteristics was his willingness to gamble. His position as Philip's successor was extremely precarious. His safety as king depended solely on the pact made with Parmenion, and the Greek cities who, counting on his youth and inexperience, could be expected to break away at once from the shackles imposed on them by Philip. A lesser man would have adopted the obvious but cautious approach of staying in Greece to secure his rule. Alexander, however, decided to press ahead with the invasion of Persia.

When the campaigning season of 335 BC opened in the spring Alexander moved against the wild tribesmen who inhabited the area between Macedonia and the Danube. He had several reasons for this preliminary campaign. He wanted to bring his boundaries to the natural frontier of the Danube, to secure his rear for the time when he should invade Persia, and to give his troops some valuable military practice against the fierce tribesmen. Alexander showed remarkable prowess by completely defeating the Triballi and the Getae in a series of lightning moves. In particular, his surprise crossing of the Danube at night was an outstanding example of his daring and organizational ability.

Alexander had just suppressed a revolt among the Illyrian tribesmen under their chieftain Cleitus and was marching back in triumph to Pella, when news was brought to him that Thebes had revolted. This was extremely serious, for other Greek cities were wavering on the brink of revolt. It seemed as if the unity achieved by the League of Corinth was to be shattered for ever. Decisive action was needed. In thirteen days Alexander marched 250 miles and camped before the walls of the astounded Thebans. In a desperate battle they were defeated, and the Macedonians stormed into the city to kill 6,000 of its inhabitants regardless of age or sex.

Alexander then took a ruthless and quite deliberate step. At a hurriedly convened meeting of some members of the League of Corinth, a terrible sentence was passed on Thebes, there can be no doubt wholly at the instigation of Alexander. The city was razed to the ground, and all its surviving inhabitants were sold into slavery. The effect of this obliteration on one of the proudest and strongest Greek cities on the rest of the Greeks was devastating. Throughout Alexander's campaign in Persia they remained cowed and subservient to Macedonian rule. By this one ruthless blow Alexander had thus obtained the submission of Greece which allowed him to invade Persia.

172

The Macedonian army

In 334 BC the invading army, which included contingents from the members of the Corinthian League, gathered at Amphipolis. The army which Alexander had collected numbered 43,000 infantry and about 6,000 cavalry.

The nucleus of this army was the 15,000 Macedonian troops who were divided into two regiments of infantry and two of cavalry. The most formidable of the cavalry regiments were the Companions, who were recruited entirely from the land-owning aristocracy of Macedonia. They were heavy cavalry and wore helmets, greaves and breast-plates, and were armed with a short thrusting lance and a sword. The Companions were undoubtedly the elite troops of the Macedonian army, and it was, their wedge-shaped charge which again and again smashed their enemies' lines.

Their nominal commander was Philotas, son of Parmenion, but in practice Alexander himself usually led their charge. The other Macedonian cavalry were the Lancers. They wore no body armour and their main function was to act as reconnaissance and skirmishing troops. The Macedonian infantry were divided into two corps, the Hypaspists and the phalanxes. Though they did not differ in their armament from the ordinary phalanx troops, the Hypaspists had a different function and status. After the Companions had broken the main line they were used to widen and exploit the breach which had been made and thus were essentially offensive troops.

The phalanxes were basically defensive troops, whose task was to hold the enemy. They were also Alexander's personal bodyguard and there was an *esprit de corps* among them which raised them above the ordinary Macedonian trooper. Alexander's debt to Parmenion for his support is also shown by the fact that another of the latter's sons, Nicanor, commanded the Hypaspists.

Besides these formidable troops, Alexander had 15,000 Greek mercenaries and 9,000 light-armed cavalry and infantry from among the very Balkan tribes against whom he had waged his recent campaign. The most

Above, obverse and reverse of a coin depicting Philip II of Macedon. British Museum, London.

Above left, bust of Alexander the Great, c. 330 BC, a Roman copy of a statue of Alexander with a lance by Lysippus, Alexander's favourite sculptor. Musée du Louvre, Paris.

Opposite, bust of Ptolemy (reigned 323–283 BC) dating from c. 280 BC: Ptolemy was one of Alexander the Great's most trusted generals and founded the dynasty that ruled Egypt from 323 to 30 BC. Ny Carlsberg Glyptotek, Copenhagen.

valuable of these were the 1,000 Agranians, armed with javelins, who were famous for their guerrilla warfare. The remainder of his troops were made up of the allied contingents sent by the Greek cities.

In addition to the remarkable innovations made by Philip the Macedonian army differed in one other important respect from other armies—its use of siege warfare. In the fifth century BC the only hope a Greek general had of successfully besieging a city was to invest it or to build up a mound against its walls. The use of siege-towers and ladders was impossible because the besiegers could not keep the defending troops from attacking and throwing them down. Philip II, however, had developed a catapult which shot a heavy arrow from a long distance. With this device he could keep a city's walls clear of defenders while his assault troops moved in with their ladders and siege towers.

This development in siege warfare explains why Athens surrendered immediately after Chaeronea, whereas, throughout the Peloponnesian War, the Spartans did not even consider a direct assault on the city worth attempting. The relative sophistication of Macedonian siege warfare contributed to one of Alexander's greatest victories, the capture of Tyre. It made his army a deadly and balanced force which was, to all intents and purposes, invincible in every theatre of war. In 334 BC Alexander ferried this army across the Hellespont and began his invasion of the Persian Empire.

The Battle of the Granicus

Since the bridgehead across the Hellespont had been secured for Alexander by a Macedonian force sent over by Philip two years before, the Macedonian army was ferried across this crucial passage without mishap. The Persian king, Darius, did not concentrate his troops at this point, but tamely allowed Alexander to gain a first vital foothold. Darius probably did not expect Philip's plan of invasion to be taken up by his son, or even if he did, thought that Alexander's ambitions extended only to the satrapies of Lydia and Hellespontine Phrygia. If this were so then the satraps on the spot, helped by the capable mercenary, General Memnon of Rhodes, would be able to contain, if not defeat, the Macedonians. This was a serious miscalculation but one frequently made by men in their first dealings with Alexander.

After making a sacrifice on the tomb of Achilles at Troy, Alexander marched northwards to the River Granicus. There the satraps of Lydia, Ionia and Hellespontine Phrygia had hurriedly gathered together an army of levies and aristocratic cavalry, which was strengthened by Memnon's Greek mercenaries. It is not surprising that Greeks were willing to fight for the Persians against fellow Greeks and Macedonians.

Apart from the natural cynicism of the mercenary, many of the Greeks in the pay of the Persians (such as the Thebans) had little reason to love the Macedonians.

Alexander reached the Granicus at evening, and found the Persian forces, numbering 30,000, drawn up on the far side of the river, lining the steep banks. Wisely following Parmenion's advice, he decided not to risk a night engagement and made camp. Early the next morning Alexander led his cavalry across the river in a surprise charge. A fierce battle followed, in which the Persian and Macedonian cavalry fought packed together like infantry. Alexander was almost killed by Spithridates, the satrap of Ionia, but was saved by his friend Cleitus. Eventually, the heavier weapons of the Macedonian cavalry began to tell and the Persian cavalry broke. The Persian infantry was swept away by the cavalry and by the phalanxes who had now crossed the river.

The Greek mercenaries in the Persian army retired in good order to a small hill and put up a furious resistance to repeated cavalry and infantry attacks. Eventually they were all killed except for 2,000 of them who were captured and sent back to Greece to work as slaves in the Macedonian mines. Alexander had deliberately refused them a safe passage in return for their surrender because he hoped that his savage treatment would act as a deterrent to the Greeks already serving or intending to serve as mercenaries in Persian armies. In fact this policy had exactly the opposite effect and he was forced later to reverse it.

Immediately after the Granicus, Alexander marched to Sardis, the capital of Lydia, and the main administrative centre for Asia Minor. The town's commander, Mithrines, wisely surrendered Sardis to the Macedonians and Alexander, ever aware of the importance of propaganda, spared Mithrines and gave him an honourable position in his own retinue. From Sardis he

moved to Ephesus, which was surrendered to him by the large democratic (and therefore anti-Persian) party.

Alexander rested at Ephesus and in the meantime sent one of his officers to carry out one of the avowed objectives of the invasion—the liberation of the Greek cities on the Ionian coast. Alchimachus, the officer in charge of this operation, carried it out with little difficulty and set up democracies in place of the Persian-backed oligarchies. This was not because Alexander had any overriding sympathy for democratic government, but because democracy represented, in this case, a convenient political alternative to oligarchy. In mainland Greece, when it suited him, Alexander supported oligarchies.

It is not clear if the Ionian Greek cities were brought into the League of Corinth or left completely autonomous. In practice, however, they were no more than subject states in Alexander's growing empire.

A new threat now presented itself—the powerful Persian fleet, which suddenly made

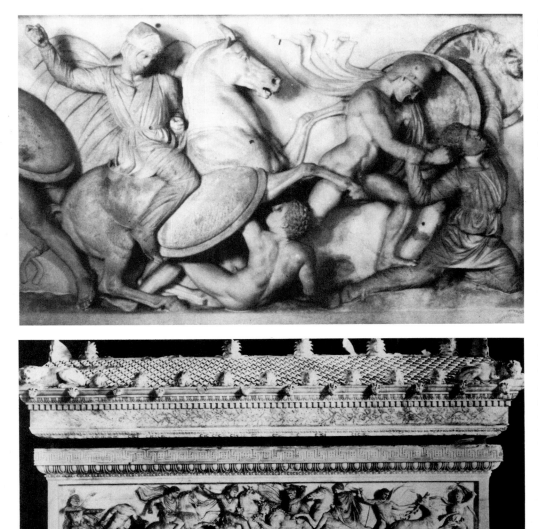

a bid for the important base of Miletus. Alexander had a fleet mainly composed of contingents from the more nautical Greek cities of the League of Corinth. This fleet managed to blockade Miletus before the Persians could reach it, and the town itself was captured by Macedonian troops. The Persian fleet retired to Halicarnassus and so the immediate threat from the sea was avoided. However, it was obvious that the Persian fleet would have to be put out of action. The Macedonians, like the Spartans, were temperamentally averse to naval warfare and Alexander shared this national characteristic. He therefore took the dangerous and unprecedented step of disbanding his fleet and sending it home.

The strategy he adopted was to neutralize the Persian fleet by capturing all its land bases. This was a hazardous policy because it would take a certain amount of time to effect, and in the meanwhile the Persian fleet was free to do as it pleased. It might cut off Alexander's supply lines from Macedonia and could possibly even be used to foment a revolution in Greece. Obviously its bases had to be in Alexander's hands as quickly as possible.

At this particular time the Persian fleet was using the large, well-fortified coastal town of Halicarnassus. Alexander immediately marched to besieged it. After a fierce resistance by its garrison of Greek mercenaries under Memnon, who had been appointed admiral of the fleet by Darius, Macedonia discipline and superior siege craft won the day. A breach was made in the walls, and Memnon, cutting his losses, fired the city and withdrew the fleet and the main body of his troops to the island of Cos. He left behind a token resistance force in the citadel inside the walls.

Because speed was imperative in order to neutralize the Persian fleet, Alexander did not rest his forces, although it was now winter. Taking with him his light-armed troops, he spent the winter subduing the remaining cities on the seaboard of Asia Minor, and in the spring met Parmenion, who had been subjugating northern Phrygia, at Gordium. From here he was well placed to break out through the Cicilian Gates into the plans of northern Syria. From there he could march down into Phoenicia, which was the main centre of Persian naval power. Alexander forced the Cicilian Gates, a high and narrow pass, by a surprise night attack and drove the satrap of Cicilia, Arsames, out into the plains of lower Cicilia. He was unable, however, to strike at the Phoenician cities because of a new but not unwelcome turn of events. News reached him as he was finishing the subjection of Cicilia that Darius was marching north towards him with the imperial army.

Victory at Issus

Darius III of Persia would undoubtedly have been a most successful king if he had not been unfortunate enough to have Alexander as an enemy. He was a competent general and an intelligent politician. The measures he took to defend his empire would probably have succeeded against an ordinary opponent. Unluckily for him neither Alexander nor the army he commanded were in any sense ordinary.

The army which Darius gathered in 333 BC to bring north check Alexander's advances was not the huge imperial army of popular imagination. Darius had deliberately selected a small army composed mainly of Iranian cavalry and Greek mercenaries. He had almost completely discarded the customary horde of satrapal levies, which were generally a useless burden. His aim was to come to grips as quickly as possible with Alexander and thus prevent his navy from being eliminated from the fight. In doing this he showed a sound grasp of the military and political situation.

Leaving his baggage train at Damascus, he marched north until he was divided from Alexander only by the range of the Amanus Mountains. Alexander had expected Darius to cross into the coastal plain by the pass known as the Syrian Gates, and sent Parmenion ahead with the Thessalian cavalry to hold it. He himself followed Parmenion more slowly down the coast of the Gulf of Alexandretta.

At this point Darius displayed his tactical skill and gave Alexander a most unpleasant surprise. Instead of advancing towards the Syrian Gates and waiting for the Macedonians to march out from them to give battle in the Syrian desert, he moved north in a wide detour, crossed the mountains at the Amanic Gates and came down to the coast at Issus. He thus placed himself across Alexander's lines of communication and behind the Macedonian army. At Issus he massacred the Macedonian wounded who had been left there, and then proceeded south down the coast, taking up a defensive position on the River Pinarus across a small plain between the mountains and the sea. Alexander did not allow his troops to brood on

the fact that they had been out-manoeuvred, but immediately turned round and marched north, arriving at the Pinarus late in the afternoon of the second day.

Instead of waiting for the morning he decided to give battle immediately and began to deploy his troops. He placed himself with the Companions and Hypaspists on the right wing and put Parmenion in command of the centre and left wing, which were made up of the phalanxes, the light-armed archers and javelin men and the cavalry provided by the League of Corinth. Darius put his best troops, the Greek mercenaries, in the centre of the line opposite the phalanxes and placed the Cardaces (experimental Persian heavy infantry) opposite the menacing lines of the Companions. This was to prove a fatal mistake. At the last moment Darius switched the whole of his cavalry to the right wing with the aim of breaking Alexander's line at its weakest point. Alexander countered this move by putting the Thessalian cavalry on his left wing right up to the seashore. Slowly the Macedonians advanced towards the river and the Persian lines. Suddenly the Companions, with Alexander at their head, charged forward across the river and in a moment the Persian left wing was in disarray.

This, however, was not the end of the battle. On the left wing the evenly matched Thessalian and Iranian cavalry were locked in a fierce fight. In the centre Darius' Greek mercenaries had poured into the gap left by the speed of the charge made by the Hypaspists and the Companions and were inflicting terrible damage on the exposed phalanxes. However, as soon as the Companions had finally put the Persian left wing to flight, they swung round to relieve the phalanxes. At this point Darius fled from the battlefield.

The Persian cavalry and most of the Greek mercenaries retired in good order but the great majority of the Persian infantry were killed by the Macedonians who swept on to Issus to capture the Persian baggage train and the wife, mother and daughters of Darius. Darius was pursued far into the night but he escaped. He has often been called a coward for his flight, but he had perfectly good and honourable reasons for fleeing. His safety was more important to the Persian Empire than any army, for he was the focal point of resistance and had he not fled from the battle when he did, he might well have been trapped and killed by the Companions.

The political impact of Issus was enormous. Agis, the Spartan king, who was about to lead a revolt in Greece against Macedonian rule, was forced to abandon his plans when the Persian admirals helping him returned to their bases on the news of the defeat. Above all, Alexander was now free to march into Phoenicia and deliver his body blow to the dangerous Persian navy.

The siege of Tyre

Phoenicia, which Alexander invaded late in the winter of 33 BC, was a narrow coastal plain lined with important maritime cities, which provided the Persians with most of their sailors and ships. Ten years previously

the cities (with the exception of Tyre) had revolted against Persian rule, and this revolt had been savagely repressed. The Phoenicians, therefore, welcomed Alexander as a liberator. The power of their puppet kings was ratified, and in return they placed their resources at Alexander's disposal.

Tyre, however, which was the most powerful of the cities, remained loyal to Darius and closed its gates to Alexander. Its citizens were confident that Alexander, in spite of his proven abilities at siege warfare, would be unable to capture their town. They had some justification for making such a calculation. The main part of Tyre was on an island half a mile from the coast, and was surrounded by walls which in some places arose to a height of 150 feet. They had a powerful navy deployed in three harbours round the island, and Alexander was obviously handicapped by his lack of ships. Apart from these military considerations they had a strong political incentive. The longer they pinned Alexander before their walls the more time Darius would have to recruit a new army. Alexander had equally strong motives for undertaking the seemingly impossible task of capturing the island fortress. So long as Tyre remained active his strategy of crippling the Persian navy from the land would remain uncompleted.

The siege lasted seven months and was perhaps Alexander's finest military achievement. It showed in particular his amazing tenacity and his ability to keep up the spirits of his troops. Because he did not have any ships Alexander began to build a causeway or mole out towards the island, using the rubble from the houses of old Tyre on the coast. This tactic, however, was not particularly successful, for the siege-towers he placed at its end were constantly being attacked by missiles from the walls and by Tyrian ships and fire-ships.

He was saved from failure because suddenly and dramatically his anti-Persian naval policy reaped its reward. The news

that most of the Phoenician cities had sided with the Macedonians reached the Persian fleet, and the Phoenician sailors promptly deserted their Persian masters and came flocking back to their homes. Suddenly Alexander found himself in command of a great part of the former Persian fleet. Yet even now his problems were not over, for the Tyrians' walls were still virtually undamaged. Alexander had an ingenious solution—floating siege-towers. He placed conventional siege-towers on two ships lashed together and these sailed round Tyre, battering at the walls. In spite of the Tyrians' desperate efforts to stop them, these floating battering rams did their damage and eventually, after a concentrated attack on their main harbour by the fleet and on a weakened section of the wall by the Hypaspists, Tyre was captured.

The Tyrians paid heavily for their loyalty The town was sacked and those of the inhabitants who were not massacred were sold into slavery.

Alexander in Egypt

To avoid any recrudescence of Persian naval power, Alexander decided to occupy the last possible base in the Mediterranean the Persians could have used, and invaded Egypt. The word 'invasion' is perhaps misleading. Egypt had never been a loyal satrapy of Persia because of the hostility of its powerful priests, which was exacerbated by an uncharacteristic Persian obtuseness and intolerance. The satrapy had revolted at the end of the fifth century BC and was only brought back into the Persian Empire as late as 343 BC by the brutal Artaxerxes Ochus. The only resistance Alexander encountered was from the Persian garrison at Gaza, which was captured after a fierce fight.

In order to impress upon the world his descent from Achilles, Alexander dragged the Persian commander, Batis, behind his chariot round the walls of Gaza in emulation of Achilles' treatment of Hector in the *Iliad*. The rest of his march into Egypt as far as Memphis, the capital of the satrapy, was a triumphal progress. At Memphis, Alexander was crowned pharaoh, an act which had considerable propaganda value. As Darius had been acknowledged as pharaoh before this, in the eyes of the world he had now been deposed by Alexander.

After spending a short time at Memphis where he rested his troops and gave a series of splendid games, Alexander set out up the Nile to inspect his new kingdom. When he reached the mouth of the Nile near Lake Mareotis he decided to build a city on the isthmus which jutted out from the coast. In this way Alexandria was founded. The ancient authorities have always implied that this was a sudden decision on the part of Alexander, but this does not seem likely.

Above, the ancient city of Taxila, Pakistan, first occupied in the sixth century BC: here Alexander halted en route *to India, 326 BC.*

Opposite top, the ruins of Persepolis, Darius' ceremonial capital, destroyed by Alexander the Great in 331 BC.

Left, the ruins of the port of Tyre, the Persian stronghold whose eventual capture by Alexander in 332 BC opened the way to Egypt.

Opposite bottom, the theatre at Sidon, through which Alexander passed before the Battle of Issus.

Alexandria was founded at a very healthy spot on the coast, and the isthmus formed a natural harbour. Alexander probably intended to found a city which would take the place of Tyre as the main *entrepôt* of the eastern Mediterranean, and chose his site with care.

From Alexandria he marched into the Libyan desert to the oasis of Siwah in order to consult the famous oracle of Ammon, whom the Greeks regarded as the Egyptian equivalent of Zeus. No one knows what the priest of Ammon told Alexander when they went in alone to consult the oracle. Arrian, the Greek historian of the second century BC, states enigmatically that Alexander heard what he wanted, and it is possible to make a reasonable guess as to what this was. As pharaoh, Alexander had become the son of Ammon and, therefore, in Greek eyes, the son of Zeus. No doubt the priest confirmed to Alexander that he was the son of the god and probably gave him hopes of further conquests.

This visit to the oracle of Ammon marks a most important step in the development of Alexander's character. He really believed that he had become the son of a god, just as before he really believed that he was descended from Achilles. Henceforth he began to behave more and more like an oriental despot, and the deterioration of his relations with his practical and down-to-earth Macedonian countrymen dates from this Egyptian episode.

After reorganizing the government of Egypt, Alexander left for Tyre where he intended to regroup his forces in preparation for his decisive battle with Darius.

The end of the Persian Empire

Although Alexander had conquered large tracts of the Persian Empire, defeated Darius at Issus and wrested from him the title of pharaoh, nevertheless Darius' position was far from hopeless. He still controlled the greater part of his empire, the important cities of Babylon, Susa, Persepolis and Ecbatana, and the vast areas of his eastern satrapies. Alexander had to defeat Darius decisively, preferably kill him, and gain control of the cities before he could call himself the new king of Persia with any degree of confidence.

After completing some necessary administrative changes from his base at Tyre, Alexander set out in the spring of 331 BC to strike at the heart of the Persian Empire. Darius, who had gathered a new army of 100,000 men, waited for him at Babylon on the Euphrates, expecting Alexander to advance down the Euphrates as all previous invaders had done. This would give Darius the advantage of being able to choose a favourable site at which to make his stand. Unfortunately, Alexander did not do as he was expected. Instead, he decided to keep away from the central Mesopotamian valley and cross the Tigris in order to approach Babylon from the east. By doing this he would avoid the enervating heat of the central valley and be able to fight on neutral ground. Moreover, with luck, he might unnerve the Persian army, which, because of its size, had much difficulty in manoeuvring.

Darius fell back on an alternative plan, which was to ambush Alexander as he made the difficult passage of the fast-flowing Tigris. This scheme too, however, went awry when Alexander captured some Persian scouts and compelled them to disclose this vital information. Avoiding the Mosul ford, which Darius was watching, he crossed the Tigris further north, and swung south round the ruins of Nineveh to confront Darius on more equal terms.

The two armies met at Gaugamela, a small village lying on the open plain. At night-time they camped opposite each other, separated by a flat strip of land three and a half miles wide. The Macedonians slept but Darius kept his troops at battle stations throughout the night, since he feared a surprise attack. Parmenion, in fact, had suggested such a plan to Alexander, who had rejected it. The result of Darius' justifiable cautiousness was that on the morning of the battle his troops were tired and nervous, while the Macedonians were relaxed and confident after a sound night's sleep.

The Battle of Gaugamela was the decisive action in the dual between Darius and Alexander. It was a victory for Alexander's generalship, since the Persians fought very bravely. The Macedonians were drawn up in exactly the same manner as they had been at Issus. Alexander commanded the Companions and lancers on the right wing, and Parmenion the phalanxes and Thessalian cavalry on the left. Darius arranged his cavalry on the left and right wings under two satraps, Bessus and Mazaeus. He himself took command of the centre, which was made up of cavalry and the powerful infantry regiments consisting of royal bodyguards and Greek mercenaries.

The main difference between Gaugamela and Issus was the enormous numbers that Darius had at his disposal. Because the battlefield was far wider, Alexander curved his line at each end to avoid a flanking movement by the Persians. During the battle the troops from these bunched flanks were fed into the centre to hold the tremendous pressure exerted by the Persian weight of numbers. Because of Persian numerical superiority Alexander had to delay the decisive charge of the Companions which, had it come too soon, would have been swamped by the densely-packed Persian cavalry.

Alexander's tactics were successful. After waiting until all Darius' cavalry was engaged he broke through the Persian left wing with the Companions. On the Macedonian left wing Parmenion with his Thessalian cavalry was being hard pressed by Persian cavalry led by Mazaeus, and Alexander turned to come to his help. On his way Alexander and the Companions ran into the Indian cavalry of the Persian centre and, after one of the sharpest encounters of the battle, these too were turned.

In the meantime Parmenion had not only held the Persians' cavalry charge but was driving them back at the head of his tough Thessalians. Darius, seeing his army in retreat on all sides, fled the battlefield, hotly pursued by Alexander. Parmenion's cavalry and the Macedonian infantry dealt with the rest of the disintegrating Persian army.

The immediate importance of the victory was that it opened up to the Macedonians the key cities of the Persian Empire. Alexander advanced to Babylon whose servile population accepted him with enthusiasm. Mazaeus, who displayed a fine contempt for loyalty, was reinstated as satrap. The Macedonian troops gave themselves over to the riotous pleasures of Babylon, much to the disapproval of Alexander's more ascetic biographers.

Alexander himself, however, did not allow them long to enjoy themselves, and quickly followed up his advantage. Susa and Persepolis both fell, and Alexander's conquest of Persia was virtually completed.

As a reward to his troops, he allowed them to loot Persepolis, and was himself responsible for burning the beautiful palace built there by Darius I and his son Xerxes.

He has been roundly condemned for this barbarous act, but there were several mitigating circumstances. The Macedonians' anger had been aroused on their entry into Persepolis by the sight of Greek prisoners-of-war whom the Persians had horribly mutilated, and Persepolis was the sop Alexander threw to his troops' outraged feelings. As for the burning of the palace, this may have been, as has been suggested, merely the deplorable result of a fit of drunkenness, but it would be unwise to underestimate Alexander's intelligence and political acumen. By burning the Achaemenid's palace Alexander showed the whole world that their rule had finally ceased.

At this point he could well have ceased his exertions, but his restless genius drove him on to hound the unfortunate Darius to death and add more vast tracts of land to his empire.

Guerrilla warfare

The huge eastern satrapies of Parthia, Aria, Sogdiana, Bactria and Aricosia were not as attractive to a conqueror as the rest of the Persian Empire. They were inhabited by rough, nomadic tribesmen, ruled by feudal barons, and the Persians themselves had never properly assimilated or civilized them. However, apart from his insatiable desire for conquest, Alexander had sound strategic reasons for subduing these vast desolate tracts. Their inhabitants and the even wilder tribes—the Sacae and the Massagetae who roamed the plains to the north of Sogdiana—would present a perpetual threat to his new empire unless they were properly cowed. Accordingly Alexander spent the next few years subjugating the area from the Mesopotamian valley to the River Jaxartes in the north and the River Indus in the southeast.

The nature of this campaign was entirely different to the previous ones he had fought.

His chief opponent, Spitamenes of Sogdiana, used the different terrain and the hit-and-run tactics of his nomadic cavalry to great advantage, and Alexander had all the infuriating difficulties of a general confronted with guerilla tactics. Yet he managed, as always, to adapt his fighting methods, which the less imaginative Roman generals, who later fought unsuccessfully in this area, failed to do.

Two examples of the versatility of Alexander and his troops are worth mentioning. The first, taken from Alexander's campaign against the Sacae, shows how he met the danger of the nomadic cavalry tactics in the open plains. The Sacae's usual procedure was to ride round and round an enemy force, gradually wearing them down. When they were charged they would retreat out of danger and then return to begin their circling movement once again.

Instead of concentrating his troops, Alexander sent out a light force to lure the Sacae into an attack. Then, having carefully cut off all their avenues of escape with his infantry, he sprang his trap by attacking them with the Companions. The light horsemen of the Sacae found themselves hemmed in on every side and were severely mauled.

The other problem Alexander had to deal with was the high mountains of the area.

Above, onyx cameo of an Egyptian king and queen of the Ptolemaic dynasty; the dynasty is named after one of Alexander's generals, who became king of Egypt in 311 BC. Kunsthistorisches Museum, Vienna.

Opposite, second-century AD reliefs from the theatre at Corinth depicting a battle between the Greeks and Romans.

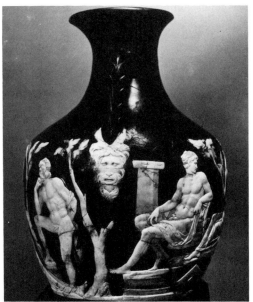

Many of his troops soon developed remarkable mountaineering talents and, on one occasion, Alexander used this new skill in a most dramatic fashion. He was in Sogdiana soon after Spitamenes had been finally defeated, subduing the few remaining feudal barons. One of these, Oxiartes, had retired to a mountain surrounded by sheer cliffs, known as the Sogdianian Rock. The fortress at its top was seemingly impregnable. Oxiartes had taunted Alexander that he would need soldiers with wings if he wanted to capture it.

Alexander chose a small force of 300 from among his most skilful climbers and sent them up the rock face at night, using crampons and ropes. Oxiartes was so amazed by this feat of mountaineering that he did not bother to see how many soldiers had reached the summit, but immediately surrendered. Alexander treated him well and married his daughter Roxane, who was a noted beauty. This policy of clemency soon induced the remaining hostile chiefs to surrender.

The final conquests

The second half of Alexander's career was varied and eventful, politically as well as militarily. His chief opponent, Darius, had been betrayed and murdered by the satrap of Bactria, Bessus, who thus saved Alexander the embarrassment of having to kill Darius when he finally caught him. Although Darius' career had ended in the most pitiable circumstances (he was found dying alone in an ox-cart) Alexander was magnanimous enough to appreciate his true worth. When he finally caught Bessus he had him put to death in a barbarous manner.

However, any credit Alexander gained by the justice with which he dealt with Persian treachery is offset by his own treachery to his followers at this period. His principal victims were Parmenion and Philotas, Parmenion's son. Nicanor, Parmenion's other son, luckily died of natural causes before he could be implicated in his family's downfall.

Philotas was executed on a trumped-up charge of not having reported some treasonable, but very unimportant, talk to Alexander. Then Parmenion, who had been left at Ecbatana, was condemned and summarily executed on false evidence which had been extracted from Philotas by torture. Alexander, who resented his early debt to Parmenion, had for a long time been attempting to discredit or, better, kill the elderly general and his sons, and so their deaths were for the most part the result of political calculation. But they were also symptoms of Alexander's increasing habit of behaving like an oriental despot. He wore oriental dress and imitated the servile court procedure of the Achaemenid kings. Much of this was dictated by the need to win over the Persians, but this does not entirely explain Alexander's transformation.

Many of the Macedonians quite justfiably resented Alexander's behaviour, and the knowledge of their resentment made Alexander even more suspicious. Two victims of this clash of wills were the philosopher Callisthenes, Aristotle's nephew, and Cleitus, both of whom remonstrated with Alexander over his oriental ways and fell victims to his anger. Alexander did show remorse at the death of Cleitus in particular, whom he himself had killed in a drunken rage, but he did not change his ways.

Alexander was now intent on a policy which was to have more far-reaching effects than a mere change in his court ceremonial and his personal dress. He had a cadet force of 30,000 young Iranians whom he trained in Macedonian military techniques, and he also arranged mass marriages between his troops and Persian women.

Discontent was slow to filter down to the ordinary troops, but eventually, when Alexander invaded India and, having defeated the Indian king, Porus, at the Battle of the Hydaspes, seemed intent on marching deeper into the subcontinent, they too mutinied. Alexander attempted bribery and threats, but the troops remained adamant. They wanted to return home and have a chance to spend the enormous bounties they had won.

Alexander finally gave way and turned back. He sailed triumphantly down the Indus to the sea, and began the long march westwards to the great cities of Persia. On this journey he made one of the most glaring mistakes of his career. Instead of keeping to the coast of southern Iran, he attempted to cross the Gedrosian Desert, the hottest stretch of land in the northern hemisphere. The march was a disaster and Alexander completed it having lost three-quarters of his army.

The last year of his life, 324 BC was marred by increasingly frequent fits of anger, and he infuriated the Macedonians by a demand to be deified. He finally died at Babylon of a fever at the age of thirty-two. When he was asked on his death-bed to whom he bequeathed his empire, he replied 'to the strongest'. Even then his political foresight did not desert him, for his generals were soon engaged in the murderous wars of succession from which the Hellenistic empires emerged—paltry kingdoms compared with the vast empire that Alexander had won so spectacularly in such a short time.

The reputation of Alexander

Alexander was a man who aroused either great admiration or great hatred among his contemporaries, and it is therefore difficult to give a balanced assessment of his character and achievements. Although he has come down in history with the title of 'great', he fully merits this only in one respect. Alexander was one of the greatest soldiers the world has ever seen. His skill as a strategist and tactician has always evoked the whole-hearted admiration of military historians, and he backed up this fundamental skill with an uncanny ability to inspire his men to do their best on every occasion. His own personal bravery, which sometimes bordered on recklessness, was the basis of his powers of leadership.

Alexander the ruler, however, is a figure of completely different calibre from Alexander the conqueror and general. Although he had a talent for short-term political manipulation, as an administrator he never matched his father, Philip. The arrangements he made for the cities and satrapies he conquered did not in most cases survive his death, and they were rarely an improvement on the previous government. His appointments were dictated mainly by political expediency or by the need to reward loyal supporters.

Alexander has been extravagantly praised as a founder of cities. However, with the exception of Alexandria, he never founded a great city. Most of those towns which he did establish were in the eastern satrapies of Persia, and they were little more than fortified garrisons, inhabited by Greek and Macedonian army veterans, who soon abandoned their uncongenial surroundings.

Alexander's so-called 'vision of the brotherhood of man', the racial and cultural fusion of east and west, has similarly been exaggerated. It is doubtful whether Alexander, off the battlefield, was ever clearheaded enough to have visions of this nature. What is certain is that Alexander developed a genuine taste for the luxurious life of an oriental despot. To be able to lead such a life he had to move away from his early role as a Macedonian king, which

involved a rough and easy familiarity with his fellow Macedonians. All his 'Persianising' manoeuvres (mixed marriages and the adoption of Persian court ceremonial) must therefore be seen as measures to weaken and sap the independence of his Macedonian supporters. They were not a deep-seated plan to mix the two races, thus establishing a new culture for the peoples of the Mediterranean and Middle East. The fact that such a fusion of the two cultures did take place later in the kingdom established by his successors, even being given a distinct name 'Hellenistic', is not relevant. There is no conclusive evidence to suggest that Alexander was aiming at such a state of affairs.

Alexander's character usually arouses a chorus of moral disapproval. He was a very heavy drinker; he could be cruel and treacherous; and there seems little doubt that he was more amorously inclined towards men than women—although he made several marriages of political convenience. However, all the Macedonians were extremely heavy drinkers, and intrigue and assassination had always been accepted methods of settling political differences among the Macedonian nobility. In these respects Alexander was a perfectly normal example of a Macedonian king. Alexander's homosexuality (certainly more acceptable then than now) is usually attributed to the overpowering influence of his mother, Olympias. Olympias is usually blamed for Alexander's naive belief in his heroic and divine origins, which culminated in his demand for deification at the end of his life. Such ideas may seem grotesque, but Alexander's successors adopted them, and the de facto deification of the king became a significant feature of certain Hellenistic kingdoms.

Alexander's worst fault would seem to have been his ungovernable temper. He frequently flew into violent rages, especially when he was drunk. These fits of anger often had tragic results, as when he murdered his

Above, the Medici Vase, first century BC: the relief portrays an episode from Greek mythology, perhaps the sacrifice of Iphigenia. Uffizi Gallery, Florence.

Above left, Laocoon and his two sons being killed by serpents, marble sculpture, c. 50 BC: Laocoon, a priest of Apollo, warned the Trojans of the dangers of the wooden horse; the Trojans disbelieved Laocoon, had him killed and brought the horse within the walls of Troy, thus admitting the Greek troops concealed within it. Vatican Museum, Rome.

Opposite top right, the Portland Vase, a blue and white glass amphora, thought to depict Peleus and the goddess Thetis. British Museum, London.

Opposite top centre, bronze head of a satyr dating from the Hellenistic age, the term used to describe the predominantly—though not exclusively —Greek culture and civilization of the eastern Mediterranean after the reign of Alexander the Great. Staatliche Antikensammlungen, Munich.

Opposite top left and bottom, two scenes from Alexander's sarcophagus, last quarter of fourth century BC. Archaeological Museum, Istanbul.

THRACE · Byzantium

MACEDONIA
Pella
Amphipolis
Methone
Olynthus
Pydna
Potidaea

Epidamnus

PROPONTIS

THASOS
CHERSONESUS
Aegospotami
Abydus
Cyzicus

Sigeum

PHRYGIA

EPIRUS

CORCYRA

THESSALY

LEMNOS

AEGEAN SEA

PERSIAN
EMPIRE

Thermopylae

AETOLIA
Delphi

Chaeronea EUBOEA
Thebes Chalcis
Leuctra Eretria
Megara

MYTILENE
LESBOS ARGINUSAE

Phocaea

Sardis

LYDIA

CHIOS

Elis
Sicyon
Olympia Corinth
Mantinea
Sphacteria Sparta

Athens
Argos

ANDROS

SAMOS

Ephesus

Miletus
Halicarnassus

NAXOS

Philip and the Phalanx

Athenians and Thebans

Cephisus

Alexander

marsh

Acropolis of Chaeronea

MELOS

CYTHERA

BATTLE OF CHAERONEA

RHODES

CRETE

MEDITERRANEAN SEA

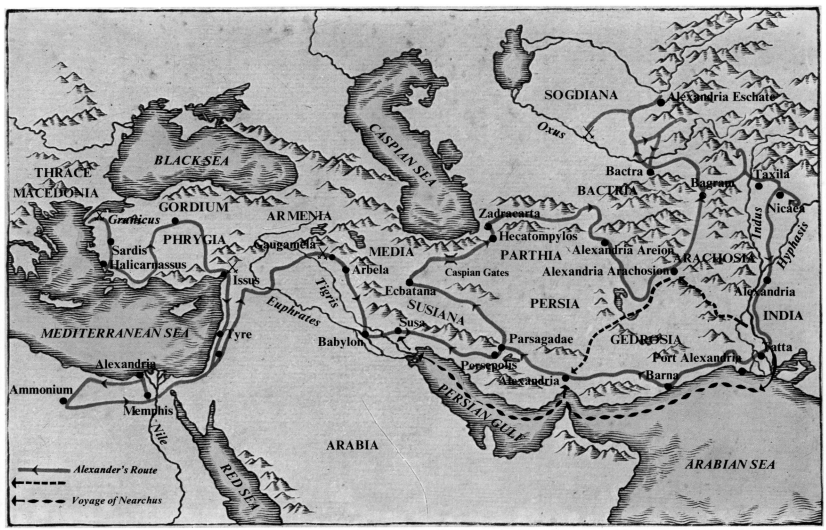

Above, map of the conquests of Alexander the Great.

friend Cleitus. Yet Alexander's temper was only one manifestation of a basic trait in his character—his impetuosity. This impetuosity was fatal to his reputation when unleashed at the banqueting table, but, properly restrained on the battlefield, it was one of the cornerstones of his amazing success.

It is of course, essential not to isolate the man from his times. Alexander's career was more than a solo and virtuoso military performance. His actions affected the whole of the then civilized world. The Macedonian conquest of Greece and Persia involved such an enormous social upheaval that the Greek cities found it impossible to revert to their old values. Alexander's career marks the end

of the classical era in Greece and the beginning of the Hellenistic period.

To the impartial observer it may seem a fine and spectacular ending to such a long and important span of history. The Greeks knew better. When the news of Alexander's death was announced at Athens one politician remarked, 'If it were true the whole world would stink of his corpse.' This remark contains more than just political rancour and hatred for a tyrant. It is a bitter reflection on the basic difference between the Greeks and Alexander that when the Greeks destroyed it was in order to build again. Alexander destroyed for the sake of destruction. It is they, the Greeks, who really deserve the title 'great'.

Opposite right, the Victory of Samothrace, early second century BC: this marble statue, of victory alighting on the prow of a ship, found on the island of Samothrace in 1803, commemorates a naval victory. Musée du Louvre, Paris.

Opposite centre, statue of the goddess Diana.

Opposite left, the Venus de Milo, c. 100 BC, the celebrated statue of the goddess Aphrodite found on the island of Melos in 1820. Musée du Louvre, Paris.

THE EMPIRE OF ALEXANDER THE GREAT

Date	Conquests	Culture	Rome	Date	Conquests	Culture	Rome
360	Philip of Macedon Birth of Alexander			330	Persepolis burnt Conquest of the eastern satrapies	Demosthenes: On the Crown Theatre at Epidauros	
		Demosthenes: first Philippics	Foundation of Ostia		Alexander murders Cleitus		
350	Philip invades Chalcidice				Alexander in India		Second Samnite War
		Aristotle			Return of Alexander and Nearchus		Treaty between Rome and Carthage
	Philip advances into Greece League of Corinth	Demosthenes: second and third Philippics	First Samnite War		Alexander at Susa		
340	Accession of Alexander Suppression of the Greek revolt	Aristotle founds the Lyceum			Death of Alexander		
	Alexander victorious at Granicus		Plebians admitted to the magistracy		Division of the Empire	Death of Aristotle and Demosthenes	
	Alexander defeats Darius at Issus		Victory of Rome over the Latins				
	Tyre—Alexander in Egypt Arbela	Foundation of Alexandria					

Part III

THE DOMINANCE OF ROME

Introduction

Rome began as a collection of villages beside the lower Tiber. Today we can see the handiwork of Rome flung defiantly across the moors of northern Britain, along the dusty margin of the Sahara and in the sands of Mesopotamia. If we look at a list of the rulers of Rome, we find there not merely Romans nor even Italians. The list includes provincials from Spain, Africa, the Balkans and Syria. Among them are the son of an Arabian brigand and a freebooter from the Low Countries. From the Euphrates to the Atlantic, every sort of language and colour was encompassed by the Roman Empire. Rome, unlike the relatively coherent world of Greece, was an amalgam of disparate traditions and peoples such as the world has rarely seen.

This amalgam was bound together by a reasonably simple, comprehensible and humane legal system and by a uniform technology. The overall mechanism was the official use of a logical language, Latin, although other, local languages, above all Greek, which remained the *lingua franca* of the eastern Mediterranean, played their part.

The interlocking relationship of the Greek and Roman contributions to the arts has long been the subject of much misunderstanding. Without going so far as Mrs Benjamin Disraeli, who 'never could remember which came first, the Greeks or the Romans', responsible critics have in the past been only too ready to underrate the qualities of Rome as the creative successor of Greece, not merely in the skills of the camp and the market-place but also in sculpture, painting and architecture. Statements such as 'Roman art is decadent Greek art' or 'in Greek archaeology, any object you turn up is beautiful; in Roman, you are delighted if you can argue that it is second-rate' are evidence of a widespread, unintelligent and wholly misleading trend.

On a small-scale map it is possible to run a pencil line around the Greek lands of the climactic Hellenic period, the fifth century BC, with a considerable measure of precision. Within that outline, in the homelands, cities of no great magnitude but jealously independent were maintained by territories of modest size and by seaborne trade. In the outlands, such as the fertile margins of the Black Sea or southern Italy, the population

surplus from mainland Greece planted full-grown colonies which retained little more than a sentimental link with the mother-city. There was at this time no Greek Empire in any political sense, but there was an appreciable diffusion of a uniform Hellenic culture, with singularly little local deviation.

Representational art at this early period was still characterized aesthetically by the restrictive instincts of all child art, in the sense that it was concerned with generalization rather than with individuality. Generalization had, however, been carried to an astonishing degree of perfection by the Greek intelligence, with its bias towards mathematical calculation and proportion. For example, in the previous century the great philosopher Pythagoras had 'supposed the elements of number to be the elements of all things', and in the middle of the fifth century BC the sculptor Polyclitus proclaimed the same principle. Greek architects, too, produced treatises on precise architectural proportions. In short, Greek thinking was primarily concerned with abstract ideas. For example, the young celebrants in procession on the Parthenon frieze (*c.* 440 BC), were all 'identical twins', of perfect shape but without an individual feature, reaction or emotion among them.

In accordance with this aesthetic principle, fifth-century Greek art was devoid of portraiture in any valid sense of the term. The famous 'portrait' of Pericles by Cresilas has no more individuality than a barber's dummy. Not until the fourth century BC was well advanced did any approach to deliberate portrayal become manifest. The earliest surviving example is probably the majestic figure which almost certainly represents Mausolus himself, from his monument, the Mausoleum at Halicarnassus,

dating from the middle of the century. According to literary tradition, at about the same time a sculptor called Demetrios acquired the nickname 'maker of men', as distinct from 'maker of statues', by virtue of his new naturalism. He is said to have portrayed a Corinthian general as 'high-bellied, bald, his clothes half off him, some of the hairs of his beard caught by the wind, his veins prominent'. Above all, in the latter half of the century, Alexander the Great's features left their mark on an era in individualistic portraits by the sculptor Lysippus and his contemporaries. Portraiture had at last entered into the consciousness of Greek art. It had already begun to point the way to the Roman sculptors and medallists, who in subsequent centuries were to develop the trend and to produce some of the finest portraits in the history of sculpture.

In more ways than one, Alexander and his age from the end of the fourth century BC marked the emergence of those ideas, political and cultural, which were to permeate the later Republic and Empire of Rome. From the time of Alexander onwards, the individual was to dominate the social and cultural scene. This revolution, or rather evolution, in art was accompanied by parallel political changes. The town or village polity, with its little democracies and transient leaders, was now enlarged into kingdoms and empires with impressively individual totalitarian rulers. In that sense Alexander and his powerful successors were the forerunners of the emperors of Rome. Upon each of them, as an individual, depended at any one time the destiny of an appreciable part of the civilized world. Whether politically, domestically or aesthetically, we have moved from the impersonal pageantry of the Parthenon to the

vivid personality, for example, of the 'Altar of Peace' at Rome (13–9 BC), where a life-like parade of the Roman aristocracy, warts and all, screens an aesthetically secondary altar.

Nor was this all. Alongside the increasing dominance of the individual emerged a growing sense of his environment. Thus it was that the Greek artists of the fifth century BC showed no awareness of landscape, except in the most symbolical form. However, when their successors began to think of individual human beings as such, whether kings or candlestick-makers, they inevitably began to think of specific and appropriate surroundings; the great man in his ceremonial setting, the lesser man in his shop or workshop or tending his herds. Landscape and townscape were born. The parallel developments of pastoral poetry and of domestic or romantic comedy in the third century BC were part of this trend. By the time Rome was ready, either directly or through its great provincial capitals such as Alexandria, to assume, at least in name, the cultural leadership of the Mediterranean, landscape was beginning to suffice the artist and his public as a subject worthy of depiction in its own right. Pliny goes so far as to ascribe 'the pleasant fashion of painting walls with pictures of country houses, landscape gardens, groves, hills, fishponds, rivers, coasts to the invention of a particular artist of the time of Augustus (27 BC–AD 14). This is of course excessive precision, but when Pompeii and its neighbouring towns were destroyed by Vesuvius in AD 79 many of their wall-paintings were of that kind. Moreover, the unlighted corridors of Nero's Golden House at Rome a dozen years earlier had imitation windows with landscapes painted upon them as a matter of course.

These are examples, chosen from many, to show that, in the arts no less than in politics, Rome discovered or carried on and developed trends of thought that either had not been manifest in the Greek experience or had at most been in a rudimentary stage. Greece in the fifth century BC, the Hellenistic age after Alexander the Great, the later Republic and the Empire of Rome were each with its own qualities successive, not competitive, phases in the organic, evolutionary expansion of human aspiration and expression.

Chapter 11

The Foundation of the Roman Republic

The history of the rise and dominance of Rome is the story of how, from obscure and lowly origins, the descendants of a few primitive Iron-Age peasants, squatting on some knolls of land on the River Tiber, worked and fought to win ultimate mastery over the known world.

In about 616 BC the village settlements of these peasants were taken over by the Etruscans who, in the space of a hundred years, turned them into a city. Profiting by Rome's strategic site controlling the last ford across the river taking trade routes to Mediterranean salt pans, the Etruscans began a few industries to cater for their more developed, sophisticated tastes, giving Rome a prosperity it had never known. Skilful builders, they drained the site for the Forum, replaced huts with houses, made roads, showed the Romans how to build with arches and adorned the city's Capitol Hill with the largest and most elaborate temple in central Italy. In it they placed a colossal statue of Jupiter, the presiding deity of the city.

The more primitive Romans, unable to fashion such images, revered innumerable unseen spirits, as real to them as the existence of their neighbours, and by whom they thought all their acts and their destiny were guided. In every Roman household, moreover, daily reverence was paid to the domestic *Lares*, the deities of the farm and the home, and to the 'gods in the store cupboard', the *Di Penates*. The Romans were deeply attached to their hearth and home and they had great reason to fear famine. Unlike the Greeks they had no great romances about the deeds, the loves and the hates of gods and goddesses. Priests did not play much part in their lives and the head of every household conducted the domestic rites. Some ancient companies or 'colleges' of priests, such as those of the dancing priests, the *Salii*, were of immemorial antiquity, the very language of their chants already being obsolete. From the weird superstitions of the Etruscans, the Romans took over the haruspices and the augurs, who claimed to be able to guide action by inspecting the entrails of sacrificed animals or by observing thunder, the flight of birds and other natural phenomena. However, Romans did not become obsessed, as many of the Etruscans appear to have been, by morbid fears of the underworld. Etruscan literature, music, painting, sculpture, metalwork and jewellery were beyond the average, boorish Roman, for whom Etruscan practical skills had a more direct appeal.

Creating a republic

In 509 BC, after over a century of Etruscan rule, the Romans rose in revolt under Lucius Junius Brutus, outraged by the rape of the Roman matron Lucretia. Her violator was a son of the Etruscan king, Tarquin. The heads of all the most important Roman families in the city took part in the revolt, and the king himself was expelled. Legend tells of the heroic single-handed defence of the narrow bridge across the Tiber waged by Horatius against an avenging force of Etruscans under Lars Porsena.

If the Etruscans did indeed eventually retake the city, it could not have been for long. Having taken the responsibility for ousting their king, the ringleaders of the conspiracy had to rule in his stead. They were the heads of the great family clans, the *patres* or patricians, who wielded absolute authority (the *patria potestas*) over all their relatives and dependants. They controlled their property, including their earnings, and

Left, fourth-century BC Etruscan tomb-painting from Orvieto. Archaeological Museum, Florence.

Below, Etruscan statue of Ajax falling on his sword; Greek influence on Etruscan art and mythology was considerable.

Below left, fifth-century BC Etruscan bronze figure of Mars or a warrior. British Museum, London.

Opposite right, the Ficoroni Cista, c. 330 BC, found in an Etruscan tomb: the vase depicts an episode from the story of the Argonauts.

Opposite left, the main thoroughfare of the necropolis at Caere, one of the most flourishing Etruscan ports: the ruts made by cartwheels in the soft stone of the roadway are still visible; on each side of the street are circle graves, popular in the seventh and sixth centuries BC.

had the power to sell them into slavery or even to have them killed. A council of one hundred or more of these patricians was said to have advised the king, and so, as the Roman Senate, they continued to advise the new rulers. These rulers were two consuls, each having equal powers chosen by popular election. They commanded the army, decided disputes, and were responsible for collecting taxes and for public expenditure. To prevent them from making any attempt to perpetuate their authority, they had to lay down their office after one year. Only a dictator, appointed at times of dire emergency for a period of six months, had more power.

To continue Rome's other pious duties to the gods, a *rex sacrorum* ('king of sacrifices') was appointed for life, subordinate to the *pontifex maximus* or chief priest—the head of all religious offices. The common people were brought into partnership in the new Republic by being able to elect the consuls and by being asked to agree to all declarations of war or peace, as well as to new taxes and new laws. Power to beat or behead any Roman citizen within the city, symbolized by the *fasces*, axes bound with rods, carried before Etruscan kings, was made dependent

upon a vote of the people. Outside the city the consuls had full power over the life of any Roman.

Thus, the consuls, the Senate and the Roman people (*senatus populusque romanus*) were organized in such a way as to exert real power and authority. They were soon to need every ounce they could muster, for they were surrounded by enemies, as greedy as they were for more land and slaves, and coveting the 350 square miles of territory which Rome had acquired while under the domination of the Etruscans.

During the first 200 years of its existence republican Rome was constantly engaged in desperate and bloody warfare with Etruscans, with invading Gauls and with Rome's Italian neighbours, particularly the tough hill men. who coveted the city's fields, crops and herds.

Left, gold brooch from Caere, c. 650 BC: Etruscan goldsmiths were skilled in the art of filigree and granulation. Vatican Museum, Rome.

Left below, war elephant and calf as depicted on a Etruscan plate, first half of third century BC. Elephants, brought to Italy for military purposes, were popular subjects among artists. Villa Giulia, Rome.

Far left above, portrait of Velia, from the Tomb of Orcus at Tarquinia, late fourth century BC.

Far left below, detail of a fresco from the tomb of the Triclinium at the Etruscan city of Tarquinia, fifth century BC.

Below, detail of a fresco depicting a banquet—a popular event among the Etruscan nobility—from the Tomb of the Leopards, Tarquinia, early fifth century BC.

Opposite top, detail of a relief from a sarcophagus at Caere, sixth century BC. Villa Giulia, Rome.

Opposite centre, interior view of a tomb in the necropolis at Caere.

Opposite bottom, the temple of Apollo at Corinth, Greece, sixth century BC; Greek art and architecture had considerable influence on early Etruscan and Roman styles, which only slowly developed their own characteristics.

Opposite far left, statue of a Samnite warrior. Musée du Louvre, Paris.

Rich and poor

The first three centuries of republican Rome were justly regarded as the heroic age of the Roman people. During this time they conquered Italy and laid the foundations of their power in the Mediterranean which was to carry them forward to a world empire. There seemed to be no limits to the Roman's bravery in battle, self-sacrifice and devotion to the city and its gods. Allowing for the desire of later historians to shame the lax morality of their own age by painting idealized pictures of the heroes of the early Republic, it is nevertheless evident that those antique Romans were men of no common stamp. Yet their virtues were dedicated to a simple ideal in which individual human needs played little part. In war they were not only brave; they were ruthless and often utterly inhumane. The same hardness of character was evident also in times of peace.

Their family life was pure, they helped scores of dependent 'clients', but they insisted rigorously upon their property rights. In all primitive agricultural communities with increasing populations the poor greatly outnumber the rich. When war took small farmers off their land, when their harvests failed and taxes were due, they were forced to borrow to restock and survive. Many lost their land—their only security—to their rich creditors who, backed by the law, demanded repayment at an interest of often twelve percent and more. The dispossessed and their families could then be sold as slaves. All efforts to change the laws permitting such outrageous greed were firmly opposed by the patricians who effectively controlled the Republic.

Since wars were continuous and the patricians could not fight alone, the poorer plebeians needed only organization and leadership in order to make their army service conditional upon the guarantee of more social justice. So great was the common danger to all Romans from outside that nothing in the nature of a violent upheaval seems to have been contemplated by the plebeians. They did, however, use force to prevent some insolvent debtors from being sold in chains as slaves.

Failing to get satisfaction, in 494 BC the disaffected plebeians left in a body to camp on the Sacred Mount three miles from Rome. They were induced to return by being allowed to elect two of their number to a new office of 'tribune of the plebs'. The tribunes' powers were preventive. They could protect anyone in Rome against the consuls and they could prevent the introduction of new laws. Only a dictator could override them, but dictators were rarely appointed. Everything depended, therefore, on the character of the tribunes. As they were elected by the assembly of the Roman people, the *comitia centuriata*, they did not completely represent the masses. The simplest way to organize a meeting of Roman voters was to call out the army in which all fit Roman men served. Since they fought for Rome, it seemed right that they should decide all vital matters. However, armies are not organized and managed according to the democratic principle of 'one man, one vote', and the Roman army was no exception. Its ranks reflected the varying wealth of the men of Rome because army service was unpaid at first and the troops had to provide their own equipment. Since none but the most wealthy Romans were able to bring their own horses, this group, the *equites*, were a class apart.

The army was divided into five classes according to their wealth, measured probably by the land they owned and the amount of equipment they could bring. Those owning a complete set of armour—helmet, breast-plate, leg-guards, shield, spears and sword—formed the first three classes of the main fighting force, occupying the positions of greatest danger. They had most at stake. In the Roman legion of 4,000 to 6,000 men, which was probably as old as the Republic, the five classes were divided up into 'centuries' of fifty to sixty men, each commanded by a centurion.

When the soldiers assembled outside the walls of Rome, (no armed men were allowed in the city) in order to give their vote, it was the vote of each century, not of each man, that was counted, which made the counting easier and quicker. As a result the wealthier Romans in the first three centuries were always in a majority. The great mass of poor men outside the army classes, and, of course, the slaves, never had any influence. Before the plebeians could effectively curtail patrician privilege, they needed to reform the constitution of the Assembly. Such was the stubborn conservatism of the patricians that they never succeeded. After a great struggle the plebeians were allowed a new assembly to elect their tribunes. This was the *comitia tributa plebis*, a purely plebeian assembly, whose conclusions were plebiscites applicable only to its own members.

Soon a similar but larger body followed, the *comitia tributa populi*, representing the whole people. Both were formed on a basis of their membership of the 'tribes' or 'wards' of the city and surrounding Roman territory. As there were only four city tribes, the remaining tribes (ultimately thirty-one in number) being rural, the country landowners were in the majority. Thus the city poor could never have things their own way

Above, head of a Roman girl. Museo delle Terme, Rome.

Left, statue of a Roman lady: her husband's wealth is indicated by her clothes, which were probably made of linen or silk.

Below left, relief depicting a sacrifice. Vatican Museum, Rome.

Opposite, Romulus and Remus, the twin founders in legend of Rome, who, washed ashore from the River Tiber, were suckled by a she-wolf. Museo Nuovo nei Palazzo dei Conservatori, Rome.

because the voting, again, was by tribes and not by individuals.

The later political history of the Republic is the story of the slow rise of the *comitia tributa* to become the chief public assembly and of the equally slow reduction of patrician privileges. A landmark was the first public declaration of Rome's laws, engraved on twelve tablets (about 450 BC). A few years later mixed marriages of patricians and plebeians were permitted. In 367 BC an effort was made to limit the private ownership of land and to scale down the interest due on debts.

In the same year it was decreed that one of the two consuls was henceforth to be plebeian. Soon plebeians won the right to be elected to the other offices of the Republic which were required to help the consuls in their heavy duties. Quaestors, who were concerned with money matters, were first elected by the *comitia tributa* in 449 BC. Aediles, at first appointed by plebeians to aid the tribunes, were joined by two patrician aediles in 367 BC. They were in charge of public building, streets, games and shows, and the archives. After 337 BC plebeians could become candidates for the praetorship (founded in 366 BC), whose holder acted as a judge in law suits. Patrician censors (instituted about 443 BC) compiled the census of Roman citizens upon the basis of which army service and taxation depended. Moral matters and the fitness of Romans to be senators were among the problems scrutinized. Plebeians were not eligible as censors before about 351 BC. Finally, in 287 BC, plebiscites passed by the *comitia tributa* were recognized as part of the law of Rome.

Conquer of perish

While these offices were being created and fought over, the Romans had vastly greater perils to overcome on battlefields in central

Italy. For more than a hundred years their former Etruscan masters remained a menace. Nine miles north of Rome the rich Etruscan city of Veii, whose walls were seven miles in circumference, was a perpetual threat. Rome's neighbouring Latin peoples were not subdued and brought into alliance until they were narrowly defeated at the Battle of Lake Regillus (*c.* 496 BC). The resulting Latin League, led by Rome in the fifth century BC, successfully withstood and overcame other neighbouring Italian peoples —the Aequi, Volsci and Sabines—all land-hungry, all wanting to capture slaves and all envying Rome's cultivated land. It was only now that the Romans were able to settle accounts with the Etruscans of Veii, though it needed a ten-year siege before Veii was captured and destroyed (405–396 BC).

Then a more fearful danger descended upon the whole of Italy, when a vast horde of savage, marauding Gauls poured over the Alpine passes bringing fire and slaughter. In 387 BC, after routing the Roman army at the grim battle of the Allia, they burned and pillaged Rome, killing many of the aged senators.

The members of the Latin League then fell upon the weakened Romans who eventually managed to reassert themselves and to force the Latins into alliance (338 BC). Samnite hill people to the east and south of Rome became formidable enemies as they contended with Rome for the rich alluvial plain of Campania. Not until 295 BC, after the Romans had suffered a number of humiliating defeats, notably the Battle of the Caudine Forks (331 BC), were they victorious in a mighty battle at Sentinum (295 BC) when Gauls joined the Samnite warriors.

By 280 BC the Romans were supreme from the Gallic north to the Greek colonies of southern Italy. Drawn into quarrels between some Greek cities, the Romans encountered a truly formidable enemy in Pyrrhus, King of Epirus. In 280 BC, at Heraclea, the Greek phalanx overcame the Roman legion; Pyrrhus also brought into the battle twenty elephants, which the terrified Romans had never seen before. So well did the Romans fight, however, that Greek successes were won at a cost that made a 'Pyrrhic victory' thereafter proverbial. By 272 BC through dogged persistence, the Romans had become the most powerful people in Italy south of the territory of the Po, already occupied by the Gauls.

The struggle with Carthage

If the Romans had lost in their struggles with Italians and Greeks, the nature of European civilization might not have been so very different from what it ultimately became. However, if the Carthaginians had triumphed over the Romans, the future cultural development of the western world cannot easily be imagined.

International traders with commercial colonies lying to the east and the west, the Carthaginians used their command of the sea to make their country the wealthiest state in the western part of the Mediterranean in the third century BC. Their horrible religious practices involved human sacrifice and their cultural activities were of little account. Rome's earlier alliance with them lasted until Rome had overcome the Etruscans and the Greek cities in Italy, for both were seafaring rivals of Carthage.

Sicily, partly occupied by the Carthaginians and partly by Greeks, became the disputed prize for which the first Carthaginian or Punic War was fought between 264 and 241 BC. To win this war Rome had to become a sea power, incurring enormous losses in men and ships, a result of storms as much as the efforts of the Carthaginians. After an exhausting struggle. Sicily and a huge indemnity of gold fell to the indomitable Romans, who soon made use of a

shabby pretext to steal Sardinia and Corsica also. The Carthaginians sought compensation by occupying Spain where, in 219 BC, their brilliant young commander, Hannibal, sworn to eternal enmity to Rome, besieged and captured a town allied to Rome—Saguntum, the present-day Sagunto, a few miles north of Valencia. The Second Punic War had begun.

After an epic but costly passage across the Alps (the exact route is still a matter of controversy), Hannibal emerged on the northern Italian plains, which the Romans had very recently taken from the Gauls. Despite huge losses of men and elephants he then dealt the Romans a series of blows so crushing that they felt that their gods had deserted them. Each Roman defeat—on the Trebia by Lake Trasimene and at Cannae —was more shattering than the one before.

Humbled, it would seem, to the dust, the Senate refused to accept defeat. An army which was desperately needed at home was

Left, Marcello, Roman victor at Syracuse in 212 BC against the Carthaginians.

Below, wall decoration—of marquetry work in coloured marble—from the basiliea of Junius Bassus (d. AD 359), consul of Rome in AD 331, showing a consul in his chariot at the circus.

Opposite, bronze figure of Publius Cornelius Scipio. National Museum, Naples.

sent to Spain. In 210 BC it was put under the command of a general in his mid-twenties, Publius Cornelius Scipio. While Hannibal roamed at will in Italy, Scipio fought doggedly but was unable to prevent Hannibal's brother Hasdrubal from bringing another army from Spain to join the Carthaginians in Italy (207 BC). As Rome shuddered with dread, an army secretly sent north by forced marches defeated and killed Hasdrubal in a great Roman triumph at the Metaurus river. Three years later Scipio invaded Africa. Hannibal was recalled to repulse him. The two armies met at Zama in 202 BC when Scipio earned the undying fame as 'Scipio Africanus', the first Roman commander to defeat Hannibal.

Momentous consequences followed Rome's hard-won victory. Carthage was rendered powerless by the surrender of its navy and by a crushing indemnity of 200 talents a year for fifty years. One gold talent, a Greek measure, was roughly as much as a man could carry (about 81 pounds). Although the Romans did not annex African territory they were undisputed masters of the western Mediterranean. Their losses, however, had been frightful.

The immense disasters of the Punic wars were probably one of the main causes of the latter decline in the old, traditional Roman way of life.

Many of Rome's elite had been wiped out. Moreover, its wealth in livestock, crops, cultivated land, houses and equipment had been destroyed over vast areas. Southern Italy never really recovered. To restore productivity to the land quickly required a capital outlay which made large ranches managed by a few slaves more attractive than intensive, piecemeal cultivation by many small-scale farmers.

The Macedonian wars

Secure in the west, the Senate drove a reluctant, war-weary people to the east, against Macedonia. The King of Macedonia, Philip V, had attacked Rome when it lay prostrate after Cannae, and had begun to harass the Greeks, who appealed to Rome for help. In 197 BC Titus Quinctius Flamininus overthrew Philip in battle at Cynoscephalae in Thessaly, ending the four years' war (200–196 BC) against Macedonia. Philip's ally, Antiochus III of Syria, then attacked Greece, whereupon the Romans returned, driving him back into Asia Minor. There a Roman army under Scipio Africanus and his brother crushed Antiochus at the Battle of Magnesia in 190 BC.

Macedonia broke the treaty it had signed with Rome, provoking a third Macedonian campaign in 171–167 BC. Again the Macedonians were defeated but this time Macedonia and Greece were forced to pay Rome an annual tribute. Hitherto the Romans had waged war because their aggressiveness had been combined with a resolute determination never to be enslaved or to see wives, daughters and sons outraged and led away in captivity by powerful enemies, never to lose land, cattle and food stores, and never to have homes and temples desecrated by impious men. As the victories they were compelled to win gave them the power to enslave or despoil others, many Romans discovered that no other calling was more lucrative than war. Every victory, of course, had always yielded valuable spoils, unless it was over the savage Gauls. Nothing was more coveted at first than enemy farmland, so quarrels over spoils arose from the distribution of the land to the victors. In 396 BC Veii's acreage went to support four new Roman country tribes, and its gold, silver and jewels to the temples of the gods. To have stripped a vanquished enemy was always a mark of honour for the Romans, who hung their trophies religiously in their houses as sacred objects, where they had to remain even when the house was sold.

The sheer quantity of loot resulting from Rome's wars in the second century BC became such that the stern old Roman character of the heroic age, already weakening, proved unable to withstand the tremendous temptations. Romans themselves recognized the change, but it was first described to an observant Greek, Polybius, brought a prisoner to Rome after the Battle of Pydna in 168 BC, which ended the third Macedonian War. 'Some Romans', he said, 'were all out for women, others for homosexuality and many for shows and drink and for all the extravagance which shows and drink occasion'. What is especially striking is that Polybius noticed that his own fellow-countrymen, since their heroic age, had developed in the same way. In the second century BC Scipio Africanus was the first eminent Roman to fall under the influence of Greek culture. Scipio Aemilianus, the second son of L. Aemilius Paulus, the victor at Pydna, who was adopted by Scipio's eldest son, followed the great Scipio in his admiration for Greek civilization, Polybius was his tutor and constant companion. Yet both belonged to the old school.

What they reverenced in the Greek tradition was the cultural achievement of the heroic and idealistic period of Greek civilization. They were attacked by die-hard Romans, also of the old school, who knew little of that Greek culture but too much of the softer, sensual life of many Hellenistic Greeks, who were no longer able to sustain the heroic virtues which had distinguished their predecessors during Greece's period of greatness.

The Scipios held no brief for them, but their enemies and their modern commentators failed to make such a distinction. Here is the key to explain much in subsequent Roman social, cultural and political life that would otherwise seem muddled and confused. If, in comparison with the Greeks of the fifth century BC, most Romans seem brutal warriors or clodhopping yokels, no other Mediterranean peoples were better. The Phoenicians were sordid hucksters, the Etruscans had become obese sensualists, while the Egyptians had for centuries been the impotent custodians of the artefacts of a culture long since dead. Alone in the East a small Hebraic remnant clung passionately to a creed of no interest whatever to their contemporaries but one which withstood time's changes, to spread later throughout the world.

The Roman virtues of honesty, abhorrence of bribery and corruption, adaptability in changing circumstances and respect for law and the admirable balance of their government between the powers of the consuls, the Senate and the Public Assembly still drew admiration from Polybius in about 150 BC. Having witnessed the decay of civic virtues in his own land, he marvelled at the eager rivalry shown by all classes in Rome whenever danger threatened.

He was also to witness two shocking manifestations of Roman savagery. In 146 BC he accompanied Scipio Aemilianus on the last, wanton war against defenceless Carthage, which was burnt and obliterated amid frightful sufferings. The same year, in the last Greek campaign, another Roman army invaded and finally reduced Macedonia. The Romans destroyed Corinth, from which they returned laden with looted treasures of Greek craftsmanship, dragging back to Rome many accomplished Greeks to be sold as slaves. With remarkable insight, Polybius prophesied that in Rome 'a high pitch of prosperity and undisputed power, the prolonged continuance of great wealth leading to more extravagance and rivalry for office . . . will prove the beginning of a deterioration'. The upshot would at length be 'not liberty or democracy, but the worst of all governments—mob rule'.

Above, bust of Hannibal (247–182 BC), Carthaginian commander and lifelong opponent of Rome.

Opposite, a Roman patrician carrying busts of his ancestors.

Statue of a patrician prince, c. second century BC. Archaeological Museum, Teheran.

The Gracchan new deal

No agricultural community in ancient times was able for long to provide a satisfactory livelihood for all its members. Despite their immense conquests of land, too many Romans suffered poverty and want, disease and famine. Any plans for relief inevitably involved some infraction of private property rights and that proved fatal to their adoption. The martyrdom which some eminent Romans had incurred in the cause of alleviating Roman poverty might be thought sufficiently notorious to deter emulation. Nevertheless, Rome had barely achieved supremacy in the known western world before Tiberius Gracchus, the public-spirited son of one of Rome's most eminent aristocrats (whose wife was the daughter of Scipio Africanus) felt the need to take urgent action to relieve the destitute. Oppressed by the poverty and unemployment of many Roman citizens, and the great need for more free, independent farmers and soldiers. Tiberius as tribune proposed in 133 BC to settle many of them on huge landed estates. This land had been captured by the Republic in its many wars in Italy and then leased to wealthy ranchers. Despite his efforts to placate the rich landowners, his plan was vetoed by another tribune. Tiberius then enacted a law deposing his opponent, an entirely unprecedented procedure.

His land law was passed but his opponents saw to it that he was murdered, along with many of his followers, when he came up for re-election. Nevertheless, some redistribution of land went on, actively promoted by his younger brother Gaius, who ten years later got himself elected tribune with some well-thought-out plans for reforms. Not only did he introduce more vigorous agricultural measures but also proposed public works, including road-making. The fiercest controversy arose over his large-scale purchases of corn for resale at low, stable prices to the Roman poor. His constitutional changes, which, by giving more economic and legal weight to the businessmen, as the old class of *equites* were now mostly becoming, diminished the power of the Senate, so adding to the hatred which he excited among the ruling classes. Nevertheless, he secured re-election for a second year as tribune in 122 BC but his attempt to win office a third term failed through the machinations of the disgruntled aristocrats. No longer protected by the immunity of his office, he was murdered, and thousands of his supporters were cut down amid frightful scenes of bloodshed, more violent than the riots in which his brother had perished. Murder on a large scale had for the first time become a political weapon which could be used to prevent the implementation of sensible, much needed reforms. 'So the plebeians lost everything', wrote a later Greek historian of Rome. 'What resulted was a still further decline in the numbers of both citizens, and soldiers ... about fifteen years after, the laws of Gracchus fell into abeyance.'

A professional army

All was not quiet on Rome's frontiers. Trouble threatened from the east, where Mithradates VI of Pontus was expanding at the expense of other states in Asia Minor, stirring up hatred of Roman tax-gatherers and traders. In the north, Rome's traditional deadly enemies, the Celts and Gauls, joined now by ferocious Teutones, were on the move. Rome's failure to stop the Gauls culminated in the destruction of two Roman armies in a frightful defeat at Arausio in 105 BC.

In the south an African prince, Jugurtha, was murduring his rivals in order to unite Numidia (an ally of Rome) under his rule. It was not until 107 BC that Marius, a consul of the people, began to make real progress against the wily Jugurtha, who had found that he could now blunt Roman swords by a new weapon—bribery. In 106 BC Jugurtha was captured by Sulla, an ambitious aristocrat under the command of Marius.

Free to turn his attentions to the Gauls, Marius was able to test in action his own reformed, streamlined Roman army of paid professional soldiers. This force of state-equipped and state-paid soldiers included recruited members of the proletariat, that class which had no personal property to defend and no means with which to provide itself with military equipment. It was a momentous change from the old republican army.

Crossing the Alps in 103 BC, Marius won a resounding victory over the Teutones near Aquae Sextiae in the following year. He had then been elected consul for four consecutive years, an unprecedented event. His military successes and his care for his veteran soldiers had made him very popular.

The interests of the soldiers and the common people were also taken up, apparently on Gracchan lines, by a tribune, Saturninus, and a praetor, Glaucia, both of whom held office in 100 BC, when Marius was elected consul for the sixth time. They managed to secure more land for Marius' veterans but failed to achieve a greater share-out for the hungry mobs of Rome, possibly because they proposed some concessions for Italians as well as sops for the Romans. Demagogic politics and the violent disorders they provoked apparently went too far even for Marius. When they involved the murder of a candidate for the consulship of 99 BC towards the end of the year 100 BC, Marius

Date	Rome: internal history	Rome: foreign relations	Rome: culture	The Greek world
509	Foundation of the Republic Tribunes of the plebs Laws of the Twelve Tablets	Victory over the Latins Etruscans defeated at Cumae	Temple of Jupiter Capitolinus	Salamis Athenian hegemony
450	Marriage between patricians and plebians Creation of the censors	Wars against the Volsci and the Aequi		Pericles Peloponnesian War Surrender of Athens
400	Plebians gain admittance to the consulate Creation of the praetors	Capture of Veii by Camillus The Gauls in Rome Conquest of Etruria begun	Temple of Concordia	Death of Socrates Spartan hegemony Leuctra: Theban hegemony
350	Revolt and disbandment of the Latin League Plebians admitted to the pontificate	1st Samnite War 2nd Samnite War	Foundation of Ostia Via Appia	Philip of Macedon Accession of Alexander Death of Alexander
300	Laws favouring the plebeians introduced by L. Hortensius	3rd Samnite War Capture of Tarentum Capture of Volsinii 1st Punic War	Gladiators introduced	Struggle between the great Hellenistic kingdoms over the division of Alexander's empire
250	Fabius Maximus dictator	Annexation of Sicily Victory of Cape Telamon 2nd Punic War Zama	Via Aurelia Via Flaminia Death of Archimedes Plautus	Attalus I King of Pergamum Antiochus III
200	Cato Consul	Cynoscephalae Pydna: end of Macedon	Ennius Terence Death of Cato	Magnesia
150	Consulate of Scipio Aemilianus Tiberius Gracchus	Destruction of Carthage Numantia Annexation of southern Gaul	Lucilius	Macedonia a Roman province Attalus III bequeaths the kingdoms of Pergamum to Rome
120	Caius Gracchus			

Left, fragment of a relief depicting a battle between Roman forces and the Gauls. Palazzo Ducale, Mantua.

Below, statue of a Gaul killing his wife, c. 240–200 BC. National Museum, Rome.

Opposite, limestone statue and cremation urns from Carthage, fifth century BC.

gratified the Senate by massacring the rioters. With the blood of Saturninus and Glaucia on his hands, he soon lost popularity with the mob and disappeared for ten years.

Public discontents with the rigid, conservative attitude of the senators was meanwhile everywhere exacerbated. Roman businessmen were shamelessly extorting wealth from oppressed provincials, but complaints about their crimes went unheeded. City mobs, unemployed and half starved, were liable to erupt on any provocation. Neighbouring Italians, increasingly restive at being at the mercy of Roman officials and despised as not being citizens, having many duties but few privileges, were enraged in 95 BC when those Italians residing in Rome were suddenly expelled. To satisfy so many competing, self-seeking interests was impossible as a wealthy senator, M. Livius Drusus, found when, in 91 BC, as tribune he introduced some sensible conciliatory and reforming measures. Gaining supporters from a few of the more intelligent leaders, he was hated by the majority of all classes, and was murdered in his own home.

The Italian frustrations that Drusus had sought to relieve then exploded with great violence, unleashing a war in which Roman armies went down to defeat with the loss of two consular commanders. While the slaughter continued, with every prospect of attacks from the Etruscans and Umbrians in the north, Mithradates of Pontus began more warlike moves. Slowly the Romans made headway against the Italians but at the cost of immense destruction and bloodshed. By promising Roman citizenship to all who did not revolt or who could lay down their arms, the Senate belatedly acknowledged the folly of its opposition to Drusus. Then the revolt was slowly suppressed. It had brought old Marius from exile to defeat the Marsi (90 BC) and to scheme to be given command of the Roman army which had to fight Mithradates in Asia Minor.

Sulla versus Marius

The Senate had already appointed Sulla to the command in Asia Minor. However, with the help of a demagogue tribune, Sulpicius Rufus, the Roman popular assembly was induced to take the unprecedented step of passing a law transferring the command to Marius (88 BC). Sulla did not want to stand down, and, more ominously, neither did his troops. They were eager for the war against Mithradates', the historian Appian records, 'because it promised much plunder and they feared that Marius would enlist other soldiers instead of themselves.'

By working upon such feelings, Sulla, deserted by most of his senior officers, marched his men to Rome. Marius and Sulpicius hastily collected troops to fight a pitched battle of Romans against Romans in and around the sacred city itself—'the first', said Appian, 'that was regularly fought in Rome with trumpet and signal under the rules of war, not at all like a faction fight. Now for the first time an army of her own citizens had invaded Rome as a hostile country. From this time civil dissensions were decided only by the arbitrament of arm.' Sulla was victorious and Marius barely escaped with his life. Sulpicius, an 'inviolable tribune', was caught and killed, and his head was severed and nailed to the rostra in the Forum, an unheard-of barbarity. Sulla, as consul, hastily tried to reform the government by strengthening the Senate and by reviving the army assembly, the *comitia centuriata*, to replace the more representative *comitia tributa*.

Leaving two consuls, Cinna and Octavius, sworn to protect the new constitution, Sulla had to hurry away with his loot-hungry troops to despoil the east. He had not long gone before Cinna impeached him and proposed to recall Marius. Deposed by the Senate, Cinna fled to raise an army and to besiege Rome. Marius returned and together they overcame all resistance, again capturing Rome with a Roman army. If that was no longer unprecedented, their behaviour in Rome certainly was. With a cruelty beyond belief, they hunted down their opponents.

The consul Octavius, together with leading senators and *equites*, was brutally slain. 'All the heads of senators were exposed in front of the rostra', wrote Appian. 'They killed remorselessly. . . . All Sulla's friends were put to death, his house was razed to the ground, his property confiscated and himself voted a public enemy. Search was made for his wife and children but they escaped.' Marius, who was chiefly responsible for these outrages, died early in 86 BC, leaving Cinna to lord it over Rome. He was supreme as consul for that year and the two succeeding years.

Sulla fulfilled all the hopes of his troops. In three years he had reduced the east, slain many tens of thousands and collected a vast treasure. He now prepared to return with a well-equipped, seasoned army to exact the terrible revenge he had been planning all the time in cold blood. Cinna, under no illusions about his fate, also collected an army, intending to sail to Greece to intercept Sulla there. However, since Cinna's forces did not relish the prospect of so hazardous an expedition, they murdered him in a mutiny at Brundisium and the fleet did not sail. Nevertheless, the followers of Cinna and Marius would not yield in Italy with a struggle.

Sulla's dictatorship

Sulla landed in Italy in 83 BC, and at the Colline Gate he destroyed an opposing army, massacring to a man the Samnites who had joined it, virtually eliminating the Samnite race. With a planned, ruthless barbarity, he pursued thousands he regarded as enemies posting up proscription lists of their names with rewards for those who murdered them or informed against them. Many innocent rich were probably included so that their property could be stolen. Nowhere in Italy was safe. Towns were attacked, houses destroyed, walls demolished and heavy fines imposed. The whole of Italy was prostrate in terror of Sulla's name.

One of the proscribed, Quintus Sertorius, escaped to hold Spain against Sulla from 80 until 72 BC. In that year he was defeated by Pompey, who had been sent by Sulla to deal with him. Meanwhile, Sulla, who was now absolute master of Italy, reshaped Roman government to suit his conservative ideas. He made the Senate the most powerful body in the state, weakened the authority of the tribunes and subjected magistrates to strict accountability. He also regulated the age at which Romans could be elected to all the principal posts of authority in the Republic, deprived the businessmen of the privilege granted to them by Gaius Gracchus of being judges in their own cause, sought to improve the quality of the men sent to govern the Republic's growing empire and tight-

ened up the whole machinery of government. No longer would the state sell cheap grain to the poor. By settling thousands of his veterans on land in Italy which had been stolen from the families of the vast numbers who had perished or been proscribed in the frightful slaughter he had let loose, he sought to maintain his influence long after his death. When he retired in 79 BC he counted upon his aristocratic friends not to allow any infraction of his revived form of senatorial government. He died in the following year.

Elderly Romans who were boys in the days of the Gracchi had seen their world overturned. Young men such as Pompey and Cicero, who were both twenty-eight, and Julius Caesar, who was twenty-one, when Sulla retired, had lived through horrors utterly alien to the traditional, idealized notions which they had held about their country.

Pompey and Crassus

In the heroic days, when the very survival of Rome was in doubt, the Senate had won power through the respect given to wise, courageous leadership. Unfortunately the power Sulla conferred upon the senators made them neither wise nor courageous.

Ambitious, energetic young men soon saw that their road to advancement did not lie along the carefully measured path devised for them by Sulla. He himself had shown them a very different road to fame, one that could successfully be traversed by anyone with a loyal army behind him. Two young commanders, Pompey and Marcus Crassus, were in such a position in 71 BC. Pompey, then thirty-six, had overcome several of Sulla's opponents in Sicily, Africa and Spain. He returned to Rome in time to join forces with Marcus Crassus, six years his senior, then on the point of extinguishing a revolt of slaves led by a gladiator, Spartacus, who between 73 and 71 BC had devastated Italy like a second Hannibal.

Pompey and Crassus, rivals though they were, compelled the Senate to make them the two consuls for 70 BC. Together they dismantled much of the rest of Sulla's painfully constructed machinery of government. Tribunes and censors were restored with their former powers. The courts which tried corrupt governors and businessmen on charges of extortion were freed from senatorial control. That these courts had not hitherto been effective is evident from the incredible rapacity with which the governor Verres had bled Sicily white between 73 and 71 BC. He would have easily got away with his vast spoils if Cicero had not listened to the pleas of the Sicilians, whom he had helped to govern as quaestor in 75 BC. He prosecuted Verres in a series of indictments which, in blasting the reputation of that

odious man, condemned to eternal obloquy the system in which he operated.

Pompey was rewarded when the tribunes and businessmen gave him immense resources in 67 BC to wage war on the pirates who made any sea voyage a desperate hazard. Crassus, now immensely rich but intensely jealous of Pompey, feared that the latter would return, another Sulla, to dominate Rome. Julius Caesar, who was already dazzling Roman society, was equally concerned. Their fears increased when, between spring and summer of 66 BC, Pompey, having swept the seas free of pirates, was rewarded by being given, irregularly, by popular vote, command of the campaign which Lucullus was patiently waging against Sulla's enemy, Mithradates. The latter had again taken the field in 74 BC, counting upon aid from Rome's numerous enemies.

A century of conflict

Looking back upon what is recorded of Roman life, it is clear that a century of civil discord, culminating in ruinous civil wars, can be dated from the murder of Tiberius Gracchus in 133 BC. Life before then had by no means always been peaceful and contented, but Romans were sufficiently ready to endure its frustrations and miseries without wrecking the tolerable harmony of Roman social life as a whole. After 133 BC that harmony was increasingly disrupted as private interests and ambitions and sectional jealousies and animosities were given free rein.

Intelligent men such as Drusus, who could see the paramount need for greater social unity, proved unable to persuade their countrymen to put this above a narrow self-interest. The best measure of his wisdom was the appalling catastrophe which followed its rejection. After the tremendous devastation brought about by the social and civil

wars Sulla was able by force of arms to impose an order rather than that peace which a harmonious social life should have automatically guaranteed. Rome's tragedy was that a dictator's sword was necessary to enforce a uniformity and an obedience alien to Roman tradition. Because it was imposed by force, it was unlikely to endure when that force was withdrawn. Fresh upheavals were therefore inevitable unless other methods could be found to produce a more natural harmony.

The uneasy period following Sulla's disappearance is a long, involved record of personal rivalries given free rein by the progressive decline of the already supine and increasingly futile authority wielded by the magistrates and the Senate. Only a few able and honourable men among the magistrates and senators had survived the social war, the Marian and Sullan massacres, and

Above, sculptured relief from Trajan's column showing Roman soldiers crossing the Danube on a bridge of boats, first century AD. Museo della Civilta Romana, Rome.

Above left, statue of winged victory, second or first century BC; this was a contemporary model of one of the statues flanking the Altar of Rome and Augustus at Lyons, built to engender provincial loyalty to Rome. Musée de la Civilisation Gallo-Romaine, Lyons.

the devastations of the Slave War. These few were to be faced by the necessity of opposing by military action a number of self-seeking ambitious men backed by professional troops of the new kind of army created by Marius, who gave their loyalty not to the Republic, but to their commander as long as he paid them and put them in the way of collecting booty, with the promise of a farm for their retirement. Political ambitions were, therefore, no longer to be satisfied by one year of high office and life-long membership of the Senate. A military command with a campaign and a triumphant return to Rome were now not merely desirable as an avenue to untold wealth but increasingly necessary for political survival.

Pompey gave the most spectacular demonstration of this fundamental change in Roman public life. After a long, patient campaign, he finally subdued all the warring factions in Asia Minor and overcame Mithradates who committed suicide. He also annexed Syria, organized Judaea, as a client kingdom, founded colonies and created large, new tribute-paying dependencies for Rome. Methodically he amassed treasure, booty and slaves on a vastly greater scale than his predecessors, Lucullus and Sulla. No Roman commander had previously so enriched the treasury, or rewarded so many of his staff and troops with enough wealth to keep them in comfort for the rest of their lives (after reserving a colossal share for himself). Such was his authority and influence that when he returned in 62 BC Rome would have accepted him more willingly than Sulla, if he had installed himself as dictator. Instead, to the amazement of all, after a superb triumph (61 BC), unprecedented for its lavish display, he disbanded his troops, asking for no more than the promised rewards for his veterans and the confirmation of all that he had achieved in the east. The senators, to whom these requests were directed, with incredible folly raised every variety of objection.

Their blindness to the political realities of the hour gave a heaven-sent opportunity to Julius Caesar and his wealthy backer, Crassus. The two had been engaged in all manner of abortive schemes in their desperate search for some way to build themselves into a position of security against Pompey. After sponsoring a demagogic, irresponsible land-reform measure, which Cicero defeated in 63 BC, Caesar, a notorious free thinker and free liver, had got himself elected *pontifex maximus*. He and Crassus had also at one stage a crazy scheme for conquering Egypt as a means of obtaining an army command. They had apparently even flirted with Catiline, who had stood trial for gross extortion during his governorship of the province of Africa.

Disappointed in his hopes of becoming consul, Catiline planned a conspiracy to seize power as a means of freeing himself from debt. Cicero was consul in 63 BC when Catiline's treason was detected. Acting with

unusual energy, Cicero arrested and executed the ringleaders in Rome, sending a consular force to fight a pitched battle near Pistoria with the nondescript gang of adventurers and slaves recruited by Catiline, who perished with them. Reckless, destitute of moral principle, with no other motive for his treason than to defraud his creditors, and having no statesmanlike plan for Rome, should he succeed, Catiline nevertheless had among a few later writers the apologists he lacked in Rome, apparently for no better reasons than that some of the Roman poor thought him their champion.

For exposing and defeating Catiline, who naturally alarmed those who remembered the terrible years of Marius, Cinna and other demagogues, Cicero was proclaimed 'the father of the country'. It was an honour that he merited for more serious reasons, to which, however, his countrymen were blind. Alone of the leading public figures of Rome Cicero seems, like Drusus, to have seen that social harmony springing from mutual understanding, the readiness to make sacrifices and to work for the common good, could alone save the Republic. So interpreted, his *concordia ordinum* ('harmony of all classes'), the sane, simple doctrine which he proclaimed to his countrymen was no platitude but deep political wisdom.

Cicero, like Marius, was from Apinum, and was also regarded as a 'new man' because none of his ancestors had been ennobled by reaching high office. Nothing but exceptional ability, energy, ambition and determination enabled him to achieve political distinction. Cicero rose by his consummate rhetorical skill exhibited as an advocate, usually for the defence, in the legal hearings held in public, which always attracted a critically appreciative crowd.

Left, bust of Lucius Cornelius Sulla.
Archaeological Museum, Venice.

Opposite top, relief showing Roman soldiers ready
to disembark from a war galley.

Opposite bottom, bust of Cicero (106–43 BC),
c. 50–40 BC, though possibly a late first-century-
AD copy owned by an admirer of Cicero; the head
and neck have been set in a modern bust. Uffizi
Gallery, Florence.

CIVIL WARS FROM CAESAR TO AUGUSTUS

Date	Rome: internal history	Rome: foreign relations	Rome: culture	The outside world	Date	Rome internal history	Rome: foreign relations	Rome: culture	The outside world
120	Tribunate of Marius	Invasion of the Cimbri and Teutoni Numidian War		Mithridates King of Pontus	60	Consulate of Caesar Sedition in Rome (58–51 BC) 2nd Consulate of Pompey and Crassus	Beginning of the Gallic War Death of Crassus at Carrhae End of the Gallic War	Caesar's *De Bello Gallico* Cicero's *De Oratore*	
110	1st Consulate of Marius 6th Consulate of Marius	Defeat of Jugurtha Marius victorious over the Cimbri and Teutoni	Birth of Cicero Death of Lucilius		50	War between Pompey and Caesar Death of Pompey Assassination of Caesar 2nd Triumvirate Octavian master of Italy	Caesar in Egypt and in Asia Pharsalus Philippi Anthony in Egypt	Assassination of Cicero Virgil's *Eclogues* and *Georgics*	Burning of the Alexandria Library
100	Sedition in Rome Italian rebellion								
90	End of Social War Death of Marius Dictatorship of Sulla	1st war against Mithridates Sulla takes Athens Defeat of Mithridates	Tabularium built at Rome Cicero's first speeches	Parthians invade Syria	40		Actium	Horaces' *Satires* Death of Sallust	
80	Death of Sulla Consulate of Pompey and Crassus	Rebellion of Sertorius 2nd war against Mithridates Failure of Sertorius	Pompey's theatre at Rome		30	Triumph of Octavian			
70	Consulate of Cicero 1st Triumvirate	Wars against the pirates	Cicero's Verrine orations	Civil war in Judaea					

Chapter 12

The End of the Republic

The defeat of Catiline did not restore the Republic to the healthy condition of Cicero's dreams. On the contrary, the fate of the Republic seemed to Cicero to be sealed when it became evident that Pompey, Caesar and Crassus, instead of fighting one another, had concluded a secret pact, known later as the 'First Triumvirate'.

Caesar's prize was to become consul in 59 BC with a nonentity, Bibulus, as colleague. Caesar promptly honoured his part of the bargain. Pompey's veterans got their reward and his eastern settlements were ratified. The furious senators put up Bibulus to obstruct Caesar by declaring unfavourable omens, so making illegal the public assembly which approved Caesar's proposals. It was, said the wits, the consulate of Julius and Caesar. Pompey married Caesar's beloved daughter, Julia. Crassus and his business friends benefited as Caesar shamelessly altered one of their tax-collecting contracts to give them a profit instead of a loss. To provide for his own safety, Caesar, despite Bibulus, had already secured from the public assembly command of Roman Gaul for five years.

Before he left for Gaul in 58 BC Caesar selected a young aristocrat, Clodius, to act as his agent during his absence. This step involved a certain amount of trickery; by means of a fictitious adoption Clodius became a plebeian in order that Caesar could make him a tribune. Whatever Caesar's original intention had been, his actions resulted in a firebrand being thrust into the city's affairs.

Never had such a violent demagogue been seen in Rome. He made every effort to further disrupt social order. He demolished venerable constitutional safeguards, attacked the Senate, converted low-price grain for Romans into a free dole at a vast cost to the treasury, collected gangs of thugs by passing a law allowing working men to meet in clubs or societies, and sent Cicero into exile. Intoxicated by his unrestrained excesses, he kept Pompey a frightened prisoner in his own house. Pompey got Caesar to agree to pardon Cicero, but Clodius delayed his return for six months by bloody riots, which continued long after Cicero's arrival.

Caesar meanwhile was involved in desperate difficulties through his attacks on the Gauls and Teutones. Returning hurriedly to northern Italy in 56 BC, he renewed his pact with Pompey and Crassus. In the following year he crossed the Rhine for a brief show of force, later reconnoitring in Britain where he returned in 54 BC to vanquish the British in battle. When Julia died in 54 BC a vital link between Pompey and Caesar was broken. Crassus was then on his way to attack the Parthians, having achieved a great military command, his life's ambition. He never returned to Rome. Mounted Persian bowmen shot his army to pieces and he was killed on retreating to Carrhae in 53 BC.

Gang warfare continued to rage in Rome until the Senate, in despair, made Pompey sole consul in 52 BC with the task of restoring order. Clodius was murdered by a rival gang. The great question now was who should command when Caesar returned to Rome in 49 BC. Neither he nor Pompey would give up their legions without guarantees which nobody could provide, and the situation deteriorated to the point where Caesar, realizing that his life was at stake, invaded Italy with one legion. Pompey, for all his confident talk, was caught unprepared, and Caesar always managed to keep the initiative. Pompey hurriedly left Italy to collect an army in the east, which Caesar met at Pharsalus in 48 BC and routed. Pompey escaped to Egypt only to be killed by the Egyptians as he landed, a fate which threatened Caesar who had followed him.

Besieged in Alexandria by Egyptian forces, Caesar fought his way out of a trap. He then established Cleopatra as queen after her brother, the Egyptian king, had been drowned during his retreat after being defeated by Caesar. A Macedonian princess of twenty-two, Cleopatra captivated Caesar, who remained three months in Egypt. He went on to fight further battles in Asia, Africa and Spain. By 45 BC all remnants of what could be called Republican opposition was at an end and Caesar, in Rome, celebrated his conquest of Gaul and his victories over his fellow Romans with two great triumphs.

Master of the Roman world

Both the ruthless slaughter on the battlefields and the lessons of past history deepened the fear that Rome was about to suffer at the hands of its new master a dictatorship like Sulla's. Yet Cicero confessed that he was 'struck with astonishment at Caesar's sobriety, fairness and wisdom'. The dread proscriptions he feared did not take place. Despite his hazardous life in the maelstrom of Roman politics and his ten years of campaigning among fierce enemies in Gaul and Germany, culminating in the bitter civil wars of Roman against Roman, Caesar had never lost the instincts of a cultivated Roman noble. If Rome had to have a dictator for life, as he became in

44 BC, they could not have had anyone more able, intelligent and farsighted than Julius Caesar to rescue the Romans, whose failure to achieve a unified society had irreparably weakened the old republican way of life long before he destroyed it altogether, Caesar could do no more than impose an order within which harmonious relations might have a chance to develop. Unfortunately his time was too short. After the events of the previous years, conditions were chaotic. Thousands of legionary soldiers clamoured for their rewards and Caesar's friends expected generous treatment. Everyone feared the future. Some reforms were, however, made: the wild extravagances of Clodius were remedied; the supply of free corn was drastically reduced; workmen's clubs were abolished; and citizenship was awarded widely outside Italy in Gaul. Caesar also tried to settle more free men on Roman farms and to help others to emigrate to new colonies. He enlarged the Senate, reformed local government and introduced the Julian calendar by making 46 BC a year of fifteen months.

Useful as these and other improvements were, they did not touch the heart of the real problem, which was that of re-creating a genuine harmony among the conflicting elements in Roman society. To expect that Caesar would have had any master plan to reform and reorganize Rome would be completely to misunderstand the circumstances of his time. His aim was self-preservation at all costs, in a world that had degenerated to the point where no wealthy man could be prominent, independent and active in public life without the support of ample physical force. Caesar, Pompey and Crassus were merely the more eminent of those of whom their contemporary, the historian Sallust (86–34 BC) wrote:

To tell the truth in a few words, from Sulla's time onwards, while all those active in public life may have professed honourable motives, such as the defence of the rights of the people, or the enlargement of the powers of the Senate, what they were really out for was their own ends which they disguised as measures for the good of the Republic.

Cicero knew that Caesar had no great political remedies. 'While we are his slaves', he said in 46 BC, 'he is the slave to circumstance. . . . He is unable to say what is going to happen.'

By 46 BC there was no military, legislative, administrative or financial authority of any importance in Rome which Caesar did not completely control. Peace and order were at last restored.

The Ides of March

Caesar was a king in all but name. He had been offered the title and a crown but refused both, sensing violent public aversion

204

to the very word 'king'. A Brutus had expelled the last king centuries before. Another Brutus and twenty-two others assassinated Caesar in the Senate on 15 March 44 BC. Those, like Cicero, who rejoiced at the death of a tyrant, soon realized their folly. The conspirators had removed the one guarantee of internal peace and order without having the means to provide either themselves. All the old discords which Caesar had quelled broke out once more.

As Caesar's genius then stood clearly revealed, so public rage at his murder bred hatred for the assassins. They feebly allowed Mark Anthony to inherit the authority of the dead man and to lay his hands on the vast treasure Caesar had accumulated. He soon began to use both against them and against the Senate they championed. Both sides amassed troops. For some time the issue was in doubt, complicated by the arrival of Caesar's great-nephew and heir, Octavian, a lad of nineteen. His early association with the Senate, secured by Cicero, did not last. In April 43 BC Anthony was defeated in two battles with the senatorial forces, but he did not have to fight another because the men of the senatorial army, under Lepidus, deserted to him.

Octavian soon saw that it might pay him to do likewise and in November 43 BC he, Anthony and Lepidus formed the Second Triumvirate, which spelt doom for all the republicans in Italy. With a cold brutality, which far exceeded that of Sulla, they proscribed their enemies and stole their possessions. Three hundred senators, including Cicero, and two thousand *equites* were butchered in cold blood. After two of Caesar's assassins, Brutus and Cassius, who had raised an army in Macedonia, were defeated by Anthony in two battles in Philippi, all resistance collapsed in October 42 BC.

The achievements of the Roman Republic

When the last of the eminent republicans perished at the hands of assassins and on the bloodstained field of Philippi, nearly a hundred years of civil strife seemed at last to have come to an end. In almost perpetual warfare during a period of 250 years, the Republic had slowly achieved supremacy throughout Italy. Then, in less than a century, it had won mastery of the Mediterranean world, commanding a tribute-paying empire from Asia Minor and Greece to North Africa and most of Spain, completely subject to its military governors, tax collectors, businessmen and slave traders. Julius Caesar added the whole of Gaul (covering roughly the area of France and the Low Countries) and Switzerland. By far the greater part of this large empire had been acquired during the century of civil conflict beginning with the Gracchi in 133 BC. At home, Roman farmers made Italy fertile, despite vast grain imports.

It was at this period too, that Roman literature reached the peak of its achievements from its first faint beginnings during the Punic wars between about 243 and 204 BC. During the last two hundred years of the Republic there was a flowering of poetry and drama, history and oratory as well as literary and scholastic works and a number of manuals on practical subjects. Philosophy was notably absent until the first century BC, when Cicero provided somewhat simplified, watered-down versions of ideas he had gleaned from Plato, Aristotle and the Stoics. Books of a religious nature also date from Cicero's time. Although an impressive number of such works survive today, they are only a pitiful remnant of a greater heritage. The plays of Plautus (*c.* 250–184 BC) and Terence (*c.* 195–159 BC), adapted from the Greek, found audiences among whom were men who had campaigned against the Carthaginians in Sicily where, in Greek amphitheatres, they first witnessed dramatic performances. Ennius (236–169 BC), Rome's first epic poet, was also a prolific dramatist, but less than a thousand lines of his works survive. Even less has been preserved of the tragedies of Accius (170–85 BC), the most renowned Roman dramatist. Cicero's

Bust of Julius Caesar (102 or 100–44 BC); consul of Rome, conqueror of Rome's western European lands, he was assassinated by a group of aristocrats allegedly because he was aiming to set up a hereditary monarchy. Composanto, Pisa.

speeches, and his treatises on oratory, political theory, ethics and religion brought Latin prose to the summit of power, eloquence and elegance. His letters and his philippic orations denouncing Mark Anthony are the main detailed source of knowledge of the last tragic years of the Republic.

Lucretius, the only Roman writer able to stand comparison with a Greek, expounded in somewhat rough verse the atomic, rationalist philosophy of Epicurus, counselling against religious superstition with a stern, passionate depth of conviction. In complete contrast are the gay, passionate verses reflecting the vicissitudes in the life and amorous adventures of Catullus (84–c. 54 BC), a young man, who brought a new note of lyricism and eroticism into Roman writing. Sallust (86–c. 34 BC) made history vivid and interesting, but only his shorter accounts of Catiline's conspiracy and the war with Jugurtha remain. Caesar's own accounts of his Gallic and Civil wars, as destitute of artistic embellishment as his head was of hair, were not without a strong propaganda motive, despite their apparent objectivity.

The Republic therefore bequeathed a legacy of mature writing. In no other cultural activity did the Romans have any comparable achievement. Their medicine was derived from the Greeks, and was long to remain dependent upon Greek slaves and Greek freedmen. Roman sculpture and painting also were largely dependent upon Greek originals and Greek artists, although mosaic art was greatly developed. Music to the early Romans was mainly the trumpet call to battle. Their often elegantly lettered inscriptions also had Greek antecedents.

In the practical arts, notably in the channelling of an abundant supply of fresh water to the city through a long system of great aqueducts. Rome far outshone any ancient, medieval and not a few modern cities. Three great systems—the Aqua Appia (312–308 BC), the Anio Vetus (279–269 BC) and the Aqua Marcia (144 BC)—poured fifty million gallons into Rome every twenty-four hours.

Architecture, building, roadmaking, and townplanning, for which the Romans have always been renowned, flourish in times of peace and prosperity, which the Republic did not long enjoy. Nevertheless, the huge war booty and the great influx of slaves enabled the relatively rich to build splendid houses. Garden art, known only in times of some cultural sophistication, began notably with the gardens of Lucullus, Pompey and Sallust, on and near the Pincian Hill.

Anthony and Octavian

Before the Romans had time to recover from the horror and devastation of Caesar's Civil War, his assassination plunged them into still worse troubles. Octavian and Anthony in uneasy partnership (for Lepidus was of no account) sought more money and land than their proscriptions had so far yielded. Anthony went to look for resources in the east and Octavian in Rome, where he had become 'the son of the god Julius', after the appearance in 43 BC of Halley's comet, which was regarded as a sign of the deification of Caesar. Octavian's legions gave him supreme power, creating for him a sycophantic following, despite the hatred which his ruthless methods must have aroused and despite his lack of any constitutional position. For ten years he tried to live down the

odium of his past, trading on the name of Caesar, cultivating the loyalty of Italians, and supported by Agrippa, an able military commander, and Maecenas, a rich and clever Etruscan. It was inevitable that before long Octavian and Anthony would come into conflict. Theirs had been the alliance of successful gangsters which Anthony's marriage to Octavia, the angelic sister of Octavian, in 40 BC, did little to improve.

Anthony had encountered Cleopatra, and was soon to fall under her spell and to repudiate Octavia. His Egyptian connection and his favours to Cleopatra and their children at the expense of Roman territory gave Octavian a pretext for a propaganda campaign, on the basis of which he forced a declaration of war against Cleopatra from the captive and emasculated Senate. Nevertheless, some senators left to join Anthony when the clash came in 31 BC. Despite his unsuccessful war on the Parthians in 36 BC, Anthony should have given a better account of himself. Defeated at Actium, he and Cleopatra fled back to Egypt, where he committed suicide. After Cleopatra had become Octavian's prisoner, the estimate she formed of his character and intentions led her to take her own life. Octavian then seized the treasure of the Ptolemies, making Egypt his private estate. He was to remain for two years in the east before returning to Rome as undoubted master of the Mediterranean world.

Chapter 13

The early Empire

Instead, Octavian had him murdered. Julius Caesar instituted no proscriptions. His fate may have shown Octavian the folly of sparing a defeated enemy, but it is an excuse upon which that mean and sadistic man would have been only too ready to lean. Octavian richly merited this harsh description by his murder of Cleopatra's sons and his ferocious reaction to any hint of a conspiracy against him. His enormities are frequently overlooked in the light of the later achievements of the Augustan era, in the course of which his character changed a great deal.

Imperator was a good old-fashioned word denoting the man who made decisions and gave orders in the home or on the field of battle. Commanders had long been hailed as *imperator* by their troops after a victory, and were often rewarded by a triumph on their return to Rome. When Octavian returned in 29 BC he celebrated a three-fold triumph and closed the gates of the temple of Janus, which were always open in time of war. Caesar had used *imperator* as part of his name so Octavian adopted it as though he were a royal heir. No Roman in 43 BC and later could imagine that Octavian at the age of nineteen should be entitled to take any part in ruling the world because his great-uncle, who had made himself dictator, had left him his goods and chattels. His power rested on the loyalty of Caesar's legions, for he had no defined constitutional position, not even that of consul until 33 BC.

In 28 or 27 BC, with Agrippa as his colleague, Octavian overhauled the machinery of government. He assumed the title of *princeps*. The Senate was further tamed, two hundred senators being removed. In 27 BC he made a show of handing over all his powers, without disclosing their origin, to the Senate, only, of course, to have all real power promptly returned to him. The senators agreed to look after a few peaceful provinces while Octavian retained command of the armies in Spain, Gaul and the east. He was dignified with the new title 'Augustus', by which henceforth he was known.

A similar farce was enacted in 23 BC when he refused renomination as consul, only to be rewarded with command of all the armed forces and the unprecedented right of bringing armed troops within the city walls. Furthermore, his authority was declared superior to that of the tribunes of the people by the award of the new tribunician power in perpetuity. In 19 BC a matching supreme authority over the consuls was also possibly given to him.

If it is true that the republicans themselves had completely destroyed the republican spirit, Caesar spoke the truth when he said that 'the Republic is a sham'. Cicero thought so too, but he did not despair of its revival. If he had been spared and heeded, things could have turned out differently.

Augustus

Augustus began to rule in exceptionally favourable circumstances. He was backed by overwhelming military support, with the wealth of Egypt and the entire Roman world under his control, at a time when the great majority of the people of Rome and Italy and in the provinces wanted nothing more ardently than peace and security. Augustus made peace and security possible, so that human energies, yoked to an insistent urge for a better life, were devoted to ensuring recovery and forgetting past miseries.

Augustus' long reign provided the majority of the people with a more agreeable existence than they had ever previously experienced. The Republic then ceased to be a living memory. Its heroes, Cicero and Cato of Utica, were shadowy figures, besmirched by association with the murder of Julius Caesar, the greatest figure of the recent past.

Writing a hundred years later the Roman historian Tacitus explained the advent of Augustus by saying that 'after the Battle of Actium all power had to be concentrated in the hands of one man for the sake of peace'. Equally concisely he summed up the achievement of Augustus:

He first won over the army by bounties, the populace with cheap corn and all men with the delights of peace. Then he grew in power, step by step, concentrating in himself the functions of the Senate, the magistrates and the laws. He met no opposition; the boldest spirits had fallen in battle or by proscription.

The remaining nobility gained wealth and fame more quickly in proportion to their acceptance of slavery, so that having prospered through revolution, they preferred the new order and safety to the old order and its dangers. Nor was the new state of affairs unpopular in the provinces where the rule of the Senate and people had become odious because of the feuds between the great and the greed of the Roman governors; where laws gave no protection because they were overturned by violence, intrigue and finally by corruption.

Thus did an embittered, freedom-loving aristocrat reveal the reality of the one-man rule by Augustus and the reason for its acceptance, which developed into active and eager approval on the part of the vast majority of Rome's subjects.

Augustus tried his best, despite poor health, to rise to his responsibilities. He worked hard, travelled widely, cautiously strengthened and extended the empire, and selected with care the hundreds of men on whom he had to rely for the day-to-day administration of his armies and civil government. He provided an example of plain, sober living in his efforts to restrain luxury, sending his only child, Julia, into a miserable exile for her profligacy, as part of his stern campaign against the lax moral standards by which the old Roman way of life was steadily being eroded. Augustus also gave notable encouragement to literature.

It is not easy to fill in the details of events during the rule of Augustus and his successors because, as the Ancient Greek historian Dio Cassius discovered:

Most things were done in secrecy and were concealed. If some were occasionally made public, yet because there is no means of verifying them, such publication inspires little confidence as long as there is reason to believe that everything was said or done according to the wishes of the emperor and those in power around him.

Despite the deficiencies of statistical evidence, there seems no doubt that 'the delights of peace' included a substantial surge forward in economic prosperity. During the principate of Augustus, the number of male citizens rose from just over 4,000,000 to almost 5,000,000.

By suppressing pirates and brigands, making new roads, extending provincial boundaries and providing sound money and, above all, a sense of security, he gave farmers, craftsmen and traders opportunities to enrich themselves and their communities. Such benefits spread far into the provinces, aiding the Romanization, then beginning, of modern France, the Low Countries west of the Rhine, Spain, Portugal and Britain. In the east, Judaea became a province. Egypt's southern frontier was secured and the country's grain supply fed the people of Rome. An effort to move the frontier of Gaul from the Rhine to the Elbe proved disastrous. An entire Roman army of three legions under the command of Quinctilius Varus was slaughtered by savage Teutons in the forests of Germany in AD 9, a disaster which so preyed on the mind of Augustus that he was said to walk about muttering 'Varus, give me back my legions'. The Romans then tried to maintain the Rhine as their frontier with Gaul.

Without over-emphasizing the virtues of Rome's republican past, Augustus strove to stem the predominating tendency to seek those sensuous satisfactions from life to which his own form of government was powerfully contributing. His laws against luxury continued a respectable tradition at least as old as the Second Punic War. However, they proved failures as did his efforts to foster family life and to increase the population by making adultery a crime and by making marriage virtually compulsory (18 and 17 BC). In a similar spirit he sought—unsuccessfully as it proved to revive ancient pieties by patching up more than eighty old temples and by the construction of new ones.

A more enduring contribution was made by the poets Virgil, Horace, Ovid, Propertius and Tibullus, and the historian Livy, all of whom, although born during the period of the Republic, wrote during the lifetime of Augustus, adding lustre to his laurels—Virgil particularly. Maecenas made handsome amends for the sufferings endured by Virgil after the proscriptions. He helped Horace also and is rightly remembered as a prince among patrons of literature.

Above, banqueting scene and, below, preparations in the kitchen: third-century AD relief. Trier Museum, Neumagen.

Opposite right, Augustus (63 BC–AD 14), the first Roman Emperor and ruler of the Roman world for forty-five years. Museo delle Terme, Rome.

Opposite left, marble statue of Augustus, c. AD 14, erected by the emperor's widow in the garden of her villa; modelled on a fifth-century BC original, it depicts a Roman general addressing his army. Vatican Museum, Rome.

The imperial succession: Tiberius

Nothing more clearly reveals where real power lay in the alleged partnership of Augustus with the Senate and the people in the government of Rome and its empire than the supreme importance in Roman life of Augustus' family connections, his selection from his relatives of his stepson Tiberius to succeed him, and the acquiescence of the Senate in the arrangement when in AD 14 the death of Augustus was belatedly announced. Other heirs from the family had been more favoured, but they had died young. Tiberius, then fifty-six, and the son of Livia, the third wife of Augustus, by her previous marriage, had been forced to marry Julia whom he hated and whom Augustus at last exiled.

After a brilliant military career under Augustus to whom he was always loyal, Tiberius had retired from public life for some time in disgust. A grim, suspicious and unamiable figure, he undertook his imperial duties seriously for a time, accepting all Augustus' authority as a matter of course. A nephew of Tiberius, Germanicus, a much more popular and sympathetic figure, bore the main military burdens of this period: an inconclusive campaign of revenge in Germany (AD 13–16) and more successful activities in the east, where poison may have caused his death in his thirty-fourth year. Tiberius' rule now degenerated into a hateful tyranny. He began by ordering the murder of his wife, Julia, as well as of a possible young rival.

In AD 17 Lucius Aelius Sejanus became commander or prefect of the Praetorian Guard, the troops which Augustus had dispersed throughout Rome. In AD 23 Sejanus grouped the Praetorians in a single camp just outside the walls of Rome. His ambition grew as his influence over Tiberius increased. When Tiberius withdrew from Rome to Campania and Capri in AD 26, where he remained for eleven years, the power of Sejanus was steadily enhanced.

Hitherto Tiberius had made light of stories of plots against his person. However, Sejanus now proceeded to enflame Tiberius' morbid fears of assassination, and the emperor sent a stream of letters condemning his supposed enemies. A reign of terror began. After five years Tiberius was persuaded that his trusted Praetorian prefect was plotting to seize imperial powers. A further letter in AD 31 then denounced Sejanus, not long after he had been appointed joint consul with Tiberius for five years and been given proconsular powers of command. A new campaign of terror then began, Sejanus was immediately killed and his two children were strangled. No accomplice or beneficiary of Sejanus—and there were many—was safe.

Amid scenes of horror during which eminent men and women, innocent and guilty alike, suffered torture and death in enormous numbers, routine trials and executions daily occurring in Rome's far distant provinces under local laws and administrations would have seemed matters of minor interest. So Pontius Pilate, who had for seven years been presiding as Roman procurator in Judaea, probably thought it unnecessary to report that on the third of April AD 33, a young Jew, Jesus Christ, had been crucified along with certain criminals whom he had also condemned. He may not have heard or heeded a rumour that his victim had later again been seen alive after his corpse had mysteriously disappeared, and that a few Judaeans who had followed him as a religious teacher having revolutionary new doctrines of love, charity and contempt for the material satisfactions of the world attached great significance to the whole event.

The Romans themselves were busy spreading a new cult, that of the divinity of their ruler. In Greece Alexander the Great had received similar adulation, which was an exaggerated form of political deference rather than the more superstitious veneration paid by orientals and Egyptians to their kings. The remarkable honours paid to Octavian as 'son of the god Julius' and 'Augustus' came nearer such oriental practices, particularly when his *genius* or 'vital spirit' was worshipped throughout Italy in civic as well as in individual ceremonies. It seems to have been a spontaneous tribute of gratitude to the man who had made life tolerable one more. In the eastern provinces the cult was more developed. Rome also established the cult of 'Augustus the God' after his death, and temples for the purpose were set up in many parts of the Empire. Such attitudes were increasingly to influence Rome.

Rome's eastern wars filled the slave markets. Most of the men, women and children sold there to do the work and to satisfy the lusts of their conquerors, came from lands of autocratic rulers and they brought strange cults and superstitions to infect the Roman way of life. Many of their descendants had become freedmen and freedwomen, a second-rate class of citizen, whose traditions, experiences and servile

past were alien to the robust, self-reliant heroes of the Republic. The newcomers rapidly accelerated the already existing tendency of Romans to seek greater sensual satisfactions, which was to become the predominant characteristic of Roman society during the ensuing centuries.

Gaius Caesar 'Caligula'

In AD 37 Rome rejoiced at the news that Tiberius, then seventy-seven, lay dead in his southern retreat. Several more promising heirs having died, Gaius, his great-nephew, was declared his successor. Then a young man of twenty-five, he was better known by his childhood nickname Caligula ('Little Boot'), bestowed upon him by his father's troops. As prodigal of public treasure as his great-uncle had been mean, he delighted the mob by spending lavishly on magnificent chariot races.

A serious illness in the first year of his reign was thought to have affected his brain because insanity alone could account for his subsequent extraordinary behaviour. He murdered his wife and sister as well as many Roman aristocrats. The familiar tag, *oderint dum metuant* ('let them hate provided they are afraid'), served as the motto of many vicious emperors. No woman Caligula

fancied was safe, still less her male relatives. His negligible military achievements, such as his feigned invasion of Britain, were excuses for tremendous ovations in Rome. Soon money ran out, new taxes were imposed and temple treasures filched. Even the subservient Romans had endured enough over four years, and in AD 41 Caligula was assassinated.

Claudius

No suitable successor was apparent but the Senate's hopes of recovering its lost authority were speedily ended by the Praetorian Guard, when they produced Caligula's uncle Claudius, whom they found hiding in fear in the palace.

The Senate was compelled to recognize him as emperor. He was then fifty-one. He had been overlooked as a doddering old fool during the exilings and assassinations which marked the reigns of Tiberius and Caligula, but his feeble-mindedness seems to have been simulated, for his rule restored sanity and peace to public life. Treason charges were discouraged and the malicious informers punished.

A number of his pronouncements and edicts have been discovered, which are characterized by an extraordinary and inimitable longwindedness. Literary composition was his hobby. He understood Etruscan, and wrote about Etruscan history and religion. None of these works or his autobiography has survived. Because he took his administrative duties seriously he relied on his secretaries, thereby giving them influence which free Romans bitterly resented. Pallas and Narcissus, his two principal aides, became immensely rich and therefore targets for revenge. Claudius extended the empire

Below, statue of a Roman actor. Petit Palais Museum, Paris.

Left, Roman cameo depicting the triumph of Tiberius: the emperor is descending from his triumphal car, attended by Augustus and Germanicus; below are soldiers, captives and trophies. Bibliothèque Nationale, Paris.

Below left, the head of a chief of the Celtic Helvetii tribe of the first century AD. Bernisches Historisches Museum, Bern.

Opposite top, marble relief of a race in the Circus Maximus, Rome. Museo Civico, Foligno.

Opposite bottom, the Emperor Claudius (10 BC– AD 54, ruled AD 41–54). Vatican Museum, Rome.

by adding Mauretania and Britain. He himself took part in the invasion of Britain of AD 43, defeating Caractacus and capturing Colchester (Camulodunum), leaving Aulus Plautius to complete the conquest.

His wives were his undoing: Messalina, the third, sent many innocent people to their deaths before she was murdered for her outrageous sexual licence. Claudius, then failing, married his niece Agrippina in AD 49. She poisoned him five years later, contriving that her son Nero should succeed instead of Britannicus, son of Claudius.

Nero

Nero, aged seventeen, was guided by his tutor, Seneca, and by Burrus, the prefect of the Praetorian Guard, to behave as he had promised, 'in the spirit of Augustus'.

Slighted and neglected, Agrippina turned against Nero to intrigue on behalf of Britannicus, then only fourteen, whom Nero murdered (AD 55). Thereafter he increasingly indulged his vanity, extravagance and arbitrary power, while his morbid fears and hates made him a monster. In AD 59 he acquired a mistress, Poppaea Sabina, wife of his friend Otho, who was sent off to govern Lusitania. A heartless gold-digger, she had Nero's mother murdered. Later his aunt, Domitia, and his wife, Octavia, shared her fate. By then he was already increasingly hated. He had revived the laws against treason, using them to kill people for their wealth because his riotous life and expensive wars in Britain had drained the treasury and depreciated the coinage.

His ambitions as poet, singer and public performer made him ridiculous in the eyes of his fellow countrymen. Roman arms suffered a disaster in Britain when in AD 61 Boadicea, queen of the Iceni, led a revolt which ended in a massacre of the Romans. A greater disaster occurred in AD 64 when much of the centre of Rome was utterly destroyed in a vast fire. While thousands died or were left homeless, Nero planned a 'golden house' surrounded by a huge pleasure park, which was created on the site of the fire. Rumours said that he had started the fire, during which he strummed his lyre, for this very purpose.

He tried to divert public odium by blaming the catastrophe on 'a sect notorious for their abominations known as Christians after their leader, Christus, who had been executed by Pontius Pilate during the reign of Tiberius'. Tacitus, who reported this charge, which he did not believe, records the excruciating tortures inflicted upon the Christians. Some were crucified; others, covered by animal skins, were torn by dogs; and others were burnt at night as human candles.

Nero's delights at such spectacles caused pity for the victims and a powerful revulsion

of feeling. He was further hated for his exactions throughout the Roman world to pay for the building of his new palace and park and for the restoration of Rome. As disgust deepened, Calpurnius Piso and many others conspired to kill him in AD 65, but they were betrayed, to meet a fate that only a monster such as Nero could devise. 'Make them feel they are dying', he commanded. Seneca, the philosopher, and Lucan the poet were forced to kill themselves. Stoic philosophy and Christian faith steeled hundreds to endure the barbarities inflicted on them. In sulphurous prose Tacitus, sickened and disgusted, catalogued the fortitude of many and the servility of the weak during the mounting toll of torture and death.

Nero bribed every man of the Praetorian Guard with money and free rations. His vicious temper knew no restraint. Poppaea, whom he had married in AD 62, died from a blow he gave her in a fit of rage (AD 65). To add to the general misery, Italy was decimated by a terrible plague, from which 30,000 were said to have died in Rome alone. In AD 66, Judaea revolted, and the Jews furiously resisted the legions under Vespasian and his son Titus. Nero meanwhile was giving performances in Greece where, carried away by vociferous sycophantic applause, he irresponsibly proclaimed the 'freedom of Greece' from Roman rule. While in Athens he summoned one of his most successful commanders, Corbulo, ordering him to commit suicide. A similar command went to two generals in Germany. No army commander could now feel safe. In Gaul, Spain and Africa his generals revolted. Nero met the threat by dreaming of a fiendish revenge. The Senate declared him a public enemy and the Praetorian Guard deserted him. Without a friend, he fled and committed suicide in June of AD 68.

Left and above, coins portraying the Emperor Nero (AD 37–68, ruled AD 54–68) and his wife. British Museum, London.

Opposite, wall-painting from the Golden House, the palace built by Nero after AD 64.

The year of four emperors

Nero was the last of the Julio–Claudian line of rulers founded by Augustus. Imperial power now became the prize of a successful army commander. Galba was the first. His career had been brilliant, but he was over seventy and afflicted by gout. With him came Otho, former husband of Poppaea. The Senate accepted Galba who, 'had he not ruled, would have been thought fit to rule by everybody'. He was a stern commander of the old school, unpopular because of his cruelty and meanness.

Early in AD 69 Otho murdered him and was proclaimed emperor by the Praetorians. Public order collapsed. Tacitus describes the chaos that once again came to Rome:

Crammed with catastrophes; made ghastly by battles; torn by seditions; peace itself savage; four rulers put to the sword; three civil wars, many foreign wars, very often both together; . . . Italy smitten by fresh disasters . . . Rome itself devastated by fire . . . sacred rites profaned; scandalous adulteries; every sea carrying exiles; rocks strewn with corpses; yet more atrocious savagery in the city; nobility, wealth, the refusal or acceptance of office alike the ground for condemnation; no more certain reward for virtue than death; informers sharing prizes as loathsome as their crimes; . . . slaves suborned against their masters; freedmen against their patrons; finally, any who lacked enemies were destroyed by their friends.

Vitellius was hailed as emperor in Cologne. Otho marched against him but was overthrown. Vitellius then became emperor in April, but in December he also was slain to make way for Vespasian from Alexandria, after bloody scenes in which the Capitol, including the ancient Temple of Jupiter, was burnt.

Chapter 14

The Flavian and Antonine Emperors

So desperate was the need for order and so great was the devastation during the terrible anarchy which had followed the removal of Nero that the Senate welcomed Vespasian. They enhanced the political power of the *princeps* which he had won by force of arms, with 'the right and power to do all such things as he may consider to serve the interests of the state and the dignity of all things, divine and human, public and private'. So specific an endowment with absolute power is an indication of the rapid decline that had taken place in the influence of the Senate.

With peace assured at home, Rome had little difficulty in coping with the revolts which had broken out in many parts of the empire during the previous two years. In AD 70 the Jews, who had rebelled in AD 66, were overcome and massacred, and Jerusalem destroyed (although a remnant held out at Masada until AD 72). By the end of AD 70 peace had been restored. By strict administration at home and in the provinces, by raising the annual tribute and by stringent economy measures, Vespasian began to repair the financial ruin of the state.

He made his son Titus the prefect of the Praetorian Guard and named him as his successor, with his younger brother Domitian as next in line. Gaps in the senatorial ranks resulting from the slaughter of Nero's reign and after were filled, partly by eminent Italians and provincials. Freedmen were no longer advanced to posts of great responsibility. Romanization progressed in the provinces as careful watch was kept on governors and their staffs. Frontiers were well guarded. Careers such as that of Agricola (AD 40–93), whose daughter married Tacitus, show that the old Roman virtues were by no means extinct. Legate in Britain for Vespasian, Agricola conquered Wales and advanced into southern Scotland up to the Highlands. His fleet sailed round the British Isles, reporting that the sea was unusually dense and heavy in the extreme north, unaware that it had encountered the tidal race in the Pentland Firth.

In Rome the dismemberment of Nero's Roman Park was begun. The Flavian amphitheatre, or Colosseum, built on the site of his lake and designed to gratify the blood lusts of the Roman mobs, opened in

AD 80 with a tremendous series of ferocious fights to the death between gladiators and wild beasts, lasting one hundred days.

On the Capitol the great temple of Jupiter, Juno and Minerva was rebuilt, a Temple of Peace was begun and roads and aqueducts were repaired. In the rest of Italy and in the Empire there was also considerable material progress.

Titus

In AD 79 Titus, generous, intelligent and popular, succeeded Vespasian; but hopes placed upon him were disappointed by his death at the age of forty-two in AD 81. On 23–25 August AD 79, Vesuvius, with a grim reminder of Italy's volcanic past, overwhelmed the adjacent towns of Herculaneum and Pompeii. In the following year another huge fire raged for three days in Rome, destroying the new Capitoline temple, the Pantheon, the library of Augustus and other great buildings. Once more a plague raged in the city.

Domitian

Domitian, as dour as Titus had been genial, ruled firmly and justly at first, although he reduced the Senate to a mere instrument of his own will. He increased taxation because of his need for funds for rebuilding in Rome as well as for bribing the troops and the Roman mob. As discontent mounted conspiracies for his removal began. As each in turn was discovered, his subsequent reprisals were increasingly savage. In an atmosphere poisoned by suspicion, informers again flourished, and hatred of him grew still

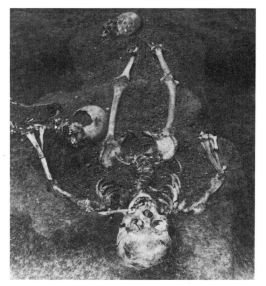

further. In this horrible insecurity his own wife was a party, with two praetorian prefects, to his assassination in AD 96.

Nerva

As no successor was in sight, the Senate momentarily revived to nominate one of themselves, an elderly lawyer called Nerva, once (AD 71) consul with Domitian. It was a good choice except that Nerva was no soldier, and many of the Praetorian Guard, enraged by the murder of Domitian, were not appeased by Nerva's money bribe. They would not rest until the two men mainly responsible for killing Domitian were executed. Troubles might have increased had not Nerva adopted as heir a seasoned soldier, the Spanish-born Trajan. Nerva's reign was short, but before he died, early in

AD 98, he began the system of *alimenta*—
loans to farmers from public funds, using
the interest to support poor children, mainly
boys, as future legionaries. Small farmers
were helped at the same time.

Senators were relieved when he stopped
treason charges and condemned informers.
Accusations of slaves and freedmen against
their masters were no longer entertained,
and slaves who had betrayed their masters
were executed.

Trajan

When Nerva died Trajan was campaigning
in Germany. He was a popular commander
sharing the life and hardships of his men,
and accepting and discharging his responsibilities with energy, resource and success.
With calm self-confidence, he did not hurry
to Rome, which he did not know well, but
first saw to strengthening Rome's frontiers
on the Rhine and Danube. He did not arrive
in the city until AD 99.

Determined to stand no nonsense from
the Praetorian Guard, he executed the
mutinous, giving the rest only half the money
bribe expected from a new emperor. By no
means parsimonious, however, he was
lavish with the occasional gifts of money
(*congiaria*) which emperors since the time of
Augustus had made to the Romans receiving the free state wheat supply. He subsequently added to the numbers benefiting
from the free distribution. From AD 101 to
106 Trajan was almost continuously campaigning against the Dacians living in the

region occupied by much of modern Hungary and Rumania, north of the Danube.
At the end of bitter fighting in two wars,
after the first of which the Dacian king
agreed to become an independent vassal,
only soon to rebel, the area was made the
new Roman province of Dacia. Its gold
mines made it an important acquisition. A
vast amount of looted gold and silver was
brought to Rome to provide the greatest
congiarium the impoverished Roman mobs
had ever received—500 *denarii* a head.
Nerva's *alimenta* grants were increased and
extended throughout Italy.

Far less admirable were the 100 days
following Trajan's celebration of his colossal

*Above, relief from the Arch of Titus of soldiers
parading through the arch carrying the spoils of
victory, including a candelabrum from the Temple
of Jerusalem.*

*Below left, street in Pompeii; built at the foot of
Vesuvius not far from Naples, Pompeii was buried
when Vesuvius erupted in AD 79, destroying the
city and killing about 2,000 people, some ten
percent of the inhabitants.*

*Opposite top right, the arch (partly restored) of
Titus, erected at the top of the Via Sacra, Rome,
by the Emperor Domitian in AD 81, to celebrate
Titus' and Vespasian's capture of Jerusalem in
AD 70 after a long siege.*

*Opposite bottom, human skeleton found at
Pompeii.*

*Opposite top left, the Emperor Vespasian (AD 9–
79, ruled AD 70–9). National Museum, Naples.*

triumph, for they were given up to revolting slaughter in the amphitheatre, where innumerable wild animals as well as some 10,000 gladiators are said to have perished. Great building plans resulted in better roads and bridges as well as the huge new market, Trajan's Forum, in Rome. His column in the middle commemorating his Dacian exploits still stands.

Trajan also gave Rome two new *thermae*. These were the public recreation centres and great baths contained in huge marble palaces, set in gardens which had been begun modestly by Agrippa around 20 BC and were later to become vaster and more numerous. Some taxes were reduced, both

in Rome and in the provinces, where a more vigorous expansion of Roman influence through colonies and new towns was notable, as in Numidia. In the East Trajan was less successful. The province of Arabia was formed in AD 105–106 with Petra and its rock-hewn temples as its religious centre.

Meanwhile the Jews were in a constant ferment. Vespasian had destroyed Jerusalem, diverting to the Temple of Jupiter in Rome the contribution which every Jew had paid to the great Temple of Jerusalem. The Jews were regarded as fanatical and obnoxious because of their private synagogues and their Mosaic Law decreeing death for anyone who attempted to persuade a Jew to

worship any other god but his own. Similar reasons explain popular animosity to the Christians whom the Jews hated also. Their influence was growing despite fierce persecution, which some fanatical Christians actually encouraged in the ardour of their faith, their contempt for all earthly things and their glory in martyrdom. Because they not only refused to honour the ancient gods and sacred spirits of the Romans, but regarded those who did so as devil-worshippers, it was impossible even for tolerant emperors to overlook their affront to established ways. Moreover, they met in secret for rites which nobody understood. Nevertheless the purity of the lives of many

of them could not fail to impress fair-minded Romans. One of these was Pliny, called 'the younger' (*c.* AD 61–*c.* 113).

While commanding the fleet at Misenum in AD 79 his uncle, Pliny 'the elder' (AD 23–78), observed the eruption of Vesuvius. Taking his ships in to have a closer view and to rescue refugees, he remained too long and was suffocated under a rain of ashes, pumice and fumes. His nephew, a friend of Trajan, was sent about AD 112 to govern Bithynia and Pontus, east of Byzantium. He sent Trajan a stream of dispatches, including many on minor matters which a resourceful governor might be expected to resolve himself. One question he raised in his correspondence was whether Christians should be punished because they were Christians, or only because they had committed some crime. Pliny had given anyone accused of being a Christian three chances to deny the fact, telling them that their refusal would

Above, fragment from Trajan's column, c. AD 106–113, depicting Roman legionaries taking cover beneath a protecting wall of interlocked shields, known as a 'tortoise'. Museo della Civiltà Romana, Rome.

Top, the Forum of Trajan, Rome; in the centre background stands Trajan's Column.

Above left, the Forum at Pompeii, destroyed in AD 79.

Left, aerial view of the fortress of Masada on the Dead Sea: here, in AD 73, the Jews made their last stand against the triumphant Roman forces.

Far left, oscillum from Pompeii in the form of a mask of tragedy, first century AD. National Museum, Naples.

Opposite top, portrait of a man and his wife from Pompeii, before AD 79. National Museum, Naples.

Opposite bottom, pig found at Pompeii. National Museum, Naples

of the offenders as customary law plainly allowed, or how many simply tried to ignore the Christians.

It is difficult to believe that men whose characters had been trained by soldiering with Trajan would constantly be asking him for instructions on many of the minor matters with which Pliny filled his letters to the emperor. Most of the replies are likely to have been drafted by secretaries, although some scholars believe that Trajan himself wrote many. Their correspondence is the only clear indication of the sort of problems with which the governor of a Roman province had to deal. Should victors in athletic contests receive the pension provided by the emperor from the day when they were crowned victor, or not until they entered their native city in triumph? Might the daughter of a centurion who had been given Roman citizenship receive it also? Would Trajan please excuse Pliny for allowing his wife to travel in a post-chaise to visit her afflicted aunt? Might the city of Prusa build its bath, already authorized by Trajan, on the ruins of an old house bequeathed to the Emperor Claudius? Should not soldiers replace public slaves as prison guards? Trajan said no in reply to this last question. Could Nicodemia, after a devastating fire, be allowed a guild of firemen, not more than 250 strong? Trajan refused this request on the grounds that they might become a political association. Could two cities please have architects from Rome to supervise the building of a theatre and a gymnasium? 'No', said Trajan, 'every province has skilled architects and in any case it is from Greece, not Rome that they usually come.' It seems hardly credible that Trajan could have found time to deal with such small details.

More important matters demanded all his attention, as he prepared his expedition against the Parthians in AD 113. Not merely a constant menace on Rome's eastern frontiers, they commanded the silk and spice route to the Far East. In the following year Trajan overran Armenia. He then grouped his forces for a campaign in Mesopotamia in AD 115. Avoiding the fate of all previous Roman commanders, he overcame the Parthians and built ships to explore the Euphrates. In AD 116 he captured Babylon and Ctesiphon, the Parthian capital, and marched to the Persian Gulf, where he arrived before his fleet. In that year the Jews rebelled in Egypt, Cyrene and Cyprus, only to be very firmly suppressed. His health failing, Trajan turned back. He died in AD 117 aged sixty-three.

mean death. To clear themselves they had to worship Trajan's image and curse Christ. After executing all who refused to recant, unless they were Roman citizens (whom he sent to Rome), Pliny began to have doubts. 'This contagious superstition', he reported, 'is not confined to the cities only, but has spread through the villages and rural districts.' Moreover, 'persons of all ranks and ages, and of both sexes are, and will be, involved in the prosecution.' He had tortured two women slaves called *ministrae* ('deaconesses') but learnt nothing except about 'their depraved and extravagant superstition'.

Trajan's reply is the first recorded official decision about Rome's attitude to the Christians. He did not think any general rule could apply:

They should not be hunted out. Any who might be accused and found guilty should be punished unless they deny that they are Christians and prove it by worshipping our gods. Anonymous denunciations must not be accepted against anybody because they would be both a bad example and contrary to the spirit of our times.

Politics as much as religious fervour called for such firmness. The ancient religious observances of the Romans were steadily declining. The temples lacked worshippers, festivals were either ignored or forgotten, and few were ready to buy animals for sacrifice. At the same time the Romans were unwilling to permit the old ways to be directly challenged by a religious fervour then foreign to the spirit of the age. The early Christians, in the first years of their existence, sought to abolish practices hallowed by immemorial tradition by spreading the new gospel completely, and so stirred up violent opposition. It is impossible to say how many other provincial governors, faced with Pliny's problem, resorted to execution

Hadrian

In the reign of Hadrian, the Roman Empire reached the height of its power. Trajan had already pushed forward its frontiers to

Left, the Emperor Hadrian (AD 76–138, ruled AD 117–138): he reorganized the imperial administrations, travelled widely, and was a benefactor of all the arts.

Below, the aqueduct at Segovia, Spain: built during Trajan's reign, it has 128 arches and is about half a mile long.

Opposite, stairway leading to the top of the citadel at the desert city of Petra, Jordan; the city was an important centre of the caravan trade between the first century BC and the third AD and became part of the Roman Empire in AD 106.

their farthest extent. He and Hadrian were cousins, both born in Seville. Hadrian's two great enthusiasms were Greek culture and hunting. The childless Trajan had summoned him to Rome in AD 93 at the age of seventeen. He never adopted Hadrian but treated him as a son, ensuring him a widening experience and promotion, and marrying him to a young grand-niece, Vibia Sabina. Hadrian was therefore the natural heir.

Hadrian was governor of Syria at the time of Trajan's death. Not without military experience, for he was a firm disciplinarian and a keen tactician, he was not, however, a campaigning emperor of Trajan's stamp. More realistically, Hadrian concentrated on ensuring the imperial defences. Trajan's eastern conquests had been very costly, yielding no great booty. They were also precarious. Consequently Hadrian relinquished Armenia, Mesopotamia, Assyria and Parthia, retaining only Arabia Petraea. Dacia in Europe, already being colonized, was also retained.

Vigorous economy was necessary if taxes were not to be increased or the currency depreciated. Hadrian restored the finances, although at the same time he wrote off a huge sum due to Rome as unpaid taxes by publicly burning all record of them in AD 118. To improve administrative services he filled higher posts with members of the *equites*, second only to senators in social distinction, eliminating freedmen for whom he had a true Roman disdain. Qualified auditors inspected provincial accounting.

Here was the beginning of that extension of the bureaucracy which was later to stifle enterprise. Senators were treated with a consideration all the greater because four of the most eminent of their number, suspected of a conspiracy, had been summarily executed during the first months of his reign before Hadrian had arrived in Rome. He tried to prevent his new privy council, to which he added some businessmen, from offending senatorial susceptibilities, since he also felt it necessary to conceal their complete subordination to the emperor. Hadrian devoted untiring energy to a thorough organization of the provinces, spending two-thirds of his reign away from Rome. Army organization and discipline were everywhere tightened up as though war were imminent. Strict, detailed army orders were enforced, the emperor setting an example by living a camp life on army rations, marching with his troops on their twenty-mile route marches with full kit, witnessing drill and frequent manoeuvres, inspecting trenches and ramparts, visiting military hospitals and making his presence felt everywhere.

No better symbol exists of his defensive policy than the great Hadrian's Wall across the North of England from Tyne to Solway. He ordered its construction in AD 121–122 on one of his first provincial tours. He endowed many cities with aqueducts, public buildings, harbours and other improvements, some of this work being undertaken by his armies. Greece, and particularly Athens, which he visited in AD 125–126 and in AD 128, were specially favoured. A lifelong admirer of Greek philosophy and literature, he expressed his gratitude by giving Greece great buildings, temples, aqueducts and roads. In Greece he acquired Antinous, a youth of great beauty and charm, whom he took to Egypt as his page in AD 130. When the young man was drowned in the Nile, Hadrian's grief was so intense that he decreed his worship as a new god—a cult which flourished for decades in the east.

Good government needs good law and good judges. Hadrian gave Salvius Julianus, a brilliant young lawyer, the task of compiling a code of Roman law, resulting in the *Edictum Julianum,* the foundation of the later, more celebrated work of Ulpian and Justinian. Four circuit judges of appeal were appointed.

The greatest tragedy of his reign was the Jewish rebellion under Bar Cocheba of AD 132–135. Failing to understand Jewish religious and nationalist fanaticism inspired by the Mosaic Law, the Romans faced perpetual unrest in Judaea. Constant provocation, notably the destruction of the Temple of Solomon and its replacement by a temple of Zeus, stirred up another fierce rebellion. After savage struggles the Jews were at last overcome. Hundreds of thousands were killed or sold, glutting the slave-markets. Christian prophecy was fulfilled, Jerusalem was utterly destroyed and the Jews were driven away. With the exception of this campaign, Hadrian, from AD 131 to 138, enjoyed, with literature and music, some of the golden years secured by his labours. He adorned Rome, rebuilding Agrippa's Pantheon and constructing his own great mausoleum. Near Tivoli he created a vast palace and pleasure park, 'Hadrian's Villa'. During his last, long, painful illness, still anxious for Rome, he named Antoninus as his successor, to be followed by Marcus Verus.

The Antonines

Hadrian had early made Antoninus consul (AD 120) and a member of his privy council, and had given him legal duties in Italy before sending him to govern Asia (AD 133–136). Antoninus was a wealthy country gentleman, whose accession gratified the Senate, to which he continued to be respectful. In AD 139 he fulfilled Hadrian's wishes and adopted Marcus Annius Verus 'Aurelius', to whom he betrothed his own daughter, Annia Faustina.

Antoninus was fortunate in inheriting an efficient, well-run empire, needing little more

than capable leadership to maintain the momentum imparted by Hadrian and by the able officials he had appointed. Their activities strengthened both bureaucratic tendencies and his own position. However, the general feeling of security contributed to a spirit of confidence without which economic progress or improvement in social welfare would be difficult to achieve. Threats to peace were not lacking but none seriously disturbed the general tranquility—not even the sporadic revolts in Britain, Numidia, Mauretania, Judaea and Egypt, all of which were easily suppressed. From the rest of the Empire and Italy, encouraged by Hadrian's liberality, came a stream of petitions for imperial favour: for baths, temples, aqueducts and for succour after fire or earthquake. In Rome itself the greedy, feckless mob was avid for the donatives which Antoninus distributed on nine occasions. The mob lived for doles, the excitement of circus races and the bloodbaths of the arena.

Deification after death, which was customary for good Roman emperors, and which Antoninus had secured from a reluctant Senate for Hadrian, was spontaneously awarded to Antoninus also when his beneficent rule ended in his seventy-fourth year in AD 161.

Left, Hadrian's Wall at Housesteads on the border between England and Scotland.

Below, equestrian statue of the Emperor Marcus Aurelius, AD 165–173.

Opposite, map of the Roman Empire at the beginning of the second century AD, the period of its greatest extent.

While still a boy in Rome, Marcus Annius Verus had won special favour from Hadrian, which continued as he developed qualities and interests akin to the emperor's own, through a life of austerity and endurance. Marcus, a keen student of Greek and Latin literature, was early attracted by Stoic doctrines, upon which he sought to model his life. His was a hard fate, calling for all the consolations philosophy could bring, for the first shadows of the grim times ahead began to fall as his reign progressed. Like Antoninus, he was from a wealthy family, driven on by his sense of duty. He and his adoptive brother Lucius, ten years younger, were both consuls in AD 161 when Antoninus died. Although recognized as *princeps* and 'Augustus', Marcus insisted upon having his brother as 'Caesar' and co-regent.

Within a year serious trouble began, of which a war with the Parthians was the worst. They had defeated two Roman armies and occupied Armenia. Lucius was sent against them with powerful reinforcements. Local commanders had, however, recovered Armenia and reduced Mesopotamia to a Roman protectorate, so that Lucius was able to return in triumph in AD 166. However, he and his army brought a disastrous contagion with them from the plague raging in Babylonia.

Panic struck Rome in AD 167 as news arrived in the city, already smitten with disease and famine, that German tribes were pouring into Dacia and across the Danube into Raetia, Noricum and Pannonia, where Roman defences had been weakened by the withdrawal of troops needed for the Parthian war and by the effects of the plague. Northern Italy itself was threatened as the invading hordes surged onward. With one intermission (AD 175–177), war was continuous until AD 180, compelling Marcus Aurelius to spend his life soldiering. A crisis arose in AD 175 when Avidus Cassius, the governor of Syria, a harsh but effective commander, proclaimed himself emperor, apparently believing the Empire to be at the mercy of a weak, ineffective ruler. Another story was that he had received false reports of the death of Marcus Aurelius. Cilicia, Judaea, as well as his own Syria, supported him. His treason was more serious when Egyptian forces joined him, for they were in control of a large part of Rome's wheat supply. News of the peril was sent to Marcus by the loyal commander of the small Roman force in Cappadocia.

After three months panic was allayed when a centurion assassinated Cassius. Marcus left at once for a tour of the disaffected provinces, which had been easily reduced by the Cappadocian commander. While he was in Asia, his loyal, devoted wife died. A grave, saddened man, he returned home with his young son Commodus. Both were hailed as *imperator*, and Commodus, then only fifteen, was named as consul for AD 177, with the title of Augustus and tribunician powers. Soon both were called

north again when a German tribe, the Marcomanni, challenged the Romans to a final fierce battle, in which the former were decisively beaten. In AD 179–180 Marcus prepared for a final campaign which would secure a shorter and safer defensive frontier in the north. Overtaken by illness, before he died he urged Commodus to finish his task.

At the age of eighteen Commodus may have been thought by his father to be young enough to profit by his own example and to have his character shaped by the weight of responsibility suddenly to be thrust upon him. Having trained and promoted him to be almost a co-ruler, Marcus could not suddenly select a rival without risking terrible internal conflicts of loyalty. Yet he has been blamed for failing to foresee the young man's weakness and instability of character. A greater contrast to his father—that stern, stoic, ascetic slave to duty—can scarcely be imagined. Commodus sacrificed the fruits of his father's victories and hurried to Rome, where he soon revealed his character to be that of a gross sensualist. His own sister, Lucilla, planned with her cousin to have him removed. Their failure unleashed a campaign of vengeance in which Lucilla, after a brief exile, was murdered. As Commodus struck down one senator after another on account of their probable sympathy with the conspirators, power increasingly fell into the hands of Perennis, who was prefect of the Praetorian Guard. Eventually he, too, was accused of aspiring to the imperial authority, which, in fact, he had already been exercising in the name of Commodus. In AD 185 he and all his family were butchered. In the following year Cleander, a former slave, and chamberlain of Commodus, became Praetorian prefect. With cool effrontery he sold public offices, governorships and magistracies. In January of AD 189 he made twenty-five men consuls. Judgements in the courts were reversed for cash payments and freedmen became senators. Criticism was soon stifled by a treason charge as he murdered the emperor's brother-in-law, senators and knights and sent the empress to exile and death. Then he was sacrificed by Commodus to the mob, by making him responsible for a serious food shortage and a delay in distributing a promised cash bribe. Commodus further outraged sober sentiments by claiming to be Hercules after acting the gladiator and slaying a lion in the arena in AD 191. Then on 1 January AD 193, Marcia, his favourite concubine, had him murdered.

Decline and fall

While Marcus Aurelius and the legionaries valiantly defended the Empire, his subjects everywhere enjoyed a prosperity probably as great as any society had known until the rise of modern industrial civilization. Ruled by a succession of tolerant, cultivated and

well-intentioned emperors, both Romans and provincials had enjoyed nearly 100 years of freedom from arbitrary interference.

Above all, they were set standards by which to steer their lives, from the senators and the aristocracy down to the humblest peasants, who no longer went in fear of their lives at the sight of Roman legionaries, tax collectors and officials. Magistrates and civil servants observed high standards of justice and efficiency. Traders were able to move about freely, aided by the universal readiness to accept Roman money, the value of which was no longer liable to be debased by some debauched emperor. They were also helped by an almost universal knowledge of Latin, although Greek remained essential in the East.

The rule of law was on the whole respected. The twenty-eight provinces over which Augustus ruled had increased in number to forty-five under Marcus Aurelius. Most provincials depended on their ability to wrest a livelihood from the land, so sharing the relatively hard fate of such primary producers, particularly of those in somewhat primitive times. Nevertheless, as villas for the wealthy sprang up, small townships developed, until there were said to have been three times as many of them under Marcus Aurelius as there had been under Augustus. Peasants were therefore often able to become acquainted with higher standards of life. Even the slaves, that vast, silent substratum upon which the economic life of the ancient world had always rested, began to see some improvements in their miserable condition.

Thus the Empire which Commodus inherited from his father, and which he proceeded to mismanage, was not only firmly established but thriving and seemed to hold promise of a slow rather than spectacular improvement in living conditions for its more lowly inhabitants, and continued prosperity for the more wealthy minority. But the decline of the Empire was to be no less swift and traumatic than its creation.

Chapter 15

Roman Civilization

Long before the Roman Empire had reached its widest extent in the second century AD, Cicero had recognized the predatory character of his countrymen, 'indeed the most just of men', who nevertheless continually stole the property of others by force 'until they acquired possession of the whole world'. If they had to restore what they had grabbed, 'they would have to return to hovels, to lie in misery and want'. More than 200 years later another of the relatively few eminent Romans with philosophical interests. Marcus Aurelius, who had been forced to kill and capture nomadic, invading Sarmatians, likened himself in a melancholy mood to a predatory huntsman.

The short, sharp, thrusting sword of the Roman legionaries was the instrument of empire, an empire yielding a continuous supply of tribute and slaves—a vast domain for trade, colonization and imperial rule, providing employment and prestige for thousands of Roman commanders, governors, administrators, and merchants.

Marius had created a professional army; Augustus established it as a permanent standing army of Roman citizens, commanded by senatorial officers. It was supplemented by auxiliary troops recruited from the provinces, who were given citizenship on completion of satisfactory service. They were commanded by officers of the Equestrian class, and their numbers grew steadily as Roman citizens no longer found twenty-five years in the ranks an attractive way of life, despite the extra pay and largesse given to ensure their continuing loyalty to the emperor, who was their supreme commander and paymaster. The Praetorian Guard, recruited mainly from Italy and stationed at Rome, was also established by Augustus to become, as the history of his successors shows, an élite corps of about 5,000 men with growing consciousness of the power of its leader if not of the men themselves. For the defence of the whole Empire about 150,000 men were kept under arms, grouped in some thirty legions, each with its distinctive, sacred standard—the 'eagle'—accompanying the commanding officer. The locally recruited auxiliary troops were perhaps equal in number to the legions.

The Romans of the Republic had been well aware of the danger of a standing army as an instrument of tyranny. They took every precaution against its occurrence by electing annually two civilian heads of state having equal powers, by limiting the rule of a dictator to six months and by maintaining an army of citizens serving at their own expense, owing loyalty to the gods, the Senate and people of Rome over and above obedience to their local commander. No armed men were allowed within the city walls. Mobilization, drill and civilian voting (then also conducted in army formation), had to take place outside the walls, on the Campus Martius.

Nothing more clearly symbolizes the radical revolution in Roman public life than the disregard of the emperors for all those ancient safeguards. There was a dramatic change from the republican idea that law should be supreme to the imperial practice that whatever the emperor should decree must override all other considerations. His was now the power to ensure his supremacy, so long as his troops remained loyal. Already, before the relatively well-intentioned orderly administration of the Flavian and Antonine emperors had restored respect for the rule of law, Romans had witnessed the disastrous consequences of its disappearance in the times of Tiberius, Caligula and

Nero, and during the horrors of AD 69–70. After Augustus might became right, so that, unless the emperor was indeed righteous, life for his subjects could be hazardous.

A prosperous interlude

Three generations of Romans came to maturity between AD 96 and AD 180, when their world seemed firmly established and protected by stoutly defended frontiers, while law and order ruled within. Many Romans and provincials grew rich. Until the wars and the plague weakened Rome and

Italy under Marcus Aurelius, the treasury was well filled, as a result of measures taken by Hadrian and Antoninus Pius, despite the huge expense of free food and money gifts to the Roman people. The cost was met from resources taken mainly as tribute and taxation from Rome's dependent provinces. Taxation fell lightly upon Roman citizens. There was an inheritance tax of five percent on money left to charities, a tax of one percent on public auctions, a five percent tax on sellers of slaves and a five percent tax payable when a slave was set free. Gold and silver mines became imperial property, their products being required for the coinage.

In the absence of sufficient reliable statistics it is impossible to guess what the revenue and expenditure of the Empire actually were. More tangible evidence of economic growth is provided by the massive buildings which were added to Rome and the provinces as well as by the roads made during the first two centuries of the Empire. Augustus had begun with building schemes which he boasted had turned a city of brick into one of marble. It was not so much the marble he himself bought as that paid for by Romans who grew rich during the newly found peace after the Battle of Actium. As always, the number of very rich Romans

was small, but they indulged in the most ostentatious and lavish expenditure, particularly after the failure of the efforts of Augustus to commend modest living by his own example and by his laws. The rich soon found, under Tiberius, Caligula and Nero, that they were signing their own death warrants by their display because it marked them down for destruction by informers and by yet more wildly extravagant emperors. Nevertheless many lived in great luxury on their estates or in their magnificent town houses.

There are few better indices of advancing wealth and civilization than the creation of pleasure gardens. Alone of the peoples of antiquity, the Egyptians and Romans were able to develop and enjoy them. Gardens need security, water and a trained labour force. The Egyptians had the Nile; the Romans their aqueducts and slaves. Little is heard of Roman gardens until the end of the Republic. Their full expansion occurred during the Empire, when many came under imperial control as a result of obsequious bequest or of confiscation. More than one wealthy Roman was condemned on some trumped-up charge because the emperor or his favourites coveted his gardens. Sufficient were acquired in these ways to provide something in the nature of a green belt around the city from which everybody benefited, even though the gardens were not open to all.

Gardens were not the only feature which made imperial Rome a city of far greater sophistication than the republican capital had been. It was more extensive, much more crowded, more dangerous and noisier. As the centre of the known world, politically, administratively and culturally, it was populous to the point of overcrowding. Rents rose steeply and the poverty-stricken mob were miserably housed. Their chance of paid employment was usually small because of the competition of slave labour in the wholesale and retail trades, in city crafts and in services.

Visitors seeing Rome's skyline towards the end of the second century AD for the first time were lost in astonishment. Most Romans lived in apartment houses. Augustus had tried to limit their height to seventy feet, but even that seemed an impressive altitude to the vast majority outside Rome, living mainly in single-storey homes.

Far more astounding, however, were the great temples, baths and other public buildings. The Colosseum required about 200,000 tons of facing stone and the same quantity of brick, tufa and concrete, all of which had to be brought by ox carts. To carry the facing stone alone probably required about 200 wagon-loads a day for four years. An earlier enterprise, the aqueduct of Claudius, rising at some points to seventy-five feet in its seven miles above ground, required 600,000 tons of stone, which involved shifting about 100 loads every working day throughout fourteen years.

Not all Roman citizens lacked employment when operations of this magnitude were involved. Less spectacular building enterprises also added up to a vast total. There were also great works outside Rome. Claudius had begun to enlarge the city's port at Ostia, which, by the time of Trajan, had been made into a splendid harbour. It was

Above, legionaries presenting a captive barbarian to the Emperor Marcus Aurelius: detail from a relief on the Arch of Constantine, c. AD 313–315. Museo Capitolino, Rome.

Above left, procession of senators and priests, first century BC.

Opposite, interior of the House of the Neptune: mosaic at Herculaneum, before AD 79.

227

further developed with warehouses, granaries and offices, becoming under Hadrian a vast trading centre humming with commercial life. Rows of tall, well-built, brick houses with large windows, a novelty for Romans, added dignity. By comparison, Rome itself still had too many plague spots —narrow, ill-lit streets made filthy by sewage. The satires of Juvenal and the poems of Martial contain vivid descriptions of the mean, poverty-stricken way of life for many a Roman citizen about AD 100.

Baths, bread and circuses

Mediterranean summer sunshine drove people into the rivers and led them to construct baths on a scale unknown further north for many centuries. While the wealthy had their own private bathrooms, at first small, others were already able to go to public bathing establishments. In Pompeii the public Stabian baths date from the second century BC. Agrippa provided the first in Rome in AD 20. Others were added by Nero, Titus and Trajan. From baths, they were to develop in public recreation and social centres in which, from sunrise to sunset, at the price of the smallest Roman coin (or often free at the emperor's cost like the dole of bread), any Roman—man or woman or child—could spend the day in a luxurious marble palace, keeping cool in summer and warm in winter. Huge fires stoked by slaves kept warm and hot baths going. In time the baths became more luxurious. Nero perfumed his baths; many lolled about in them all the time, taking seven or eight baths a day after the manner of Commodus, whose custom it was to have his meals in them.

There were numerous other distractions to fill the empty lives of the common people. Conjurors, clowns, fortune-tellers, jugglers and street-musicians sought their reward at street corners and in market places. Serious theatrical performances, begun by Terence and Plautus in the second century BC, did not appeal to the mob, which called for knockabout farces and salacious stage shows. Even these palled before the thrills

of chariot races in the huge Circus Maximus of immemorial age. In 221 BC the consul Flaminius had constructed a circus in the Campus Martius. Nero's circus was across the Tiber near the site of St Peter's. Everyone had their favourite among the four teams of competing drivers distinguished by their colours—the reds, greens, blues and whites. Consuls and emperors witnessed many races which went on all day, as huge bets were placed and violent passions stirred.

During the Empire the people demanded ever stronger excitements, which even the ghastly daily slaughter of men and animals in the great Colosseum could barely satisfy. One of the most notable emperors, Titus, endeared himself to the mob in AD 80 by opening the great Colosseum, built by his father, for an inaugural series of 100 days of continuous fighting and slaughter. In brutal times, when the safety of many a man and his family depended upon his ability to kill his enemies, such scenes were defended as a good introduction to the realities of life. A few unusually sensitive souls, such as Cicero during the Republic and Seneca in Nero's reign, were exceptional in loathing these performances. (Cicero's beloved daughter was not so squeamish as her father.) The human victims were slaves, trained to fight

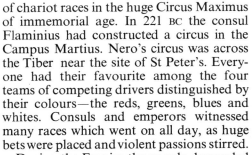

as gladiators, and criminals. Christians who met martyrdom there under emperors as abominable as Nero or as saintly as Marcus Aurelius were regarded as a fitting sacrifice because of their criminal rejection of the gods of Rome.

Roman peace and civilization

Augustus struck a new note when in a decree to the provinces of the Roman Empire, he wanted 'all who are cared for by us' to be assured 'how much care I and the Senate take to prevent any of our subjects suffering unjust treatment or extortion'. How greatly such an assurance was welcomed can easily be realized from stories of republican mal-treatment of helpless provincials.

Cicero made a name for himself as a powerful advocate when, on behalf of the cruelly victimized Sicilians, he drove into exile the detestable Verres who, for three years from 73 to 71 BC, had used his power as governor to rob, loot and murder the wretched islanders, relying upon the use of colossal bribes to defeat any attempt to prosecute him. Julius Caesar cleared himself of an enormous burden of debt by one year's campaign of looting and slaving in

Spain in 61 BC. Before the Roman conquest, Gaul was not regarded as a particularly rich source of treasure but during his campaigns there (58 to 49 BC), Julius Caesar acquired vast wealth.

Cicero was regarded almost as a god in his province of Cilicia in 51 BC because he made the troops under his command live under canvas without taking the usual bribes the provincials had to pay to avoid having the men billeted upon them. His friend Brutus was at that time trying to collect interest on money he had lent to the Cypriots at the rate of forty-eight percent; his agent indignantly rejected an offer of twelve percent. After the armies of Lucullus, Sulla and Pompey had wreaked their will on the countries of the Near East, there was little left to steal, but later Roman governors did their best. Therefore, it is not surprising that Augustus should be revered as a god for having done something to end such practices. His division of the provinces between those to whom

he appointed governors and commanders of armies and those who received governors nominated by the Senate, was part of the pretence by which he affected to share power with that pillar of the old Republic he had overthrown.

From the earliest times Rome's most urgent economic concern was to grow and import sufficient wheat to satisfy her ever-growing population. Otherwise it had no special economic policy. During the Empire there should as a rule have been no great difficulty in obtaining wheat. Imperial conquests were few. Augustus added Egypt and four northern provinces to secure the Danube as a frontier. Claudius annexed Britain and the Flavian emperors took a considerable slice of southwest Germany between the Rhine and the Danube. Trajan's only lasting gain was Dacia. Secure frontiers,

were also copied abroad, such as the forum, baths and, of course, temples. From these new civic centres a Romanizing influence could radiate. As provincial life settled down in peace and prosperity, villas sprang up over the countryside. Naturally, the pace of such development varied from province to province.

The extent of empire

That stretch of southern Gaul from the Alps to the Rhone and from Marseilles to Lyons, called Gallia Narbonensis, had been steadily Romanized from the first century BC, but civilizing influences had already reached there at an earlier stage with the Greek colony at Marseilles. It was a peaceful senatorial province during the Empire when, as the elder Pliny observed, it was little different from Italy. Climate and people were similar.

With Rome already in southern Gaul, the process of Romanization began to influence the less amenable 'long-haired' Gauls, as the remainder were called. Savagely mauled by Caesar, they had small reason for gratitude to the Romans. In time, towns developed, but country dwellers, although accepting the towns as centres, had a vigorous life of their own, sometimes clustered around large country villas. Druidism was suppressed, but the native gods were assimilated to those of the Romans without great difficulty. Corn, fruit and vegetables were grown in abundance, some of which were exported, together with hides, ham and cheese as the animal population increased. Great forests fed the furnaces of many small-scale metal workers and glass blowers. Their products, with jewellery and textiles, were dispatched by river and road.

New discoveries revealing the presence of Rome or Romanizing influences in Britain are continually being made. The sites of several hundred villas, mainly south of the Wash, and many permanent forts in Wales and north of York, are known. Most of the villas lay south of a line roughly from Gloucester (Glevum) to Colchester (Camulodunum). A connecting network of roads did not go beyond Hadrian's Wall in the north or Exeter in the south. Devon and Cornwall were not occupied. Wheat, lead, iron and gold were the main products. Coal was worked and iron was wrought in the Wealden forest. Despite some striking discoveries at Bath, at Fishbourne near Chichester, in London and elsewhere, it seems that Rome's civilizing influence was less than in Gaul, as might be expected in a country on the periphery of the Empire. The most enduring artistic achievements of Roman Britain were architecture, some sculpture, mosaics, wall paintings and some splendidly cut inscriptions.

Upper Germany (roughly modern Luxembourg, Flanders and Belgium) and Lower

tribute and interest on investments in land were the main rewards. Some trade in provincial goods over and above large imports of foodstuffs, grain, oil, fish sauce, etc., resulted, but while such one-way traffic went on more subtle forces were at work whose influence was to prove remarkably potent. Rome had some exports in manufactures such as the famous Arretine pottery, glass and bronzeware, but these soon declined as provincials learnt to produce them at home. It was the Roman way of life that was to prove the most enduring of Rome's exports.

Civilization and civic virtues developed and spread from Rome with the growth of city life. Throughout the provinces Romanized urban centres began to arise whose remains have survived all over western Europe. Their very form was often modelled upon the Roman military camp with its central axes and chequer-board streets. Greek cities had earlier shown a similar, regular rectangular pattern. Just as the Greeks built theatres where they settled, so Romans had to have amphitheatres. Older characteristics of Roman cities

Above, mosaic of a sea leopard from the Roman palace at Fishbourne, England.

Left and opposite below, two reliefs depicting the interior of a cloth's merchant's warehouse and a pharmacy, where soap is being made. Uffizi Gallery, Florence.

Opposite top, terracotta depicting a circus scene in which a bestiarius *is fighting two lions. Museo Nazionale delle Terme, Rome.*

THE EMPIRE IN THE FIRST CENTURY

Date	Rome: internal history	Rome: foreign relations	Rome: culture	The outside world	Date	Rome: internal history	Rome: foreign relations	Rome: culture	The outside world
30 BC		Annexation of Egypt	The Baths of Agrippa	Indian embassy to Augustus	40	Fall of Sejanus Caligula Emperor	Intervention in Parthia		Death of Christ Conversion of St Paul
		Treaty with the Parthians				Claudius Emperor	Conquest of Britain	Work on the harbour at Ostia	1st Council of Jerusalem
20 BC	Agrippa favoured by Augustus	Annexation of Illyria	Death of Virgil Ludi Saecultares		50			Pont du Gard	
10 BC	Augustus Pontifex Maximus	Annexation of Germania	Ara Pacis		60	Nero Emperor			
0			Death of Maecenas and of Horace	Birth of Christ		Great fire of Rome	Rising of the Jews	Golden House	
	Tiberius favoured by Augustus					Galba—Otho— Vitellius	Capture of Jerusalem	Death of Seneca	
10	Lex Papia Poppaea	Disaster under Varus			70	Vespasian Emperor			
	Death of Augustus		Death of Ovid and of Livy	Artabanus King of the Parthians		Titus Emperor Destruction of Pompeii		Arch of Titus Construction of the Colosseum	
	Tiberius				80			Death of Pliny the Elder	
20	Sejanus Prefect of the Praetorian Guard					Domitian Emperor			
		Rebellion in Gaul		Death of Juba II of Mauretania	90		1st Dacian War		
30					96	Assassination of Domitian			

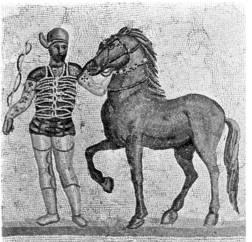

Germany (roughly the Palatinate) lay west of the Rhine. This remained the Roman frontier after the earlier failure to reach the Elbe, except during the period AD 74–274 when the *Agri Decumates* (the Black Forest, the Neckar basin and Swabian Alps came under Roman control. A large force of eight legions or more manned the defences, also providing a Romanizing influence, which was further strengthened by settling army veterans, now Roman citizens, on farms up to the frontier. There is evidence that cultural interests fostered by Roman examples grew stronger as the provinces grew in prosperity and well-being. Education, costume, domestic building and decoration—all copied the Roman and Italian manner. Adjacent Celtic Gaul, with which relations were naturally close, aided the process. Crafts, notably the glassware of Cologne, developed, but agriculture, as everywhere, was the mainstay.

A critical point in the imperial defences was the gap between the Rhine and Danube, linking Germany and Gaul with the Danubian provinces conquered under Augustus and Dacia won by Trajan—roughly southern Bavaria, Austria, Hungary, Romania and Yugoslavia. Commodus lamentably failed to carry out his father's plan to assure control of the area now occupied by Czechoslovakia. Their rich agriculture and the gold of Dacia made these lands valuable acquisitions, and a vigorous policy of colonization went forward. Towns on the chequer-board plan, provided with water, drainage, amphitheatres and other adjuncts of Roman city life were created, and veterans were settled, not always successfully, for much of the land was mountainous, barren and agriculturally unproductive.

After defeating the Carthaginians at the end of the third century BC, the Romans gradually established their influence both in North Africa and in Spain where they already had territory. Carthaginian Africa (roughly modern Tunisia) became public land. Gaius Gracchus failed in his colonizing programme but Romans and Italians later settled there. Elsewhere Romanization was largely left to the influence of the army, the

officials and the merchants. In the early years of the Empire there were three legions in Spain, two in Africa and two in Egypt. As in other provinces, but perhaps more particularly in Africa and Spain, the Romans could count upon a willingness on the part of the more able native inhabitants to assimilate a superior culture opening up wider horizons on the world. Prized from the first for its abundant wheat harvests as Rome's chief granary, Africa was later to add a considerable export of olive oil because Italy could no longer meet the demands. Towns began to develop from colonies of army veterans such as Thamugadi (Timgad) in Algeria. Although the mass of the large and growing population was little influenced by Roman ways, a profoundly Romanized social élite grew up which, later in the history of the Empire, was to make a great impact upon Rome itself.

One of the earliest provinces of the Republic, Spain long resisted conquest. During the Empire it enjoyed a period of peace and economic prosperity. The country was rich in minerals wanted by everyone—gold, silver and lead. To those valuable products, won by harsh exploitation of slaves and the proletarian poor, were later added wheat, olive oil and wine. Domitian had prohibited the planting of vineyards in the provinces in order to protect the Roman growers, but it was not long before Rome needed Spanish wine. Tough Spanish fighters were enlisted by the Romans in the earlier years of the Empire, but as peaceful activities softened the Spanish character the supply of cavalrymen and infantry diminished. Vespasian reduced the Roman force in Spain to one legion. Trajan, a most successful commander, and his cousin, Hadrian, were both from Roman families long settled in Seville. Among writers of the first century AD who were famous in Latin literature, Seneca, Lucan, Quintilian and Martial were all Spaniards. As everywhere else in the Roman world, political, administrative and cultural activities were confined to an élite.

The Greeks, well endowed with native talent, inheriting a civilization and culture older than that of Rome itself, benefited

when firm Roman rule stopped them fighting one another. In general the imperial administration also prevented Roman depredations, except when Nero laid hands on Greek sculptures and other works of art. A corrupt and venal republican Roman administration had plunged the Asian provinces into near ruin, and their recovery of economic prosperity under the Empire was remarkable. However, it is doubtful whether such prosperity was shared by much of the population. The great mass of people were probably always poor. Both Greece and Asia had suffered much more than a loss of material property. Thousands of their inhabitants, many of whom might have built up their native lands, had been sold into slavery to toil for Roman taskmasters. Some clever Greeks profited by their opportunities to exercise crafts which were beyond the duller wits of their masters, so that Greek tutors, scribes, artists, craftsmen, architects and doctors won an assured position in Rome.

During the Republic, Cicero and Caesar had gone to study in Greece. It is therefore difficult to guess how much Roman art, architecture and mechanical skills were the product of native talent and how much was Greek in inspiration and execution. Much that is admired as Roman today would not have been there had it not been for such pervasive Greek skills. To Rome however belongs the merit of first realizing the

Above, the theatre at Arles, southern France, built in the first or second century AD.

Below, fragments of Roman gilded glass showing a gladiator, c. 400 AD. British Museum, London.

Opposite top, mosaic depicting four Roman charioteers.

Opposite centre, relief from Vaucluse, France, of a boat being hauled ashore. Avignon Museum.

Opposite below, the Pont du Gard, Nimes, France: constructed c. 19 BC by Agrippa, Augustus' stepson and a provincial governor, it is part of the aqueduct built to bring water to the city.

relied upon Rome and how much they were able to do for themselves. Rome is often given credit for allowing the cities in the provinces self-government, but it is difficult to square this with the only recorded official correspondence between a provincial governor and the emperor.

When a city on the fringe of the Empire could not have a fire brigade without the emperor's sanction, which Trajan instructed Pliny to refuse, it is not easy to imagine that local initiative had much scope. It is possible that this single instance was not typical. It is also possible that, if permission had to be sought, as it was by Pliny, for such things as temples, markets, amphitheatres, baths, libraries and schools, it was freely granted. Certainly such adjuncts to city life sprang up all over the Empire. Moreover, since local civic dignity was thought to be enhanced by election to local office, it seems hardly likely that such an election conferred no real responsibility. Some of these amenities may have been needed, not only by the local inhabitants, but also by the Roman citizens from Italy on the staff of the governors, by local legionary forces, and by visiting merchants, contractors and tax collectors.

excellence of the best Greek work. Moreover, the Romans were the principal agency by which the priceless heritage of the great age of Greek culture was made available to the rest of the known world. Finally, it was Roman enthusiasm for Greek light and learning that first inspired later ages to seek themselves to recover every scrap of Greek writing they could find.

The rule of the strongest

Such were the main provinces forming the Empire, then virtually equivalent to the known world, for, although trade routes brought silks and spices from the Far East in exchange for gold, few Romans had any direct knowledge of the lands from which they came. History has shown how the Roman Empire came together as the result everywhere of Roman victories in brutal, bloody warfare. 'Kill or be killed' was the law of life. It explains the rise of Caesar, who resolved not to be killed, and the fall of Pompey, his opponent. It explains Mark Anthony's murder of Cicero and his own death when he failed to kill Augustus. More cunning than his great-uncle, Augustus took good precautions not to be killed. Most of his more dangerous enemies had already gone down before he achieved world domination.

If the Romans had lost to the Etruscans, to the Greeks, or to the Carthaginians they would have become as insignificant in world history as the Sabines they conquered or the Samnites they exterminated. Having established their supremacy, however, they were

for centuries able to maintain themselves against all comers.

At last they too went down to defeat. Over too much of the world, the Romans, in the mordant phrase of Tacitus, had made a wilderness and called it peace. After the destruction the work of renewing life had to begin. In that great task the Romans could at first do little more than to provide conditions under which those who remained of the peoples they had defeated could rebuild and renew.

Roman rule should not be denied great credit for that care (*providentia*) promised by Augustus and honoured by the best of his successors. Trajan, Hadrian and Antoninus Pius were the emperors who responded most liberally to provincial petitions for help. Many inscriptions have been recovered in which eminent provincial citizens record their gratitude for imperial aid. It is impossible to discover how much the provinces

The quality of Roman culture

What was the nature and quality of that culture which the Romans helped to spread throughout their Empire, and how far was it superior to native traditions? Nowhere, not even in Britain or Germany, did the Romans enter a cultural vacuum. Indeed, Tacitus gave a somewhat idyllic account of the merits of the barbaric Germans. Although he derived much from previous writers, as destitute of much first-hand experience of the country as he was, and although he was concerned to castigate the vices of his own age by contrasting the superior merits of the noble savage, nevertheless archaeological evidence confirms part of his story. German craftsmanship in metalwork was respectable, already providing the basis of some trading or bartering relationships with other peoples. In Britain the situation was somewhat similar. To all such peoples, still bound by immemorial tradition, the appearance, the manners and the interests of Romans, who had long since shaken themselves free from their own Iron Age past with its set traditional ways, must have formed a striking contrast.

Roman culture was slow in winning converts except among the more intelligent, emancipated provincial élite. They were first to acquire knowledge of the Latin language, the main universal link between the provinces of Rome and between the provinces themselves. For the first time in human history it was possible to travel throughout the known world with the aid of

Left, the theatre at Thugga, Tunisia, one of the best preserved in North Africa.

Opposite top, mosaic of the seasons at Corinium (modern Cirencester), England. Corinium Museum, Cirencester.

Opposite below, Roman road leading into Antiquarium at Carthage.

a universal language. Latin also made a literature accessible to many provinces with no written traditions. Within a few generations, men from southern Gaul, Spain and North Africa began to make contributions to Roman literature. Greeks alone left Latin to the Romans, and with good reasons, for Romans as eminent as Cicero and Lucretius testified to the superiority of Greek. Hadrian was more Hellenic than the Greeks in his practical admiration of their glorious past. His successor, Marcus Aurelius, used Greek and not Latin when he wrote his private meditations.

In the search for knowledge over and above a readiness to repeat what others have said the Romans have no particular title to fame. Roman science was of no account.

Such scientific works as were written in Latin were all translations or adaptations of previous work, directly or indirectly based upon Greek originals. In medicine the situation was no better, though it was somewhat redeemed by Celsus (AD 14–37), who wrote a useful summary of the history of medicine. Romans were ready purchasers of handbooks and manuals of a practical nature, almost all of which are unfortunately lost. They also welcomed encyclopedic guides to knowledge, again compiled from various Greek writings. Old Cato the Censor began in about 180 BC with a summary, written for his son, of all extant knowledge about medicine, farming and oratory, but his work was later surpassed by the more comprehensive compilation of Cicero's learned

Left, the theatre at Sabratha, Libya, restored by a team of Italian archaeologists: 5,000 spectators could be accommodated here.

friend Varro. The latter's nine books on grammar, dialectic, rhetoric, geometry, arithmetic, astronomy, music, medicine and architecture formed, after omitting medicine and architecture, the seven liberal arts of the Middle Ages. Celsus' work on medicine is the only surviving fragment of his encyclopedia. Varro's has been lost but the later work of Pliny the Elder—his famous *Natural History* of AD 77—has survived. Despite its bulk and variety, no Roman felt prompted to correct its many errors or to follow up questions which Pliny admitted that he could not answer.

Romans, said Pliny, had become lazy and degenerate because knowledge was not being sought by research, despite the great rewards this would bring. He is not always given credit for such personal observations as he made, notably on plants, probably because with equal zest he records a host of absurd opinions he had met with in the conversation or the writings of others. Most of his great work was compiled from other sources, just as in his *Natural Questions* Seneca relied mainly on Aristotle. In the search for truth the Romans failed to develop adequate scientific critiera, and it was, therefore, unfortunate that the work of Seneca and Pliny (regarded almost as oracular) survived until the Middle Ages instead of Greek writings. Meanwhile, the Greeks were not idle. In the time of Marcus Aurelius, Ptolemy's works on astronomy and geography and Galen's medical works broke new ground, but it does not appear that the Romans took any interest in either geography or medicine.

Theoretical work such as mathematics seems to have been beyond the capacity of the Romans. Cicero's expression for an insoluble mystery—'an Archimedean problem'—shows that he at least expected his hearers to have had some knowledge of the great mathematician even although the vast majority of them must have understood his work as little as the boorish Roman soldier can have who killed Archimedes in Syracuse in 121 BC.

All that the Romans were able to absorb from Greek work in natural science was that digested in brief, practical, elementary manuals. As great numbers were in circulation, some may well have reached the provinces. Whatever use was made of them there did not, however, stimulate any similar writing, practical or theoretical. In mechanical invention the Romans made a somewhat better showing. Their vast military works, their battering rams, their slings and their forts and ramparts were all instruments of victory. Their skill in road making, in constructing huge, efficient aqueducts and their colossal buildings have understandably astonished mankind, for it was not until modern times that they have been rivalled. Vitruvius, who lived in the reign of Augustus, described an undershot water-wheel, which was the first known example of the use of gearing to transmit power. By its means the exhausting daily task of corn grinding could be eased. If the Romans had valued mechanical progress, if they had any pity for the slaves and the donkeys whom they compelled under the lash to turn their heavy corn-grinding mills, it might be thought that such miseries would rapidly have been abolished by the greater use of water power. Yet at the end of the fourth century AD, long after Rome had reached its full development, there were no more than twenty to thirty mills near the Tiber—which may mean that some used water power—in contrast with a total of more than 200 mills in other parts of the city which certainly did not make use of water.

Another conclusion may be derived from the failure of the Romans to progress far even in those practical matters in which they are commonly thought to have been superior to their contemporaries: namely, that without theoretical science the practical way of life is so limited that it cannot progress far. Similarly, great curiosity or nimble inventiveness will stop short of real achievement when the urge to reduce toil or to achieve great production is lacking. The Greeks had cut gears with a skill and precision that

would have put watch-making within their capabilities. Archimedes had constructed a mechanical model of the movement of the planets which was still to be seen in Rome in Cicero's time. Yet no Roman contributed anything of value to astronomy. It is doubtful whether any of them could have understood such remarkable advances as those made by Hipparchus of Bithynia in the second century AD. He was the first to use trigonometry and he also made new instruments, catalogued 850 stars and discovered the precession of the equinoxes.

Heron of Alexandria had at some period invented heat engines, jet propulsion, screw-cutting, a double-cylinder force pump and many other ingenious devices, but they mostly died with him. In comparison with this immense and varied creative power of Greece not one single Roman can be said to have possessed an original, creative mind, except possibly the poet Lucretius. Yet it was he, with Cicero, who made the fullest and frankest confession of his and Rome's indebtedness. 'To set in clear light the dark discoveries of the Greeks', he said, 'is a hard task, above all when new works must be found for many things because of the poverty of our tongue and the newness of the theme.'

Literature and oratory

In the world of facts, not merely had the Romans nothing original to offer but they were unequal to the task of understanding and transmitting all that Greek genius had discovered. In the world of values (beauty and aesthetic satisfaction, morality and ethical standards) their inferiority was less pronounced.

For the first three centuries in the history of the Republic the Romans had no wider cultural horizons than those which their traditional way of life afforded. This meant in practice that they had virtually no appreciation of literature, painting, sculpture or the decorative arts. 'In those rough and warlike days', said Suetonius in the second century AD, 'there was no time to spare for civilized studies.' He dated the beginning of literary studies from 'the poets Livius and Ennius who were half Greek, and who only translated from the Greek'.

Livius (c. 284– c. 294 BC) produced a rough Latin translation of Homer's *Odyssey* as well as of Greek comedies and tragedies. Ennius (239–169 BC) copying Homer, composed an epic poem on the history of Rome down to 171 BC. He, like Livius, was from the south of Italy, long occupied by the Greeks. Fragments alone remain of their work and of that of Naevius (c. 270–201 BC), who was imprisoned and exiled because of his free comments upon Roman statesmen in his plays. Plautus (c. 250–184 BC) and Terence (c. 195–159 BC) adapted Greek dramatic themes. Theatrical performances

Left, the discus-thrower, a Roman copy of a bronze figure made by the Athenian sculptor Myron, c. 450 BC. Museo delle Terme, Roma.

Opposite left, Roman standard-bearers.

Opposite right, relief from a sarcophagus of a Roman farmer milking a goat, a common domestic animal in the fourth-century AD. Museo della Civilta Romana, Rome.

became more spectacular, with ambitious scenic effects, but the popular plays in Cicero's time were nearly all revivals. Thereafter the theatre lost its attraction as the common people sought ever stronger excitements from pantomime (after 22 BC), circus races and the bloodbaths of the amphitheatre. Literature, having reached maturity in the first centuries BC and AD, thereafter faded. Roman poets, who scorned rhyme as childish, used metres copied from Greek verse, but the pronunciation of Latin words, with their sequences of long and short syllables, compelled modification. Lyric verse using varied metres was written by Catullus under the Republic and by Horace, Martial and Seneca in the early Empire. The great Roman epic poets—Lucretius, Virgil and Lucan—wrote in lines of six feet (hexameters). When words of five syllables (pentameters) were used by these poets after a hexameter, they together formed a distich and were known as elegiacs. Propertius, Tibullus and Ovid were the principal remaining elegiac poets. Their transformation of Latin poetry ended with Ovid. There were of course infinite subtle variations of stress and quantity.

Roman prose, depending also on skilful use of the sonorous, stressed quality of Latin, achieved at the hands of a master such as Cicero a majestic cadence in oratory, declamation and in written form. Here again styles changed. People got tired of trying to write like Cicero, even when the style was skilfully varied as by the historian Livy. The enduring fame of Tacitus was made by his more pungent, graphic and almost telegraphic phrases. The Elder Pliny, preoccupied entirely with his facts, neglected style,

whereas his nephew, the Younger Pliny, without anything of great moment to impart, tried in the volumes of his letters which he published in his lifetime to polish his language with such care that artifice took the place of art.

In oratory a similar decline was lamented by Tacitus himself. When it truly flourished —in the last years of the Republic—the tradition of outspoken, free speech was still vigorous, despite the dictatorial interlude in which it had been suppressed by Sulla. Already by AD 85, as Tacitus declared, 'the great imperial system has imposed a hush upon eloquence as it has indeed upon the world at large.' A contemporary of his, usually known as Longinus, who compiled the treatise on *The Sublime*, was more direct in attributing the decline of all oratory and

literature to the loss of that democratic freedom which 'had power to feed the imagination of the high-minded and to inspire hope'. In imperial Rome, he declared, 'we seem to learn the lessons of a righteous servitude in our boyhood.' It was therefore useless to expect creative work to be produced because 'no slave ever becomes an orator'.

Tacitus praised the restoration of freedom by Nerva after AD 96 as 'a blessed period in which a man might think what he liked and say what he thought', but although this era lasted for nearly 100 years, creative literature failed to revive. Suetonius and Apuleius, who survived into the reign of Antoninus Pius, were the last Latin authors of any distinction. With Suetonius the recording of Roman history virtually came to an end and even as a biographer he had no worthy successor. History had been one of the earliest and most impressive forms of Roman literature but it did not survive long into the imperial period, dying out before any considered Roman theory of history or historiography could arise. Down to the time of Livy history had been written with considerable regard for both literary work and moralizing effect. Tacitus, who introduced a more astringent treatment, was by no means free from such tendencies. Nevertheless, he showed a devotion to truth which even his strong dislike of the imperial system did not obscure.

It will never be known how many Roman parchment rolls or vellum codices reached the provinces. Complaining that they brought him no profit, Martial said that his poems were hummed in Britain and thumbed by centurions stationed on the Danube.

Artistic development

'At Rome the works of art are legion', said the Elder Pliny, but 'the great and constant pressure of business and other duties are too heavy for most people to enjoy them.' For two or three centuries Romans had been looting pictures, statuary and other works of art. Commanders celebrating their triumphs in Rome followed the example first given by Marcellus after his capture of Syracuse in 211 BC, by parading works of art taken from the enemy which were subsequently dedicated as public spoils to be stored in temples in the city. Later, other places such as the *Porticus Octaviae*—the library and other buildings erected by Augustus in memory of his sister Octavia—housed many works of art. All the most

famous of such pictures, statues, works in bronze and other treasures seem, without exception, to have been Greek. No history of Roman art, if there were such, has survived.

From what the Elder Pliny reports in his *Natural History*, it is evident that some Roman artists had been at work from early times. Pliny said that 'there was an ancient art of bronze statuary native to Italy', but he is silent upon its merits. Etruscan sculpture, often of great distinction, had been created from the seventh to the first centuries BC. In other parts of Italy there was some local sculpture but little is known in Rome until the first century BC. Probably few if any of these sculptors working in Rome were in fact Romans, otherwise their names would have been mentioned by Pliny

Below, statue from the House of the Deer at Herculaneum, a Roman town near Naples destroyed at the same time as Pompeii when Vesuvius erupted in AD 79.

Opposite top, a slave mocks two lovers: detail from a mosaic at Pompeii, before AD 79.

Opposite bottom, the ruins of Leptis Magna, Libya: originally a Phoenician port, the city was founded in 650 BC; the Emperor Septimius Severus was born there and carried out considerable improvements to the city.

and others. A huge bronze statue of Apollo which Augustus commissioned for the library of his temple on the Palatine was called the Tuscan Apollo. The colossal statue of himself which Nero commissioned was entrusted to Zenodoros, probably an Alexandrian Greek who had made a name for himself in Gaul as a sculptor.

In painting there seems to have been virtually no great Roman work. It is true, however, that as early as 304–302 BC Quintus Fabius, a patrician of the famous Fabia clan, was commissioned to paint on the walls of the new temple of Salus what was probably a battle scene in the war against the Samnites. As a result of this work he received the name 'Pictor', by which his family was thereafter known. Pliny himself saw the painting before the temple was burnt down in the reign of Claudius. Fabius had no successor and his family was probably not at all proud of its nickname. This illustrates the fundamental difference between the Greeks, who honoured artists and craftsmen for their work and the Romans, who valued the art but despised the artists.

Slavery and contempt for the vanquished contributed to produce such an attitude because the Romans looked down upon Etruscans and Greeks alike. Pliny records that in Greece after 367 BC 'painting on tablets of boxwood was the earliest subject taught to free-born boys, while slaves were always strictly forbidden to learn the art.' Cicero, trying to rescue the Romans' cultural reputation, could only ask 'do we

imagine that if it had been thought praise-worthy for Fabius, a Roman of the highest rank, to paint, we should not have had many artists equal to Polyclitus and Parrhasios?'

'Since the days of the poet Pacuvius', said Pliny, 'the profession of painter has had no honour from the well-born, except in our own time Turpilius, a Roman *eques* from Venetia whose beautiful works are in Verona.' Painting was considered a permissible pastime for a noble Roman boy who was dumb. Pliny tells how the mute grandson of the consul Quintus Pedius, was taught to paint and was progressing well before he died.

Never having been taught at school the elements of drawing or of any other craft and knowing that their Greek slaves or Etruscan hirelings were excellent craftsmen, the Romans left artistic production to them, well content to enjoy the results. Roman connoisseurs competed with one another for the works of famous Greek painters such as Apelles, Mikomachos, Melanthios and

Aetion until, as Pliny said, 'the wealth of a city could hardly buy one of their works.'

The possession of works of art, like fine houses and gardens, was at once a title to distinction and a hostage to fortune. Mark Anthony was said to have proscribed Verres in order to steal his Corinthian bronzes and Nonius to obtain possession of a fine opal. Old silverware was similarly the object of fierce competition, particularly if it was designed and decorated by some famous silversmith such as Myron. Silver cups, engraved or embossed with hunting scenes or battles, or recalling some fable from mythology, were greatly prized. During the greatest days of the Empire, when more Romans enjoyed wealth and leisure than ever before. Pliny remarked that 'it is extraordinary that while huge sums are given for works of art, the ability to create them has vanished.' It is interesting to read Pliny's explanation for this: 'the aim of the artist as of everyone else in our times is personal gain.'

Above, mosaic fountain at Pompeii, before AD 79.

Opposite, portrait of a Neapolitan girl. National Museum, Naples

In older times the artist's skill was regarded with more religious feeling as a god-like gift. Creative artistic ability, like sacred love and beauty of character, achieves its greatest feats in the service of ideals and in forgetfulness of self. Instinctive realization of this is seen in the high reputation of Greek art down to the fifth century BC. When money, personal fame, social distinction and competitive superiority become the real motives, as in the early Roman Empire, true inspiration evaporates. A great trade in copies, reproductions and, of course, forgeries was stimulated. According to the fictional character, Trimalchio, a rich freedman in the novel by Petronius, self-made men in the early Empire paid huge prices for fakes in order to be able to boast and to impress their guests with rarities, which everyone else coveted but could not afford.

The Romans had neither wallpaper nor tapestries, but the walls of their houses were lavishly painted with a great variety of scenes and designs. Some remarkable specimens have survived, the earliest from Rome being from about 200 BC. Whether Roman or Italian, they are more realistic than the otherworldly Etruscan tomb paintings, by which Roman wall painting may have been inspired. Later examples in Rome include some from the home of Augustus on the Palatine and from the remains of Nero's Golden House. Far more numerous and better preserved are those which have been unearthed from the buried tombs of Herculaneum, Pompeii and Stabiae. From these examples, relatively few in number, it is possible to trace considerable variations in style during a period of about 200 years. Greek influence was strong in and around Naples, so the pictured scenes and designs are often Greek in conception and execution.

Where Roman or Italian artists are thought to have created any such pictures, it seems likely that they were Greek-taught. In colouring, draughtsmanship and composition these artists often attain high quality, making the total loss of all paints by the great masters of Greek art infinitely regrettable. From being merely patterns of colour, Roman murals developed to include a great variety of themes and topics: architectural vistas, scenes from mythology and legend, portraits, theatrical episodes, landscapes, gardens, still life, hunting scenes and scenes from everyday life. Pliny thought that landscapes were first painted on walls in the reign of Augustus. Certainly the garden scene in the Villa of Livia in Rome has a fresh appeal to city dwellers and testifies to the growing pleasure which Romans derived from their gardens.

No account of Roman painting would be complete that did not refer to the general practice, in both Greece and Rome, of colouring the marble statues displayed in

public places as well as the sculptured reliefs and friezes of their temples. From faint remaining traces of the colouring used, it is possible to imagine the vivid appearance given to figures which we see as white, polished marble. As the Romans depended for their colours upon vegetable sources such as saffron, madder and gall nuts, or upon shellfish such as the murex, which yielded the famous imperial purple, some of their colouring would probably appear crude today.

Decorative patterns and scenes using small pieces of stone or marble of varying colours had been made by the Greeks and others long before the Romans (who did not make or use carpets) adopted the practice of covering the floors of their dwellings with such pictures in stone. Some of these patterns were so pictorial that only a man with the skill of a painter could have designed them. Throughout western Europe and North Africa the ruins of many large villas have revealed striking examples of this distinctive Roman art. Adapted later for the adornment of Christian churches, mosaic pictures of sacred subjects were exhibited on walls and ceilings.

Vase painting, in which the Greeks had attained great distinction between the eighth and fourth centuries BC, had been practised in the Greek colonies in southern Italy for about a century and a half, to decline and disappear in the third century BC. It seems to have excited little interest among the Romans.

Their only pottery of any distinction was that from Arretium, a former Etruscan town, where it was made in moulds cut to provide designs in relief. Manufacture began only after 30 BC and lasted barely 100 years. Widely exported this red glazed Arretine ware carried some excellently designed pottery through the Roman world. As the

Above, marble relief showing a walled hill-town: counting-houses stand outside the walls. Museo Torlonia, Avezzano.

Opposite, relief from a funeral stela showing the deceased and his family enjoying a meal. Cologne Museum.

best designs are Hellenistic in style, it seems probable that the artists were Greek or of eastern origin.

Competition from Gaul and elsewhere soon diminished Rome's export trade in glazed pottery. In Rome itself glassware was increasingly coming into use in the early Empire after the invention of glass blowing, probably in Syria, in the first century BC. Bowls, cups, vases, and other domestic forms of glassware in various colours were sometimes engraved or adorned by ornament in relief. Martial mentions a tough form of glass, 'dreadnought', used by the common people.

Roman taste

Despite the crudities of the uncultivated rich and the need to appeal to the mob, a tradition of good taste nevertheless survived in Rome because both craftsmen and their customers seem instinctively to have welcomed those virtues of symmetry, balance and proportion which come naturally to human minds. Thus the furnishings and equipment of the average well-to-do household, the only place where the decorative and adorning arts would appear, did not lack aesthetic merit. Pompeii and Herculaneum, preserved in the mud and ashes by which they were buried in August AD 79, are not the only source of examples of the artistic quality of Roman homes, because artefacts of all kinds and of many periods have also come to light elsewhere.

Many museums have examples of such things as pottery, glass, silverware, jewellery, mirrors, coins, seals, medallions, cameos, reconstructed chairs, chests and couches, bronze and silver lamps and lamp-stands, braziers, and even kitchen utensils. Homes well equipped with all these articles would

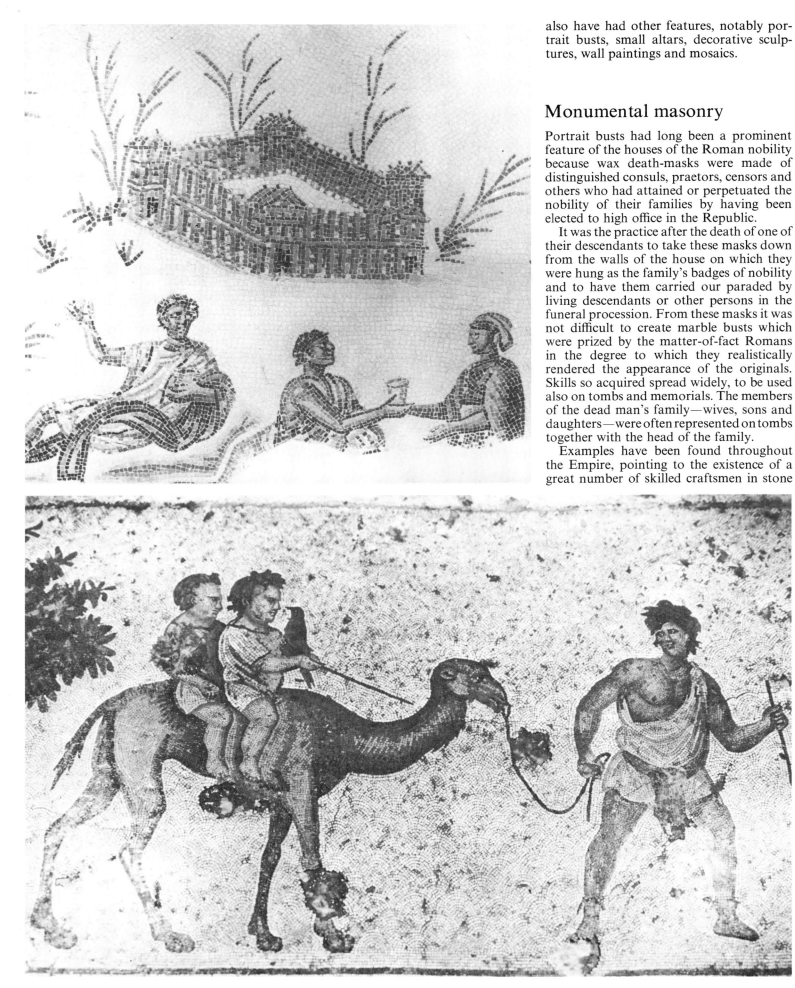

also have had other features, notably portrait busts, small altars, decorative sculptures, wall paintings and mosaics.

Monumental masonry

Portrait busts had long been a prominent feature of the houses of the Roman nobility because wax death-masks were made of distinguished consuls, praetors, censors and others who had attained or perpetuated the nobility of their families by having been elected to high office in the Republic.

It was the practice after the death of one of their descendants to take these masks down from the walls of the house on which they were hung as the family's badges of nobility and to have them carried our paraded by living descendants or other persons in the funeral procession. From these masks it was not difficult to create marble busts which were prized by the matter-of-fact Romans in the degree to which they realistically rendered the appearance of the originals. Skills so acquired spread widely, to be used also on tombs and memorials. The members of the dead man's family—wives, sons and daughters—were often represented on tombs together with the head of the family.

Examples have been found throughout the Empire, pointing to the existence of a great number of skilled craftsmen in stone

and marble. Who they were, whether slave or free, Roman or provincial, is unknown. Such craftsmanship, again anonymous, adorned many of the thousands of altars, large and small, which were also to be found in every city, as well as in many private houses and gardens, as shrines to the *lares*, the spirits of the home.

One of the finest remaining public monuments, strangely ignored by Pliny in his comments on Rome, is the great Altar of Peace, *Ara Pacis*, dedicated in 9 BC by the Senate to commemorate the safe return of Augustus from Gaul and Spain. The altar, decorated with reliefs representing the animals sacrificed at the dedication ceremony, stood within four walls, splendidly decorated externally by gracefully patterned foliage on the power panels. Two sides of the upper panels were covered by reliefs realistically representing Augustus, the imperial family, prominent senators and others taking part in the stately procession at the dedication ceremony.

Controversy about the aesthetic quality of these reliefs suffers when the works in question are not related to the quality of the total culture in which they are produced. Because the *Ara Pacis* does not show the amazing creative genius of the Parthenon frieze, and because it has something of the 'made to order' character of the best commercial art, some critics have refused it the praise which others willingly give to its pleasing design and high technical compe-

tence. When it is seen as part of the endeavour of Augustus and his friends to recapture the virtues of past, idealistic ages, to make a stand for dignity, decorum, piety and contentment in an era when all the old values seemed to have been rejected, it is possible to judge its quality more satisfactorily.

More extraordinary is the pictorial, sculptured narrative illustrating Trajan's campaings in Dacia which spirals up the great column in his Forum. Despite its lack of perspective, a skill which the Romans never quite attained, it presents, with more than 2,500 human figures, a vivid record of the Roman army in action at the culmination of the power of the Empire.

It is impossible to leave Roman work in stone and marble without a reminder of the aesthetic excellence of the letter forms used in the inscriptions. Some of the very finest examples date from the early Empire. Here again there was a Greek precedent, for, as might be expected, the superb artistry of the Greeks is apparent in many of the remaining inscriptions. Of the many inscriptions the Romans had cut on their memorials, both public and private, in Rome and in the provinces, those on Trajan's column are deservedly renowned. They have for centuries formed a model of forceful beauty in the expression of the written word. Anyone alert to the change in the quality of Roman inscriptions, apart from the often somewhat crude efforts of some barely literate provincial craftsmen, has another clue to the

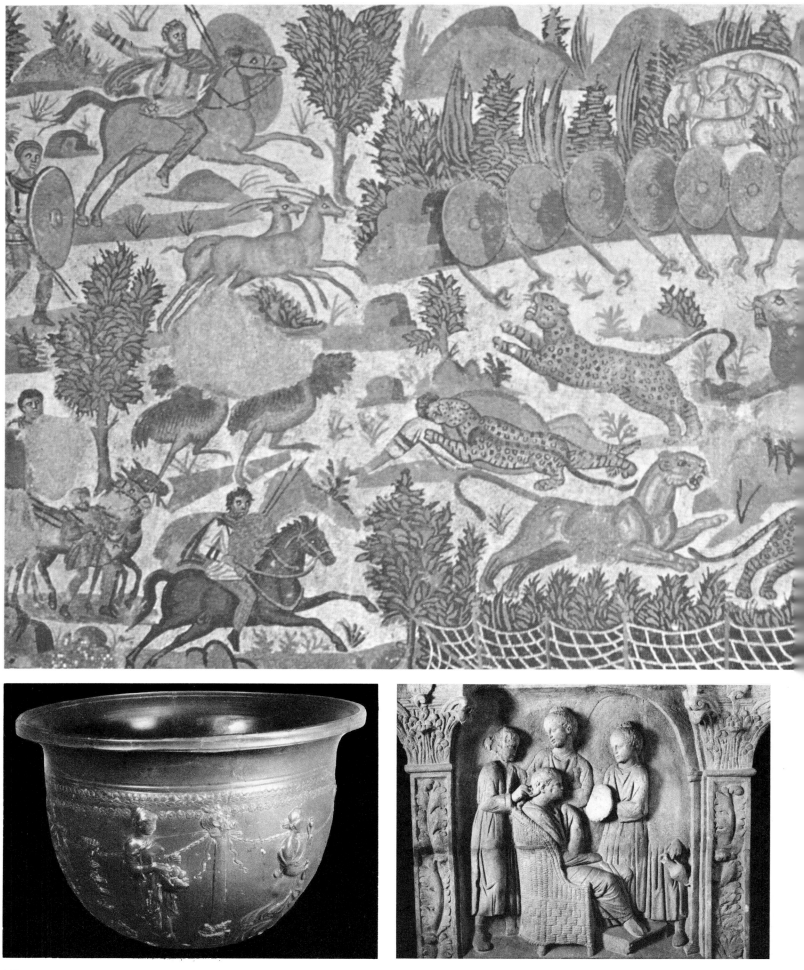

changing nature of Roman culture and civilization. The special clarity and assurance of the best lettering begins to show a remarkable deterioration in the troubled times of the later Empire.

Seals and gems show a similar good quality during the first two centuries of the Empire but their craftsmanship probably owed more to the Greeks than to native talent. When the traditions by which the Republic had been maintained lost their force, the coinage became an instrument of imperial policy. Julius Caesar was the first living Roman to be depicted upon a coin. Hitherto the Romans had always honoured their gods or some traditional hero of old. In the Empire the propaganda motive became increasingly apparent in the design of the coinage. Roman mints were kept busy. In a single year of Hadrian's reign more than 100 types of coin were struck. Without attaining the magnificence of the best Greek work, the Roman die-cutters maintained a respectably high standard up to the end of the second century AD. Some of their best work appears on the medallions, commemorative pieces not always related to the coinage, which Trajan first began to issue as rewards to loyal subjects.

Throughout the western world and Mediterranean lands there were innumerable reminders of the Roman presence to command respect, to set standards. Some of them—arenas, aqueducts, bridges, baths, temples, and memorials—were no doubt welcome amenities. These were the outward visible signs of Roman dominance which inevitably directed attention to Rome, canalizing thoughts, emotions and ambitions in the hearts of many provincials.

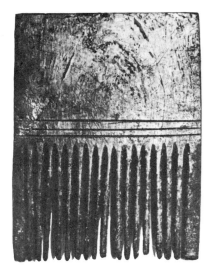

Religion

Aspiring provincials who looked to Rome for guidance in the direction of their lives and, for some, for faith to live by, did not, however, meet with as direct and satisfying a response as that often given to requests for tangible physical aid. Many were unconscious of any spiritual needs, content, if they were recruits to the legions, with their oath of loyalty to the emperor.

When it came to finding sustenance for minds as well as for bodies, the Romans themselves were at a loss. Their scanty regard for the progress of knowledge and their lack of all interest in scientific research were symptoms of a general cultural deficiency. It was all very well for Virgil to utter his much quoted opinion, 'happy the man who is able to understand the reasons for things.' Too many Romans did not believe him or else were content with perfunctory explanations. Roman attitudes to religion and to philosophy were little different.

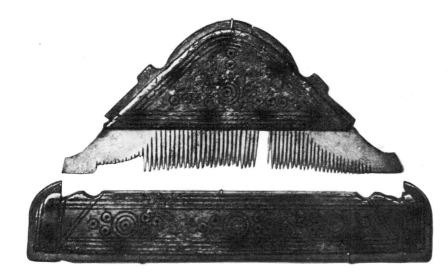

Above and top of both pages, ivory combs and pins; one, decorated with a small hand endowed with supernatural powers, was worn as a charm.

Left, frieze from the Altar of Peace of the imperial family in procession.

Opposite right, detail of a crane from Trajan's Column; the pulley and ropes and the men inside the treadmill are clearly visible. Vatican Museum, Rome.

Opposite left, the marble impluvium *in the House of the Faun at Pompeii, before AD 79: the statuette in the centre gives the house its name.*

Essentially conservative by nature, the Romans continued to honour their old customary religious practices, just as they maintained old political forms and titles, long after they had ceased to have any real meaning. It is indeed difficult to believe that the religion of the early Republic, although long honoured as the *mos maiorum* ('the ways of the departed'), ever had deep meaning. Whatever it may have signified in those early times, small traces of this religion remained because it produced no coherent mythology. It was not depicted in art, nor was it supported by any theology, metaphysics or by regular religious services.

Custom alone kept religion alive as it was handed down from parents to children. By the early Empire many fewer families were conscious of any living religious tradition. Civil wars, the Social War, slave revolts, famine, pestilence, proscriptions, confiscations and banishments had shattered the entire social fabric. Physical sufferings and premature deaths were not the only explanation for the bankruptcy of older beliefs. Even if they had been continuously taught, they would have been powerless against other overwhelming forces. Romans who had survived such terrible upheavals lived with fears for which the traditional Roman religion provided no consolation.

A nation that erected altars and temples to appease such divinities as Misfortune, Fever, Storms and other evils to which mankind is a victim, might well despair as those evils multiplied. Lucretius was a sound counsellor when he made the need to

rescue his countrymen from the plague of their religious beliefs among the principal themes of his poem *On The Nature of Things*. After recounting some of the atrocities in his own lifetime, Tacitus declared that it was plain that the punishment of the Romans and not their salvation was the concern of their gods. Even if traditional Roman religious practices had not been faced with the need to surmount such a terrible series of challenges, they increasingly encountered, from about the end of the first century BC onwards, the competition of religious beliefs from other lands, among them some that were better attuned to basic human needs.

Roman religion was singularly ill-equipped to provide consolation or encouragement, or to develop human understanding or affection. At the best it provided a series of customary, decent observances to accompany the civil ceremonies attending birth, marriage and death. If supernatural aid was sought by a pious visit to a temple, it would be to ask a god for some worldly advantage.

In such a spiritual vacuum, oriental religious beliefs began to make headway. Roman legionaries may have encountered them in the east, but they were mainly brought to Italy by the thousands who had been enslaved during Rome's campaigns of loot and conquest. The Egyptian goddess Isis, wife of Osiris, god of the underworld, had reached Athens by the fourth century BC. Her cult had a fraternity or 'college' in Rome by the time of Sulla, but her temple was later destroyed in 53 BC by order of the Senate. Serapis or Sarapis, a more recent god, also from Egypt, found a welcome in Rome although Augustus wanted no Egyptian gods to remind Rome of Cleopatra. Ovid recommended young men to linger near the temple of Isis because it was popular with young women. Tiberius destroyed the sanctuary of Isis and Serapis in the Campus Martius, but it was rebuilt by Caligula, only to be destroyed by fire in AD 80. Domitian caused it to be reconstructed in grand style because on one occasion he escaped from his enemies disguised as a priest of Isis.

Under the Flavian emperors the cult of Mithras, a sun god whose worship by the Persians has been thought to have had its origins in Vedic India, began to spread throughout the Roman Empire. These eastern religions brought the Roman people into contact with new and strange forms of worship, conducted by priests who were not elected or appointed as Roman religious officials were, like magistrates for the performance of a routine duty, and who after discharging it returned as an ordinary citizen to everyday life. These priests of the eastern cults were dedicated devotees.

Above, the Ludovisi Battle Sarcophagus, c. AD 250, depicting a battle between the Romans and a barbarian tribe, probably the Dacians; the figure of the dead man, a Roman general, dominates the relief. Museo della Terme, Rome.

Opposite, cameo of the Emperor Augustus, first century AD: the emperor is wearing an aegis *and* gorgoneion, *symbols of his power; the diadem is medieval addition. British Museum, London.*

A new spiritual force was brought into Roman life by these oriental religions. Their purpose was to win converts to the faith; in short they sought to stir human souls to a belief in what they held to be a reality not of this world. Their ceremonies became private religious services regularly conducted by priests who sought to confirm and deepen the faith of their congregation by addresses or sermons. These newcomers were slow in making headway among the practical, conservative Romans. Other superstitions contended with them for Roman interest, notably astrology. Traditional Roman policy firmly opposed the pretences of astrologers, who were expelled from Rome in 139 BC. Like similar expulsions of Greek philosophers, the ban was forgotten. Cicero denounced the pretences of these astrologers with arguments that would have convinced the very few then willing to listen to the voice of reason, but the superstition gained ground rapidly among the upper classes of Rome.

Such were merely some of the main currents of opinion in Rome during the first two centuries AD. After the crucifixion of Christ,

at some time during the governorship of Pontius Pilate in Judaea (AD 29–36), news soon spread about His life, teaching, death and resurrection. Already between about AD 50 and 64 Paul was travelling and making converts in Corinth, Thessalonica, Galatia, Rome, Philippi and elsewhere, with whom he kept in touch by sending letters of counsel and encouragement. By about AD 65 the main facts in the life of Christ had been shortly summarized in the Gospel of Mark. Between about AD 89 and 100 the gospels of Matthew and Luke repeated the story, adding more about Christ's actual message. All were based, it is believed, upon an earlier statement which has disappeared.

The new faith spoke in a language not heard before, of a personal God of a very different kind, enjoining forms of worship and a new way of life, with a promise of redemption from sin and evil and an assurance of immortality, all of which would have been strange indeed to Roman ears. 'If any man is in Christ', the Romans were told, 'he is a new creature; the old things are passed away.' Such 'possession by the spirit' brought 'love, joy, peace, long-suffering,

gentleness, goodness, faith, meekness and temperance'. All sharing in it infallibly became a community of disciples, who met together for payer, sacraments, worship and exhortation. They shared a common way of life and their possessions also if necessary. As it seemed only recently that Christ had been a living presence sharing the lives of the men who had been spreading His gospel, God had indeed come near to man in a very direct and personal way. 'Thus spake the Lord, could therefore introduce the Christian message without reserve and without seeming to make exaggerated claims or any suggestions of spiritual arrogance. Those who passed on such teaching spoke, therefore, with an authority to which the advocates of other new religious beliefs could hardly aspire.

For all bewildered, troubled people in the Roman Empire and for all those for whom the life of the poor was a meaningless burden as well as those for whom the life of the rich came to seem empty, there were a number of gratifying new beliefs and religions whose devotees were eager for converts. It would, however, be misleading to suggest that vast numbers of Rome's subjects were painfully searching for religious consolations. Most were content to repeat traditional rites and observances without vexing their minds by thoughts about human destiny and the hereafter.

The local gods, their household spirits, their magic charms and incantations, and the soothing words of an itinerant astrologer easily satisfied their severely practical (and, therefore, seriously limited) outlook on life. Their lethargic minds may have been stirred sufficiently to watch the public ceremonies of the cult of Mithras, in which devotees bathed in the blood of a sacrificial bull, the *taurobolium*. They could hardly witness unmoved the frenzied demeanour and actions of the self-mutilated fanatics accompanying the splendid celebrations in mid-March in honour of Cybele, the Great Mother, whose image was paraded over streets strewn with flowers.

Although the Christians as yet dared not parade their faith, for they were suspect still as enemies of Roman religion and as a dangerous private sect of conspirators, some of them succeeded in creating a favourable impression and in gaining converts to their faith.

Philosophy

Perhaps the clearest indication of the shallowness of the philosophical speculation of the Romans is their lack of concern with logic, Cicero, who revered Plato, also spoke with great admiration both for Aristotle and the Peripatetic school of philosophy and for the Megarian or Stoic school. An unnecessary antagonism had developed between the logical doctrines of these two main schools of thought, but Cicero, who was much influenced by the Stoics, was not concerned to try to reconcile them. Yet he saw that logical aids to reasoning might improve speeches and convince juries, judges and public assemblies. No Roman whose works have survived is known to have taken any deeper interest in speculative philosophy. Powerful forces prevented its study.

The Republic's ban on philosophers in Rome had public support because they were regarded as enemies of the established order. Not until the advent of Nerva and Trajan

abusing the society in which they were parasitic, with nothing positive to offer in return. Far worthier were the Stoics, who held that virtue is knowledge, and that it is virtuous to live in harmony with reason because reason partakes of the divine. Stoicism, after about 300 BC had been taught in Athens by Zeno and his disciple Chrysippus, and the doctrine had been brought to Rome by Panaetius. Its firm ethical principles made a strong appeal to many practical minded Romans of the Republican era. It profoundly influenced Scipio Aemilianus and his friends, and later served to harden the resolve of Caesar's opponents, Cato and Brutus; and to some extent that of the less resolute Cicero.

Stoic belief in the divine nature of reason not only tended to produce an unwavering sternness among its adherents; it gave many Romans, as it had given Greeks, a special kind of courage. Convinced that, in the light of reason, such things as pain, pleasure and death are not the concern of the wise man, many of the victims of Caligula, Nero and Comitian were enabled to face torture and death.

A Greek slave from Phrygia, Epictetus (c. AD 55–135), set free in the reign of Domitian, acquired great renown by teaching the Stoic attitude to life and by emphasizing as he did so the brotherhood of mankind and the unity of humanity. Hadrian exhibited many of the best Stoic qualities but its most notable convert was Marcus Aurelius, a kind of Stoic saint.

was the prohibition lifted. By then, however, it was too late because Roman education had been perverted by rhetoric.

'Perplexing problems which offer small scope for ornamentation', Seneca reported, were neglected by the rhetorician, 'who wants to win approval for himself, not his cause.' So contrary was such an attitude to the best traditions of republican Rome that it was not until 92 BC that a school of rhetoric was opened, only to be quickly forbidden by the censors.

Paradoxically, it was during the Empire, when the occasion for free speech and rhetorical declamation on public themes became too dangerous, that rhetoric, with grammar, became the main element in the education of youth, with disastrous effects on all other subjects also, notably philosophy.

As an effort to solve the riddle of the universe, philosophy, despite the valiant effort of Lucretius, had no future among the Romans. When philosophy was taken up by followers of one or other of the new religions, all its mysteries received magical solutions. Stoics and Epicureans were still to be found, and in Alexandria some Greeks, of whom the physician Galen (about AD 129–199) was probably the most eminent, endeavoured to follow the guidance of Aristotle. In Rome at about the time of Vespasian, there was a brief revival of the Cynics who went about, dirty and unkempt,

Left, relief from Trajan's column showing Trajan talking to his soldiers in camp: the column, built between AD 106 and 113, is based on the sketches of participants in the campaigns in Dacia.

Below, detail from a second-century AD sculpture of a Roman haruspice, or soothsayer, consulting the entrails of a bull. Musée du Louvre, Paris.

Opposite, relief depicting the Emperor Marcus Aurelius (ruled AD 161–180) attending a sacrifice. Museo Capitolino, Rome.

THE GOLDEN AGE OF THE ANTONINES (AD 96–192)

Date	Rome: internal history	Rome: foreign relations	Rome: culture	The outside world	Date	Rome: internal history	Rome: foreign relations	Rome: culture	The outside World
96				Indian embassy to Rome		Marcus Aurelius adopted as successor to the Empire		Antoninus' Column	Vologeses III King of the Parthians
100	Trajan ascends the throne				160		Campaigns in Mauretania		
		2nd Dacian War	Trajan's works in the harbour at Ostia and the Forum in Rome			Marcus Aurelius ascends the throne	Campaigns in Armenia and against the Parthians	Lucian's *Portraits*	
	Pliny the Younger special commissioner in Bithynia	Annexation of Dacia		Roman embassy to India					
		Annexation of Palmyra	Trajan's Column			Persecutions in Rome	The Germans besiege Aquileia	Theatre of Herodes Atticus at Athens	Roman embassy to China
	Hadrian ascends the throne	Conquest of Mesopotamia	*Annals* of Tacitus			Persecutions at Lyons and in Africa			
120		Insurrection in Judaea			180		Campaigns on the Danube	Aurelius' Column	
	Hadrian travels throughout the Empire	Construction of Hadrian's Wall in Britain	*Lives of the Twelve Caesars* by Suetonius			Commodus ascends the throne	Peace with the Germans	Birth of Origen	
	Perpetual edicts	Insurrection in Judaea	Hadrian's Villa		190	Assassination of Commodus (192)			
140	Antoninus ascends the throne		Death of Juvenal						

Chapter 16

The third Century

After Commodus had been strangled, the Praetorian Guard took command, installing Pertinax as emperor after he had promised each man a large bribe. Although this was paid, he then tried to reinforce the discipline which Commodus had relaxed. Three months later disgruntled praetorians invaded the palace and killed him. They then held a kind of mock auction, choosing as emperor a rich senator, Didius Julianus, because he promised them the largest bribe. Two months later he, too, was killed after Septimius Severus had been proclaimed emperor by his troops.

The new emperor, was a North African born in Leptis. He had to fight for the supremacy because a rival, Pescennius Niger, was also proclaimed emperor in Egypt and Syria. After a long compaign Niger was defeated and killed. Byzantium held out against Severus for two years, only to fall victim to his fury in the end. Another claimant, Albinus, governor of Britain, had reached Lyons with his army before he, too, was overcome.

Vindictively cruel, greedy and unscrupulous, Severus, described as 'an African Sulla' was nevertheless resourceful and energetic and was ably backed by his more cultured, philosophical wife, the Syrian Julia Domna. He dismissed the members of the Praetorian Guard, filling its ranks with 15,000 of his own troops. Plautianus, another African, was appointed prefect, and his daughter married Caracalla, the elder of the two sons of Severus. This ambitious prefect exercised an influence resented both by Julia Domna and by Caracalla. Tired of his wife, Caracalla accused Plautianus of plotting against the emperor and had him murdered. Severus had many large landowners throughout the Empire put to death, confiscating their property in order to become owner of most of the Empire's good arable land. No single act did more to weaken the Empire.

The administrative civil service was re-organized on a military pattern, posts being given to ex-army officers and centurions. Africans and Syrians were favoured instead of Romans and Italians, and Roman senators, deprived of their provinces, lost their political influence.

Their social standing was reduced as well as they were swamped by the influx of provincials, notably from Africa and the East. All power resided in the emperor and his council. When between AD 203 and 212 its vice-president was the judicious Papinian, an able and hardworking jurist, the voice of sanity was heard. His legal writings profoundly impressed succeeding generations. His powers were increased as he became head of a supreme court for all criminal cases in areas more than 100 miles from Rome. Administration of the free corn supply was also added to his office.

Public revenues were concentrated in the hands of the emperor, who now became dignified by a new title *Dominus*, or supreme lord, a description which Augustus had refused. Then for the first time the pernicious legal doctrine began to be heard that 'the wish of the emperor has the force of law'. Already troubles were growing. Italy and the provinces were infested with bandits, partly recruited from the political enemies of Severus. At huge expense Severus bribed the mob with gifts of oil and medicines in addition to the free corn. Great new buildings arose such as the seven-storey *Septizonium* (House of Seven Planets), a testimony to Severus' faith in astrology. His large triumphal arch dominated the Forum. There were also vast building plans in the provinces, prominent among them a series of ornate public buildings for the Emperor's birthplace, Leptis.

The departure of Albinus with his troops to make an abortive bid for imperial power had a disastrous effect in Roman Britain. Northern tribes, taking advantage of the weakened opposition, overran Hadrian's wall. To complete the restoration of peace and order, Severus himself joined his son Caracalla in Britain in AD 208, remaining there until he died at York in AD 211.

Caracalla's assassin Macrinus, another Aurelius Antoninus to cover the fiction that Severus had been adopted by the Antonines. Ignoring his father's wish that he should share power with his more popular younger brother he murdered him in his mother's arms. He later campaigned for a long time on the Danube. He was assassinated in AD 217, as he was about to attack Parthia.

After Caracalla, the imperial purple must have seemed somewhat tawdry, particularly since the Senate had been compelled to deify the madman Commodus and to swear allegiance to one usurper after another. Roman citizenship had been devalued by being conferred by Caracalla upon all provincials in AD 212. This had been done simply as a financial expedient because they all then became liable to pay an inheritance tax and other taxes. Caracalla badly needed money to bribe his army to pay for extravagances such as his colossal Baths at Rome.

Caracalla's assassin Macrinus, another African, was Praetorian prefect and became the first emperor who was not even a senator. Julia Domna, Caracalla's mother, and her sister, Julia Maesa, then conspired to get the succession for Maesa's grandson,

a boy of fourteen, already a priest of the Baal of Emesa. In AD 218 Marcrinus was defeated in battle by disaffected troops, whereupon the boy, under the name Elagabulus, was proclaimed emperor without regard to the Roman Senate.

He eventually arrived in Rome with a body of Syrian supporters in train. These had to be rewarded by admission to the Senate and by imperial appointments. Young as he was, Elagabulus soon earned the active loathing of society, despite the fact that Rome was by now accustomed to all kinds of enormities. In AD 222 he was murdered and his body flung into the Tiber, whereupon his young cousin, aged thirteen and a half, was hailed as emperor, assuming the title of Alexander Severus. His imperious and ambitious mother, Mamaea, became a power behind the throne. She wisely got Ulpian appointed Praetorian prefect.

This learned jurist wrote copiously upon Roman law, compiling commentaries, treatises upon case-law and legal textbooks which had a permanent and profound influence. Failing to retain the confidence of the Praetorians, whose licence he sought to restrain, he was murdered in AD 228.

During these troubled times, Rome's enemies beyond the frontiers became more aggressive. In AD 224 Persia had become united under Ardashir, proclaimed Shahanshah, 'king of kings'. The Roman army which met his attacks was unable to do more than to check his onslaught upon the Empire. His son, Shapur I, who succeeded him in about AD 240, proved even more formidable.

In the north there were other threats to the Empire's frontiers which called urgently for action, and it was while with the army on the Rhine in AD 235 that the emperor, Alexander Severus, and his mother met their deaths at the hands of their own troops.

Above, the Emperor Caracalla (AD 176–217, ruled 211–217) as portrayed on a Roman coin. Musée du Louvre, Paris.

Left, Ardashir I (left) receiving the diadem and gift of kingship.

Below left, the triumphal Arch of Septimius Severus, which records the emperor's successful campaigns against the Arabs and the Parthians, AD 203.

Opposite, rock carving dating from Taq-i-Bustan, late Sassanian dynasty.

Military anarchy and imperial crisis

During the succeeding fifty years about thirty men were proclaimed as emperor, only one of whom escaped assassination. A period of anarchy made life miserable, wrecking the confidence and hope of the previous 100 years. No reliable detailed history is available for these chaotic years, and it is therefore not possible to follow the fortunes of all those who aspired to, or were able to inherit, imperial power. That there were still men ready to risk their lives for so hazardous a responsibility is a remarkable tribute to the might and majesty of empire. Certainly Rome could still give proof of a surprising vitality and vigour, despite the virtual breakdown of orderly government.

Insofar as Roman citizens depended upon their government for support, and as time went on more and more were being reduced to such a condition, they were still served to some extent by the imperial bureaucracy, although its ranks had been seriously depleted. Armies could still be recruited, maintained and led against Sarmatians, Dacians, Goths, Alemanni and Persians. Such struggles were becoming increasingly severe, and Rome suffered several serious defeats. In AD 254 the

Marcomanni overran Pannonia, penetrating as far as Ravenna. Shapur led the Persians to victory, in AD 260, capturing the Roman emperor Valerian and burning Antioch before being driven back.

For about ten years a violent plague had been raging, further weakening the power of Rome, already seriously diminished by the anarchy which it seemed beyond the power of even such able emperors as Gallienus (? AD 260–268) or Aurelian (AD 270–275) to quell.

Both were murdered. When men of such ability and courage could be found to face the appalling chaos of their times, it may seem too soon to speak of a 'decline and fall'. Nevertheless great disasters had a catastrophic effect on the old Roman way of life. Their origin has been traced back to the seemingly golden age of Trajan, Hadrian, and Marcus Aurelius. It was in their time that the defence of the vast Empire began to demand resources which proved increasingly difficult to supply. A well-disciplined, efficient army of some 400,000 men should not have been beyond the resources of an Empire of anything from 50,000,000 to 75,000,000 inhabitants. However, the army was undisciplined often murdering its commanders. Moreover, the economic life of the empire was handicapped by totalitarian controls. Taxes increased and became more

difficult to collect. Various other expedients were attempted by the emperors, which proved disastrous in practice because they impeded free enterprise.

During the Republic the necessity of averting famine in Rome had created the beginnings of a state-managed corn supply. During the reign of Augustus free enterprise brought back general prosperity, even if on a modest level. As usual, however, the most spectacular profits were reaped by relatively few.

Despite the disorders of the first century AD, economic progress was maintained, and there was a notable advance during the second century. It was with the legacy of troubles bequeathed by Commodus that rulers in the third century had to grapple. Constant campaiging on distant frontiers and the need to bribe troops as the price of their loyalty meant more taxes. To collect them over the whole Empire meant more officials. As taxes became more difficult to extract, other expedients were employed, of which the worst was the debasement and ruin of the coinage.

Rome's silver *denarius*, whose steady value had facilitated commerce and industry in the second century AD, had, in less than 100 years, lost its silver content and virtually all its value. In Egypt, where the provincial coinage was less badly depreciated, the

creeping inflation of earlier times became a galloping inflation in the last quarter of the third century AD. Industrious, enterprising men were reduced to poverty or ruin. Since it was upon their resource and energy that the proletariat depended for employment and direction, they too became the helpless victims of the state's economic expedients. All those who received fixed incomes, interest on loans and rents, and all officials and soldiers found their standard of life was being reduced. Military unrest and the constant need for bribes or donatives were a direct result of inflation.

Egypt had not been invaded, it was not a country which suffered from exhaustion of the soil and it possessed its own coinage. Yet the evils from which the Empire suffered were to be found there in full measure. More is known in detail about Egypt from the considerable number of papyri recovered from the desert. Galen had already described how peasants were forced by taxes, rents and requisitions to part with so much of their grain, beans and lentils and that they were forced to eat the bark of trees, roots and other substitutes, which gave them ulcers and killed many.

By the end of the third century AD, plague, taxation and poverty had wrought havoc among once prosperous communities in a land of abundant, annually renewed fertility. Farms and villages were deserted. Irrigation systems which kept Egyptian agriculture alive could no longer be maintained. When petitions to the emperor for relief were made in vain, countless wretched Egyptians, faced with utter ruin, had only three questions to put to their religious oracles. 'Am I to become a beggar? Shall I take flight? Is my flight to be stopped?' Many fled to become bandits preying upon the community.

Faced by the consequences of its own harsh rule, the state sought still harsher remedies. Work was made compulsory for all. No one was allowed to leave his profession, trade or labour. The emperor was the largest land-holder, so agricultural labourers were bound to the soil and their children after them. Those employed in the many state-owned brickyards, in state textile and grinding mills, in mines, quarries and metal working, in arsenals manufacturing arms and in workshops were similarly made prisoners of their calling. Quotas for taxation were fixed and their collection was made the personal responsiblity of the leading inhabitants of a community.

If by such means the most urgent needs of state were partly satisfied, it was at the expense of the great majority. State workers needed a state bureaucracy for their management, so more taxes had to be raised to pay them. Neither state officials nor state workers had the incentives which working on their own account would have provided. Yet their products, whose real cost was excessive, deprived free labour of a market and the community of the goods that they might have produced, had they been free to do so.

Above, cameo depicting the Emperor Valerian (c. AD 193–260, ruled 253–260) taken captive by King Sapor of Persia after his defeat at Edessa. Musée du Louvre, Paris.

Left, sunrise over the tetrapylon at Palmyra.

Opposite, the Emperor Septimius Severus and his family, third century AD; this family portrait was later amended to remove the figure of one of Severus' sons after the child's death. Staatliche Museen zu Berlin.

Such evils were aggravated by the disasters of war. The province of Dacia, with its gold mines, was lost during the reign of Aurelian. His victories could also be very costly, as when in AD 273, he not only carried off Zenobia, the rebel queen of Palmyra, but destroyed her city in the desert, the vital link on the caravan route to the Far East.

The decline into which the outlying parts of the Empire were sliding was for a time delayed in Britian. Yet even here Roman towns decayed. Under Hadrian a splendid town was built at Verulamium. However, by about AD 275 it was in ruins, although occupation continued in one form or another until the fifth century. Other towns such as Wroxeter shared a similar fate. Yet large villas, built by prosperous Romanized Britons, continued to spread in the south. There was in fact a flight from towns to the country, provoked, it would seem, by imperial rapacity demanding ever greater taxes, and also by the destruction of the value of money, which effectively ended the independent production of goods for sale on free markets.

Owners of large villas, with their own considerable labour force, tried to satisfy most of their needs at home. In Gaul such a development was more pronounced. Articles not easily made in villas, such as pottery and metalware, would have been produced in or near forests by small independent craftsmen, who would either sell their work to itinerant pedlars or go on the road themselves.

Small, self-sufficient communities were more easily able to do without money and to evade the harsh taxes levied upon towns. As long as peace and security were assured, they survived reasonably well. The poorer peasants continued a miserable existence in their little huts of one or two rooms, seeking the bare means of survival from their small plots. When their conditions of life became too harsh, like the poor in Egypt they took to brigandage. In Gaul especially there was little to choose between these dispossessed, discontented and ruined men, the *Bagaudae*, and the barbarian invaders. Travel was dangerous. A menace hung over every villa. Coins of silverware were better buried than kept in the house.

Aurelian was the first of the 'barrack-room emperors' (those set up by the soldiers only to be quickly murdered) who proved able to do something to stop the rot. A tough, valiant commander and a stern disciplinarian, he defeated the Vandals and invading Marcomanni, and overthrew Queen Zenobia of Palmyra. He threw a new defensive wall round Rome—an ominous precaution. In Rome he changed the corn dole to two pounds of baked bread, sometimes with pork, salt and oil also. On three occasions 500 debased *denarii* were given to all citizens in Rome. After his murder in AD 275 and a brief interlude, his work was valiantly continued by Probus.

During a year of strenuous campaigning Probus vanquished hordes of German invaders in Gaul, pacified Asia Minor and celebrated a great triumph in Rome in AD 282. Then he also fell a victim of some disaffected troops. Carus, prefect of the Praetorian Guard, who succeeded him, won a great victory over the Persians before dying—probably murdered—in the following year. His two sons, one appointed Caesar of the East, the other Caesar of the West, did not live long. In the spring of AD 285, after a bloody battle, the succession passed to a Dalmatian of humble origin, Diocles, who was an astute and capable soldier rather than a brilliant one.

The new emperor, who took the name Diocletian, reigned for twenty-one years, abdicating in AD 305 to die peacefully in retirement. He owed his success to his administrative ability backed by great force of character. With greater insistence than any of his predecessors, he demanded an oriental subservience, emphasizing the divine nature of his office. His policy was 'divide and rule'. Sensing the terrible responsibilities and dangers of one-man rule, he divided the duties and the risks by separating the eastern part of the Empire from the western part. The eastern part he ruled as Augustus from Nicomedia, on the Sea of Marmora about ninety miles from Byzantium, entrusting the western part to his old comrade-in-arms, Maximian, who ruled from Milan. Two emperors, whose position was reminiscent of that of the two consuls, were now supreme. Both had some hard fighting against frontier foes, Maximian being faced with the additional task of stamping out the bandits (*bagaudae*) in Gaul. In AD 293 each Augustus took a deputy as caesar and heir: Galerius was deputy to Diocletian and Constantius Chlorus to Maximian. Both had to divorce their wives and to marry the daughter of their Augustus. There were now four emperors, forming the famous 'tetrarchy'.

Barbarian invasions or internal insurrections continued to assail the Empire in the east, in Egypt and in the north. Carausius,

admiral of the Roman fleet in Britain, rebelled, and ruled the country from AD 286–87 until AD 293 when he was murdered by Allectus. The latter governed Britain until he was killed in battle in AD 296. There were campaigns in Africa, Egypt and Persia, in all of which Roman armies triumphed.

Immense tasks faced the tetrarchs within the empire. Despite the valiant efforts of Aurelian and Probus, the ruin and desolation of fifty years of anarchy had not been repaired. Probably the dominance of Rome was irretrievably shaken during that terrible time. Many were robbed by the merciless, undisciplined legionaries. Army pay had lost most of its value along with all other incomes, but whoever starved it was not the legionaries. Their plundering raids struck such terror in the minds of peasants and

townsfolk alike that threats of barbarian invasions could hardly have been more feared. Many of the legionaries were in fact barbarians and more had to be recruited or hired as mercenaries as many Romans lost the will to fight and their numbers dwindled as a result of plague, economic ruin and starvation.

Diocletian further divided authority by subdividing the provinces into smaller administrative units, thus tightening control and at the same time diminisihing the risks of military uprisings and their creation of pretenders to the throne. All economic measures could be more sternly enforced. Because the 'barrack-room emperors' had nearly destroyed the purchasing power of the coinage, Diocletian demanded payment of taxes in kind. In order to obtain this he bound tenants of the vast imperial estates to

the soil, further diminishing the recruiting ground for the army. These were not his only expedients to overcome the ruin of inflation. Small issues of gold and silver coin of good quality were struck, but as vast quantities of the old, base, silver-washed copper coins still appeared, the rise in prices was not halted. Officially the scale was: one *aureus* or gold piece was equal to 200 silver pieces which were equal to 8,000 *denarii*.

To stem the inevitable rise in prices, Diocletian made an elaborate attempt to control wages and prices. In his famous 'Edict of Maximum Prices' of AD 301 he published a long catalogue of all common and some luxury goods, many arranged according to their quality and place of origin. He also listed some salaries, wages, and costs of transport. It is the only record of many such prices in the 1,000 years of Rome's history. Where it is possible to compare his prices with those of earlier periods, the effect of inflation is very evident. In the second century AD a *modius* (rather less than a quarter of a bushel of wheat in normal times) had not cost a *denarius*. Diocletian forbad anyone, under pain of death, to sell it for more than 100 *denarii*. The monthly payment which an elementary teacher received for each pupil was fifty *denarii*. A teacher of architecture could expect 100 *denarii* a month for each pupil.

In his denunciation of 'limitless and furious avarice with no thought for mankind' Diocletian damned the 'most cruel inhumanity of the enemies of the individual and state' by which profiteers 'abounding in great riches capture smaller fortunes'. Offenders were to be punished with death. In such a manner did an autocrat seek to repair the economic havoc caused by the crimes of his predecessors. Like all such attempts to fasten the guilt of inflation upon its victims, Diocletian's edict failed completely. Three years after it had been published the imperial government was offering rich Egyptians ten times the official price for a pound of gold. For wheat, the staple of Roman life, the record from Egypt

Below, a ship from Palmyra, Syria, third century AD; Roman control was established there in AD 30, and the city reached the peak of its political and commercial importance in the third century AD.

Below left, the triumphal arch at Palmyra.

Opposite right, bust of a woman and child from Palmyra, late second century AD. British Museum, London.

Opposite left, relief from Palmyra of Baal Shamin between the gods of the sun and the moon, first century AD. Musée du Louvre, Paris.

was the same. Using Egyptian units, a price of about 1,300 *drachmae* in AD 301 had become 10,000 *drachmae* in AD 314 and 2,000,000 drachmae twenty years later. At that rate sixteen tons of bronze coins would have bought only fifty pounds of wheat. Money transactions on such a scale were clearly impossible. In AD 304 Diocletian had a breakdown. In the following year he abdicated, compelling his reluctant co-emperor, Augustus Maximian, to retire as well.

Chapter 17

The later Empire

At first, the two caesars, Galerius and Constantius, became Augustuses as Diocletian had planned, each appointing caesars in their turn. When Constantius died at York in AD 306 his son Constantine was acclaimed Augustus by his troops. Galerius, unable to resist, reluctantly made him Caesar of the West, subordinate to Flavius Severus, formerly caesar and now Augustus of the West. Tension increased when, prompted by the rise of Constantine, the Praetorian Guard in Rome set up Maxentius, the son of Maximian, as Augustus.

After Severus had been treacherously murdered in AD 307 there was a general jockeying for positions which resulted for a time in six men, each bearing the title Augustus, dividing the Empire between them. This brought to an end the relatively tranquil age of Diocletian, although the peace he had won was not immediately disturbed. Inevitably there was a struggle for power. By AD 314 the contenders were reduced to two, Constantine and Licinius, dividing the Roman world between them. There followed ten years of an increasingly uneasy partnership, which ended in AD 324 when Licinius, twice defeated by Constantine, was exiled and murdered. Henceforth Constantine was supreme.

His reign inaugurated more than a new political chapter in the stormy history of the later Roman Empire. Throughout this period cultural life, already singularly artificial and unproductive, even during the so-called golden age of the second century, had been virtually extinguished. Classics upon which many generations had been nourished were unread. Plautus, Terence and even Virgil were no longer appreciated or understood without explanation from a few scholars who somehow managed to preserve some continuity. Nevertheless, in this cultural desert a great new force was stirring.

Christianity's growing influence

Despite public aversion and despite exclusion and persecution, those who called themselves Christians had steadily attracted more converts. They were, however, still a minority sect, consisting mainly of the poorer city dwellers, and many women, as well as freedmen and slaves, for the Church made no distinction between bond or free. With its message of comfort and hope for all distressed in mind, body or social condition, with its promise of a glorious salvation for all true believers, with its scorn for the things of this world and its faith in the second coming of the Redeemer by whom all things were to be made new, the Christian message made an immediate appeal to many frustrated, afflicted, and impoverished people.

Some converts were also to be found among those who were sensitive to human miseries and wrongs. Some richer citizens who shared the disillusionment which results when great wealth is found to provide distractions rather than real satisfactions were also attracted, as were many ordinary people who found the daily round of baths, circus races and gladiatorial fights becoming progressively less rewarding.

Christians were, however, greatly outnumbered by the vast masses of people who relied, insofar as they needed otherworldly influences, upon traditional superstitions or foreign mystery religions. Magic charms and incantations, the pronouncements of oracles and of astrologers, satisfied such urges as they had beyond the narrow bounds of their own outlook. Because Christians spurned all such ancient practices and because they rejected as idolatrous the worship of Isis, Osiris, or Mithras, and refused to believe in the divinity of Roman emperors, they provoked general animosity.

By AD 300 Christians had lived through more than two and a half centuries of scorn,

Above, head of the Emperor Constantine the Great (c. AD 274–337): he chose Byzantium as his imperial capital and named the city after himself.

Top, ivory panel of Christ, c. AD 420, one of the first extant representations of Christ on the Cross: at the far left, Judas Iscariot has hanged himself from a tree; the words above Christ's head mean 'King of the Jews'. British Museum, London.

Opposite, the 'Urn Tomb' at Petra, the Roman city in the Jordanian desert.

enmity and waves of persecution. Difficulties arise when the detailed history of the early Christian is studied, as many of the documents purporting to describe the fate of the primitive Christians have been found to be forgeries. Zealous scribes glorifying heroes and heroines of the early Church freely invented stories to edify the faithful. Doubts have therefore sometimes arisen about the only two circumstantial references to Christians, in which Tacitus described the persecutions of Nero and the younger Pliny appealed for guidance in dealing with the Christians of Bithynia.

Nevertheless, when a critical review has discounted all falsifications, it remains evident that the Christians had a vitality and a power of growth able to overcome all obstacles. At times they were indeed forced to undergo sufferings as terrible as those which Nero had inflicted in AD 64. How many were tortured and executed by provincial governors as the routine duty about which the younger Pliny became uneasy will never be known. In about AD 200–202 Septimius Severus, who had already made conversion to Judaism an offence in Palestine, prohibited the propagation of Christianity and attempts at conversion, but there is no record of great persecution. Philippus, during whose short rule (AD 244–249) Rome celebrated its first 1,000 years, was reputed by later, unconfirmed tradition to have been the first Christian Roman emperor.

After Philippus had been murdered by Decius, resolute steps were taken against Christians. In AD 250 they were ordered to take part in pagan religious ceremonies and to renounce Christianity, but persecutions ceased in the following year, after some

illustrious martyrs, including Fabianus, Bishop of Rome, had met their deaths. Said to have been 'chosen by the whole Christian community' in AD 236, he was the seventeenth to have held the office which in the sixth century became that of 'pope'. In AD 258 Valerian renewed the persecutions, in which Cyprian the able Bishop of Carthage died, as well as Sixtus II, Bishop of Rome. Gallienus, who became emperor after Valerian had been captured by the Persians, stopped the persecutions in AD 260. Much the worst persecution of which there is reliable testimony was that initiated by Diocletian in AD 303, which included ruthless executions, torture, deaths in the arena and condemnations to imprisonment or to work in the mines. Diocletian's abdication in AD 305 did not halt the terror, except where it was in the power of the usurper, Constantine, to suspend persecutions in Britain and Gaul.

Where and how Constantine was influenced to take some interest in Christianity is a mystery. His mother, whom a pious legend later credited with the discovery of the True Cross while on a pilgrimage at the age of eighty to the Holy Places of Jerusalem, did not inspire her son, for he was later to convert her. All that is known is that while on his way to challenge Maxentius for imperial power in the west, he set out as a pagan commander and arrived in Rome in AD 312 with his troops bearing the Christian monogram—the Greek equivalent letters 'Ch', 'r' and 'i'—on his standard, the *Labarum*. His way lay over the mountains where solar phenomena are not unusual. Late one afternoon as the sun was setting a luminous cross was observed in the sky. Later, perhaps in a dream, came the promise

'by this sign you will triumph'. At the fierce battle before the Milvian Bridge, across the Tiber, Constantine did indeed triumph.

He and his colleague Licinius, Augustus of the East, then published the Edict of Milan in AD 313, allowing freedom of worship and ordering the restoration of all property seized from the Christians, giving them the right, as a corporation, to own property. The text of the edict is lost, but it began a new epoch in human history. Apart from the intense relief of the Christians at so miraculous a delivery from a diabolical persecution, the immediate results were not spectacular.

Constantine remained *pontifex maximus*, and the ancient pagan observances continued. When placed upon an even footing, Christianity eventually triumphed, although its following was at that time very small. Christians had not merely survived physical repression, they had been attacked by some keen scholars who subjected their beliefs to sharp scrutiny, criticism and ridicule. Celsus was the first to write a sustained attack in his *True Discourse* in about AD 180. More searching and damaging was the later work of a Hellenized Syrian, Porphyry (AD 232 or 233–305), pupil of the Egyptian or Alexandrian philosopher Plotinus, whose lectures he edited. His book *Against Christianity*, written in about AD 270, has been called the most extensive and most learned work written against Christianity in the ancient world. Like the works of Celsus and other critics of the new religion, it was banned and destroyed, so they are now known only by extracts quoted by their Christian opponents. The positive Gospel message was not to be nullified by mere negative criticism on behalf of traditional beliefs.

Imperial totalitarianism

Diocletian is supposed to have ended his days in his magnificent palace at Salonae (Split) on the Dalmatian coast in AD 313, saddened by the hard fate of his family and friends and by the collapse of his great plans for the government of the Roman Empire. Nevertheless, sufficient of his work remained to be carried on by Constantine, who made his break with the past real and final. Imperial rule was still divided between two men, Constantine and Licinius, until the final rupture, ending with the defeat and subsequent execution of Licinius by Constantine in AD 324. It was imperial rule of a new type, oriental in its ostentation. Reverence for emperors, despite the most solemn oaths of loyalty, had vanished as bearers of the title had been assassinated every other year or so during the fifty years before Diocletian. So he had assumed a crown and magnificent robes, with majestic titles to match, requiring oriental prostration by all who were admitted to his sacred and heavily guarded presence.

Worship of the emperor as a god, which had begun, mainly in eastern provinces, in favour of Augustus, had been something of an embarrassment to his more realistic successors. Nero relished it, and Caligula and Domitian, who were not normal, demanded it.

Constantine, who relinquished none of the trappings of empire, could not, as a Christian, accept divine honour, although his pagan subjects offered it as a matter of course. Instead, he regarded himself under specially divine protection, so originating the theory, which was to vex political thought later, that kings rule by divine right.

Emperors were thus cut off from the realities of life in a way that a campaigning emperor such as Trajan, Hadrian or Marcus Aurelius had not been. Bureaucracy, already formidable, now further developed to impose an almost insurmountable barrier between emperor and subject. There were both military and civil officials, whereas during republican days one man combined both duties. Diocletian imposed a strict separation between military and civil authority as part of his efforts to reduce the power of provincial rulers to revolt.

Under Constantine the supreme Privy Council consisted of the heads of the various civil service departments, each given exotic oriental titles. The treasury was in the charge of the Count of Sacred Largesses. Court and palace administration was the responsibility of the Lord of the Sacred Bedchamber, the chief eunuch, who was influential, often corrupt, and therefore feared and detested.

One privy councillor managed the vast imperial domains or crown lands; another drafted laws and acted as chief legal official. The Master of Offices controlled the civil service, the imperial records, the arsenals and the imperial guard. In addition, he was in charge of the secret police or imperial secret service. His spies were everywhere, often corrupt, and more sinister and more evil than the criminals they were supposed to unmask. It was as though the informers, the sycophants who had profited by provoking degenerate emperors to strike down many of the noblest Romans, had become a permanent, well-paid and full-time profession.

Early in the Republic the praetor had become a greatly respected official, for he was both judge and interpreter of the law and of legal procedure. During the later Empire three, and sometimes four, praetorian prefects were entrusted with these duties in Italy, in Asia, in Gaul and sometimes in the Balkans. Under each of Constantine's praetorian prefects were the dioceses, twelve in all, headed by vicars, who were the superiors of the governors of the 120 provinces into which the Empire had been subdivided. Local government went on, nominally at least, in all large cities, each being governed by its town council or senate, and local officials called *decuriones* or *curiales*. A very tight web of political control thus enmeshed every town dweller. There was not everywhere the same grip upon rural districts, although the procurators on the vast imperial estates and the stewards or bailiffs on the large private estates of the wealthy were often held to a strict accountability for the profitableness of their charge. Under the weight of all these bureaucratic controls, the ordinary citizens or *humiliores* were powerless.

One great and enduring contribution of the Roman Republic to political and administrative activity had been to give practical effect to the discovery of the Greeks that in political life the law should be supreme. Rome's 'rule of law' faded as the contrary principle emerged in the third century that 'what the emperor desires shall have the force of law'. Such had been the reality ever since the rule of law had been broken during the Republic. Sulla and Caesar prepared the way for Augustus and the principate. Augustus described himself as *princeps* to mask the reality of his absolute power, saying that 'although my rank and influence (*auctoritas*) was superior, I had no greater powers than those confided in my colleagues and me alike'. Tiberius maintained the verbal distinction by saying, 'I am *dominus* to my slaves, *imperator* to my troops and *princeps* of the rest.'

Dominium for a Roman meant an absolute, exclusive and unrestricted right of control, which Augustus did not exercise, although he could have done so if he chose. The *dominium* which, with Septimius Severus, replaced the principate no longer respected the convention that *princeps* and citizen were equally subject to the rule of law. As long as the emperor refrained from undue meddling in the private lives of ordinary citizens, the rule of law could still be invoked by them over wide areas of contract, tort, property rights and so forth. As time went on, however, imperial demands became much more exacting.

The political condition of the *humiliores* was made all the more hopeless through their lack of any opportunity of getting together to express their ideas, hopes and desires. They were forbidden to form political associations, they had no newspapers and nothing in the nature of a parliament. Some of the more sympathetic, alert rulers were aware of the vast sea of discontent among their subjects and they tried through their laws to help them. However, the laws could operate only to the extent that the bureaucrats in control were ready to execute them. So there was no escape for the downtrodden. During the fourth and fifth centuries many of the *humiliores* who tilled the soil found mere survival more and more difficult. Taxation and rent, often taken as a share of their annual harvest, left them with insufficient food for themselves and their families in the winter. Money did not easily come their way and inflation destroyed nearly all the purchasing power of such coins as they got. From their desperate condition there was no escape because all men were compelled to pursue the craft or trade to which they were committed by birth and early training.

Everyone was victimized. Diocletian had tried to assess taxes fairly according to the estimated productivity of each administrative area of the Empire. Every year the amounts to be paid were estimated afresh. On top of this levy was a poll tax on every inhabitant. In the towns there was a sales tax, and tradesmen and craftsmen were heavily taxed in addition. The harshest treatment was, however, reserved for the town notables—the *curiales* or *decuriones*. Civic officials had not only to pay all such general taxes, but, in addition, every five years a sum amounting to a capital levy. Worst of all, they were made personally responsible for collecting the taxes from their town and the surrounding country, and for making good from their own resources any deficiency between the fixed quota due to the emperor and the amounts contributed by the citizens. To escape the ruin which such a rule often involved was made impossible. Men could be tortured until they disclosed their wealth and crucified if they lied, although in AD 349 such punishments were banned.

Once an honour for which men competed, the dignity of *duumvir* or *decurio* was hated and shunned. Men had to be compelled to serve and their sons or heirs after them. If they absconded or died without a male heir their colleagues in office had to take over their property and their responsibilities. Before long nomination as a *decurio* was regarded as a punishment. If there were any wealthy, noble landowners—known as *clarissimi*—in the area, they also were liable for heavy taxes.

Both politically and economically, therefore, the emperor's subjects were captive and heavily exploited. Moreover, since arbitrary authority of this kind depended upon a network of minor bureaucrats whose power was much greater than their actual responsibility, bribery and corruption were rampant.

The Christian refuge

In such circumstances the Christian bishops and presbyters gained increasing influence, for they stood outside the official bureaucratic machinery. After the adoption of Christianity by the emperors, the bishops and clergy began slowly to enlarge their claims upon the loyalty and obedience of their Christian congregations, so that even the emperors themselves were subsequently to feel the weight of the spiritual authority which the Church had been allowed to develop.

Apart from spiritual consolation, the Church began to provide a new way of escape—the only one for many a tortured soul. In Egypt where bureaucratic oppression and mismanagement together with inflation had made life intolerable for many, Christian zeal created a new institution and a new way of life for thousands, which were destined to become the sole repository of those cultural values which the Roman Empire was able ultimately to bequeath to the western world.

When Anthony (*c*.AD 250–356), an Egyptian peasant, after serving the Church as a novice for fifteen years, shut himself up in a disused old fort for twenty years, his example attracted others who wished to share his rigorous, ascetic life. At their request he planned a somewhat loosely organized communal society, in which a colony of hermits could cooperate for religious services and for the production of their barest necessities. A more tightly controlled religious community was created by another Egyptian, Pachomius (*c*.AD 290–345). His followers lived in buildings of their own, subject to a strict rule, with daily readings of the Scriptures, religious services and other pious observances. Similar retreats were made for women. A monk, *monachus*, 'one who lives alone', was also called a *nonnus*, of which the feminine form, *nonna*, is the origin of the English word 'nun'. These communities of monks or nuns were expected to be self-supporting as far as possible.

Before the end of the fourth century monasteries and nunneries were arising in Italy, to spread rapidly throughout the Empire. Difficult as the struggle for existence continued to be, the Christian Church prospered. In the Roman Empire many left their wealth to the Church, which was at last able, thanks to Constantine, to hold and administer property. Some of the legacies were probably large houses with their concealed gardens surrounded by a peristyle, the prototype in miniature of the later monastic cloister. Within the privileged seclusions of such splendid surroundings the monks and nuns could lead a less troubled existence than they would have otherwise had to experience. They worked for themselves on the lands they had inherited, and so with good organization they became self-sufficient, often having surplus produce to sell or give to the poor. They were cared for when sick and were not neglected or cast out helpless into the world in their old age.

Roman cameo of the Emperor Kusadak trampling over barbarians, fourth-century AD. National Museum, Belgrade.

The assured supply of food and drink and other benefits provided by monasteries and nunneries, especially to those who might otherwise have been destitute, does not necessarily mean that monasticism owed its success solely to the material advantages it offered. Some may of course have looked for no more, but, if they were admitted, they had to observe the rigours and austerities of founders of the order. Since asceticism, founders of the order. Since ascetism, mysticism and religious fervour were the qualities which the monastic way of life was designed to promote, no concessions were granted to those who sought, under the protection of the Church, an easier life than they would otherwise have had. Fasting, prayer, early rising, daily readings and religious services, with recurrent observances of the festivals of the Church, accompanied by unquestioning obedience and willing service at any task, however menial, imposed a way of life to which few Romans had been accustomed since the early days of the Republic. Monasteries and nunneries represented a complete break with the life of the Roman Empire, replacing it by a new way of life, governed by otherworldly thoughts and values.

So great was the contrast that self-contained and isolated communities were essential if full expression were to be given to the Christian denial of almost all the values by which the world was then governed. Those who chose it often renounced a life of physical ease and comfort provided by great wealth and the obsequious services of an army of slaves and diversified by the daily round of baths, circus races and bloodshed in the arena, followed by an endless round of banquets.

Nothing more clearly indicates the break between the history of the ancient world and the medieval world than this reversal of cultural values. Nothing but the attraction of the new religious and ethical values explains the rush to enter religious communities of monks and nuns. During the fourth century AD they developed to such an extent that the imperial authorities became uneasy at the withdrawal from the active life of the community of able-bodied

men and women, whose labours were needed in the emperor's service. Monks and nuns paid no taxes. They had first claim to the food they grew, the cloth they spun, the baskets they wove and all other products of assiduous monastic industry when hundreds of thousands might be facing acute shortages or famine. Above all, monks escaped military service at a time when the Empire was menaced from outside its frontiers as never before.

The Arian heresy

During the reign of Constantine these new influences were not very powerful. He was more preoccupied with matters of Church doctrine, already a cause of serious controversy. About AD 318 Arius, a priest in Egypt, endeavoured to relate the divinity of Christ and of God the Father in such a way that made Christ seem inferior, if not a second, subordinate God. Known as the Arian heresy, this interpretation aroused such fierce opposition that Constantine summoned what was to be the first of a series of great councils of the Church. In AD 325, 300 bishops met at Nicaea in Bithynia to resolve the difficulty.

Constantine himself provided the solution in a form of words acceptable to the great majority. His simple formula was that God the Father and God the Son were of the same substance (*homousious*). Many would have preferred 'of like substance', but, incorporated in the original Nicene Creed, Constantine's interpretation proved successful for the moment. Athanasius was satisfied. Arius and others who would not accept this interpretation were exiled, Arius' writings were destroyed and the possessors of any of these writings who refused to burn them were put to death.

THE THIRD CENTURY AND THE DECLINE OF THE EMPIRE (AD 193–395)

Date	Rome: internal history	Rome: foreign relations	Rome: culture	The outside world	Date	Rome: internal history	Rome: foreign relations	Rome: culture	The outside world
193	Septimius Severus Emperor	Annexation of Mesopotamia			300	Persecution of Diocletian Constantine Augustus Edict of Milan Constantine sole ruler		Basilica of Maxentius	
200	Caracalla Emperor Edict on the right of citizenship	Campaigns in Britain	Arch of Septimius Severus Baths of Caracalla	Birth of Mani				Arch of Constantine at Rome Council of Nicaea	Reign of Shapur II
		Peace with the Parthians	Death of Tertullian	End of the Parthian dynasty	325	Constantinople capital of Empire Death of Constantine Reign of Constantine's sons	Victory over the Goths Persian War	Great building works at Constantinople	
225	Military anarchy	1st Persian War		The Sassanids come to power					
		2nd Persian War	Plotinus teaching in Rome	Accession of Shapur I	350	Julian emperor Valentinian and Valens Emperors	Invasion of the Alamanni in Gaul		Franks in Gaul
	Millenary of Rome								
250	Gallienus' edict of toleration Aurelian Emperor	Valerianus prisoner of the Persians Fall of Palmyra	Aurelian's ramparts at Rome St Anthony in the desert	Invasion of the Goths Invasion of the Alemanni	375	Theodosius Emperor	Defeat at Hadrianople		Reign of Shapur III
					395	Division of the Empire	Treaty with Persia		
275	Diocletian Emperor The Tetrarchy	Treaty with Persia	Porta Nigra at Trier Baths of Diocletian Palace at Salonae (Split)	Salian Franks in Zealand					

By prohibiting sacrifices, by stripping pagan temples of their gold and silver, by confiscating temple estates and by prohibiting gladiatorial combats, Constantine struck hard at the old ways. He used the gold to mint the *solidus*, which remained a standard monetary unit, and was not debased until the eleventh century.

In AD 326 Constantine left Rome, which he never saw again. He spent his time travelling in the provinces and residing in his new capital, Constantinople, which was solemnly dedicated in AD 330. Work there and religious quarrels kept him busy. Arius, recalled to explain his ideas, succeeded in getting Constantine in AD 331 to ask Athanasius, now patriarch of Alexandria, to reinstate him, which he refused to do. In AD 336 Athanasius was exiled but, although Arius then died, his heresy continued to flourish. Beset by these fierce controversies, Constantine died in AD 337 aged sixty-three. A few hours before he died he received Christian baptism. Christianity seems to have been a kind of talisman for him, ensuring the success of his tasks in this world.

By his encouragement of Christianity during more than twenty years, he had helped to consolidate and strengthen doctrines whose outcome he could not have imagined.

Constantine's successors

How little Christian principles meant to those with power was made evident when, to clear the way for Constantine's sons—Constantine, Constantius and Constans—and eliminate possible rivals, soldiers murdered the whole imperial family except for two young nephews of the dead emperor, Gallus and Julian, who were made virtual prisoners. As senior of the three Augustuses, the eldest brother ruled the west as Constantine II. In AD 340 he set off to eliminate his young brother, Constans who was ruling Italy and Illyricum, but lost his life on the way. Constans who then took over his heritage, was soon struggling to stem the tide of Franks who were pouring into Gaul, as well as the Picts and Scots invading Britain.

Meanwhile, his brother, Constantius II, as Emperor of the East, was hard pressed by the Persians. In AD 350 Magnentius, a semi-barbarian commander of German origin, led a revolt in Gaul which ended in the death of Constans. Constantius II concluded a truce with the Persians which set him free to deal with Magnentius, whom he defeated in AD 351. However, he lost more than 50,000 men, which meant a serious weakening in the defences of the Empire.

Above, relief from the Arch of Constantine, erected in Rome AD 312 to commemorate the emperor's victories, depicting Constantine addressing the Roman people in the Forum; he is flanked by statues of former emperors.

Below, fourth-century AD cameo thought to portray the Emperor Constantine II (d. AD 340) and his wife. Rothschild Collections, Paris.

Opposite, interior of the Basilica of Constantine, begun between AD 306 and 310 and completed by Constantine.

Constantius II, now sole Augustus, had to rely upon his imprisoned young cousins, Gallus and Julian, as subordinates and possible successors.

Gallus proved a failure, so Constantius had him executed in AD 354. However, his studious half-brother, Julian, who was sent to Gaul, showed remarkable ability as a commander and administrator. After some strenuous fighting in AD 356, he recaptured Cologne, which had been overrun and largely destroyed by the Franks in the previous year. Given supreme command in Gaul in AD 357, he valiantly threw back invading Letts, Franks, Germans and others, carrying the offensive into Germany and receiving the submission of some tribes. By AD 359 he controlled the whole of the Rhine. As ruler of Gaul, he sought to reduce the crushing weight of taxation. In AD 361 he renounced Christianity and declared war on his cousin, Constantius II, who was on the eastern frontiers and was about to attack the Persians. Constantius II had not been popular with the Church or the people. Cruel, intolerant, always fearing threats to his throne, he was badly served by toadying subordinates. Civil war was averted by his sudden death in AD 361, which left the succession to Julian.

For the second time the Roman Empire had a noble, soldier-philosopher and writer as its ruler. Julian put an end to some of the worst abuses and extravagances of the court at Constantinople before resuming the campaign against the Persians. He also speedily set about restoring pagan rites and ceremonies, re-opening and restoring pagan temples and reducing Christian privileges. Although he did not persecute Christians, others did. Tolerant of all religions, he required the Churches to restore pagan property, so that many Christian sanctuaries were forced to close. However, he recalled the bishops banished by Constantine during the Arian dispute, restoring their possessions. Christians were made liable to serve as *decuriones*. They were forbidden to teach rhetoric and Greek literature despite a desire to restore the study of Greek and Roman literature. Naturally he was hated by the Church to whom he was 'Julian the Apostate'. In AD 363 he left Constantinople, crossed the Euphrates, but, after some successes, died of wounds received in battle. His army was in such difficulties that his successor, Jovian, had to accept Persian terms which included the surrender of Armenia, as well as five provinces across the Tigris.

Jovian died suddenly in AD 364, succeeded by Valentinian I in the west (AD 364–375) and his brother Valens in the east (AD 364–378). Henceforward the dominance of Rome was increasingly threatened by northern and eastern tribes. Not long after AD 360 the Huns, a fierce, nomadic Mongol people, swept across south central Asia, crossed the Dneister, and erupted into the heart of Europe, spreading death and destruction, and inflicting appalling cruelties.

The Barbarian onslaughts

Tough fighters though they were, Ostrogoths, Visigoths and Vandals proved themselves to be no match for the Huns. So great was the fear they aroused that survivors fleeing before them clamoured for admission into the Empire. Valens allowed thousands into Moesia in AD 375. Valentinian I held the Germans at bay but the defence of Britain against Picts and Scots from the north and Saxons and Franks from the sea involved the Romans in desperate struggles. In AD 368 Valentinian I had sent to Britain his best general, Theodosius, who managed to hunt down the invaders, repair Hadrian's Wall and restore some stability. After a victorious onslaught on Sarmatians and Quadi across the Danube, Valentinian I died of apoplexy in AD 375. Gratian, his son by his first wife, succeeded him as Emperor of the West, accepting as co-emperor his little half-brother, Valentinian II, who was thus proclaimed by the Illyrian army.

In AD 378 the Visigoths, who had been admitted into Moesia, were so badly treated by Roman imperial officials that they rebelled. Valens, who marched against them, was defeated and killed at the battle of Hadrianople, before Gratian arrived with reinforcements. Early in AD 379, Theodosius was chosen by Gratian as Emperor of the

East; he was son of the murdered general who had restored order in Britain. With great courage and resource, Theodosius trained his army and halted the invading Goths. There was now no hope of throwing them out of the Empire. Gratian and Theodosius accepted the inevitable by allowing them to settle, as allies, south of the Danube, in Pannonia and Moesia. These brief interludes were bought at the price of the slow decay of Roman rule, but they gave Theodosius a few years of relative peace in Constantinople. They were, however, a symptom of the approaching collapse of the Roman Empire. This was, in fact, a long drawn-out process.

Viewed from Rome itself, it became at last an agonizing reality, the end of the world. For the nomadic tribesmen of northern and eastern Europe it was the dawn of a better life in a land where there were richer foods and drink, where servile labour could be put to work and where well-built villas provided the luxury of warm winter quarters. It was a land where they could acquire strange habits, such as a daily bath and where they could associate, if they wished, as superiors with sophisticated, cultured people whose ancestors had for generations confined their forbears to harsher lands and forests east of the Rhine and north of the Danube.

Above, gold medal of Constantine II struck at Antioch, Turkey, AD 343/4.

Left, breviary of Alaric II, King of the Visigoths: completed in 506 AD, it contains a detailed summary of Roman law. Bibliothèque Nationale, Paris.

Opposite, detail of a silver disc depicting the Emperor Theodosius I (c. AD 346–395, ruled 379–395) between his two sons. Academia de la Historia, Madrid.

While these changes were slowly coming about, Rome was increasingly relying upon tough barbarians or semi-barbarians to fill great gaps in the legions and to produce able commanders to lead them to victory against other barbarian tribes with whom they themselves often had no great quarrel.

It is difficult to be certain why the once warlike Romans and Italians could provide so few soldiers. There are no reliable statistics, but Romans seem to have been unable to recruit an army such as that with which Marius had routed huge forces of

Teutones near Aquae Sextiae in 102 BC. Grisly scenes of human carnage over which Roman mobs had continuously gloated for two centuries, instead of making the Romans warlike, seem to have made them believe that victory or death by the sword was a fate reserved for slaves and criminals. Their morale and their will to fight had gone.

Christianity, with its message of peace, may partially explain the lack of martial qualities but Christians were to be found in the army, often among senior officers. They were willing to fight pagan invaders, and

many Germanic tribes were still pagan. A considerable number of the Goths, however, were Christians. Wulfila (AD 310–381), a Goth who had been converted in Constantinople, had spread the Gospel among his people, translating the New Testament. It was the first book written in Gothic, for which he had devised a script.

However, the new religion failed to become a real bond between those accepting it. The Arian doctrines spread by Wulfilla and other missionaries were detested by the Catholics of Rome. Religion failed to become a bond because the absolutionist, totalitarian spirit of imperial rule also infected Church politics, with deplorable results as Christians began to create dogmatic theology out of their interpretation of the Gospel message. A doctrine whose purpose was to spread charity and human affection paradoxically produced hatred and fierce dissent over different theories, incapable by their nature of verification. Christians had cause to recall the poet's lament, made already in pagan times, that religion could promote so many evil deeds.

Meanwhile life in Rome went on with the endless round of baths, circus races, and sordid scenes in the arenas, where animals were the principal victims, because gladiatorial slaughter had at last been stopped. Poets still exalted the marvels of Rome, predicting its glorious future.

The empire crumbles

Although the collapse of Roman resistance to barbarian incursions was to become disastrous, it was still true in AD 400 that the greatest sources of the weakness of the Empire had been plague, civil wars and gross mismanagement. Warring commanders fighting each other with legionaries badly needed to repel barbarians squandered Rome's most precious assets—fighting forces and the moral force that comes from loyalty to ideals and to the men who should have symbolized those ideals. Every legionary took a solemn oath of loyalty and devotion to the emperor. There were no protestations of servility and adulation too gross or too exaggerated for the senators to repeat in proclaiming their grovelling abasement before the emperor's commands. So low had Roman morale sunk that neither legionaries nor senators honoured their promises a moment longer than it seemed expedient.

Dereliction of duty on a grand scale occurred as personal ambition overrode all considerations of the wider interests of the Empire and its inhabitants. In AD 383 Maximus abandoned Britain to take his army on a foray with the aim of seizing imperial power. Theodosius was able to crush the revolt, but four years later had to suppress another would-be emperor. For Britain the cost was disastrous. Hadrian's Wall stood deserted, and the country could no longer be held against Picts, Scots and sea-borne invasions of Saxons. One after another, magnificent villas began to be abandoned as their owners fled.

It was a reduced, threatened and divided Empire that Theodosius bequeathed to his two sons in AD 395. Arcadius, then aged seventeen, had the mainly Greek-speaking eastern half of the Empire; Honorius, then eleven years old, the western half. From then onwards the fortunes of the two Empires diverged. The east, as the Byzantine Empire, ruled from Constantinople, survived for a thousand years. The west, ruled ineffectively from Ravenna, was steadily eroded.

When the legionaries were led by an exceptionally able commander, they could still win victories. Such was Stilicho (c.AD 359–408), who held off the Goths, despite their formidable chieftain Alaric. But Stilicho was not in Gaul when Alans, Suevi and Vandals crossed the Rhine in force in AD 406 to swarm over northern Gaul, burning, raping, looting and destroying.

Stilicho, a Vandal, was murdered by insanely jealous Romans in AD 408, with the fatal facility with which they killed many of their most able men. Alaric, seizing his opportunity, invaded Italy in AD 410, and reached Rome. On a fateful day in August, the sacred capital, preserved from foreign invasion for more than 800 years, was taken and plundered by Alaric and his Visigoths. Many once prosperous citizens were deported as slaves. Consternation and horror shook the entire Roman world as the dreadful news was spread.

No clear picture can be drawn of the extent of the barbarian influx bringing new peoples to take over the Western Roman Empire. Northern Gaul and Britain were lost before the middle of the fifth century AD. Southern Gaul was also overrun by Vandals coming from Northern Gaul, until the Visigoths moved in, forcing the Vandals into Spain. Native Roman subjects greatly outnumbered them but there is no evidence that they put up any serious resistance. Instead they accepted Visigoths as they had been forced to accept billeted Roman legionaries, to whom they had had to yield a third of their houses and property. The Visigoths took two-thirds.

Co-existence, forced upon the Romans, did not lead to fraternization. Intermarriage was still forbidden. Neither common humanity nor a common religion could overcome the repugnance both peoples felt for alien habits and customs. Sophisticated, wealthy Roman subjects owning vast estates, living a life of fairly cultured ease, had to accept

Attila

as superiors crude and illiterate people, destitute of the elements of civilized life. Their domestic and sanitary habits, the stench of their bodies and clothes, their food and the way they ate it, their beer and their drunken bouts—all poisoned life for the Romans. In Aquitaine and southern Gaul co-existence was unavoidable, with the Visigoths as nominal allies of the emperors, none of whom was able to interfere.

The Visigoths honoured the alliance when a vast hord of nomadic Huns, under their fierce warrior-king, Attila, 'the scourge of God', assailed the Empire, after massacring, slave-hunting and looting their way through eastern Europe between AD 433 and 441.

To buy off Attila, the Emperor of the East had paid a colossal bribe in gold which

Above, medallion depicting Attila the Hun.

Opposite, the Mausoleum of Theodoric (AD 455–526), founder of the Ostrogothic monarchy at Ravenna, sixth century AD.

did not prevent Attila trying, in vain, to capture Constantinople. After devastating the Balkans, he moved westwards, claiming Aquitaine. He was confronted by the last Roman general of great ability, Aëtius. In a mighty battle Aëtius and the allies he had collected defeated Attila in AD 451 in the heart of Gaul.

Attila was still powerful. He invaded northern Italy in the following year, but Pope Leo persuaded him to withdraw. In AD 453 Attila took a German wife, dying suddenly in the bridal bed. Thereafter his hordes withdrew to the east. Again a military genius was sacrificed when Aëtius was killed in AD 454 by the worthless Valentinian III, the last emperor with some pretence to a hereditary title. He, too, was slain in revenge in AD 455. Immediately the crafty King Gaiseric (or Genseric), who had taken his Vandals from Spain in AD 429 to luxuriate in Rome's granary in Africa, invaded Italy. They fell upon an undefended Rome in AD 455, which was systematically looted of all the valuable property the Vandals could carry away. Gaiseric then took over the whole of Roman Africa.

All real power now lay with the Germanic tribes. Ricimer, a Suevic commander of some of Rome's mercenaries, made and unmade emperors. The best was Majorian (AD 457–61), whose ability and sensible reforming efforts provoked resentment and ultimately led to his assassination.

Pagan tribes to the north were in constant ferment, but Gaiseric and his Vandals in Africa, commanding the Mediterranean with their fleet, remained the greatest threat. Rome, despoiled and depopulated, suffered horribly from the lack of African wheat. Before Gaiseric's death in AD 477, which ended the danger from the Vandals, Gaul had been finally lost to the Empire.

All that remained of the Empire was Italy, under the nominal rule of a small boy, Romulus Augustus, son of a Pannonian who had married a Roman woman after having been secretary to Attila. In AD 476, after a nominal reign of a year he, the last Roman emperor, was deposed by mercenary German troops under Odovacar. Italy, the bastion of the Western Empire now fell to the barbarians. Odovacar sought to preserve a semblance of legitimacy by asking the Emperor of the East to fill the imperial position and to make him his lieutenant in Italy.

After AD 476 the history of the lands once ruled from Rome becomes the story of the barbarian kingdoms, although several generations of Roman, Italian and Romanised provincials preserved what they could of the way of life to which they had been accustomed. Such is the tenacity of a vital cultural tradition that it can survive acute political and economic crises. That tradition, created during the many centuries when Rome was the dominant world power, was helped by strict rules against intermarriage, by the need to employ Roman officials to collect taxes and to maintain some administrative services, especially correspondence in Latin, and by the retention of Roman law and practice in separate courts alongside the tribal law of the barbarians.

Because the barbarian kings wanted to raise taxes, many wealthy proprietors were left to manage their huge estates, although the barbarians took over much land, including vast imperial domains. From the letters of Sidonius Apollinaris (c. AD 430–c. AD 487) some glimpses can be had of life in Aquitaine during the fifth century. He and his friends among about a hundred wealthy villa owners with large estates and pleasant gardens managed to maintain a civilized life and to indulge in some intellectual interests, while affecting an attitude of snobbish aloofness towards their barbarian masters. Such a situation could not and did not last for long.

In Italy the situation was somewhat different. The Ostrogoth invaders were less numerous, as there was so much vacant land for them to occupy; and many established proprietors were not dispossessed.

In AD 489 the eastern emperor called upon Theodoric, an Ostrogoth, to replace Odovacar. Fierce fighting took place until Theodoric treacherously killed his enemy in AD 493, massacring his troops. Italy now became part of an Ostrogothic empire. By wise rule, Theodoric secured the food supply and internal peace. To him also are due some of the buildings and mosaics of Ravenna. In AD 507 one of his grandsons, Amalaric, inherited the Visigothic Kingdom of Spain which Theodoric ruled for him, so extending Ostrogothic dominion over a considerable part of the old Roman Empire, a rule maintained after the death of Theodoric in AD 526 by Amalaric (–AD 531) and later by Theudis (–AD 548).

New forces were keeping the former Roman world in a ferment. From the north came the Franks, after consolidating their hold on lands between the Rhine and Brittany. Led by the Merovingian branch of the Salian Franks, under the fierce Clovis, a barbarian pagan, who became king at the age of fifteen in AD 481, they began to look southwards. In AD 493 Clovis married Clotilda, the Catholic daughter of the king of the Burgundians, becoming Catholic himself. The fact that he was converted to Catholicism and not Arianism was to be a fatal bar to any understanding with the Arian Ostrogoths. The marriage between Clovis' sister, Audofleda, and Theodoric did not stop Theodoric from vigorously preventing seizure of the coastal strip of old Roman Gaul by Clovis. Renewal of religious persecution by the Arians embittered life for the Catholic majority in Italy, and more so in Africa and Spain where persecution sometimes went to savage lengths. Arianism survived for some decades underground in Spain after the victory of Catholicism there in AD 589.

Gaul, united at last under Clovis after much fighting, remained Catholic after his

death in AD 511, when his kingdom was divided among his four sons. Theodoric's Ostrogothic empire did not long survive his death in AD 526 when he had been about to intensify his oppression of his Catholic subjects and to embark on a campaign against the Vandals in Africa. They had renounced their alliance with him in AD 523 and were preparing to side with the Byzantine emperor, Justin, who had declared war on Arianism. Such were the divided and shattered remnants of the once dominant Roman Empire of the West.

The Roman Empire of the East

Almost an outpost of the Roman Empire, Byzantium was dangerously exposed to the wild tribes of the east into whose hinterland no Roman had penetrated far. Its military power was at first negligible; that of its potential enemies seemed unlimited. Yet it had assets which were exploited, with varying success, to secure its survival for a thousand years.

Constantinople, the capital, was the firm foundation of the power of the Byzantine Empire. Defended by sea and by a double landward wall—the first built by Constantine, the second and larger by Constantine's grandson, Theodosius II (AD 408–450) the city withstood all assaults. Its territories in Asia Minor, which had not been invaded by barbarians, commanded trade routes to the east, so many were wealthy. A professional civil service of tax collectors, and a highly paid, well-trained, privileged army of professional fighters of many nationalities, obeyed an autocratic emperor. Oriental in its dazzling magnificence, the imperial court made Constantinople a wonder of the world. It had been Christian from the start, but Byzantine Christianity was so bound up with the emperor's powers that it never secured the independent influence wielded by the Bishop of Rome. Religious zeal amounting to fanaticism bit deeply into the minds of the Byzantines, already predisposed to excitability and violence by their country's exposed and perilous position.

Left, portrait of Justinian I on a Byzantine coin. British Museum, London.

Below, detail of a Byzantine mosaic from Ravenna depicting the three kings bringing their gifts to the infant Jesus.

Opposite, mosaic from Ravenna showing the Empress Theodora with court officials, AD 584.

Constantinople was intended to be a new Rome. It had seven hills and fourteen regions, as did the old capital on the Tiber, and many of its buildings were carefully copied from the Roman originals. The old Roman provinces of the West in Britain, Gaul, Spain, Italy and Africa remained nominally subject to the Byzantine emperor, and sometimes their barbarian rulers accepted from him such honorific titles as 'consul' or 'patrician'.

Throughout its 1,000 years, the history of Byzantium bore no resemblance to the first 1,000 years of Rome's independence. Yet the Byzantines regarded themselves as Romans and Latin remained the official language. That part of Roman law which was preserved for future generations was put together during the reign of Justinian (AD 527–565). Justinian's reign, too, saw an attempted resurgence of Roman power which was for a time successful. He reconquered Africa, Italy and southern Spain, winning command of the Mediterranean, but these successes overstrained his resources. In Italy the struggle against the Goths was fierce and prolonged. What was not destroyed during the fighting became the prey of Byzantine

tax-gatherers. Rome had been entirely cleared of its inhabitants in AD 546 during the struggle which began Italy's Dark Age. Byzantium was unable to revive civilized life there or to maintain its rule for long.

Within fifty years of Justinian's death, in AD 565, his conquests were lost and the Roman Empire was never again reunited. Such disasters were catastrophic for western Roman civilization but the Empire of the East miraculously survived. It, too, was very nearly obliterated by a formidable assault by Sassanid Persians. Despite Justinian's immense fortifications, they captured the whole of Asia Minor and Egypt after AD 611. All was, however, recovered by the genius of Heraclius by AD 629.

Italy, badly depopulated, was by then overrun by Lombards from the north. The entire system of values of all kinds by which men guide their lives—their civilization and their culture—was very different among the barbarian conquerors of the Western Roman Empire from those of the Christian Eastern Empire. Both, in varying ways, would have regarded Roman values as completely alien.

Christianity was responsible for a revolution in art and music. A great Christian

Above, the Emperor Justin I (AD 450–527, ruled AD 518–527) and his successor Justinian I. British Museum, London.

Above left, imperial cross. Cappella delle Reliquie, Basilica Vaticano.

Opposite top, mosaic from Ravenna of the Emperor Justinian I and members of his court, c. AD 547.

Opposite bottom right, ruins of the walls built to guard Constantinople by Theodosius I.

Opposite bottom left, Byzantine coin of the Emperor Justinian I. British Museum, London.

THE FALL OF ROME AND THE BARBARIAN KINGDOMS

Date	Western Roman Empire	Invasions and barbarian kingdoms	Culture	Byzantium—Islam	Date	Western Roman empire	Invasions and barbarian kingdoms	Culture	Byzantium—Islam
400	Division of the Empire	Alaric invades Greece		Arcadius			Visigoths in Spain Division of the Frankish kingdom	The Salic Law	
	Honorius	The Visigoths in Gaul	St Augustine's *City of God*	Theodosius II	525				
425	Alaric takes possession of Rome						Death of Theodoric End of the Burgundian kingdom	Tomb of Theodoric San Vitale at Ravenna	Justinian'I
450	Aëtius at Ravenna	The Huns on the Rhine Invasion of Attila The Vandals settle in Africa	Death of St Augustine		550		Sack of Milan Conquest of Italy by Byzantium	St Radegonde at Poitiers	
	Sack of Rome by Gaiseric	Battle of the Catalaunian Fields	St Leo the Great		575		Lombard invasion of Italy		Birth of Mohammed
	Romulus Augustulus the last Emperor	Death of Attila	Mausoleum of Galla Placidia	Leo I	600		Treaty of Andelot Conversion of Recarred	Gregory the Great Death of Gregory of Tours	Tiberius II Maurice
475					625		Clothaire II	Mission of St Columba	Phocas Heraclius
	Ravenna taken by Odovacar	Invasion of the Herulians	Treasury of Chilperic				Dagobert	Death of Isidore of Seville	Death of Mohammed
500	End of the Western Empire	Accession of Clovis Theodoric King of the Ostrogoths—Battle of Tolbiac	Baptistery of Frejus	Anastasius I	639		Death of Dagobert		

literature arose, much more of which has been preserved than that of classical times. Christian ethical and moral values, however, were too often forgotten in fierce wars, civil strife and social upheavals.

Nevertheless, the Gospel message remained, and it was taken by Byzantine missionaries to bring the first rudiments of a more developed culture to many barbaric tribes. Constantinople itself was a melting pot for countless newcomers from strange, barbaric lands, including Huns, Arabs, Berbers, Slavs, Croats and Serbs. Its great wealth, its trade sustained by Constantine's *solidus*, its magnificent buildings, crowned by Justianian's masterpiece, St Sophia, all served as outward signs of a vital civilization. It was not Roman, but, nevertheless, it would never have come into being had not the early Romans and their descendants laboured, fought, built, schemed and written over the centuries to improve, as they thought, their own and mankind's estate on earth.

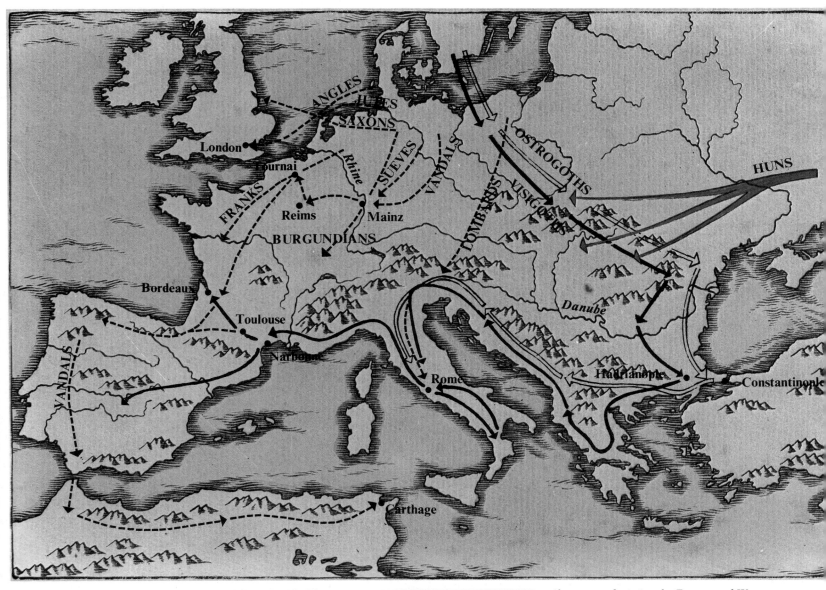

Above, map depicting the Eastern and Western Roman Empires in the fifth century AD and the barbarian invasions in the west.

Left, interior of the church of St Sophia, consecrated in AD 537.

Opposite, sixth-century AD Byzantine ivory relief depicting the Emperor Justinian I as defender of the faith. Musée du Louvre, Paris.

Part IV

THE ANCIENT EAST

Introduction

It is all too easy for historians and writers, whether consciously or unconsciously, to assume a western standpoint. The heritage of the civilizations of the eastern Mediterranean and Mesopotamia can easily be traced through the development of western European civilization and then, from the late fifteenth century onwards, out into a wider world, to the Americas and later still to Africa and Australasia; this heritage does, after all, carry with it Christianity, one of the most influential religions the world has even known.

That such attitudes were expressed during the years of European military, political and commercial hegemony is perhaps understandable; today they are no longer so acceptable. The civilizations of India and China are as old as those of Mesopotamia and Egypt, older than that of Greece. The influence of Confucius and the Buddha has been enormous, in both time and geography.

Perhaps one clue to the western view of eastern civilizations lies in the difficulties of communication. Travellers from the west did reach the east, but they were exceptional; there was certainly nothing like the frequent contact that gradually brings about cultural cross-fertilization. In addition, one might argue, though admittedly in very general terms, the relatively peaceful nature of these civilizations must be taken into account; more often invaded than invading, they lacked the aggressively proselytizing impetus of western Christendom.

The ancient civilization of the Indian subcontinent began with the invasion of the Aryans in about 1500 BC, described by one historian as one of Indian history's 'great creative forces'. It was then that the great religions of India, and of the world, were founded: Hinduism developed out of the Vedic religion of the Aryan invaders; Buddhism, originating in the Ganges Valley, slowly spread through India and then beyond her borders to become the strongest religions of Asia and the first in the world to be adopted beyond its own cultural birthplace. Successive waves of invaders—the Bactrians, the Guptas (their civilization was a milestone of literary and intellectual achievement) and finally, from the twelfth century AD onwards, the Muslims—all helped to mould Indian civilization but all were at the same time themselves modified by it.

China, like India one of the great civilizations of the ancient world, has shown remarkable cultural continuity despite political change. Under Shang and Chou rule, the distinction between those of noble and those of common birth slowly established itself, as did the pictographic nature of the Chinese language, the widespread use of which acted as a unifying influence. The conservative philosophy of Confucius, born in 551 BC, reinforced support for the established order; its very dominance too acted as a cohesive force, generations of administrators being trained to follow his precepts of 'documents, conduct, loyalty and faithfulness'. From then on, in many respects even to the present day, the continuity of Chinese civilization has been remarkable; though disturbed for quite long periods by invasions from outside, imperial unity was always restored.

Of all the great civilizations of the east, only that of Persia, by reason of its very geographical position, astride many international routes, maintained any kind of regular contact with the west. For fifteen hundred years the Persians, themselves a collection of many different peoples, vied with Greece, then with Rome and finally with Rome's eastern successor, Constantinople. The Sassanid Empire, politically strong and united in religion, was the last great flowering of Persian might. Yet, at the very moment of its greatest triumphs—when imperial armies had invaded Egypt, taken Jerusalem and Rhodes and were within sight of Constantinople—the tables were turned, and the Sassanid Empire collapsed within a few decades. Its place as the west's, and Christianity's, chief opponent was taken by Islam.

On page 284, fourth-century AD image of the Buddha. National Museum of India, New Delhi.

Opposite, Sassanian silver dish showing King Shapur II, fourth-century BC. British Museum, London.

Chapter 18

Persia under the Sassanids

The internal history of Persia has been dictated by the endless desert plateau which lies at the centre of the country. Surrounding the desert, fertile valleys reach into the Zagros Mountains in the southwest, the Elburz chain which bounds the southern shores of the Caspian and, in the northeast, the first foothills of the Hindu Kush.

It is a country of fertile pockets consisting of small towns and agricultural communities dominated by great landowners, all forming a string of separate cultures. The wandering peoples of the plateau were uncontrollable and from the desert came political chaos. The surrounding mountains were no barrier to invaders and only an exceptionally determined central government could bring cohesion to the country, unite the independent townships and subdue the nomads. Above all, only an efficient administration could protect and organize the complex irrigation systems on which so much Persian agriculture (and local authority) depended. The intricately designed subterranean watercourses were abandoned and collapsed whenever the government was unable to guarantee local security.

Despite Persia's geographical diversity and the long antagonism between its nomadic and agricultural communities, the

country has always possessed a tenacious political continuity and a distinct cultural unity. Persia has always managed to absorb and use her conquerors—Alexander the Great, the Muslim Arabs and the Mongol hordes. Its rulers all inherited the same method of uniting the country—an authoritarian, widely publicized and quasi-divine kingship, which emerges, with differing royal symbolism, under the Abbasids, the Sassanians and reaches back beyond even the glories of Xerxes and Darius to the ruthless rulers of ancient Assyria.

The kings of Persia also inherited the same ancient rivalry with the west. Greece, Rome and Byzantium were their only cultural equals. It was a case of mutual fascination. These enemies learnt more from each other

(particularly in administrative devices and forms of faith) than they would admit.

In AD 224 Ardashir, grandson of Sassan the founder of the Sassanian dynasty, deposed Artabanus V, last of the Parthian kings who had ruled Persia since the second century BC. The new king of kings (the title was practical rather than grandiose) set about strengthening an existing tradition of state bureaucracy which owed something to Persia's Greek conquerors of the past. He replaced local warlords and hereditary satraps with royal governors who could be dismissed at will. He curbed their ill-disciplined private armies and placed himself at the head of the Persian forces.

The Sassanians were highly assiduous propagandists of their own kinship. They

placarded their achievements in great rock-cut inscriptions and reliefs of cowering captives which still overlook the caravan roads of the country. Their coins, which every man handled, repeated the imperial slogans. Their sumptuous palace decoration inspired the mystery of their rule as viceroys of the divine Ormazd, the spirit of good.

The Sassanians used the magi, their Mazdean priesthood, to focus loyalty upon their throne. The Mazdean faith was based on the belief that the universe was under the dominion of two opposing principles and its prophet was Zoroaster. In the fire-temples of Persia the spirits of good and evil, light and darkness (Ohrmazd and Ahriman) fought their battle and claimed impartial devotion.

Mazdeanism was adulterated with local polytheistic cults in many parts of Persia and the prophet Mani of the third century AD adapted it further. Manichaeism, his religion, spread beyond the confines of Persia and had its most remote adherents 1,000 years later among the medieval Christian heretics of Europe.

The magi controlled important temple revenues and estates. Another recognized class of society was the warrior landowners, semi-feudatories who dominated the provinces when Sassanian power was weak. Administration, religion and soldiering were the recognized professions and the merchant and clerk classes were insignificant.

Of the shepherds and peasants who pursued their dreary seasonal cycle of work we know little, for the Sassanians have seen

to it that we learn of their rule largely through their own official version of events —a chronicle of conquests and a record of administrative decrees.

Shapur I and his successors

The reign of Shapur I (AD 241–272) marks the early heyday of the dynasty. His armies overran Armenia, Antioch and Syria and wrecked the Roman military stronghold of Dura Europos. Shapur's triumph came in 260 when he captured the Roman emperor Valerian and his invading army of 70,000 legionaries. Roman imperial prestige in the east never recovered from this shattering defeat. Shapur advertized the fact in rock-carvings and official paintings throughout Persia. The Roman captives were settled in Khuzistan where part of the extensive irrigation works which they dug is said to be still in use today.

The unity of the Sassanian state depended largely upon the character of individual kings. Shapur's successors were largely undistinguished and quarrelsome. They were finally reduced to crowning Shapur II in a quaint ceremony in 309 when he was still in his mother's womb—the magi had guaranteed a male child. Unexpectedly the second Shapur survived to reign for almost seventy years of almost constant warfare with Rome. The Roman emperor Julian the Apostate came to avenge Valerian's defeat, only to be lured to his own mysterious death in Persia.

During the long reign of Shapur II Christianity became the official religion of Rome in fact as well as name. Julian was the last emperor to look back with longing to the pagan past. Now Christian Armenia turned from Persia to Rome as its protector. Accordingly Shapur persecuted Christians in Persia and encouraged the local Christian heresies of the east which so perplexed the bishops and bureaucrats of Constantinople.

Persia became the home of one of the separated Churches of the east—the Chaldean, more usually called Nestorian. Nestorius, the patriarch of Constantinople, had been condemned in 431 for the heretical notion that the divine and human persons could be distinguished. In fact we now know that Nestorius was probably not a 'Nestorian' and that the 'Nestorians' of Persia had little concept of the heresy.

Ostracized by European Christians, the Persian 'Nestorians' turned to evangelize parts of India and central Asia. Their achievements were astonishing and by 774 they were able to set up a monument in China to record the triumph of Christianity. When in the thirteenth century the Mongols united their old mission lands the 'Nestorian' patriarch in Persia counted some 230 dioceses all over the east in his spiritual dominion. Nonetheless, the Church was

virtually extinguished in persecution and bloodshed by Timur's Mongols at the end of the fourteenth century. Very few representatives of this, the most ancient of Christian heresies, survive in the east today.

Most of Shapur II's immediate successors were feeble and overshadowed by their leading ministers. The separatist tendencies of Persia reasserted themselves. The Mazdeans challenged the state religion, the Hephtalite (White Hun) tribes lorded it in the mountains and the local nobility detached outlying provinces. It was Khosrow I (531–579) who restored the old Sassanian authority and ushered in the empire's most splendid period. He perfected the machinery of state government, continued the irrigation schemes begun by Shapur I and subdued the Huns in the north and the Yemenis in the south.

The Sassanians always regarded their western conquests as the most significant and, inevitably, Khosrow sought victory over the Roman (now Byzantine) Empire. In 540 he took Antioch and entered into the final, protracted struggle for Armenia which, with its chain of garrison fortresses and unreliable inhabitants, was the key to the Byzantine defence system.

Some strongholds, especially to the south of the Caucasus, changed hands almost annually. Armenian and Laz rulers exploited the situation for over a century until 651, when peace favourable to the Byzantines was finally signed, only because the Sassanians had themselves lost their empire.

In Ferdowsi's eleventh-century Persian work, the *Epic of the Kings*, Khosrow figures as the most heroic and attractive of all Sassanian rulers. His love for the exquisite Shirin, his spirited Christian (and possibly Greek) concubine, has passed into Persian romance. It was Shirin who, it is said, first fielded an entire harem in the Persian aristocratic sport of polo.

At Ctesiphon Khosrow chose a Byzantine architect to create the most splendid palace in the world. His offspring ruled for only a few more decades from this palace, but its ruins at Ctesiphon are still astonishing. Here the greatest unsupported brick vault in the world, almost a hundred feet wide and over a hundred feet high, stands in the desert over the banqueting hall of Khosrow.

The end of the Sassanids

The energies of the Sassanian Empire were burnt out by Khosrow's grandson, the avaricious and overweaning Khosrow II. He sent his generals to fight their way to Chalcedon and threaten Heraclius' Constantinople across the narrow waters of the Bosporus. But the Byzantine emperor penetrated deep into Persia and in 628 Khosrow II was hounded to his death. 'The realm was coming to an end; from every side foemen made their appearance', wrote Ferdowsi.

After centuries of noble rivalry with Rome the Sassanian dynasty met an unexpected and ignominious end. Eight years after the invasion by Heraclius, the patriarch of Constantinople, it was the Arabs and not the Byzantines who finally crushed Sassanian Persia and in 637 gazed with amazement upon the palace of Ctesiphon. Yazdegerd II (632–651), the last king of kings upon whom the glory of Ohrmazd shone, was murdered in obscurity at Merv.

According to tradition some Persians fled to India, where the fire-worshipping Parsees still number their years from Yazdegerd's accession. The *Epic of the Kings* concludes:

The standards of the kings of the world came to an end. Gold vanished and farthings took its place. The unseemly became good and the good unseemly; the road to Hell issued forth from Paradise. The countenance of the revolving firmament was changed, and it withheld its love from free men altogether.

Chapter 19

India before Islam

India stands almost a continent in itself, a vast tract of land in the shape of a diamond, bordered on the southern sides by the Indian Ocean and on the northern by the Himalayas and its sister ranges.

From the tip of the diamond flow two great river systems, the Indus draining southwestward, and the Ganges to the southeast, creating the fertile Indo-Gangetic plain of North India, watered by the monsoon. South of the Vindhya Mountains, which bisect the diamond from east to west, lie the tablelands of the Deccan, and the lesser ranges of the Ghats which run down the coasts to meet above the lower tip, which is South India. Pendant from the diamond is a pearl—Sri Lanka.

The sea in ancient times isolated India from the rest of mankind, except for traders from the Hellenic and Roman worlds and the spice lands further east. It was through the mountain passes of the northwest that invasion came, from the entry of the Aryans in 1500 BC to the arrival of Muslim conquerors in AD 1000.

The Aryan invasion was not the first. Two great language families were already established in India: Munda, spoken by tribal people of eastern and central India, and Dravidian, spoken by the inhabitants of the Deccan and South India.

Between the arrival of the Aryans and that of the Muslims the mountain passes admitted invaders of all kinds: Persians, Macedonians, Greeks, Scythians, Parthians, Kushans and Huns. They ruled Indian lands for a time and then withdrew, or remained and lost their identity in the Indian melting-pot.

With the coming of the Aryans began the formation of ancient Indian civilization. Aryan, Munda, Dravidian and foreign elements contributed. The civilization which resulted has, without military conquest, enriched the world. Its national religion, Hinduism, is still vigorous in the land of its birth; its international religion, Buddhism, has spread all over the Far East and south east Asia. Its writings and its architecture have shaped the culture of southeast Asia and Sri Lanka. Its numerical notation—the nine symbols and the zero we mistakenly call Arabic—has been adopted the world over.

With the coming of Islam, a religion it could not absorb into Hinduism, the history of ancient India closes. Thereafter Indian civilization developed under the influence of new ideas from Persia and the Middle East working on the ancient heritage. That heritage was transformed, but it persists.

The Indus Valley civilization

In the 1920s archaeologists began unearthing the remains of a great civilization which preceded the coming of the Aryans. Its two main cities, Mohenjodaro in Sind and Harappa in the Punjab, have been extensively excavated, and as many as a hundred other sites have been found which belong to the same civilization. This civilization extended along the greater part of the Indus to the upper Gangetic watershed, some 1000 miles in length, and commanded 800 miles of seaboard in both directions from the Indus delta.

The Indus folk were confirmed city-dwellers. The houses of the more well-to-do had courtyards and bathrooms. The elaborate system of covered drains with manholes and soakpits, the rubbish chutes and public wells show an advanced appreciation of the hygienic requirements of city life. The gridiron pattern of their main streets is in striking contrast with the meandering streets of their Mesopotamian contemporaries.

Above the city rose a citadel on a platform of mud brick, walled and bastioned, enclosing (at Mohenjodaro) a pillared hall and a great bath of brick sealed with bitumen. North of the citadel was a workers' compound and the granaries which housed the Indus peoples' main form of subsistence and, perhaps, tribute.

Steatite seals, many of them masterpieces of the engraver's art, have been found in great quantities. They depict the gods and animals (chiefly the humped cattle so charactersitic of India) with short inscriptions which have not yet been deciphered.

For several centuries, from 2300 to 1800 BC, the people of the Indus Valley civilization lived in their well-planned cities, raised their wheat, barley and cotton, and

Above, marble relief of the Amaravati school, second century AD: the presence of the Buddha is conveyed by the throne, furnished with cushions and placed under a tree, symbol of enlightenment. Musée Guimet, Paris.

Below, bull from Mohenjodaro, one of the two great cities the Indus valley civilization, third millennium BC.

Opposite top, bowl belonging to King Khosrow I. Musée du Louvre, Paris.

Opposite bottom, royal banquet scene as recorded on a Sassanian dish. Walters Art Gallery, Baltimore.

carried on trade with the Persian Gulf, Afghanistan and the rest of the subcontinent.

How it began, who its people were, and how it ended remain mysteries. It shows clear affinities with ancient Mesopotamia but striking differences as well. Whether its people were the ancestors of those who today speak Munda or Dravidian languages we can only guess until their script is read.

Flood, dessication of the land, and invasion may all have played a part in bringing it to an end. Very probably the Indus Valley civilization had been destroyed by the time the Aryans arrived. Its fate and its contribution to Hindu culture remain unknown.

The Aryans

The tribes calling themselves Aryans, who settled in the Punjab after the fall of the Indus Valley civilization, present a very different picture. Far from emulating their city-dwelling predecessors, they were decidedly rural, living in small stockaded villages. Their chief instrument of war was the light, swift, horse-drawn chariot. Their weapons and tools were of bronze. Their chief occupations were raising cattle and raiding the herds of others. Cattle played a great part in their economy. It is not known whether they knew the techniques of agriculture before they entered India, but in any case they quickly took up the cultivation of wheat and rice.

The Aryans spoke an archaic form of Sanskrit, a language belonging to the Indo-European family which includes, among others, Greek, Latin, the Slavic, Celtic and Germanic languages and Persian. Perhaps as early as 1500 BC these tribes crossed the mountain passes which connect the Punjab with the Iranian plateau. Their formidable chariots scattered their aboriginal enemies, whom they called *dasas*, a name which quickly came to be a synonym for 'slave'. From the Punjab they pushed eastward to the region of Delhi and the Gangetic basin, and thence south into central India. In succeeding centuries Aryan culture established its dominance over the Deccan and the south.

The age of the Aryan republics and monarchies was India's heroic age. The aristocracy were called Kshatriyas; their chief was the raja. The Kshatriya boy learned bowmanship and charioteering. He was taught to keep his honour untarnished and to seek glory on the battlefield. If he were killed, paradise was to be his reward. To slay one who submitted, to refuse hospitality to a stranger, even though he were an enemy, were heinous sins. At sixteen the Kshatriya boy was a man, ready to make war for the four lawful ends: cattle, gold, territory and women.

The Brahmins or priests presided over the great sacrifices of the more powerful

Kshatriyas, offering oblations of ghee (clarified butter) to the sacred fire and muttering the hymns of the *Vedas* or sacred writings, which ensured their success.

The common folk were called Vaishya. To them were allotted the more mundane functions of cattle-breeding, agriculture and trade. Below them were the Shudras, a servile population and probably largely non-Aryan. This classification of Aryan society into four estates is quite old and precedes the evolution of the caste system, with which it should not be confused.

Vedic religion

'Veda' is the name given to the religious literature of the Aryan tribes of India. More specifically the term is applied to the collections of hymns to the gods which are chanted as the sacrifice. The *Rig Veda* is the oldest of these collections, its earliest hymns belonging to the time when the Vedic tribes had just occupied the Punjab, and some may date from the period of their stay in Persia.

Indra, the war chief of the gods, is one of the major deities of the *Rig Veda*, destroying the forts of the Dasas and slaying demons. Varuna, whose Greek counterpart is Uranus, and Mitra, the Persian Mithra, guarantee oaths and mete out justice. The gods of the *Rig Veda* are largely the sky and elemental deities of the sort common to all the early Indo-European religions.

The gods were humoured and propitiated in sacrifices to the sacred fire, *Agni*, conducted in the hearth or in the open air. In its spirit as in its practices it was far removed from the worship of idols in temples of later Hinduism. A second stratum of Vedic literature, the *Brahmanas*, sets out the details

of the sacrifice which grew more and more complex and became increasingly the speciality of the class of priestly Brahmins.

A third stratum of the *Vedas*, the *Upanishads*, marks a new departure in the evolution of religious concepts. They assert the greater efficacy of meditation and renunciation over the sacrifice. The doctrine of transmigration, which holds that one is reborn after death in a higher or lower form of life according to one's deserts, was by this time accepted as self-evident. The object of meditation is knowledge of the identity of the inmost self with the absolute, knowledge which can release one from the endless cycle of rebirth and death and bring union with the over-soul.

Of the Indo-European religious heritage little remains in modern India except the wedding ritual round the sacred fire and the daily domestic sacrifice. But the mystical speculations embodied in the *Upanishads* are the spiritual forebears of Jainism, Buddhism, and the philosophical schools of Hinduism.

Jainism

At the close of the Vedic age, eastern India, especially the region round Magadha in the present state of Bihar, where the dominance of Brahmins was not fully established, saw the birth of a number of ascetic movements. These rejected the authority of the *Vedas*, but their metaphysical doctrines show an affinity with those of the *Upanishads*. One of the earliest and most successful of these new religions was Jainism, which today claims some 1,500,000 adherents among the merchants and traders of western India and the south.

According to Jain doctrine the entire universe is filled with living souls, whose

primeval purity is clouded by action and which are bound thereby to material things and the endless cycle of transmigration. The remedy is an attitude of passive devotional contemplation and the observance of the doctrine of *ahimsa* or non-violence. The monks wear gauze over their mouths and sweep the path before them as they walk to avoid inhaling or treading on insects or microbes.

Buddhism

The Mahavira ('Great Hero'), founder of Jainism, and the Buddha ('the Enlightened') both lived in the sixth century BC in eastern India, and both were said to be of princely birth. According to legend, at the Buddha's birth it was prophesied that he would be either a great ascetic or a universal emperor. His father, wishing him to follow in his footsteps, raised him in circumstances of ease and luxury to prevent him from developing any unworldly tendencies.

One day, however, as the son was driving about in his chariot, he saw a birth, a sick man, an old man, and a corpse. Filled with a sense of the sorrow inherent in life, he renounced his family and patrimony and stole away at night to discover the source of suffering. Enlightenment came while he meditated under a tree, and the disciples he acquired through his preaching became the Buddhist monkhood. Thus began the long career of Buddhism, now extinguished in the land of its birth but with millions of adherents in all the countries of the Far East.

Buddhism propounds a middle way between the indulgence of the senses and the severe self-mortification of the ascetic. Suffering is universal. Its root is desire and its cure is the transcendence of desire through the healing knowledge obtained in meditation. By leading an exemplary and disinterested life, and by diligent meditation, release from the cycle of rebirth and death, the final extinction of Nirvana, can be won.

Several features of the caste system were by now in evidence. However, the many ascetic movements, and the religions of release which grew out of them, rejected in some respects the principles on which caste was based. The taking of life is evil: in holding this the Mahavira and the Buddha stood opposed to the Vedic religion of sacrifice. What a man does is more important than what condition of life he is born into: in this they disturbed the pretensions of the Brahmin priests. Anyone could become a monk, regardless of rank. But for the vast majority caste remained the organizing principle of their social existence, and, whatever their higher loyalties, the Brahmin priest continued to serve their ritual needs, at birth, at marriage and at death.

Invaders from the west

The states of the Vedic age had been tribal republics and monarchies, ruled by a hereditary aristocracy, the Kshatriyas. Such states continued to prevail in the Punjab until the coming of Alexander the Great in 326 BC, and it was there that the prestige of the Brahmin was highest. In the eastern regions, however, at the same time as the appearance of Jainism and Buddhism, there arose territorial states whose policies were expansionist and whose rulers were often usurpers of low birth. The most successful of these were Magadha, whose capital, Pataliputra, was soon to become the seat of government of an empire larger than any India has since seen.

The tribal states of the Punjab had known invasion before Alexander. Gandhara and Sind had been satrapies of Darius of Persia towards the close of the sixth century BC, and Indians had served in Xerxes' host for the invasion of Greece. Alexander must have appeared to Indian eyes as the last of the Persian conquerors. He showed in the battle of the Jhelum the superiority of swift cavalry over the chariots of the Indian ruler Porus which got bogged down in mud. But Porus' elephants inflicted heavy losses on the Macedonians, and elephants soon became the most prized engines of war in the Hellenistic world. Alexander's men shortly after mutinied at the thought of endless advance through the sub-continent, and the expedition withdrew down the Indus.

Meanwhile Chandragupta Maurya had seized the throne of Magadha by virtue of a popular revolt. The tribal states of the Punjab had already been weakened by Alexander's conquests, and the authority of Alexander's governors was undermined by his death. In the consequent turmoil and uncertainty the tribal states quickly fell to Chandragupta's advance, and the last memory of Alexander's brief stay in India was soon extinguished.

Seleucus, the Macedonian general who succeeded to Alexander's eastern dominions, concluded a pact with Chandragupta, by which he obtained 500 of the elephants he so badly needed for his war against another Macedonian general, Antigonus. In exchange he ceded vast tracts west of the Indus in what is now Pakistan and Afghanistan.

Seleucus sent Megasthenes as ambassador to the Mauryan court at Pataliputra. He wrote a most valuable, though somewhat idealized, account of India in the early years of the Mauryan Empire. To Megasthenes India was a land where crime was rare, though there were no written laws, where slavery did not exist and where the peasant ploughed his land unmolested by armies engaged in battle nearby. His book was the basis of knowledge of India in the west for many centuries.

The pillared hall of Chandragupta's palace recalls that of Darius and his successors at Persepolis. The polished sandstone pillars with animal capitals of Asoka Maurya show definite Persian influence and were possibly designed by Persian workmen. But, however indebted to foreign sources,

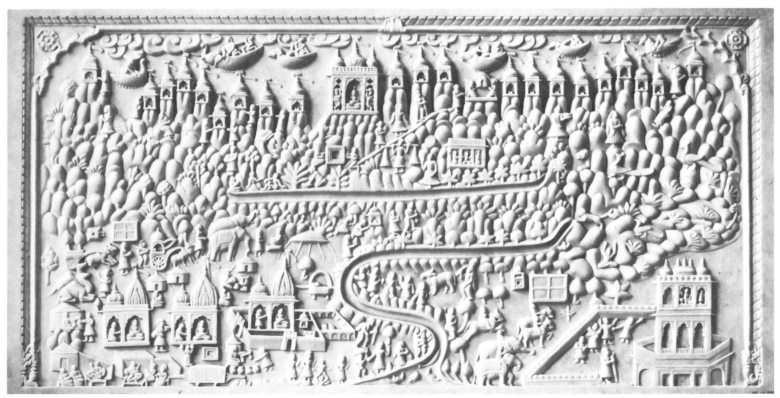

Left, stone elephant from the temple at Konarak, thirteenth century AD.

Below, seventh-century AD relief at Mahabalipuram depicting the penance of Arjuna, son of India, the god of warriors and of Nature.

Opposite top, interior of a cave in the Gupta rock sanctuary at Ajanta, sixth century AD.

Opposite bottom, nineteenth-century AD carved marble panel, a symbolic representation of a Jain holy place.

the imperial style of the Mauryas is purely Indian in spirit.

When Asoka acceded to the Mauryan throne in 268 BC the empire he inherited comprised all but the extreme southern tip of the Indian diamond and some of the eastern seaboard. He completed it by the conquest of Kalinga (Orissa) on the eastern coast below the mouths of the Ganges.

Asoka had an inclination towards Buddhism, and the deaths and suffering caused by the Kalinga campaign transformed his life. Henceforth he renounced aggressive war and made his whole aim the welfare of his subjects 'in this world and the next'. His officials were to inculcate the virtues of respect for elders and the teachers of all sects, of non-violence and of peaceableness. He sent envoys to the Hellenistic kingdom to promote his views there. Such 'conquest by righteousness' he held superior to conquest by arms.

He himself undertook tours to further this teaching and to visit the holy places of Buddhism. Above all, he had his words inscribed on rocks and pillars throughout the land. Though mostly in the dialect of Magadha, Asokan edicts in Greek and Aramic have been found in Kandahar. By virtue of these inscriptions we possess a record of the simple and direct words of one of the great figures of world history.

During Asoka's reign Buddhism prospered and spread. It was at this time that Buddhism was brought to Sri Lanka where it has flourished ever since.

The Shunga and Kushan Empires

In 250 BC Diodotus broke away from the Seleucid Empire and established an independent Greek kingdom in Bactria. But in the century which followed the pressure of central Asian tribes, the Scythians or Sakas, drove the rulers of Bactria inexorably south and east, into Gandhara and the Punjab.

The Mauryan Empire did not long survive the death of Asoka, and in 187 BC Pushyamitra raised on its ruins the more modest Shunga Empire, which was Hindu in its religion and revivalist in spirit. The two Indo-Greek kingdoms into which the Bactrian kingdom had divided were able neither to destroy the Shungas to the east nor to make common cause against the Saka menace which had appeared in the northwest and perished utterly before the beginning of the Christian era.

Menander (Milinda) was one of the few Greeks to leave a lasting impression on the Indian consciousness, thanks less to his considerable conquests than to his patronage of Buddhism. He figures in a dialogue with a Buddhist monk in *The Questions of Milinda*, a piece of early Buddhist literature, and his legend has spread all over Buddhist Asia. The Greeks minted portrait coins of superb artistry which set a pattern emulated by

succeeding kings of India. One of the last benefits of their presence in the northwest was the development of the Gandhara school of sculpture, with its image of the Buddha rather startlingly given a Greek profile, his hair and drapery sculpted in the Greek manner.

The Sakas did not knock on the gates of India in vain. It is difficult to make out the history of these invasions from the scrappy and contradictory bits of evidence that survive in half a dozen languages or even to discover the identity of the numerous people involved. But in any case we can say that western India and the northwest were in the hands of barbarian kings by the first century AD. The tradition according to which St Thomas the Apostle visited Gondopharnes, King of India, shortly after the Crucifixion, may well be true.

Some time in the first or second century AD Kanishka, king of a people called the Kushans, established an empire which straddled the mountain passes of the northwest and extended well into the heart of north India. The Kushan dress as depicted on sculpted reliefs—pointed felt cap, long riding coat trimmed with fur, baggy trousers and felt boots—suffices to show their central Asian origin. Their special mode of warfare was the swift cavalry which ended the use of the chariot in Persia, and perhaps also in India, at least in their domains.

The Kushan kings took their titles from the peoples they had conquered or with whom they were in contact: Maharaja (Indian), king of kings (Persian), son of heaven (Chinese), Caesar (Roman). They were similarly eclectic in religious matters, and, thanks to their patronage and protection, Buddhism found a foothold in central Asia and thence spread to China.

The age of invasion saw the gradual emergence of two great religious movements. The Mahayana ('Great Vehicle') form of Buddhism, with its worship of the Buddha of the past and its emphasis on the ability of laymen to achieve the highest goal, had a wider appeal than the more austere and monkish religion of the old schools, called Hinayana ('Little Vehicle'). In the course of time Mahayana Buddhism prevailed in

Above, statue of the Buddha, one of the first known colossal images, at Bamiyan, Afghanistan.

Above left, relief of the Gandhara school, third century AD, showing Siddhartha stealing away from his father's palace: prophecy revealed that the future Buddha would devote himself to asceticism if he saw old age, sickness, death and a hermit, and now the prophecy has been fulfilled. Victoria and Albert Museum, London.

Opposite, portrait of Hsuan-tsang from a painting found in the Caves of the Thousand Buddhas. (Stein Collection) British Museum, London.

Tibet, China, Japan and several of the countries of southeast Asia. The Hinayana remained strongest in Ceylon and Burma.

The second religious development was the Bhakti cult, a popular movement, setting the loving adoration of the god and dependence on his grace against the sacrifice of the *Vedas* or the gnosis of the *Upanishads*, Jainism and Buddhism. The worship of Vishnu incarnate as Krishna is the theme of the *Bhagavad Gita*, easily the most widely read of the religious classics of India.

The Guptas

In AD 320 the barbarian kingdoms of the northwest and west had either been reduced or Indianized, and the Magadhan Empire was revived by Chandra Gupta I. Under his son, Samudra Gupta, most of northern India was included within the Gupta domains, and the Deccan and the south experienced Gupta power. His son, Chandra Gupta II, ousted the descendants of the Saka invaders from western India.

The reign of Chandra Gupta II was perhaps the most brilliant ancient India was to see. From the account left by a Chinese monk, Fa-hsien, who visited India at this time, it appears that northern India enjoyed more peace and security and a milder government than it had done for many centuries. Sanskrit poetry and drama flourished under the example of the great dramatist and poet Kalidasa, and Sanskrit was widely employed at court.

From Gupta times date the first extant remains of Hindu temples. Gupta architecture set a standard of beauty, simplicity and restraint which later architecture did not achieve. Although adherents of the Hindu sects, the Gupta emperors patronized Buddhism in addition, and the Buddhist

university at Nalanda attracted monks from Sri Lanka and China.

The earliest literature of south India, the Tamil anthologies of poems on war and love, mention resident Greek merchants in a south Indian port. These were no doubt the representatives of the Roman trade which, from Augustus' time, had brought prosperity to western and southern India. This literature already shows the influence of Aryan culture, though on the whole its form and spirit is indigenous.

By Gupta times, however, the south had become a transmitter as well as a receiver of Aryan culture. It was from south India, probably the ports of the Pallava kingdom of Kanchi, that Sanskrit, the art of writing, Hinduism and Buddhism first reached the courts of southeast Asia. South India had remained largely free of north Indian control, taking to sea earlier and with more

enthusiasm than the peoples of other parts of India and perpetually interfering in the affairs of Sri Lanka. Though the Pallavas had had to bow to the forces of Samudra Gupta during his southern campaign, their submission was not lasting.

From the middle of the fifth century a new barbarian invader, the Hun, made his ominous appearance, as his kindred were doing in Europe. For a generation or so the Guptas succeeded in holding off this menace from the northwest. But toward the close of the century it reappeared in the persons of Toramana and Mihirakula, the latter holding Kashmir, western India and part of the Gangetic basin. In fifty years the Huns were pushed back to Kashmir and parts of the northwest, and they never again became a threat, losing their identity among the Rajput clans of later fame. But the Gupta Empire had perished in the ordeal.

Below left, Buddha preaching, Gandhara school, second century AD; the style is a mixture of Hellenistic and oriental characteristics. Sarnath Museum, India.

Far left, Gupta-style Buddha, fifth century AD. Calcutta Museum.

Bottom, panel dating from the third century AD showing the four main events of the Buddha's life. State Museum, Lucknow.

Opposite right, Buddha from Mathura in the Gupta style, fifth century AD.

Opposite left, interior of the Buddhist cave temple at Ellora, near Aurangabad, eighth century AD. Sarnath Museum, India.

Harsha, under whom north India of the early seventh century was again united from sea to sea, is the ancient Indian king best known to historians. This is because of the excellent biography by his court poet Bana and the memoirs of Hsuan Tsang, a Chinese Buddhist monk travelling in India who enjoyed the king's hospitality. We see Harsha as a just and efficient monarch, constantly touring his empire to hear petitions and redress grievances, holding the whole together by his energy and close personal attention to affairs of state.

His power was evenly balanced with that of the Chalukyas of the Deccan, against whose king, Pulakushin II, he could make no headway. The vast, loosely knit empire he had made unravelled at his death. In the succeeding centuries his capital, Kanya-kubja, was the prize in the interminable struggles between the Palas of Bengal, the Gurjara-Pratiharas of north India and the Rashtrakutas in the Deccan.

The decline of ancient India

Towards the close of the tenth century a Tamil power, the Cola, were laying the foundations of an empire which was to include the south and Ceylon, and whose arms were borne as far afield as the Ganges in the north and the island of Sumatra to the east. The Rashtrakutas had given way to the revived Chalukya line, the Palas were in decay and the Gurjara-Pratihara Empire was fragmenting, its feudatories growing strong at the expense of their suzerain. It had been a long time since a central Asian invader had appeared in the northwest. It was almost time for another.

The conferment of royal lands, powers and prerogatives on conquered kings, on powerful subordinates, and on great temples and monasteries had been going on for a long time. The effects of this were to fritter away the strength of the nominal overlord.

Coins grew scarce, and India's trade with foreign lands does not seem to have been as flourishing as under the Kushans and Guptas. Even in Harsha's time security of life and property had declined. Hsuan Tsang was several times set upon by bandits and very nearly lost his life.

North India's outward life was marked by provincialism, insecurity and endless dynastic warfare. The inward conviction that this was an age of decline found expression in the popular religious literature of the time. Those for whom the burden of tradition was too wearisome sought out the increasingly successful and esoteric Tantra cults.

Chapter 20

The Chinese World

string, another early form of communication. Chinese characters were then evolved during the reign of Huang Ti.

The discovery was reputedly made by one of his ministers named Ts'ang Chieh, who studied the pattern of the stars in the heavens and the footprints of birds and animals on sand and saw that things could be represented by different signs. Huang Ti is also credited with the invention of the 'south-pointing chariot', which is the modern compass. The rearing of silk worms and the manufacture of silk threads were apparently discovered by Lo Tsu, his wife.

Below, monster mask and ring of bronze dating from the period of the 'Warring States', fifth century BC.

Below centre, ritual bronze wine bucket dating from the western Chou dynasty, late eleventh or early tenth century BC.

Below left, bronze jug dating from the Shang dynasty. Minneapolis Institute of Arts.

Opposite, Bodhisattva of the Gandhara school from Shabaz-Garhi, second century AD: a Bodhisattva, or ministering spirit, acted as intermediary between god and man. Musée Guimet, Paris.

Far to the east of the ancient world, remote and inaccessible across the vast stretches of the Asian land mass, lay China, one of the three great civilizations of antiquity. Like those of early Egypt and Mesopotamia, Chinese civilization emerged along the banks of a river system, the Huang-ho or Yellow River, in northern China. But while the civilizations of the Nile and the Fertile Crescent have declined, that of China has endured. Thus the people who live in China today can claim the oldest continuously recorded history in the world.

Traditional Chinese historians trace their country's history back some five thousand years to the legendary achievements of the early pioneers of civilization and culture. Foremost among these are: P'an Ku, the creator of heaven and earth; Fu Hsi, the ox-tamer, the patron of hunting and animal husbandry; Shen Nung, the patron of agriculture and medicine; and Huang Ti, the 'Yellow Emperor', a warrior and empire builder who is supposed to have reigned in the twenty-seventh century BC.

The exploits of these early heroes in this pre-historic age reflect the transition of early Chinese civilization from a nomadic hunting existence to a more settled agricultural economy.

Other discoveries which represent the cultural origins of the Chinese people are also traced to this early period. Fu Hsi is credited with evolving the 'eight trigrams', a series of mystical diagrammatic forms which are regarded by some scholars as the first attempts at a written language. Shen Nung apparently experimented with knotted

The early dynasties

The emergence of a more closely integrated political society in the twenty-fourth and twenty-third centuries BC is recalled in the behaviour of the three model kings, Yao, Shun and Yü. Tradition has it that Yao introduced the ideal of good government by abdicating, not in favour of his son but of Shun, an able fisherman and farmer.

In turn, Shun relinquished the throne to Yü, another able commoner. Yü the Great devoted himself to engineering and water conservancy works and is credited with founding the Hsia dynasty (2000–1500BC), the first state to figure in Chinese prehistory.

The last of the Hsia rulers was so evil that the people arose in revolt and established a new dynasty, the Shang. This dynasty is described in some detail in early Chinese classical texts. Ssuma Chien, a historian who wrote in the first century BC, listed about thirty of the early Shang kings.

Despite this, for a long time many doubted whether the Shang dynasty could have had any real historical existence. However, about fifty years ago large numbers of so-called 'dragon bones' appeared on sale on the streets of Peking, to be ground up for medicinal purposes. When these were examined they were found to be inscribed with ancient styles of writing. It was realized

that they were in fact oracle bones, used in ancient times for divinistic purposes.

Archaeological excavations were made between 1929 and 1933 at the site where these 'dragon bones' had been found and about 100,000 pieces were recovered, the majority of which have been deciphered by scholars.

These excavations at the site of the ancient Shang capital near An-yang, in northern Honan province, have given us a more detailed understanding of early Chinese history. The writing on the oracle bones and the magnificent bronze urns and implements which have also been recovered show that the Shang people enjoyed a mature Bronze Age culture in northern China between 1523 and 1027 BC. Moreover, greater authenticity has been given to the traditional accounts found in the early classical texts. It is remarkable that the oracle bones so far deciphered record twenty-three of the thirty Shang kings listed by Ssuma Chien.

It is now generally accepted that by 1500 BC a highly gifted people, obviously with a long history of development behind them, had emerged with a distinctive culture in northern China. These people lived in large houses and had a highly developed agricultural economy which at one stage used cowrie shells as a medium of exchange. They employed skilled artisans who worked in bronze and jade, creating delicate ornaments and magnificent urns, which were frequently inscribed and buried as an expression of the prevailing ancestor worship practised by the early Chinese.

The first empires

In the eleventh century BC these gifted people were overwhelmed by the Chou, a nomadic tribe from the western regions. The Chou, who were consolidators rather than innovators, readily accepted much of the Shang achievement. Work in bronze, textiles and pottery continued, and the written language was developed. Politically, the Chou formalized the loose feudal structure which had emerged under the Shang. They divided their territory into fiefs under a new aristocracy and based the economy on the agricultural produce of a large peasant class.

There were clearly defined social grades and concepts of tribute and chivalrous behaviour among the nobles, which had marked similarities to the type of feudalism which was to develop more than 1,000 years later in Europe. However, the Chou failed to establish their control on a formal contractual relationship. As a result the Chou kings exercised only nominal sovereignty from their capital near Sian.

From the beginning there were signs of political instability, and the numerous small principalities tended to break away. They also failed to withstand the continual pressure from the nomadic tribes of the north and northwest.

In the eighth century BC the Chou tried to place themselves in a stronger defensive position by moving their capital eastwards to Lo-yang. The ensuing period, 722–481 BC, is known as the *Ch'un Ch'iu*, or 'Spring and Autumn period', a name which is taken from the account of these years in the annals of the state of Ly, where Confucius was born.

Over the next three hundred years about twenty-five semi-independent states contended for feudal hegemony and slowly undermined Chou authority. It was a time of population expansion, significant advances in craftsmanship, the growth of a money economy and changes in military techniques. The age also saw a gradual shift from the use of bronze to that of iron. Horse-archers, using the newly perfected crossbow, replaced the ancient and slower-moving two-wheeled chariots of the Shang.

It was also a time of significant intellectual advances. The complex political situation led to the appearance of innumerable advisers who attached themselves to the various feudal lords and formed contending schools of thought. The famous philosophers Confucius, Mencius and Chuang Tzu lived during this period of the 'hundred schools', from which sprang China's great philosophical traditions.

By the fourth century BC the fight for supremacy between the states had become harsher and more uncompromising. The chivalrous behaviour of the early feudal period was replaced by a relentless fight for survival. One after another the smaller states were absorbed by their increasingly ruthless neighbours. This change in the character of the age is reflected in a change in name, and the period from 403 to 221 BC is known as that of the 'Warring States'.

The Ch'in

The western state of Ch'in emerged triumphant in this situation. Its statesmen rejected the moral political philosophy of Confucius, with its gentle emphasis on right behaviour. Instead they adopted the uncompromising outlook of the Legalists, who offered the Machiavellian advice that the end justified the means and that the individual should be subordinated to the state. Acting on these principles, the Ch'in rulers systematically set about strengthening the central power of the state. A bureaucracy was introduced, irrigation works were carried out by forced labour, and the population was pressed into military service. One by one, the surrounding states were conquered, and in 222 BC Ch'u, the last and greatest of its opponents, was absorbed. King Cheng, who completed this task, then adopted the title Shih Huang Ti and proclaimed himself ruler of the first centralized empire in Chinese history.

The Ch'in brought about lasting changes which profoundly influenced the subsequent course of Chinese history. They introduced standard taxes, weights and measures, and laws. They rigorously controlled the thought of the educated class and reputedly burnt innumerable philosophical and political books. To improve communications, they built an elaborate network of roads and canals, largely by forced labour. Ch'in armies moved out into Mongolia and south into Vietnam.

Undoubtedly, their greatest effort was the building of the Great Wall. This stupendous achievement stretched for 1,500 miles along the northern borders of China, from the eastern coast to the mountainous ranges of the interior. The aim of the Ch'in rulers was to establish a secure bulwark between the rich agricultural land which they had conquered and the wide expanses to the north, across which the hordes of marauding nomads customarily appeared.

However, the Ch'in had lost internal control before they could test their wall. Harsh laws, enforced labour and the continuous drive for military expansion aroused a brooding sense of discontent among the people. In 210 BC Shih Huang Ti died and was succeeded by a weak son. Revolts broke out, and the empire which its founder had meant to endure for 10,000 generations passed to the second of the great dynasties of ancient China, the Han.

The Han dynasty

During the Han period (206 BC–AD 220) cultural, political and institutional developments since Shang times combined to form a sophisticated and many-sided society which was a dazzling model for the ancient world in the east.

To gain popular support, the early Han emperors repealed the stringent Ch'in laws, ostensibly supported feudalism and rejected the doctrines of the Legalists. Confucianism was encouraged, both as a state religion and as a code of moral behaviour for the individual. During the first part of the period, known as the Former Han dynasty, assemblies of scholars gathered to debate constitutional matters, examine the ancient writings, discuss the economic state of the country and decide on such abstruse problems as whether the salt and iron industries should be nationalized.

However, it soon became clear that the governmental control established by the Ch'in was to be maintained. Through a number of centralizing moves, the feudal privileges which had been restored at the beginning of the reign were gradually removed. New laws of inheritance divided

Above, interior of a Han-dynasty tomb.

Left, ivory statuette of the Emperor Huang Ti, supposed author of the oldest Chinese medical work, discussing his book with Shen Nung. Wellcome Medical Museum.

up the large estates and the status of the nobles was slowly reduced.

In their place a competent civil service was established, based on ability not birth. Entry to this elite was decided by a man's knowledge of the Confucian classics. As the system grew, it became customary for scholars to spend arduous years perfecting themselves in the classics and in mastering the intricacies of the essay, success in which was awarded by appointment to the government bureaucracy.

Inevitably, a conformist view was encouraged which strengthened Han control. By the time of Han Wu Ti (140–87 BC) a system of direct rule had been perfected. From the capital of Chang-an (modern Sian) the imperial jurisdiction and its Confucian concepts of just and ethical rule extended over north and central China.

Attempts at internal control were matched by efforts to consolidate and extend the Chinese frontiers. Punitive measures were taken against the south, which had broken away under a rebellious Ch'in governor at the beginning of the Han period. But efforts to subdue the Nam-Viet, as the area covering Kwangtung, Kwangsi and Vietnam was known, were only moderately successful, and the region remained semi-independent until pacified by the later T'ang. During Han times the threat of external invasion came not from the south but from the north.

Here the various nomadic tribes—the Hsiung-nu, Yueh-chih and Tungus—provided a constant threat. Attempts were made to repair the Great Wall and to garrison

troops along its length, but these defensive measures were only moderately effective against the fast-riding nomadic bowmen.

When Wu Ti, the 'Martial Emperor', came to the throne a new policy was adopted. He attempted to meet the growing challenge of the Hsiung-nu by forming an alliance with their historic enemies, the Yueh-chih, who had been defeated by the Hsiung-nu and driven westwards. In 138 BC he sent one of his generals, Chang Ch'ien, to the Yueh-chih, but by this time the tribe had disappeared into central Asia. Undeterred, the worthy general followed in their trail only to be captured by the Hsiung-nu and imprisoned for ten years.

When he escaped he continued his mission, crossing Ili, Ferghana and Bactria, the territory which had also been explored by Alexander the Great. Eventually he found the Yueh-chih in the region of present-day Khiva, on a tributary of the Amu Darya (Oxus). Understandably, they refused to involve themselves in Chinese affairs once more and Chang Ch'ien travelled for another year in order to report back to his imperial master, during which time he was once again imprisoned by the Huns.

Although he failed in his mission Chang Ch'ien brought back a wealth of information about Asia. In particular, Wu Ti's interest was aroused by his report of the speed and beauty of the 'heavenly' horses of Ferghana, which took on a blood-red hue when they sweated.

The Chinese emperor was determined to obtain some, so as to improve the strain of the rather puny steppe ponies then available in China, which were ineffective against the well mounted nomadic raiders. Accordingly, an envoy was sent to obtain some, but was rebuffed. Wu Ti then decided on a show of force and a Chinese army of 60,000 men was sent 2,000 miles across central Asia to enforce the imperial will.

This Chinese move into central Asia had important consequences for both east and west. For centuries the overland route was

the natural line of communication, along which the laden caravans carried the countless bales of gossamer-thin Chinese silk, the Seres cloth so highly prized in the Roman world. In return came swift Sogdanian horses, Roman gold, the steady spread of Persian and Indian influence and, above all, Buddhist religious ideals.

Wu Ti's expansive urge into central Asia gave new dimensions to the Chinese state, but it was expensive. It has been estimated that between 129 and 90 BC China lost a quarter of a million of its best fighting men there.

After Wu Ti's death, palace intrigues by ambitious eunuchs, the political activity of powerful families and rising social discontent steadily undermined the imperial authority. Large estates were built up and maintained by private armies, which destroyed the careful administrative balance originally established by the Han.

Between AD 9 and 23 a reforming minister, Wang Mang, seized control and initiated a series of reforms. Although the government later reasserted its authority, the underlying discontent encouraged unrest and rebellions. Prominent amongst these were the Yellow Turban rebellion and the revolt of the Five Pecks of Rice band, which devastated large areas and brought the country close to disaster. A military struggle for control

Left, part of the Great Wall of China near Peking.

Below, bronze figure of a flying horse, Han dynasty, second century.

Opposite top, Han-dynasty tomb relief depicting scenes of entertainment, including players, singers jugglers and dancers.

Opposite centre, stone relief portraying a mounted warrior, Han dynasty.

Opposite bottom, monumental figure in a rock temple in Hunan province, Wei dynasty, early sixth century AD.

followed which dominated the politics of the declining years of the Han dynasty.

The struggle for the succession of the Han dynasty during the third century AD is one of the most stirring episodes in Chinese history. It is known as the age of the Three Kingdoms, and the exploits of the protagonists have been immortalized in tradition and legend.

On the one side was Ts'ao Ts'ao, the villainous and powerful tyrant of Wei. Matched against him was Liu Pei, King of Shu, and his sworn brothers-in-arms, Chang Fei and Kuan Yu, the last-named being later deified as the god of war. The adventures of the three heroes and their continuing loyalty to one another are a part of the popular Chinese literary tradition. On more than one occasion they were helped by the minister Chuko Liang, a strategist whose ruses were often instrumental in saving his side from defeat.

One of these stories tells of the occasion when the heroes ran short of arrows while beleaguered on an island. The wily minister set up straw figures dressed as warriors on a boat and sailed it against the foe, who shot the figures full of arrows which were then collected and used again.

The Wei emerged victorious in the middle of the third century, but Ts'ao Ts'ao's son was not strong enough to hold the throne.

One of his generals, Ssu-ma Yen, then established the short-lived Chin dynasty, which collapsed in AD 290.

Pressure from the north

The struggle for internal control was made more complex by the pressure of the barbarian tribes strung out along China's northern borders. In both the east and the west, this was the first great age of the Turkic and Mongol peoples. For centuries they had dominated the central Asian trade routes, spilling out and driving lesser tribes before them towards the Roman and Han empires. By the fourth century this pressure proved irresistible.

In the west, the Huns drove the Ostrogoths, Visigoths, Franks, Alemanni and Vandals across the Roman frontiers, bringing about the collapse of political control. In the east, where the Huns were known as the Hsung-nu, they pushed south of the Great Wall to overrun the greater part of northern China. In China, as in the Roman west, their impact was not entirely destructive. Some of the tribes, who had already absorbed a considerable amount of Chinese culture while stationed along the northern borders, were content to settle, bringing

with them vigorous ideas and new social customs.

During the fourth and fifth centuries numerous small kingdoms were set up by these tribes in northern China. One such group, the T'o-pa clan, established the Northern Wei dynasty (AD 386–532), which achieved a considerable cultural level.

One important consequence of the barbarian invasions was that many Chinese fled into central and southern China. There they adapted to their new surroundings, growing rice instead of millet, and acquiring new social customs, among which was the practice of drinking tea. Various short-lived dynasties were also established in the south, which competed against one another as well as against the equally precarious states of their northern neighbours.

Between the fourth and sixth centuries China passed through a period of political fragmentization as well as a time of change and constructive growth. This resulted in a vastly extended political entity when the country was once again reunited in the sixth and seventh centuries by the Sui and the T'ang.

The spread of Buddhism

Mahayana Buddhism, with its emphasis on faith and participation, mutual help and the goodwill of others, had a wide appeal. It was this form of Buddhism which spread along the central Asian trade routes into China and Japan. During the barbarian invasions of the third to the sixth centuries the religion expanded rapidly, largely because the nomads who set up the numerous kingdoms in north China were more inclined to support beliefs which were already familiar to them.

In time, Indian missionaries such as the monks Dharmaraksa and Kumarajiva travelled to China to explain the faith and to translate the scriptures. In return Chinese pilgrims, the most notable of whom was Fa-hsien, made their way along the perilous Old Silk road to study Buddhism at its source.

The work of these men changed China's religious outlook. During the centuries of political disunity there was a widespread decline of Confucianism, which appealed only to the educated administrative class. Buddhism, on the other hand, offered the calm monastic life as an escape from uncertainty and the promise of salvation after death. By the sixth century, when the Sui reunited the country, Buddhism had spread among all classes of the people.

Reunification

The concept of imperial unity, which had first been achieved by the Ch'in and the

Han, was recovered in the sixth and seventh centuries by the Sui and the T'ang. There were only two emperors of the short-lived Sui dynasty, but they managed to re-establish the trend towards centralized government in China. Through their efforts the Great Wall was restored, canals were dug and communications were improved between the north and the south.

However, the numerous wars in which the second Sui emperor was involved aroused strong internal opposition. One of his officials, named Li Yuan, aided by his strong-minded son, Li Shih-min, rose in revolt and established the T'ang dynasty in 618.

During the T'ang dynasty (618–907) China experienced one of the most glorious eras of its history. A number of capable rulers

restored imperial control. In turn, T'ai Tsung (626–649), Kao Tsung (649–683), and a remarkable woman, the Empress Wu, reorganized and systematized the land-holdings of the previous centuries, opening up new agricultural areas and encouraging economic development. The growth of population and the shift in the economic centre of the country from the wheat and millet land of the north China plain to the rich rice-growing fields of central China brought prosperity and an ample income for the government.

Chang-an, the capital, conveniently located at the eastern end of the central Asian trade routes, yet strategically placed to act as a natural focus for the economic and cultural life of the country, was a

glittering metropolis which attracted travellers from all over the known world. The city, with a population of close on 2,000,000, extended five miles from north to south and six miles across. Within its walls were large, cosmopolitan markets, parks, temples and richly equipped palaces. The main thoroughfare, fully 500 feet wide, stretched the length of the city, lined by statues and stately trees and thronged with innumerable passers-by.

With their internal control assured, the T'ang systematically set out to subdue the surrounding territories. In a series of brilliant military campaigns T'ai Tsung conquered his former allies, the eastern Turks, and assumed the title of 'Heavenly Khan'. He then moved against the western Turks, occupying the Tarim Basin and extending Chinese rule right to the Oxus valley. At the same time T'ang armies drove southwards into Vietnam and set up a protectorate over the area.

Under Kao Tsung, the Chinese pushed towards the northeast, and the Korean kingdoms of Silla and Paekche were brought under their control. By the eighth century

the T'ang Empire was the largest the world had ever seen.

The high point of the T'ang achievement was reached during the reign of Hsüan Tsung (712–756). It was a brilliant age which produced matchless works of art in pottery, painting and sculpture. Above all, this was the golden age of Chinese poetry. The work of Tu Fu (712–770), Li Po (701–762), Wang Wei (699–760) and others emerges in a dazzling way from this period. Their unforgettable verse is at once an arresting landmark in the country's literary heritage and a poignant and delicate commentary on the customs and feelings of an age.

However, the high point reached at this time also marked the beginning of the decline of the T'ang. Like his predecessors, Hsüan Tsung pursued the imperial ideal and sought to extend Chinese suzerainty into central Asia. By the mid-century his armies had reached the Hindu Kush.

Here the Chinese came up against the Arabs, a different sort of foe from the Uighurs and Turks to whom they were accustomed. In 751 the westward advance of the Chinese was decisively and finally halted at the Battle of Talas near Ferghana,

the region which had previously been explored by the armies of the Han.

After the setback Hsüan Tsung never recovered his position in central Asia. During the remaining years of his reign he was increasingly preoccupied with internal difficulties. Economic hardship brought about by an expanding population, the growth of large private estates and burdensome taxation led to widespread political discontent.

A personal tragedy is woven into Hsüan Tsung's remaining years. In 745 the ageing emperor fell in love with Yang Kuei-fei, the beautiful young concubine of one of his sons. He made her his consort, raised her

brother to political power in the government, and extended his patronage to a young general named An Lu-shan, to whom Yang Kuei-fei was attracted. As public feeling grew against the emperor's behaviour, the ambitious young general rose in revolt and captured the capital, forcing the emperor to flee, accompanied by Yang Kuei-fei and her brother. On the road, Hsüan Tsung's discontented bodyguard executed the two favourites, and the heartbroken emperor then abdicated his throne.

After Hsüan Tsung, the rich and varied cultural activity of the T'ang continued. The work of the elegant stylist Han Yü (768–

824), whose essays became models for scholars of subsequent ages, and the splendid poetry of Po Chü-i, who disciplined his art to make it understandable to the common people, both appeared at this time. But the age lacked the grandeur of the earlier period.

Growing financial and economic difficulties led to widespread unrest. To an increasing extent the hard-pressed government began to covet the fabulous wealth of the Buddhist monasteries, which by this time had developed the original simple teaching into a number of complex philosophical sects. Between 841 and 845 violent

Date	India	China	The West
2300 BC	Indus Valley civilization	Hsia dynasty	Sumer
			Hittite Old Kingdom
			Egyptian Middle Kingdom
1500			Minoan civilization
	Aryans enter India	Shang dynasty	Hittite Empire
			Egyptian New Kingdom
		Ch'u dynasty	Hebrews in Palestine
1000			Mycenae
	Late Vedic period		Assyrian Empire
	Jainism	Lo-Yang becomes the Ch'u	Rise of Persia
	Buddhism	capital	Roman Republic founded
500		Spring and Autumn period	
	Death of the Buddha (483)	Death of Confucius (479)	Supremacy of Athens
400			Peloponnesian War
	Alexander the Great		Gauls sack Rome
	in India (326–325)	Period of the 'Warring States'	
	Chandragupta Maurya usurps		Alexander the Great
300	the throne of Magadha (324)		
	Asoka Maurya (273–232)	Shih Huang Ti (221–210)	Expansion of Rome
		The Great Wall (215)	First Punic War
200		Han Dynasty founded (206)	
	Pushyamitra Shunga		Destruction of Carthage (146)
	overthrows Mauryans		Tiberius Gracchus
		Han Wu Ti (140–87)	Marius
	Indo-Greek kingdoms	Chinese expansion	
100	Menander		
	Saka (Scythian		Sulla
0	invasions)		Julius Caesar
	Kushan dynasty	Later Han	Augustus
		The silk road	Nero
AD 100			Trajan
200	Kanishka	Buddhism introduced	Hadrian
			Marcus Aurelius

Date	India	China	The West
300	Buddhism	The Three Kingdoms	Sassanids in Persia
			Aurelian
	Gupta Empire	Barbarian invasions	Constantine
	founded (320)		
	Chandra Gupta II (375–414)	A succession of short-lived	Division of Roman Empire
400		barbarian states	
	White Hans overthrow		Great invasions
	Gupta Empire in north India		End of the Western
500			Roman Empire (476)
	Toromana and Mihirakula;		
600	decline of the Guptas	Sui dynasty	Justinian
	Harsha of Kanauj (606–47)	T'ang dynasty	Mohammed
		T'ai Tsung (627–49)	
700			Arab conquests
	Arabs in Sind (712)	Hsüan Tsung (721–56)	Charles Martel
800		Contact with Islam	Charlemagne
	Rajput kingdom	Decadence of the T'ang	Expansion of
	established	Persecution of Buddhists	Scandinavia
900		End of T'ang dynasty (909)	
	Chola dynasty in		Otto the Great
	south India		Hugh Capet

Left, figure of a warrior, Tang dynasty. William Rockhill Nelson Gallery of Art, Kansas City.

Far left, T'ang dynasty guardian figure.

Opposite left, Attendants on the Princess Kung T'ai: *hand copy of a painting on the princess' tomb, T'ang dynasty, AD 706.*

Opposite centre and right, details of a T'ang dynasty silk scroll depicting scenes from court life. Peking Palace Museum.

persecutions occurred and thousands of monasteries were dispossessed. In the latter part of the ninth century the familiar pattern was repeated of popular risings and military intervention, bringing the dynasty to an end in 906.

For the next fifty years China once again endured an era of division and political collapse, when five separate dynasties and ten independent kingdoms were set up, and barbarians again invaded the north.

Further reading

The most stimulating, if controversial, analysis of the world's civilizations is Arnold Toynbee, *A Study of History* (one-volume edition, Oxford University Press and Thames and Hudson, London, 1972; American Heritage Press, New York, 1972). This edition is a brilliant abridgement of the famous 12-volume study, brought to life by a clever selection of over 500 illustrations.

Good, global surveys of prehistoric societies and early civilizations from the archaeologist's viewpoint are provided by Brian M. Fagan, *Men of the Earth* (Little, Brown and Co., Boston, 1974) and Glyn Daniel, *The First Civilizations* (Penguin Books, Harmondsworth, 1971; Apollo Editions, New York, 1970). An equally useful, well-illustrated account of human progress from the first tool-makers to the Romans is Henry Hodges *Technology in the Ancient World* (Penguin Books, Harmondsworth, 1971; Alfred Knopf, New York, 1970), whose subject is rather wider than the title would suggest. Also misleadingly named is Jacquetta Hawkes, *The Atlas of Early Man* (Macmillan, London, 1976; St Martin's Press, New York, 1976), which is not really an atlas in the conventional sense but a fascinating conspectus of simultaneous developments around the world from 35,000 BC to AD 500, superbly produced and illustrated and accompanied by an excellent text.

PART I: THE AWAKENING OF MAN

New discoveries concerned with man's earliest history have come so thick and fast in recent years that many older publications on the subject are now badly out of date. Two of the best general books are Josef Wolf, *The Dawn of Man* (Thames and Hudson, London, 1978; Abrams, New York, 1978), and Bernard Wood, *The Evolution of Early Man* (Peter Lowe, London, 1976), both of which have vivid reconstruction illustrations. A more conventionally illustrated account is Desmond Collins, *The Human Revolution* (Phaidon Press, London, 1976; E. P. Dutton, New York, 1976), which gives the story of man's origins from an archaeologist's point of view, while David Pilbeam, *The Ascent of Man* (The Macmillan Co., New York, 1972; Collier-Macmillan, London, 1972) provides a clear introduction to human evolution by a physical anthropologist.

The origins and growth of the world's earliest civilizations—those in the Near East—is admirably described and illustrated in David and Joan Oates, *The Rise of Civilization* (Elsevier-Phaidon, Oxford, 1976; E. P. Dutton, New York, 1976), whose story is continued in Nicholas Postgate, *The First Empires* (Elsevier-Phaidon, Oxford, 1977; E. P. Dutton, New York, 1977). These two books in the 'Making of the Past' series cover the whole of the Near East from about 9000 BC down to 500 BC, but exclude Egypt, which is dealt with by another good volume in the same series: Rosalie David, *The Egyptian Kingdoms* (Elsevier-Phaidon, Oxford, 1975; E. P. Dutton, New York, 1975). Another reliable general account of Egyptian history is Paul Jordan, *Egypt: the Black Land* (Phaidon Press, London, 1976; E. P. Dutton, New York, 1976). For the pyramids, readers should turn to I. E. S. Edwards, *The Pyramids of Egypt* (revised edition, Penguin Books, Harmondsworth and New York, 1961).

By far the liveliest discussion of the history and cultural achievements of the Mesopotamian and Egyptian civilizations in general is given by Jacquetta Hawkes, *The First Great Civilizations* (Penguin Books, Harmondsworth, 1977; Alfred Knopf, New York, 1977); she also includes the Indus civilization for good measure. More detailed studies of the different civilizations can be found in A. L. Oppenheim, *Ancient Mesopotamia* (University of Chicago Press, Chicago and London, 1964); S. N. Kramer, *The Sumerians* (University of Chicago Press, Chicago and London, 1963); Joan Oates, *Babylon* (Thames and Hudson, London and New York, 1979); and O. R. Gurney, *The Hittites* (2nd edition, Penguin Books, Harmondsworth and New York, 1969).

PART II THE TRIUMPH OF THE GREEKS

For basic information about different aspects of Greek or Roman civilization it is best to consult the *Oxford Classical Dictionary* (2nd edition, Clarendon Press, Oxford, 1970), which is more of an encyclopedia than a dictionary.

The book the layman should read first to gain an idea of the true flavour of Greek civilization is M. I. Finley, *The Ancient Greeks* (Penguin Books, Harmondsworth, 1966, New York, 1977), a brilliant short introduction to the subject. Two new volumes in the 'History of Civilisation' series are probably the most helpful books to turn to next for a good up-to-date general history of Greece: they are R. J. Hopper, *The Early Greeks* and N. G. L. Hammond, *The Classical Age of Greece* (Weidenfeld and Nicolson, London, 1976 and 1975; Barnes and Noble, New York, 1976 and 1976). Heavily illustrated volumes giving the same story from an archaeological standpoint are Peter Warren, *The Aegean Civilizations,* Alan Johnston, *The Emergence of Greece* and Roger Ling, *The Greek World* (all in the 'Making of the Past' series, Elsevier-Phaidon, Oxford, 1975, 1976 and 1976; E. P. Dutton, New York, 1975, 1976 and 1976).

Those wishing to learn about the early periods in more detail should refer to R. F. Willetts, *The Civilization of Ancient Crete* (Batsford, London, 1977; University of California Press, Berkeley, 1977) for the Minoan period; J. V. Luce, *Homer and the Heroic Age* (Thames and Hudson, London, 1975; Harper and Row, New York, 1975) for Mycenae and the Trojan Wars; and to V. R. d'A. Desborough, *The Greek Dark Ages* (Benn, London, 1972; St Martin's Press, New York, 1972) and L. H. Jeffery, *Archaic Greece: the City States c. 700–500 BC* (Methuen, London, 1978) for the centuries preceding the classical era. Probably the best popular account of the life and conquests of Alexander is Robin Lane Fox, *Alexander the Great* (Omega/Futura, London, 1975; Dial Press, New York, 1974). John Ferguson, *The Heritage of Hellenism* (Thames and Hudson, London, 1973; Harcourt, Brace, Jovanovich, New York, 1973) is another useful source for the period.

A feast for the eye as well as the mind are the gloriously illustrated volumes currently being produced in Athens celebrating the Greek achievement: G. A. Christopoulos (ed.), *A History of the Hellenic World*, vol. I, *Prehistory and Protohistory;* vol. II, *The Archaic Period* (Ekdotike Athenon, S.A. Athens, 1970 and 1971; Heinemann Educational Books, London, 1974 and 1975). Further volumes are in preparation.

PART III: THE DOMINANCE OF ROME

Rome's Etruscan heritage is well described in M. Pallottino, *The Etruscans* (revised edition, Penguin Books, Harmondsworth, 1975; Indiana University Press, Bloomington, 1975). Two new volumes in the 'Fontana History of the Ancient World' provide the most up-to-date brief accounts of Roman history down to the end of the Republic: R. M. Ogilvie, *Early Rome and the Etruscans* and Michael Crawford, *The Roman Republic* (Fontana/Collins, London, 1976 and 1978; Humanities Press, Atlantic Highlands, New Jersey, 1976 and 1978). Michael Grant's two-volume survey in the 'History of Civilisation' series, *The World of Rome* and *The Climax of Rome* (revised editions, Weidenfeld and Nicolson, London, 1974; New American Library, New York, 1970) can also be recommended to the general reader; it carries the story to the collapse of the Empire.

More specialized books for the middle and late periods include H. H. Scullard, *From the Gracchi to Nero (133 BC–AD 68)* (4th edition, Methuen, London, 1976; Barnes and Noble, New York, 1976) and A. H. M. Jones, *The Decline of the Ancient World* (Longman, London and New York, 1966), both standard textbooks. The classic account of the Empire's demise is of course Edward Gibbon, *The Decline and Fall of the Roman Empire* (Everyman edition, Dent, London, 1960), which is still worth reading. A more digestible, infinitely shorter modern classic on much the same period is Peter Brown, *The World of Late Antiquity* (Thames and Hudson, London, 1977; Harcourt, Brace, Jovanovich, New York, 1971), also very helpful for an understanding of the early Byzantine era.

Many aspects of Roman civilization are briefly discussed in Donald Dudley, *Roman Society* (Penguin Books, Harmondsworth, 1975; New American Library, New York, 1975) within a narrative framework. Roman art is magnificently illustrated in the 'Arts of Mankind' series, R. B. Bandinelli, *Rome: the Centre of Power* and *Rome: the Late Empire* (Thames and Hudson, London, 1970 and 1971; George Braziller, New York, 1970 and 1971). Also well illustrated is Barry Cunliffe, *Rome and Her Empire* (Bodley Head, London, 1978), an archaeologist's look at Roman civilization throughout the Empire.

PART IV: THE ANCIENT EAST

Persia under the Sassanids is described in R. Ghirshman, *Iran from The Earliest Times to the Islamic Conquest* (Penguin Books, Harmondsworth, 1954).

A sound general introduction to early Indian history is provided by B. and R. Allchin, *The*

Acknowledgements

Birth of Indian Civilization (Penguin Books, Harmondsworth, 1968). W. A. Fairservis, The Roots of Ancient India: the Archaeology of Early Indian Civilization (Macmillan, New York, 1971) is also a standard work. Sir Mortimer Wheeler, The Indus Civilization (3rd edition, Cambridge University Press, Cambridge and New York, 1968) remains the classic account of this early civilization.

China and Japan are discussed together in a sumptuous volume, Arnold Toynbee (ed.), Half the World (Thames and Hudson, London, 1973; Holt, Reinhart and Winston, New York, 1973), a good general survey of their history and culture by a number of specialists. The standard account of East Asia as a whole is J. K. Fairbank, E. O. Reischauer, and A. M. Craig, A History of East Asian Civilization, vol. I: East Asia, the Great Tradition (Houghton Mifflin Co., Boston, 1958). A more approachable book on the subject is P. Fitzgerald, Ancient China in the 'Making of the Past' series (Elsevier-Phaidon, Oxford, 1978; E. P. Dutton, New York, 1978).

Colour

Jacqueline Auboyer, Paris 295 top; Erwin Böhm, Mainz 19 bottom, 26 top, 131 bottom, 266; British Museum, London 254, 287; Photographie Bulloz, Paris 18 top; Cooper-Bridgeman Library, London 215 left, 235 bottom, 310 top; Werner Forman Archive, London 30 right, 31 left, 66, 90 top, 214; Fotomas Index, London 118, 267 top; Charles Fowkes 59 top left; Photographie Giraudon, Paris 123 top; Susan Griggs Agency, London—Adam Wolfitt 58 top; Sonia Halliday, Weston Turville 178, 198, 246 top, 263 left; Hamlyn Group Picture Library 14 top, 19 top, 47 bottom, 79 top, 86 top, 138 top, 146 right, 154 top, 174 top, 239, 302; Robert Harding Associates, London 62 right, 67 top left, 106, 130 left, 298; Hirmer Fotoarchiv, Munich 35; Michael Holford, London 95 left, 102 top, 122 top, 126, 207 top left, 279 top; Mike Howgate 43 left; Kunsthistorisches Museum, Vienna 179; Eric de Maré, London 218 top, 219 top left; Metropolitan Museum of Art, New York 55 left; Photoresources 114, 186; Picturepoint, London 234–235 top; Josephine Powell, Rome 135 left; Rapho, Paris—Pierre Belzeaux 250–251; Scala, Florence 187 bottom, 191, 194–195, 203, 211, 242; Ronald Sheridan, London 67 top right, 82 top left, 190 left; Skira, Geneva 171; Snark International, Paris 275 left; Spectrum Colour Library, London 138 top; Stiftung Preussischer Kulturbesitz, Staatliche Museen, Berlin 83 left, 262; Z.E.F.A., London 70 left, 154–155, 159, 162, 226, 230, 307 top; Joseph Ziolo, Paris 74.

Black and white

Acropolis Museum, Athens 130 right; Fratelli Alinari, Florence 132, 139, 142, 164, 181 right, 187 top, 189 top, 189 bottom right, 190 top right, 191 top left, 191 centre right, 192, 194, 195 bottom, 201 right, 217 top, 219 bottom right, 227 left, 227 right, 231 bottom, 232 top, 238 right, 240 top, 244–245, 246 bottom left, 255, 256 bottom, 257, 258, 259 top, 268, 277, 280 top, 281 left; Paul Almasy, Paris 77 right, 177 top, 293 bottom, 297 bottom; Anderson 119 left, 145, 188 left, 190 centre right, 193 bottom left, 193 right, 216 left, 216 top right, 272–273, 279 bottom; Archaeological Survey of India 301 top right; Archives Photographiques, Paris 21 bottom right, 91 top left, 135 right; Arts Council of Great Britain 8, 42 top right; Bernisches Historisches Museum 213 bottom left; A. D. H. Bivar, London 288 top; Edwin Böhm, Mainz 41 bottom, 49 left, 137 top left, 137 bottom left, 140 top, 176 top, 188 bottom, 197 bottom; Boudot-Lamotte, Paris 136; British Museum, London 21 top, 21 centre right, 22 bottom, 32 bottom right, 37 bottom, 39 top, 45 centre, 80 left, 83 bottom, 89 top, 122 bottom, 169 bottom; Brooklyn Museum, Charles Edwin Wilbur Fund 60 left, 61 right, 62 left, 82 bottom; Bulloz, Paris 20 top, 20 bottom, 182 bottom right, 213 right; John Bulmer, London 237 top; Camera Press, London 219 centre bottom; J. Camponogara, Lyons 201 left; Cooper-Bridgeman Library, London 16 top right; R. Descharnes, Paris 131 left; Deutsches Archaeologisches Institut, Athens 153 bottom; Deutsches Archaeologisches Institut, Rome 182 centre bottom, 196, 212 top, 238 left, 269; Director General of Antiquities, Iraq 18 left, 18 upper right, 63 right, 67 bottom left, 72 bottom, 86 centre bottom; Fitzwilliam Museum, Cambridge 86 bottom right; Werner Forman Archive, London 36 top left, 36 centre left, 36 bottom left, 38 top, 38 bottom, 41 top, 45 right, 48 right, 53 bottom, 55 top right, 65 top right, 67 bottom right, 70 right, 72 top, 83 centre left, 85 left, 86 bottom left, 87 top, 87 bottom, 88 right, 89 bottom, 92 top, 94, 183 top right, 183 bottom right, 249, 267 bottom, 293 top, 305 right, 306 left, 306 top right, 306 bottom right, 309 bottom right, 310 centre bottom, 310 bottom right, 311 left; Fotomas Index, London 65 top left, 93, 156 top right, 250 bottom left; Fototeca Unione, Rome 210 top; Alison Frantz, Athens 119 right; Photographie Giraudon, Paris 18 bottom right, 21 bottom right, 44 top right, 69 centre, 73, 81 bottom right, 85 right, 213 top left, 221 top, 225 top, 253 bottom, 261 right, 273 bottom, 274, 282, 291 bottom, 292 top, 301 top left, 309 top left; Griffith Institute, Ashmolean Museum, Oxford 91 bottom left; Susan Griggs Agency, London 69 left; Government of India, Department of Archaeology 296 top; Sonia Halliday Photographs, Weston Turville 175 top, 190 bottom right, 231 top left, 265 left, 265 right; Hamlyn Group Picture Library 14 bottom, 53 top, 64, 65 centre right, 71, 102 bottom, 105 bottom, 140 bottom, 141 right, 152 top, 158 right, 173 left, 199 top, 223 bottom, 236 top, 252 bottom left, 264 right, 275 right, 295 bottom, 296 bottom, 299 left, 300 top right, 300–301; Robert Harding Associates, London 84 top, 149 bottom, 152 centre, 229 bottom left, 290, 303 centre, 303 right, 307 bottom, 309 top right, 310 bottom left; Hirmer Fotoarchiv, Munich 16 bottom right, 17 bottom left, 21 centre left, 24 right, 32 left, 33, 36 right, 37 top, 43 right, 44 left, 57 top, 57 bottom, 59 centre, 59 bottom, 60 left, 61 centre, 63 centre bottom, 65 bottom right, 68 right, 80 right, 81 top left, 95 right, 111 bottom, 112, 113 right, 115, 121 bottom, 123 bottom, 129 right, 148 bottom, 156 bottom right, 158 centre bottom, 165, 180 bottom, 182 bottom left, 280 bottom right; Michael Holford, London 59 top right, 98, 113 left, 116, 130, 149 top, 170, 207 bottom, 228 centre bottom, 228 bottom right, 231 centre top, 233 right, 234 right, 236 bottom, 248 top, 256 top, 272 bottom, 280 bottom left, 281 right, 305 left; Jericho Excavation Fund, Dame Kathleen Kenyon 15; A. F. Kersting, London 104, 105 top, 153 top, 176 bottom, 219 top right, 223 top, 228 top right, 261 bottom left, 294 left, 294 right, 297 top, 300 top left; Magnum, George Rodger 220; Mansell Collection, London 17 top left, 24 left, 39 bottom, 42 bottom, 45 left, 46 top, 46 bottom, 47 top, 52, 55 bottom right, 56, 58 centre left, 58 bottom right, 63 centre top, 68 left, 77 left, 78 centre, 82–83 top, 92 bottom, 109, 117 bottom, 120–121, 127, 128 left, 128 right, 129 left, 146 left, 148 top, 168 left, 168–169, 173 right, 174 bottom, 175 bottom, 180 top left, 180 top right, 184, 188 right, 189 bottom left, 191 centre left, 193 top left, 197 bottom, 199 bottom, 205, 207 top right, 208 right, 208–209, 210 bottom, 212 bottom, 215 right, 225 bottom, 228 top left, 229 top, 232 bottom, 233 left, 244 left, 247, 250 bottom right, 252–253, 259 bottom, 260, 263 right, 300 top right; Bildarchiv Foto Marburg 61 left, 75, 96, 103, 124 right, 278, 308; Eric de Maré, London 216 bottom right, 217 bottom, 218 bottom, 219 bottom left, 241; Mas, Barcelona 221 bottom; Metropolitan Museum of New York, Rogers Fund 48 left, 65 bottom left, 88 left, 91 bottom right, 167 right; Minneapolis Institute of Arts, Collection A. E. Pillsburg 303 left; Musée de l'Homme, Paris 12, 13 top; Museum of Fine Arts, Boston 158 centre top, 309 bottom left; Ny Carlsberg Glyptotek, Copengagen 134 left, 172; Oriental Institute, University of Chicago 16 left, 69 right; Antonello Perrissinotto, Padua 27 bottom, 29 right, 30 left, 261 top left; Photo Boissonas, Geneva 131 right, 156 left; Photo Hachette, Paris 44 bottom right; Picturepoint, London 276; Josephine Powell, Rome 28, 29 left, 30 centre, 31 right, 32 top left, 100, 107, 108 left, 183 left, 283 bottom; Radio Times Hulton Picture Library, London 141 left; G. Rampazzi, Turin 32 top right; Rapho, Paris 11, 13 bottom, 137 right; Jean Roubier, Paris 210 centre, 234 centre, 234 bottom; Scala, Florence 152 bottom left, 191 top right, 202 bottom, 208 left, 228 bottom left, 246 bottom right, 248 bottom; Raymond V. Schoder, S.J., Loyola University, Chicago 154 bottom, 157 top, 160 bottom; Service de Documentation Photographique des Musées Nationaux, Paris 17 right, 26 bottom, 131 top, 289; Ronald Sheridan, London 60 right, 125, 152 bottom right, 157 bottom, 167 left, 177 bottom, 264 left; Soprintendenza Antichita, Rome 117 left; Spectrum Colour Library, London 134 right; Staatliche Antikensammlungen, Munich 180 centre top; Staatliche Museen zu Berlin 49 right, 81 top right, 91 top right; Stiftung Preussischer Kulturbesitz, Staatliche Museen, Berlin 78 top, 158 left; Wim Swaan, New York 81 bottom left; University Museum, Philadelphia 22 top; Vatican Museum, Rome 181 left, 252 bottom right; Roger-Viollet, Paris 63 top left, 63 bottom left, 76 left, 76 right, 78 bottom, 84 bottom, 108 right, 110, 160 top, 161, 299 right; Wadsworth Atheneum, Hartford, Connecticut 124 left; Walters Art Gallery, Baltimore 288 bottom, 292 bottom; William Rockhill Nelson Gallery of Art, Kansas City 311 right; Roger Wood, London 111 top, 229 bottom right; Z.E.F.A., London 163, 237 bottom, 240 bottom, 243.

Index